OVID
METAMORPHOSES IX – XII

For
David West

The illustrations on the front cover is of a tondo of an Attic red-figure Kylix (525-500 B.C.) depicting Herakles in Pholos' cave. It comes from the Shefton Museum, University of Newcastle upon Tyne (inv. no. 202), and is reproduced here by courtesy of the Director, Miss L. Allason-Jones, and of the curator, Dr A.J.S. Spawforth.

OVID

Metamorphoses IX – XII

Edited with an introduction, translation and notes by

D.E. Hill

Aris & Phillips is an imprint of
Oxbow Books, Oxford, UK

© D.E. Hill 1999.
Reprinted 2011

ISBN 978-0-85668-646-7

This book is available direct from

Oxbow Books, Oxford, UK
(Phone: 01865-241249; Fax 01865-794449)

and

The David Brown Book Company
PO Box 511, Oakville, CT 06779, USA
(Phone: 860-945-9329; Fax: 860-945-9468)

or from our website
www.oxbowbooks.com

A CIP record for this book is available from the British Library.

Printed in Great Britain by
CPI Antony Rowe, Chippenham and Eastbourne

Contents

Contents

PREFACE

Fourteen years have elapsed since the appearance of my edition of the first four books of Ovid's *Metamorphoses* and seven since the appearance of my edition of books 5-8. During those years, I have been much encouraged by the warm reception they have, generally, received and I hope that books 9-12 will be felt to fill a need. Interest in Ovid continues to grow, but it continues to grow in an era less and less sympathetic to the learning of Greek and Latin. My continued hope is that the style of my editions will achieve three things. Readers should be able to extract as much as possible of the nuance of the original by simply reading the translation. Readers should be able to judge more and more certainly where they can trust the translation and where caution is required. Some readers, at least, should feel inspired to go on and learn Latin.

Once again, it is a great privilege to record my indebtedness to Professor R.J. Tarrant who has continued to provide me with a draft of his forthcoming Oxford text; once again, I must stress that the text I print does not necessarily enjoy Professor Tarrant's endorsement; it is, however, much better than it would have been without his help.

I am shocked to realize that another seven years have elapsed since I completed my edition of book 5-8; even when full allowance is made for personal indolence and the distraction of other academic ambitions, it is hard to explain so long a delay. I am sure that others will agree with me that recent developments in the way universities are managed world wide have made it increasingly difficult to give proper attention to our fundamental *rôles* of teaching and research; those of us who have unwisely accepted management functions have suffered even more than others. It would be wrong, however, not to give public acknowledgement of the way my particular colleagues have worked together to support me and render my task as light as possible. Had it not been so, this book would have been delayed for many more years yet.

Parts of this work were read in Bologna in response to a kind invitation by Professor Calboli, and other parts in Leeds, to the Classical Association there; I do hope that those who were present will see the very welcome improvements that their suggestions have prompted. The work has also been read in its entirety by Mrs R.J. Littlewood, Professor David West and, the general editor of this series, Professor Malcolm Willcock. Errors were removed by all three of these, for which I am profoundly grateful. More importantly, however, they all entered fully into the spirit of what I was doing and helped me to find better ways of doing things in my particular style, even though, if they had been doing it themselves, it is obvious that they would have done it differently. Such helpers are not easy to find, and I have been unusually lucky to secure the assistance of three. As they may well notice, I have occasionally ignored their advice and sometimes repaired error in ways different from their prescription. The reader who finds blemishes should conclude that they arise from my stubbornness and not from their oversight.

I have, as before, gained great pleasure from working on this book. My admiration of Ovid continues to grow. I do hope that this book will enable more people to share in my appreciation of one of the most imaginative, witty, urbane and humane of Latin poets.

Newcastle upon Tyne
April, 1999

INTRODUCTION

This Introduction is only slightly adapted and updated from my Introductions to Books 1-4 and 5-8. Each volume is intended to stand alone, if so desired, so that, where it is important for understanding, I have not scrupled to repeat information from the notes to 1-4 or 5-8. On the other hand, in less important matters, I have referred readers to my notes to 1-4 and 5-8, as I might to any other work.

1. *Ovid's life and works*

Ovid was born in the small Italian town of Sulmo (now Sulmona) on the 20th March 43 B.C., five days after the first anniversary of Caesar's assassination. When Octavian (soon to be known as Augustus) made himself undisputed master of the Roman world by defeating Antony and Cleopatra at Actium, Ovid was only twelve. The difference between the social and political outlook of his generation and that of Virgil, who was born only twenty-seven years before him, must have been as profound as the difference today between those who remember Europe in the tumult of the Fascist era, and those who do not.

For a century before Ovid's birth, Rome had been racked by political upheavals, frequently breaking out into violence and, eventually, full civil war. Catullus (c.84-c.54 B.C.), Virgil (70-19 B.C.), Horace (65-8 B.C.), Tibullus (55/48-19 B.C.) and Propertius (54/47-16/2 B.C.) had all been touched by these upheavals and all reflect the political issues of their day to a greater or lesser extent in their poetry. The last four lived to see the end of the civil war and the establishment of the Augustan regime. Indeed, in their more optimistic moments, Virgil and Horace can dare to hope that they are witnessing the birth of a new Golden Age, though all four clearly suffer from doubts too. With Ovid, however, politics are ignored. Just as the fall of the Greek city states and the rise of the Hellenistic world some four centuries earlier had driven poetry from the centre stage of politics into the study, the countryside and the boudoir, so again, the collapse of the Roman Republic rendered politics neither interesting nor safe for any but the most robust of poets. Even so, Ovid fell disastrously foul of Augustus' authority and spent the last years of his life, from A.D. 8 until his death about a decade later, in exile.

As a boy and young man, he received the conventional education of a reasonably prosperous and ambitious Italian family. First at home, then at Rome and finally on the Grand Tour (including Athens, Sicily and Asia Minor) he was given also the training and polish necessary for a legal or political career. At the core of this training was a grounding in rhetoric achieved largely through exercises known as *controuersiae* and *suasoriae*; in the former, the student would prepare an argument based on an unusual or even exotic situation arising out of a point of law; in the latter, he would prepare a speech to sway a figure of history or mythology confronted by some dramatic or momentous decision. No reader of Ovid will be surprised to learn that Ovid preferred the latter and, for good or ill, the influence of these exercises is to be found throughout his work.

Ovid did embark briefly on the political career his father had wanted for him but his own inclinations and genius and the influence of his friends soon drove him to abandon politics and the law in favour of poetry.

All his early work, except for his lost play *Medea*, was written in elegiac couplets (the metres are discussed in the next section), a medium well suited to his witty and epigrammatic style. His subject matter ranged from the plight of various mythological women in a whole range of disastrous love affairs to a number of mock didactic works purporting to give practical advice to both sexes on every aspect of the conduct of a love affair including even a poem on cosmetics. Such poetry did, however, have a more serious side. Ovid, like Catullus as well as the Augustan poets, was amazingly well read and his work is packed with witty and learned allusions to his predecessors in both Greek and Latin. Roman poets, such as Catullus, Tibullus and Propertius, as well as the almost entirely lost Gallus, had established elegiac as a prime form for amatory poetry, and Ovid's work was firmly established in that tradition.

He was exiled in A.D. 8, though we do not know precisely why. There is, however, no need to doubt his own account that it arose from *carmen et error*, 'a poem and a mistake'. For a brief discussion, see the note on 3.142 in the earlier volume. Ovid's rather cavalier attitude to authority and sexual propriety throughout his amatory elegiacs must have earned him disapprobation at a time when Augustus was constantly legislating in an attempt to enforce high moral standards. A single famous example must suffice here to make the point. In 23 B.C., M. Marcellus fell sick and died. He had recently married Augustus' daughter, Julia (they were cousins, for Marcellus' mother was Augustus' sister). The young man had clearly been marked out as Augustus' successor though he was only nineteen (he was the same age as Ovid) and the grief that followed his death was quite unrestrained. Virgil made him the final tragic figure in his famous parade of Roman heroes at the end of the sixth book of the *Aeneid* and, it is said, the boy's mother swooned when she heard Virgil recite the lines. Austin's note on *Aen.* 6.868 gives a full account of the elaborate memorials constructed for him by his grieving family. Among them was a marble portico and library dedicated by his mother. There must, accordingly, be real mischief in Ovid when, in a list of places which are particularly good for picking up a girl, he included this very monument (*Ars am.* 1.69-70).

However, Ovid was a man of great literary ambition. The clever trifles discussed above were so packed with wit, charm and learning that they would alone have secured him a place among the famous poets of antiquity. Nevertheless, true greatness seemed to require a major work in weighty dactylic hexameters, the metre of Homer and of Virgil whose *Aeneid* (published in 19 B.C. shortly after its author's death and when Ovid was still a young man) had come to dominate Latin letters in a wholly unprecedented way. No direct challenge to the master of epic, Virgil, was possible, but Ovid had conceived a rival plan and by the time of his exile it was essentially complete. In his *Metamor-*

phoses, Ovid turned to the dactylic hexameter to produce a mythological *tour de force* of epic scale that wholly transcended anything he had produced before. This, his greatest work, was essentially complete when he was sent into exile, and he had even completed the first half of another serious work, this time in elegiac couplets again, the *Fasti,* a calendar of the Roman year, which afforded ample scope for a display of religious, historical, mythological and astronomical learning.

The *Metamorphoses* is a very long poem (15 books in all) in the form of a highly idiosyncratic 'history' of the world from Creation to the death and deification of Julius Caesar. Its special peculiarity is that each of the stories it tells involves a metamorphosis (transformation) and each is so attached to the next that the whole gives the illusion of a seamless garment. There was, of course, a long tradition of more or less large poems using a single theme to unite a collection of stories. Hesiod (or, perhaps more probably, a sixth century imitator) had produced a *Catalogue of Women,* now largely lost, which consisted simply of a string of tales about women each starting with the simple formula, 'Or like...', the origin of its alternative title, *Eoiae.* This work had had a considerable influence on the Hellenistic writers. Callimachus' *Aetia,* for instance, an elegiac poem of over 4,000 lines (though only fragments survive now) was a string of legends united by the fact that all related the 'causes' (*aitia*) of some Greek custom, religious rite etc. In the 2nd century B.C., Nicander had composed a *Heteroeumen*a (an alternative Greek word for *Metamorphoses*; it is lost but Antoninus Liberalis, frequently cited in the notes, has left us a prose paraphrase of many of its stories) and Ovid's older contemporaries, Parthenius and Theodorus, were also each said to have composed a *Metamorphoses.* This is a very complex issue and those who wish to follow it up should consult Wilkinson, Ovid recalled (144-46), the authorities cited by him and my own notes on 1.1 and 1.4.

One of the most obvious features of Ovid's *Metamorphoses* is the attention paid to achieving the effect of a continuous narrative, or *perpetuum...carmen* as he himself put it at 1.4. He achieved this sometimes by clever links (at 6.146, we have just listened to the fate of Arachne who had scorned Minerva when we are introduced to her former neighbour, Niobe, who had not learnt from her example but...), sometimes by arranging for one character to narrate a story to another (at 8.577, Theseus' journey has been blocked by the flooded Achelous who, entertains him and, in the course of conversation, begins the story of the Echinades) and sometimes by bringing together a series of stories with a common theme (from 7.402 to 9.97, the stories are linked by the common thread of Theseus). The situation is further complicated, however, by the fact that it is possible to detect other structures, such as the simple chronological one, or more subtle groupings, such as Otis's (83) four-fold division, 'The Divine Comedy' (Books 1-2), 'The Avenging Gods' (3.1-6.400), 'The Pathos of Love' (6.401-11.795) and 'Rome and the Deified Ruler' (12-15), each section itself subdivided, according to Otis, into smaller sections as discussed in his following pages. Some readers may well find the specific analyses of Otis and others, at least in part, unconvincing, but few if any will deny that the unity of the *Metamorphoses* is achieved by Ovid's genius in relating one story to another in a bewildering variety of ways. The original decision to start this edition with the first four books was quite arbitrary; indeed, it necessitated breaking off before the Perseus story was complete. Similarly, this edition of books 5-8 leaves us wondering why Achelous is groaning. It will, however, become obvious that there are no clean breaks in the *Metamorphoses* and the whole, in this format, would make a cumbrous volume indeed. However, now that we are more than half way through, I do hope to be able to complete the whole project.

In spite of Augustus' decision to banish Ovid as an offender against public morality, many readers detect a strong moral and humane theme throughout the *Metamorphoses*. Cruelty and treachery are almost invariably punished, but all the more venial of the foibles and weaknesses of human nature are depicted with a constant, gentle humour. One of the recurrent motifs is that the metamorphosis is only the revelation of some ultimate truth about the victim (see the note on 6.97) and the mediaeval writers who treated the *Metamorphoses* as a storehouse of paradigms for moral instruction (see Rand 131-37, Wilkinson (1955) 366-98) were exaggerating rather than falsifying. There are so many verbal pyrotechnics, so much showing off of learning, so much wit and humour (some subtle, some not, but none cruel) that the fundamental humanity of Ovid can be lost sight of. Many may even agree with the elder Seneca (*Contr. 2.10.12*) who complained that Ovid did not lack the judgement to restrain his excesses but the will. For my own part, I find his charm and sensitivity too overwhelming to be much exercised by his occasional blemishes. For a particularly trenchant view of Ovid's moral purpose, see W.R. Johnson in *Ancient Writers, Greece and Rome*, ed. T.J. Ince (New York, 1982) II 783-806.

Exile was a bitter pill for Ovid, the ultimate sophisticate, to swallow. The last six months of the *Fasti* were abandoned and there flowed from his pen instead a great outpouring of elegiac verse devoted largely to complaints about his punishment, nostalgia for happier days and pleadings to a variety of friends for help to secure a return home. Eventually, some four years after the death of Augustus, he died himself, still in exile at Tomis (a small town on the Black Sea, now Constanta in modern Romania). In his ten years there, he never tired of bemoaning the climate of the place and its remoteness, but he did learn the local language and he did acknowledge the kindness that his hosts had afforded him.

A much fuller account of the issues raised in this section will be found in Wilkinson (1955) and in Kenney, *Cambridge History of Classical Literature II* (Cambridge, 1982) 420-57. See also J.C. Thibault, *The Mystery of Ovid's Exile* (Beverley and Los Angeles, 1964).

2. Metre

English verse is based on stress; it is, essentially, a recognizable pattern of stressed and unstressed syllables.

Mad dogs and Englishmen go out in the mid-day sun.

It would be possible to substitute for 'Englishmen' words such as 'antelopes' or 'terriers' without disturbing the metre because all three words have the same stress pattern; substitute 'alsatians', however, and the metre is lost, not because the number of syllables is wrong, but because the stress pattern is.

Classical Greek, on the other hand, had no stress so that its verse was not stress based. It was founded instead on a pattern of 'long' (marked —) and 'short' (marked ∪) syllables, sometimes called 'heavy' and 'light', though both sets of terms are misleading because not all 'long' syllables take longer to say than 'short' syllables and 'heavy' and 'light' suggest stress which is quite wrong. It will suffice to say that the distinction for the Greek speaker between 'long' and 'short' syllables was different from, but no less important than, the distinction between stressed and unstressed syllables for the English speaker.

The Homeric poems, and all Classical epic and didactic poetry thereafter (and much more besides), were written in the dactylic hexameter. This rhythm consists of six dactyls (— ∪ ∪) which may (in the case of the last foot, must) become spondees (——), like this:

$$\cup\cup - \cup\cup - \cup\cup - \cup\cup - \cup\cup --$$

(As in all metres, Greek and Latin, a short syllable may count long at the end of a line). By translating length into stress, it is possible to gain some sense of the rhythm from the schoolboy mnemonic:

Down in a deep dark ditch sat an old cow munching a turnip.

But, as the pattern above indicates and as any reading of the text will illustrate, the dactylic hexameter enjoys great inherent variety. Add to that the fact that sentences could, and more and more frequently did, run over from line to line, coming to rest at a considerable variety of points within the line, and it will be seen that this is a metre well suited for narrative poetry.

The elegiac couplet, on the other hand, is, as its name indicates, a two line metre and is a rhythm which clearly lends itself to end-stopping. Indeed, the second line of the couplet is often no more than a restatement of the first. It is, accordingly, a superb metre for cleverness and wit, but it lacks the epic weight of the dactylic hexameters, though it never lost its rôle in brief epitaphs where its very simplicity could lend real dignity.

Latin, like English, is a stressed language and its very earliest verse, like much of its mediaeval or modern (*gaudeamus igitur*, for instance, or *adeste fideles*), was based wholly on stress patterns, just like English verse. However, during the classical period and beyond, for at least a millenium from the second century B.C., Latin verse was based on the principles of Greek quantitative verse, as it is called, though, gradually, with some extra refinements that almost certainly arose because Latin was a stressed language.

The reader who wishes to know more should consult L.P. Wilkinson, *Golden Latin Artistry* (Cambridge, 1970) 89-134. Further exploration of the purely technical aspects of this section could usefully begin with W. Sidney Allen, *Accent and Rhythm* (Cambridge, 1973) and D.E. Hill, 'Quaestio Prosodiae', *Glotta 52* (1974) 218-31.

3. *The text*

The *Metamorphoses* was one of the most popular of classical works during the Middle Ages and, as a consequence, we possess a bewildering number of mediaeval manuscripts, though none earlier than the ninth century and no complete manuscript earlier than the twelfth. In addition, we possess a translation into Greek by the 13th century monk, Maximus Planudes. All the ordinary difficulties of such a tradition are further complicated by the apparent existence from time to time of ancient alternatives which may or may not have arisen from two editions from Ovid's own hand. For the details, see R.J. Tarrant in *Texts and Transmission*, edited L.D. Reynolds, (Oxford, 1983) *276-82*.

Professor Tarrant is preparing a text for the O.C.T. series and he has very kindly sent me copies of his draft typescript of the text for the first tweve books. In choosing between well known variants or emendations I have, far more often than not, been guided by him. His text will obviously become the standard one; in view of its imminence, I have contented myself with producing a readable text without apparatus or serious pretensions to originality. The punctuation style is my own.

4. *The translation*

Before any attempt to outline the principles on which this translation is based, it may help to consider other possible approaches and discuss why they have been discarded.

It might be argued that verse for a lengthy work is as alien to a modern audience as Latin itself and any attempt, therefore, to use verse cloaks the translation with a quaintness that is quite wrong. There are, of course, translations available for anyone of that persuasian and the theoretical position is advanced in perhaps its most trenchant form in E.V. Rieu's introduction to his Penguin translation of the *Odyssey*. This translation of the *Metamorphoses*, however, is based on the proposition that the 'otherness' of Ovid is part of his importance and appeal and that to make him seem like a contemporary is not the task of his translator.

It might be argued that Ovid's verse was composed according to the strictest rules and that the appropriate English equivalent would involve strict metre at least and, probably, rhyme as well. Arthur Golding, whose translation was known to Shakespeare, A.E. Watts (University of California Press, 1954), whose translation was lavishly praised by Otis, and now A.D. Melville (Oxford, 1986) are among the best known to have adopted this approach. On rhyme I cannot do better than cite Milton's preamble to *Paradise Lost*:

> *The measure is* English *Heroic Verse without Rime, as that of* Homer
> *in Greek and of* Virgil *in Latin; Rime being no necessary Adjunct or*
> *true Ornament of Poem or good Verse, in longer Works especially,*

but the Invention of a barbarous Age, to set off wretched matter and lame Metre; grac't indeed since by the use of some famous modern Poets, carried away by Custom, but much to thir own vexation, hindrance, and constraint to express many things otherwise, and for the most part worse than else they would have exprest them. This neglect then of Rime so little is to be taken for a defect, though it may seem so perhaps to vulgar Readers, that it rather is to be esteem'd an example set, the first in English, *of ancient liberty recover'd to Heroic Poem from the troublesome and modern bondage of Riming.*

Furthermore, rhyme must restrict vocabulary and, therefore, fidelity and, even more important, it produces either end-stopped lines or constant comic effect. For all these reasons, rhyme is possibly appropriate for Ovid's elegiacs but certainly not for his hexameter poem. Most of these arguments apply also, to a greater or lesser extent, to strict verse but, in any case, the argument for strict verse is based on something of a fallacy. While it is perfectly true that Ovidian hexameters are written to very precise rules they are, nevertheless, rules which permit an astonishing range of tempos which would be wholly lost in the strait-jacket of English strict verse. For all these reasons, I have settled on a six-beat blank verse effect though I have not scrupled, from time to time, to stretch my metre even to the point where the reader may think that it has become prose, if fidelity to Ovid's meaning was not, apparently, otherwise attainable. In broad terms, I took the view that once a rhythm had been established, it would be easier for the reader to imagine that it had been sustained than to identify and correct an infidelity. The principle advantage of the line for line translation is that it minimises the distortions inevitable in any translation. It must be wrong to use six words where Ovid uses only one, or seriously to distort the order of his ideas. I have tried to preserve either the order of Ovid's words or his sentence structure, whichever seemed more significant in each case. Where Ovid uses a common Latin word, I have sought a common English word, but where his vocabulary is highly poetic, deliberately archaic or, as so often, where he has deliberately coined a new word, I have attempted the same effect in English. In the notes, I have tried to draw attention to particular instances where the translation has failed or might mislead. I hope that I have done this often enough so that the reader never wholly forgets that this is a translation, and not so frequently that the reader loses all trust. Ideally, the reader will so enjoy the translation and the insights that it, together with the notes, provides, that he will be driven to a desire to master the Latin. For a full account of the history of Renaissance English translations of Ovid, see Wilkinson (1955) 406-38. For more on the principles behind this particular translation, see D.E. Hill, 'What sort of Translation of Virgil do we need?', *G & R 25* (1978) 59-68 (now reprinted in *Virgil* (Greece and Rome Studies) edited Ian McAuslan and Peter Walcot, Oxford, 1990, pp. 180-8).

5. *The notes*

As has already been indicated, Ovid's *Metamorphoses* is an amazingly rich poem full of learning, allusion and wit. Apart from the very important observations on the limits of the translation, as discussed above, the main purposes of the notes are to elucidate passages likely to be unclear, to indicate something of Ovid's possible sources and to discuss how he treated them, to give some indication of how Ovid's work has influenced his successors and to add anything else which seems valuable or interesting. The notes make no pretence whatsoever of completeness and, inevitably, reflect one man's tastes and prejudices. The hope is, however, that the notes will alert readers to the sort of questions that can be asked, challenge readers to notice, from their own reading, important points that have been omitted and bring to readers' attention classical authors and modern scholarly works they might otherwise have ignored. Students of classics in translation (and some readers will surely fall into that category) are often far too diffident to approach the notes of the standard editions of classical authors. In an attempt to overcome this, I have quoted from such works extensively and directed to them very freely in the hope that any reader with access to a standard university library will feel drawn to use its resources and thus, in a relatively painless way, acquire a wider and deeper knowledge of classical literature with Ovid as the spur. However, the genius of Ovid is such that, although a full appreciation does indeed depend on a close familiarity with classical literature, much profit and pleasure can still be gained from a relatively superficial reading. Accordingly, a reader coming to the work for the first time should consult the notes only when puzzled by the translation or text. Second or subsequent readings can then be enriched by following up the leads given in the notes.

The notes include almost no linguistic discussion; it would be burdensome for those without Latin and, with a facing translation present, largely superfluous for those with Latin, especially since they can turn to Anderson and Hollis for more linguistically based notes on books 6-8.

Two points about Ovid's 'sources' should be made plain. Much classical and Hellenistic literature known to Ovid is lost to us. Accordingly, it should not be assumed that a note's reference to an earlier treatment of a myth or idea necessarily involves a suggestion that it is Ovid's source. Each case must be judged on its merits; an understanding of Ovid cannot, however, be complete without as much knowledge as possible about the ancient tradition behind him and a full appreciation of his sense of detail.

Some readers may be disappointed that the notes are not much fuller on Ovid's influence on later times, though those already well versed in mediaeval literature and art will find much in the text and notes that they will recognize. The best general treatments of this subject are to be found in Rand, Wilkinson (1955), the essays by Robathan and Jameson in *Ovid*, edited J.W. Binns (London, 1973) 191-242, Hanne Carlsen, *A Bibliography to the Classical Tradition in English Literature* (Copenhagen, 1985), *Ovidian influences on literature and art from the Middle Ages to the twentieth century*, edited by Charles Martindale, Cambridge, (1988) and Jane Davidson Reid, *The Oxford Guide to Classical Mythology in the Arts*, Oxford, (1993).

METAMORPHOSES IX–XII

LIBER IX

    Quae gemitus truncaeque deo Neptunius heros
causa rogat frontis; cui sic Calydonius amnis
coepit, inornatos redimitus harundine crines:
    'triste petis munus; quis enim sua proelia uictus
5   commemorare uelit? referam tamen ordine, nec tam
turpe fuit uinci quam contendisse decorum est,
magnaque dat nobis tantus solacia uictor.
nomine si qua suo fando peruenit ad aures
Deïanira tuas, quondam pulcherrima uirgo
10   multorumque fuit spes inuidiosa procorum.
cum quibus ut soceri domus est intrata petiti,
"accipe me generum," dixi "Parthaone nate."
dixit et Alcides; alii cessere duobus.
ille Iouem socerum dare se famamque laborum,
15   et superata suae referebat iussa nouercae.
contra ego "turpe deum mortali cedere" dixi
(nondum erat ille deus); "dominum me cernis aquarum
cursibus obliquis inter tua regna fluentum.
nec gener externis hospes tibi missus ab oris,
20   sed popularis ero et rerum pars una tuarum.
tantum ne noceat quod me nec regia Iuno
odit et omnis abest iussorum poena laborum.
nam quo te iactas, Alcmena nate, creatum
Iuppiter aut falsus pater est aut crimine uerus.
25   matris adulterio patrem petis; elige fictum
esse Iouem malis an te per dedecus ortum."
talia dicentem iamdudum lumine toruo
spectat et accensae non fortiter imperat irae
uerbaque tot reddit: "melior mihi dextera lingua.
30   dummodo pugnando superem, tu uince loquendo"
congrediturque ferox. puduit modo magna locutum
cedere; reieci uiridem de corpore uestem
bracchiaque opposui tenuique a pectore uaras
in statione manus et pugnae membra paraui.
35   ille cauis hausto spargit me puluere palmis
inque uicem fuluae tactu flauescit harenae;
et modo ceruicem, modo crura micantia captat,
aut captare putes, omnique a parte lacessit.
me mea defendit grauitas frustraque petebar,
40   haud secus ac moles quam magno murmure fluctus
oppugnant; manet illa suoque est pondere tuta.
digredimur paulum rursusque ad bella coimus
inque gradu stetimus certi non cedere; eratque
cum pede pes iunctus, totoque ego pectore pronus
45   et digitos digitis et frontem fronte premebam.

BOOK 9

What was the reason for the god's groans, asked the Neptunian
hero, and for his mutilated forehead; the Calydonian river began thus
to him, his dishevelled hair wreathed with bulrushes:
   'It is a grim favour you seek; for who that has been conquered would be willing
to recall his battles? Even so, I shall tell it in order, and it was not   5
so shameful to be conquered as it is glorious to have striven,
and so great a conqueror gives me great solace.
If in talk there has come by name to your ears
some Deïanira, she was once a most beautiful maiden
and the jealous hope of many suitors.   10
And when with them the house of the sought after father-in-law had been entered,
"Take me for a son-in-law," I said, "O son of Parthaon."
Alcides said the same; the others gave way to us two.
He referred to giving Jupiter to her as a father-in-law, to the fame
of his labours and to his overcoming of the orders of his stepmother.   15
In reply, I said, "It is shameful for a god to give way to a mortal"
(he was not yet a god); "you are looking at me, lord of the waters
that flow in twisting courses within your realms.
And I am not an alien son-in-law sent from foreign lands,
but I shall be one of your people and a part of your state.   20
Only let it not hurt me that neither royal Juno
hates me nor do I have any punishment of imposed labours.
For he to whom you, son of Alcmene, boast that you were born,
Jupiter, is either a false father, or a true one through sin.
You seek a father in the adultery of your mother; choose whether you prefer   25
that Jupiter is a fictitious father or that you have sprung from dishonour."
While I was speaking thus, he had been long gazing at me with a grim
look, and, scarcely controlling his blazing anger,
he replied in so many words: "My right hand is better than my tongue.
Provided only that I win in the fighting, you may outdo me in the speaking,"   30
and he closed with me savagely. After boasting just now, I was ashamed
to give way; I threw the green clothing from my body,
and put my arms up and held my hands half-clenched,
at the ready, away from my chest, and prepared my body for the fight.
He scooped up some dust in his hollowed palms and sprinkled it on me,   35
and in his turn grew yellow with the touch of yellow sand.
And now he caught my neck, now my flashing legs,
or you would have thought that he caught them, and he assailed me from every angle.
My weight protected me and I was attacked in vain,
just like a rock on which with a great rumbling the billows   40
pound; it stays there safe in its own bulk.
We drew apart a little and then again came together in war
and stood our ground determined not to yield; and we were
joined toe to toe, and I, leaning over him with all my breast,
pressed fingers to fingers and brow to brow.   45

non aliter uidi fortes concurrere tauros,
cum pretium pugnae toto nitidissima saltu
expetitur coniunx; spectant armenta pauentque
nescia quem maneat tanti uictoria regni.
50   ter sine profectu uoluit nitentia contra
reicere Alcides a se mea pectora; quarto
excutit amplexus adductaque bracchia soluit
impulsumque manu (certum est mihi uera fateri)
protinus auertit tergoque onerosus inhaesit.
55   si qua fides (neque enim ficta mihi gloria uoce
quaeritur), imposito pressus mihi monte uidebar.
uix tamen inserui sudore fluentia multo
bracchia, uix solui duros a corpore nexus;
instat anhelanti prohibetque resumere uires
60   et ceruice mea potitur. tum denique tellus
pressa genu nostro est et harenas ore momordi.
inferior uirtute meas deuertor ad artes
elaborque uiro longum formatus in anguem.
qui postquam flexos sinuaui corpus in orbes
65   cumque fero moui linguam stridore bisulcam,
risit et inludens nostras Tirynthius artes
"cunarum labor est angues superare mearum"
dixit "et ut uincas alios, Acheloe, dracones,
pars quota Lernaeae serpens eris unus echidnae?
70   uulneribus fecunda suis erat illa nec ullum
de comitum numero caput est impune recisum
quin gemino ceruix herede ualentior esset.
hanc ego ramosam natis e caede colubris
crescentemque malo domui domitamque peremi.
75   quid fore te credis, falsum qui uersus in anguem
arma aliena moues, quem forma precaria celat?"
dixerat et summo digitorum uincula collo
inicit; angebar ceu guttura forcipe pressus
pollicibusque meas pugnabam euellere fauces.
80   sic quoque deuicto restabat tertia tauri
forma trucis; tauro mutatus membra rebello.
induit ille toris a laeua parte lacertos
admissumque trahens sequitur depressaque dura
cornua figit humo meque alta sternit harena.
85   nec satis hoc fuerat; rigidum fera dextera cornu,
dum tenet, infregit truncaque a fronte reuellit.
Naïdes hoc pomis et odoro flore repletum
sacrarunt, diuesque meo Bona Copia cornu est.'
dixerat, et nymphe ritu succincta Dianae,
90   una ministrarum, fusis utrimque capillis,
incessit totumque tulit praediuite cornu
autumnum et mensas, felicia poma, secundas.
lux subit et primo feriente cacumina sole
discedunt iuuenes; neque enim dum flumina pacem
95   et placidos habeant lapsus totaeque residant

Just so have I seen strong bulls charge together,
when the prize sought for in the fight is the sleekest wife
in all the glade; the herds look on and tremble,
not knowing for whom the victory of so great a realm waits.
Three times Alcides wanted without success to push   50
my breast away as it struggled against him; the fourth time,
he shook off my embrace, loosened my tight arms,
and, pushing me with his hand (I am determined to admit the truth),
at once turned me round and clung heavily upon my back.
If you believe me (for I do not seek glory by telling   55
falsehoods), I felt weighed down by a mountain laid upon me.
And yet I was just able to insert my arms, streaming with much
sweat, just able to loosen the strength of his hold.
He pressed upon me as I gasped, stopped me from regaining my strength
and took hold of my neck. Then at last my knee was   60
forced to the ground and I bit upon the sand.
Worsted in manly strength, I turned to my own skills
and slipped away from the man by forming myself into a long snake.
And after I had looped my body into twisted coils
and moved my forked tongue with a fierce hiss,   65
the Tirynthian laughed and, mocking my skills,
"It was the labour of my cradle to overcome snakes,"
he said, "and though you outdo, Achelous, other serpents
how small a part will you, as one snake, be of the Lernaean hydra?
She was made fertile by her injuries, and not one   70
head out of the number of its companions was cut back with impunity,
but instead the neck was strengthened by twin heirs.
She was branching out with snakes born from the slaughter
and was growing in evil, but I subdued her and, when she was subdued, dispatched her.
And what do you think will become of you, turned into a false snake,   75
wielding arms not your own and hiding in a borrowed form?"
He had spoken, and then he clapped his fingers, fetter-like, around the top
of my neck; I was being strangled as if my windpipe had been gripped by pincers,
and I was fighting to prise my throat from his thumbs.
Conquered in this shape too, I was left a third form,   80
a fierce bull; I changed my body to a bull's and fought again.
He thrust his arms onto my muscles from the left side,
let me run on, then, dragging me back, followed after, pushing my horns down
and sticking them in the hard ground, making me sprawl in the deep sand.
And this was not enough; while he held my stiff horn   85
with his fierce right hand, he broke it and tore it from my mutilated forehead.
The Naiads filled it with fruit and fragrant flowers
and sanctified it, and *Bona Copia* is wealthy because of my horn.'
     He had spoken, and a nymph girt-up in Diana's style,
one of his serving-girls, with her hair let down on both sides,   90
advanced, bearing in that most bounteous horn the whole of
autumn, that is glad fruits, for the second course.
Daylight approached and, with the first sun striking the peaks,
the young men departed; for they did not wait for the river
to have peace and a gentle flow, and for all   95

opperiuntur aquae. uultus Achelous agrestes
et lacerum cornu mediis caput abdidit undis.
      huic tamen ablati doluit iactura decoris,
cetera sospes habet; capitis quoque fronde saligna
100 aut superimposita celatur harundine damnum.
at te, Nesse ferox, eiusdem uirginis ardor
perdiderat uolucri traiectum terga sagitta.
namque noua repetens patrios cum coniuge muros
uenerat Eueni rapidas Ioue natus ad undas.
105 uberior solito nimbis hiemalibus auctus
uerticibusque frequens erat atque imperuius amnis.
intrepidum pro se, curam de coniuge agentem
Nessus adit membrisque ualens scitusque uadorum
'officio' que 'meo ripa sistetur in illa
110 haec,' ait 'Alcide; tu uiribus utere nando.'
pallentemque metu fluuiumque ipsumque timentem
tradidit Aonius pauidam Calydonida Nesso;
mox, ut erat, pharetraque grauis spolioque leonis
(nam clauam et curuos trans ripam miserat arcus)
115 'quandoquidem coepi, superentur flumina' dixit;
nec dubitat nec qua sit clementissimus amnis
quaerit et obsequio deferri spernit aquarum.
iamque tenens ripam, missos cum tolleret arcus,
coniugis agnouit uocem Nessoque paranti
120 fallere depositum 'quo te fiducia' clamat
'uana pedum, uiolente, rapit? tibi, Nesse biformis,
dicimus; exaudi, nec res intercipe nostras.
si te nulla mei reuerentia mouit, at orbes
concubitus uetitos poterant inhibere paterni.
125 haud tamen effugies, quamuis ope fidis equina;
uulnere, non pedibus te consequar.' ultima dicta
re probat et missa fugientia terga sagitta
traicit; exstabat ferrum de pectore aduncum.
quod simul euulsum est, sanguis per utrumque foramen
130 emicuit mixtus Lernaei tabe ueneni.
excipit hunc Nessus 'neque enim moriemur inulti'
secum ait et calido uelamina tincta cruore
dat munus raptae uelut inritamen amoris.
      longa fuit medii mora temporis, actaque magni
135 Herculis implerant terras odiumque nouercae.
uictor ab Oechalia Cenaeo sacra parabat
uota Ioui, cum Fama loquax praecessit ad aures,
Deianira, tuas (quae ueris addere falsa
gaudet et e minimo sua per mendacia crescit):
140 Amphitryoniaden Ioles ardore teneri.
credit amans Venerisque nouae perterrita fama
indulsit primo lacrimis flendoque dolorem
diffudit miseranda suum; mox deinde 'quid autem
flemus?' ait 'paelex lacrimis laetabitur istis.
145 quae quoniam adueniet, properandum aliquidque nouandum est,

the waters to subside. Achelous hid his rustic face
and his head stripped of a horn in the middle of the waters.
    Though grieved by the loss of this adornment now removed,
he was unscathed otherwise; and the loss to his head was concealed
by a covering of willow leaves or bulrushes.   100
But you, fierce Nessus, had been destroyed by ardour for the same
maiden, your back transfixed by a flying arrow.
For, returning with his new wife to his native walls,
Jove's son had come to the swift waters of Euenus.
The river, fuller than usual, increased by winter storms,   105
was teeming with whirlpools and impassable.
Fearless for himself but concerned for his wife,
he was approached by Nessus strong in limb and familiar with the shallows;
and, 'With my assistance, she will be set down on that bank,
Alcides,' he said; 'you must use your strength for swimming.'   110
Pale with fear and afraid both of the river and of him,
the terrified Calydonian was handed over to Nessus by the Aonian;
soon, weighed down as he was by his quiver and his lion skin
(for his club and curved bow he had thrown across to the bank),
'As I have begun, so let this river be overcome,' he said;   115
he neither hesitated nor sought out where the river was
calmest, and he scorned to be conveyed by the compliance of the waters.
And now, reaching the bank, while he was picking up the bow he had thrown,
he recognized his wife's voice and, as Nessus prepared
to breach his trust, cried out to him, 'Where, does your vain   120
trust in your feet, you savage, rush you off to? It is you, two-formed Nessus,
I am speaking to; listen, and do not purloin my property.
If no respect for me moves you, yet your father's wheel
could have restrained you from forbidden intercourse.
But you will not escape, however much you trust your horse strength; 125
with a wound, not with my feet, I shall catch you.' These last words
he confirmed with action and transfixed the fleeing back with an arrow
shot; the barbed shaft was protruding from his breast.
And as soon as it was plucked out, blood mixed with the corruption
of the Lernaean poison spurted from both holes.   130
This Nessus gathered up; 'But I shall not die unavenged,'
he said to himself, and he gave clothes soaked in his warm
blood as a gift to the girl he had seized, as though it were a love stimulant.
    There was a long intervening lapse of time, and the deeds of great
Hercules had filled the lands and the hatred of his stepmother.   135
The victor at Oechalia was preparing a sacred offering
to Cenaean Jove, when talkative Rumour came first to your
ears, Deïanira, (adding falsehood to truth
is her delight, and through her lies she grows from something very small):
to say that Amphitryoniades was in the grip of ardour for Iole.   140
She loved him, but believed it and, terrified by the rumour of a new passion,
first she gave way to tears and by her weeping piteously
spread her grief abroad; soon after, 'But why
am I weeping?' she said, 'The wench will rejoice in those tears.
Since she will be coming, there is a need to make haste and devise something 145

dum licet et nondum thalamos tenet altera nostros.
conquerar an sileam? repetam Calydona morerne?
excedam tectis an, si nihil amplius, obstem?
quid si me, Meleagre, tuam memor esse sororem
150   forte paro facinus, quantumque iniuria possit
femineusque dolor iugulata paelice testor?'
in cursus animus uarios abit; omnibus illis
praetulit imbutam Nesseo sanguine uestem
mittere, quae uires defecto reddat amori.
155   ignaroque Lichae quid tradat nescia luctus
ipsa suos tradit blandisque miserrima uerbis
dona det illa uiro mandat. capit inscius heros
induiturque umeris Lernaeae uirus echidnae.
      tura dabat primis et uerba precantia flammis
160   uinaque marmoreas patera fundebat in aras;
incaluit uis illa mali resolutaque flammis
Herculeos abiit late dilapsa per artus.
dum potuit, solita gemitum uirtute repressit;
uicta malis postquam est patientia, reppulit aras
165   impleuitque suis nemorosam uocibus Oeten.
nec mora, letiferam conatur scindere uestem;
qua trahitur, trahit illa cutem, foedumque relatu,
aut haeret membris frustra temptata reuelli
aut laceros artus et grandia detegit ossa.
170   ipse cruor, gelido ceu quondam lammina candens
tincta lacu, stridit coquiturque ardente ueneno.
nec modus est, sorbent auidae praecordia flammae
caeruleusque fluit toto de corpore sudor
ambustique sonant nerui, caecaque medullis
175   tabe liquefactis tollens ad sidera palmas
'cladibus,' exclamat 'Saturnia, pascere nostris,
pascere et hanc pestem specta, crudelis, ab alto
corque ferum satia. uel si miserandus et hostis,
[hoc est, si tibi sum, diris cruciatibus aegram]
180   inuisamque animam natamque laboribus aufer.
mors mihi munus erit; decet haec dare dona nouercam.
ergo ego foedantem peregrino templa cruore
Busirin domui saeuoque alimenta parentis
Antaeo eripui nec me pastoris Hiberi
185   forma triplex nec forma triplex tua, Cerbere, mouit?
uosne, manus, ualidi pressistis cornua tauri?
uestrum opus Elis habet, uestrum Stymphalides undae
Partheniumque nemus, uestra uirtute relatus
Thermodontiaco caelatus balteus auro
190   pomaque ab insomni concustodita dracone.
nec mihi Centauri potuere resistere nec mi
Arcadiae uastator aper, nec profuit hydrae
crescere per damnum geminasque resumere uires.
quid, cum Thracis equos humano sanguine pingues
195   plenaque corporibus laceris praesepia uidi

while I can and while that other woman does not yet occupy my bedroom.
Should I complain or be silent? Should I return to Calydon or linger here?
Should I withdraw from the house or, if nothing else, stand in her way?
What if I, mindful, Meleager, that I am your sister,
prepare a bold crime, and bear witness to how much a woman   150
wronged and in pain can do, by slaying the wench?
Her mind went off in various directions; to all of them
she preferred sending the clothing soaked in Nessean
blood, so as to restore the strength of a love that had failed.
And to Lichas, ignorant of what she was giving, she herself not knowing,   155
gave her own grief, and with coaxing words that most unhappy woman
bade him to hand those gifts to her husband. The unwitting hero took them
and put onto his shoulder the Lernaean hydra's venom.
        He was offering incense and words of prayer to the first flames
and was pouring wine onto the marble altars from a bowl;   160
the violence of that evil, warmed and melted in the flames,
went off seeping throughout the Herculean limbs.
While he could, he suppressed his groaning with his usual virtue.
After his endurance had been conquered by his sufferings, he pushed the altars back
and filled wooded Oeta with his cries.   165
And without delay, he was trying to rip the deadly clothing off;
where it was pulled, it pulled the skin and, disgusting to relate,
it either clung to the body when he tried in vain to wrench it off,
or it uncovered mangled limbs and his great bones.
His very blood, as when a white-hot metal strip is dipped   170
in a cold tank, hissed and cooked in the burning poison.
And there was no limit to it; the greedy flames consumed his breast,
a blue-green sweat flowed from the whole of his body,
his burning sinews resounded, and, as his marrow melted
in the unseen corruption, raising his hands up to the stars,   175
'Saturnia,' he cried out, 'feed yourself on my disasters,
feed yourself, and gaze upon this plague, cruel one, from on high,
and glut your fierce heart. Or, if even an enemy is to be pitied,
[that is, if I am an enemy to you, sick as it is from dreadful torture]
destroy this life hated and born for labours.   180
Death will be a favour to me; it is the gift a stepmother should give.
Is it for this that I tamed Busiris as he fouled his temples
with strangers' blood, that I snatched his mother's nourishment
from cruel Antaeus, and that neither the triple form of the Spanish
shepherd, nor your triple form, Cerberus, moved me?   185
Was it you, O my hands, that forced down the horns of the mighty bull?
Yours was the task at Elis, yours at the Stymphalian waters,
and at the Parthenian copse, by your courage was there brought back
the bāldric embossed with gold of Thermodon,
and the apples closely guarded by the sleepless snake.   190
Nor could the Centaurs resist me, nor could
the boar that ravaged Arcadia, nor did it profit the hydra
to grow by its loss and to regain double strength.
What of the Thracian's horses fattened on human blood,
and their stalls filled with mangled bodies which once I saw,   195

uisaque deieci dominumque ipsosque peremi?
his elisa iacet moles Nemeaea lacertis,
hac caelum ceruice tuli. defessa iubendo est
saeua Iouis coniunx; ego sum indefessus agendo.
200   sed noua pestis adest, cui nec uirtute resisti
nec telis armisque potest; pulmonibus errat
ignis edax imis perque omnes pascitur artus.
at ualet Eurystheus! et sunt qui credere possint
esse deos?' dixit perque altam saucius Oeten
205   haud aliter graditur, quam si uenabula taurus
corpore fixa gerat factique refugerit auctor.
saepe illum gemitus edentem, saepe frementem,
saepe retemptantem totas infringere uestes
sternentemque trabes irascentemque uideres
210   montibus aut patrio tendentem bracchia caelo.
      ecce Lichan trepidum et latitantem rupe cauata
aspicit, utque dolor rabiem conlegerat omnem,
'tune, Licha,' dixit 'feralia dona dedisti?
tune meae necis auctor eris?' tremit ille pauetque
215   pallidus et timide uerba excusantia dicit;
dicentem genibusque manus adhibere parantem
corripit Alcides et terque quaterque rotatum
mittit in Euboicas tormento fortius undas.
ille per aërias pendens induruit auras,
220   utque ferunt imbres gelidis concrescere uentis,
inde niues fieri, niuibus quoque molle rotatis
astringi et spissa glomerari grandine corpus,
sic illum ualidis iactum per inane lacertis
exsanguemque metu nec quidquam umoris habentem
225   in rigidos uersum silices prior edidit aetas.
nunc quoque in Euboico scopulus breuis eminet alto
gurgite et humanae seruat uestigia formae,
quem quasi sensurum nautae calcare uerentur
appellantque Lichan.
                at tu, Iouis inclita proles,
230   arboribus caesis quas ardua gesserat Oete
inque pyram structis, arcum pharetramque capacem
regnaque uisuras iterum Troiana sagittas
ferre iubes Poeante satum, quo flamma ministro est
subdita; dumque auidis comprenditur ignibus agger,
235   congeriem siluae Nemeaeo uellere summam
sternis et imposita clauae ceruice recumbis
haud alio uultu, quam si conuiua iaceres
inter plena meri redimitus pocula sertis.
      iamque ualens et in omne latus diffusa sonabat
240   securosque artus contemptoremque petebat
flamma suum, timuere dei pro uindice terrae.
quos ita (sensit enim) laeto Saturnius ore
Iuppiter adloquitur. 'nostra est timor iste uoluptas,
o superi, totoque libens mihi pectore grator,

and, having seen, I demolished, and destroyed both master and horses?
By these arms, the Nemean monster was strangled and lies dead,
on this neck, I bore the sky. Jove's cruel wife
is wearied from giving orders; I am unwearied from performing them.
But here is a new plague which can be resisted   200
neither by manly strength, nor by force of arms; a devouring fire
spreads through the depths of my lungs and feeds on all my limbs.
But Eurystheus is well! And are there those who can believe
that there are gods?' Thus he spoke and went stricken through high
Oeta, just as if a bull carries hunting spears   205
stuck in his body and the perpetrator of the deed has fled.
Often you would see him giving groans, often roaring,
often trying again to tear all the clothing off,
and felling trees and raging at the mountains
or stretching out his arms to his father's heaven.   210
       Look, he caught sight of Lichas terrified and hiding in a hollowed
crag, and when the pain had built up all its fury,
'Was it you, Lichas', he said, 'who gave these deadly gifts?
Will you be the perpetrator of my murder?' He trembled and grew pale
with fear and nervously spoke words of excuse;   215
and as he spoke and prepared to put hands to knees,
Alcides seized him and spun him three or four times round
and threw him more violently than a catapult into the Euboean sea.
As he hung in the airy breezes, he hardened
and, as they say that showers congeal in cold winds,   220
and then become snow and, when the snow has swirled around, its soft
mass freezes and is rounded into thick hail,
so he, thrown through the void by mighty arms,
bloodless from fear, having no moisture in him,
was turned, as an earlier age told it, into solid stone.   225
Even now there is a low protruding rock in the deep Euboean
flood which keeps traces of its human form,
and which sailors fear to tread on as if it would feel them,
and they call it Lichas.
                        But you, famed offspring of Jupiter,
when you had cut down the trees which lofty Oeta bore   230
and built them into a pyre, you ordered that your bow and capacious quiver
and your arrows that would see Troy's kingdom again
be borne by Poeas' son by whose service the flame was
put beneath; and while the greedy flames were seizing the pile,
you strewed the Nemean hide over the top of the heaped up   235
wood and reclined, your neck resting on your club,
with no other expression than if you were lying down as a dinner guest
wreathed with garlands among full cups of undiluted wine.
       And now the flame, strengthening and spreading on every side,
began noisily to seek out his calm limbs   240
and its despiser; the gods feared for the earth's defender.
And so (for he had noticed it) Saturnian Jupiter spoke to them
in joyful terms: 'That fear of yours is my delight,
O gods, and I gladly congratulate myself with all my heart,

245 quod memoris populi dicor rectorque paterque
et mea progenies uestro quoque tuta fauore est.
nam quamquam ipsius datur hoc immanibus actis,
obligor ipse tamen. sed enim ne pectora uano
fida metu paueant, Oetaeas spernite flammas!
250 omnia qui uicit uincet quos cernitis ignes,
nec nisi materna Vulcanum parte potentem
sentiet; aeternum est a me quod traxit et expers
atque immune necis nullaque domabile flamma.
idque ego defunctum terra caelestibus oris
255 accipiam, cunctisque meum laetabile factum
dis fore confido. si quis tamen Hercule, si quis
forte deo doliturus erit, data praemia nolet,
sed meruisse dari sciet inuitusque probabit.'
adsensere dei; coniunx quoque regia uisa est
260 cetera non duro, duro tamen ultima uultu
dicta tulisse Iouis seque indoluisse notatam.
interea quodcumque fuit populabile flammae
Mulciber abstulerat, nec cognoscenda remansit
Herculis effigies nec quidquam ab imagine ductum
265 matris habet, tantumque Iouis uestigia seruat.
utque nouus serpens posita cum pelle senecta
luxuriare solet squamaque nitere recenti,
sic, ubi mortales Tirynthius exuit artus,
parte sui meliore uiget maiorque uideri
270 coepit et augusta fieri grauitate uerendus.
quem pater omnipotens inter caua nubila raptum
quadriiugo curru radiantibus intulit astris.

        sensit Atlans pondus; neque adhuc Stheneleius iras
soluerat Eurystheus odiumque in prole paternum
275 exercebat atrox. at longis anxia curis,
Argolis Alcmene questus ubi ponat aniles,
cui referat nati testatos orbe labores
cuiue suos casus, Iolen habet; Herculis illam
imperiis thalamoque animoque receperat Hyllus
280 impleratque uterum generoso semine. cui sic
incipit Alcmene: 'faueant tibi numina saltem
corripiantque moras, tum cum matura uocabis
praepositam timidis parientibus Ilithyiam,
quam mihi difficilem Iunonis gratia fecit.
285 namque laboriferi cum iam natalis adesset
Herculis et decimum premeretur sidere signum,
tendebat grauitas uterum mihi, quodque ferebam
tantum erat ut posses auctorem dicere tecti
ponderis esse Iouem. nec iam tolerare labores
290 ulterius poteram; quin nunc quoque frigidus artus,
dum loquor, horror habet, parsque est meminisse doloris.
septem ego per noctes, totidem cruciata diebus,
fessa malis tendensque ad caelum bracchia magno
Lucinam Nixusque pares clamore uocabam.

that I am called ruler and father of a grateful people,   245
and that my offspring too is safe in your favour.
For although you are giving him this for his own tremendous deeds,
I am myself still in your debt. But let not your faithful hearts
tremble with vain fear, scorn the Oetaean flames!
He who has conquered everything will conquer the fires that you see,   250
and he will not feel the power of Vulcan except in his mother's
part. What he has drawn from me is eternal, free of
and exempt from death, and not to be subdued by any flame.
And when it has done with earth, I shall receive it in the heavenly
domains, and I am sure that this my act will   255
bring joy to all the gods. If anyone, however, if anyone happens
to be aggrieved that Hercules will be a god, he will not want the reward to be given,
but he will know that it deserved to be given and will unwillingly approve.'
The gods assented; the king's wife too seemed
to have borne the rest of Jove's words without a morose expression,   260
but his last ones morosely, and seemed pained at his rebuke.'
Meanwhile, whatever was ravageable by fire,
Mulciber had destroyed, and Hercules' appearance
did not survive to be recognized, nor did he have anything drawn
from his mother's looks, he kept traces of Jupiter only.   265
And as a new snake that has cast off old age with its slough
is wont to revel and gleam in its new scales,
so, when the Tirynthian had shed his mortal body,
he blossomed in his better part and began to seem
greater and to become venerable for his august solemnity.   270
The almighty father in his four-horsed chariot snatched him up
through the hollow clouds and carried him to the radiant stars.
    Atlas felt his weight; but Stheneleian Eurystheus had still not
let go of his anger, and cruelly began to work out his hatred
for the father against the offspring. But, long troubled by cares,   275
Argive Alcmene had Iole whom she could burden with her old woman's
complaints, to whom she could speak of her son's world renowned
labours, or of her own misfortunes; on Hercules' instructions,
Hyllus had received her in the marriage bed and in his heart,
and he had filled her womb with his noble seed. Thus to her   280
did Alcmene begin: 'May the gods look favourably on you at least
and then shorten the delay, when you are due and calling
Ilithyia who has been placed in charge of timid girls in child-birth,
and who was made difficult for me by the grace of Juno.
For when it was time for labour-enduring Hercules   285
to be born, and the tenth sign was being pursued by the sun,
his weight was stretching my womb and what I was carrying
was so big that you could tell that the author of the hidden
load was Jupiter. And then I could endure
my labour no longer; even now indeed, while I speak,   290
a cold shudder grips my body, and to remember is part of the pain.
Tortured through seven nights and for as many days,
tired out from my sufferings and stretching my arms to heaven, I was calling
with a great cry to Lucina and the Nixus equally.

295   illa quidem uenit, sed praecorrupta meumque
       quae donare caput Iunoni uellet iniquae.
       utque meos audit gemitus, subsedit in illa
       ante fores ara dextroque a poplite laeuum
       pressa genu et digitis inter se pectine iunctis
300   sustinuit partus; tacita quoque carmina uoce
       dixit et inceptos tenuerunt carmina partus.
       nitor et ingrato facio conuicia demens
       uana Ioui cupioque mori moturaque duros
       uerba queror silices; matres Cadmeides adsunt
305   uotaque suscipiunt exhortanturque dolentem.
       una ministrarum, media de plebe, Galanthis,
       flaua comas, aderat, faciendis strenua iussis,
       officiis dilecta suis. ea sensit iniqua
       nescioquid Iunone geri, dumque exit et intrat
310   saepe fores, diuam residentem uidit in ara
       bracchiaque in genibus digitis conexa tenentem
       et "quaecumque es," ait "dominae gratare; leuata est
       Argolis Alcmene potiturque puerpera uoto."
       exsiluit iunctasque manus pauefacta remisit
315   diua potens uteri; uinclis leuor ipsa remotis.
       numine decepto risisse Galanthida fama est;
       ridentem prensamque ipsis dea saeua capillis
       traxit et e terra corpus releuare uolentem
       arcuit inque pedes mutauit bracchia primos.
320   strenuitas antiqua manet, nec terga colorem
       amisere suum; forma est diuersa priori.
       quae quia mendaci parientem iuuerat ore,
       ore parit nostrasque domos, ut et ante, frequentat.'
            dixit et admonitu ueteris commota ministrae
325   ingemuit; quam sic nurus est adfata dolentem:
       'te tamen, o genetrix, alienae sanguine uestro
       rapta mouet facies. quid si tibi mira sororis
       fata meae referam? quamquam lacrimaeque dolorque
       impediunt prohibentque loqui. fuit unica matri
330   (me pater ex alia genuit) notissima forma
       Oechalidum Dryope, quam uirginitate carentem
       uimque dei passam Delphos Delonque tenentis
       excipit Andraemon et habetur coniuge felix.
       est lacus accliuis deuexo margine formam
335   litoris efficiens; summum myrteta coronant.
       uenerat huc Dryope fatorum nescia, quoque
       indignere magis, nymphis latura coronas;
       inque sinu puerum, qui nondum impleuerat annum,
       dulce ferebat onus tepidique ope lactis alebat.
340   haud procul a stagno Tyrios imitata colores
       in spem bacarum florebat aquatica lotos.
       carpserat hinc Dryope quos oblectamina nato
       porrigeret flores, et idem factura uidebar
       (namque aderam); uidi guttas e flore cruentas

She came indeed, but precorrupted, and someone   295
who would be willing to present my person to unjust Juno.
And as she heard my groans, she settled down upon that
altar in front of the doors and, with her left knee
pressed against the back of her right, and with her fingers interlocked in a comb,
she held up the birth; also, in a quiet voice, she recited   300
charms, and the charms stopped the birth which had begun.
I strained and insanely uttered empty insults
to ungrateful Jove, and I wanted to die and I complained in words
that would move hard flints; the Cadmeian mothers were there
and took up my prayers and encouraged me in my pain.   305
One of my serving-girls was there, Galanthis, a fair-haired girl
from amongst the plebs, zealous to carry orders out,
and loved for her readiness to serve. She realized it was something
being done by unjust Juno, and as she kept on going in
and out of the doors, she saw the goddess sitting on the altar   310
and holding her arms clasped by her fingers to her knees
and, "Whoever you are," she said, "congratulate the mistress; Argive Alcmene
has been delivered, her prayers have been answered, she is now a mother."
The powerful goddess of the womb leapt up in terror
and loosed her locked hands; and with their bonds removed, I was myself delivered. 315
The story is that Galanthis laughed when she had tricked the divinity.
As she laughed, she was caught, and the cruel goddess dragged her by her very
hair, and when she wanted to lift her body from the ground,
she prevented her and changed her arms into fore-paws.
Her zeal remained as before, and her hide did not lose   320
its colour; her form was different from earlier.
And because, to help in child-birth, she had used her deceitful mouth,
from her mouth she now gives birth and resorts, even as before, to our houses.'
        She spoke and, much moved by the warning given by her former serving-girl,
she groaned; and as she grieved, her daughter-in-law so addressed her: 325
'But you, O mother, are moved by a stranger to your
blood-line being stripped of her form. What if I were to tell you of the wondrous
fate of my sister? And yet tears and grief
impede and prevent my speaking of it. Her mother had an only daughter
(our father begot me from another woman), Dryope, the most notable   330
for beauty of the Oechalides, and, though she had lost her virginity
and suffered the violence of the god who holds Delphi and Delos,
she was accepted by Andraemon and he was considered fortunate in his wife.
There is a lake which, with its sloping edge, gives the appearance
of a steep shore; at the top it is crowned by myrtle groves.   335
Dryope had come here not knowing of her fate, and, to make you
more indignant, intending to bring garlands to the nymphs;
and in her bosom she was carrying her boy, a sweet burden,
who had not yet completed a year, and she was feeding him with her warm milk.
Not far from the pond, mimicking Tyrian colours,   340
there was flowering, with the promise of berries, a water-lotus.
Dryope had plucked flowers from it to hold out
to her son to entertain him, and I was about to do the same
(for I was there); I saw drops of blood fall

345   decidere et tremulo ramos horrore moueri.
               scilicet, ut referunt tardi nunc denique agrestes,
               Lotis in hanc nymphe fugiens obscena Priapi
               contulerat uersos, seruato nomine, uultus.
               nescierat soror hoc. quae cum perterrita retro
350   ire et adoratis uellet discedere nymphis,
               haeserunt radice pedes; conuellere pugnat
               nec quidquam nisi summa mouet. subcrescit ab imo
               totaque paulatim lentus premit inguine cortex.
               ut uidit, conata manu laniare capillos
355   fronde manum impleuit; frondes caput omne tenebant.
               at puer Amphissos (namque hoc auus Eurytus illi
               addiderat nomen) materna rigescere sentit
               ubera, nec sequitur ducentem lacteus umor.
               spectatrix aderam fati crudelis opemque
360   non poteram tibi ferre, soror; quantumque ualebam,
               crescentem truncum ramosque amplexa morabar
               et, fateor, uolui sub eodem cortice condi.
               ecce uir Andraemon genitorque miserrimus adsunt
               et quaerunt Dryopen; Dryopen quaerentibus illis
365   ostendi loton. tepido dant oscula ligno
               adfusique suae radicibus arboris haerent.
               nil nisi iam faciem, quod non foret arbor, habebat
               cara soror; lacrimae misero de corpore factis
               inrorant foliis ac, dum licet oraque praestant
370   uocis iter, tales effundit in aëra questus:
               "si qua fides miseris, hoc me per numina iuro
               non meruisse nefas; patior sine crimine poenam.
               uiximus innocuae; si mentior, arida perdam
               quas habeo frondes et caesa securibus urar.
375   hunc tamen infantem maternis demite ramis
               et date nutrici; nostraque sub arbore saepe
               lac facitote bibat nostraque sub arbore ludat,
               cumque loqui poterit, matrem facitote salutet
               et tristis dicat '"latet hoc in stipite mater."'
380   stagna tamen timeat nec carpat ab arbore flores
               et frutices omnes corpus putet esse dearum.
               care uale coniunx et tu, germana, paterque;
               qui, si qua est pietas, ab acutae uulnere falcis,
               a pecoris morsu frondes defendite nostras.
385   et quoniam mihi fas ad uos incumbere non est,
               erigite huc artus et ad oscula nostra uenite,
               dum tangi possunt, paruumque attollite natum.
               plura loqui nequeo; nam iam per candida mollis
               colla liber serpit, summoque cacumine condor.
390   ex oculis remouete manus; sine munere uestro
               contegat inductus morientia lumina cortex."
               desierant simul ora loqui, simul esse; diuque
               corpore mutato rami caluere recentes.'
                   dumque refert Iole factum mirabile, dumque

from the flower and the branches move with a trembling shudder.   345
Of course, as too late the country people now at last relate,
the nymph Lotis, fleeing from the coarseness of Priapus, had changed
her face, and turned it into this, but kept her name.
My sister did not know this. And when, terrified, she wanted
to go back and, having prayed to the nymphs, depart,   350
her feet were stuck in a root; she fought to wrench them away
but did not move them at all except at the top. A supple bark
grew up from below and pressed in little by little on the whole of her thighs.
And as she saw this, she tried to tear her hair with her hand
and filled her hand with foliage; all her head was possessed by foliage.   355
But her boy, Amphissos, (for Eurytus, his grandfather, had given him
this name) felt his mother's breast
grow hard, and the milky wetness did not follow as he sucked.
I was there, an observer of your cruel fate, but I could not,
sister, bring you help; but, as much as I was able,   360
I embraced the growing trunk and branches and slowed them down
and, I admit it, I wanted to be hidden under the same bark.
But look, her husband, Andraemon, and her most unhappy father are here,
seeking Dryope; Dryope they sought,
and I showed them the lotus. They gave kisses to the warm wood   365
and clung prostrate to the roots of their tree.
My dear sister now had nothing, except her face,
that was not tree; tears bedewed the leaves made from
her unhappy body, and, while she could and her mouth provided
a pathway for her voice, she poured forth her complaints into the air thus: 370
"If the unhappy are believed at all, I swear by the gods
that I do not deserve this wickedness; I am suffering the penalty without the crime.
I have lived innocently; if I am lying, may I dry up, lose
the foliage I have, be cut down by axes and burnt.
But take this baby from his mother's branches   375
and give him to a nurse; and see to it that he often drinks his milk
under my tree and plays under my tree,
and when he can speak, see to it that he greets his mother
and sadly says: '"My mother is hidden in this tree-trunk."'
But let him be afraid of ponds and not pluck flowers from a tree   380
and let him think that every bush is the body of a goddess.
Farewell, dear husband, and you, my sister, and my father too;
and, if you have any piety, protect my foliage
from injury by the sharp sickle and from chewing by the flock.
And, since I have not the right to lean down to you,   385
come and raise yourselves up here to my lips
while they can be touched, and lift up my little son.
I can speak no more; for soft bark is already creeping
over my white neck, and I am being hidden in a tree-top.
Take your hands from my eyes; let the spreading bark,   390
without your help, cover my dying eyes."
All at once her mouth had stopped both speaking and existing. But for a long time
after her body had been changed, the fresh branches were warm.'
     And while Iole told of the amazing event, and while

395 Eurytidos lacrimas admoto pollice siccat
 Alcmene (flet et ipsa tamen) compescuit omnem
 res noua tristitiam. nam limine constitit alto
 paene puer dubiaque tegens lanugine malas
 ora reformatus primos Iolaüs in annos.
400 hoc illi dederat Iunonia muneris Hebe,
 uicta uiri precibus; quae cum iurare pararet
 dona tributuram post hunc se talia nulli,
 non est passa Themis. 'nam iam discordia Thebae
 bella mouent,' dixit 'Capaneusque nisi ab Ioue uinci
405 haud poterit, fientque pares in uulnere fratres,
 subductaque suos manes tellure uidebit
 uiuus adhuc uates, ultusque parente parentem
 natus erit facto pius et sceleratus eodem
 attonitusque malis, exul mentisque domusque,
410 uultibus Eumenidum matrisque agitabitur umbris,
 donec eum coniunx fatale poposcerit aurum
 cognatumque latus Phegeius hauserit ensis.
 tum demum magno petet hos Acheloia supplex
 ab Ioue Callirhoë natis infantibus annos;
415 [neue necem sinat esse diu uictoris inultam]
 Iuppiter his motus priuignae dona nurusque
 praecipiet facietque uiros impubibus annis.'
      haec ubi faticano uenturi praescia dixit
 ore Themis, uario superi sermone fremebant
420 et cur non aliis eadem dare dona liceret
 murmur erat. queritur ueteres Pallantias annos
 coniugis esse sui, queritur canescere mitis
 Iasiona Ceres, repetitum Mulciber aeuum
 poscit Ericthonio; Venerem quoque cura futuri
425 tangit et Anchisae renouare paciscitur annos.
 cui studeat deus omnis habet; crescitque fauore
 turbida seditio, donec sua Iuppiter ora
 soluit et 'o nostri si qua est reuerentia,' dixit
 'quo ruitis? tantumne aliquis sibi posse uidetur
430 fata quoque ut superet? fatis Iolaüs in annos,
 quos egit, rediit; fatis iuuenescere debent
 Callirhoë geniti, non ambitione nec armis.
 uos etiam, quoque hoc animo meliore feratis,
 me quoque fata regunt. quae si mutare ualerem,
435 nec nostrum seri curuarent Aeacon anni,
 perpetuumque aeui florem Rhadamanthos haberet
 cum Minoë meo, qui propter amara senectae
 pondera despicitur nec quo prius ordine regnat.'
 dicta Iouis mouere deos, nec sustinet ullus,
440 cum uideat fessos Rhadamanthon et Aeacon annis
 et Minoa, queri; qui, dum fuit integer aeui,
 terruerat magnas ipso quoque nomine gentes,
 tunc erat inualidus Deïonidenque iuuentae
 robore Miletum Phoeboque parente superbum

Alcmene was using her thumb to dry the tears   395
of Eurytus' daughter (and yet she wept herself), a new affair
subdued all their sadness. For there stood on the high threshold
a boy almost, with a hint of down covering his cheeks
and his face reshaped as in his earliest years, Iolaüs.
Juno's Hebe had given him this favour,   400
won over by her husband's prayers; and when she was preparing to swear
that she would grant such gifts to no one after him,
Themis did not allow her to. 'For Thebes is already setting
discordant wars in motion,' she said, 'and Capaneus will be invincible
except by Jupiter, and the brothers will be made equal in their wounds,   405
and, as the ground is taken from beneath him, the prophet, still alive,
will see his own shade, and, by taking vengeance on a parent for a parent,
his son will be made pious and wicked by the same deed,
and, stunned by his sufferings, an exile from his mind and from his home,
he will be driven by the faces of the Eumenides and by his mother's ghost,   410
until his wife demands the fatal gold from him
and Phegeus' sword has gouged out the flank of his kinsman.
Then at last, Acheloian Callirhoë will supplicate great Jove
and ask him for those years for her infant sons;
[and, so that he would not let the murder of the conqueror be long unavenged,] 415
moved by these words, Jupiter will take over the gift of his stepdaughter
and daughter-in-law and will make men from beardless boys.'
     When Themis, with her foreknowledge of what is to come, had said these things
with her prophetic lips, the gods began to roar in a variety of speeches
and, why others may not give the same gifts   420
was what they were murmuring. Pallantias complained that her husband's
years were old, gentle Ceres complained
that Iasion was growing grey, Mulciber demanded that life
be given back to Erichthonius; Venus too was affected by concern
for the future and proposed to renew Anchises' years.   425
Every god had someone to favour and from their partiality
unruly revolt grew, till Jupiter opened up
his mouth and said, 'Oh, if you have any respect for me,
where are you rushing to? Is there someone who thinks he is so powerful
that he can overcome even the fates? It was through the fates that Iolaüs returned 430
to his spent years; it is through the fates that Callirhoë's sons
should grow young, not through campaigning or force of arms.
You too, and, so that you may bear this in a better spirit,
me also do the fates rule. And if I had the power to change these things,
the advancing years would not be making my Aeacus stoop   435
and Rhadamanthus would be for ever in the flower of youth
together with my Minos who, because of the bitter burdens
of old age is despised and does not rule in his former state.'
Jove's words moved the gods, and none of them, seeing
Rhadamanthus and Aeacus tired out by their years, and Minos too,   440
could maintain their complaint; for he who, when in the prime of life,
had terrified the nations with just his very name,
was then feeble, and Deïone's son, Miletus,
proud of his youthful strength and of Phoebus, his father,

445 pertimuit, credensque suis insurgere regnis
  haud tamen est patriis arcere penatibus ausus.
  sponte fugis, Milete, tua celerique carina
  Aegaeas metiris aquas et in Aside terra
  moenia constituis positoris habentia nomen.
450   hic tibi dum sequitur patriae curuamina ripae
  filia Maeandri totiens redeuntis eodem
  cognita Cyanee praestanti pignora forma,
  Byblida cum Cauno, prolem est enixa gemellam.
  Byblis in exemplo est ut ament concessa puellae,
455 Byblis Apollinei correpta cupidine fratris.
  [non soror ut fratrem nec qua debebat amabat.]
  illa quidem primo nullos intellegit ignes
  nec peccare putat quod saepius oscula iungat,
  quod sua fraterno circumdet bracchia collo,
460 mendacique diu pietatis fallitur umbra.
  paulatim declinat amor, uisuraque fratrem
  culta uenit nimiumque cupit formosa uideri,
  et si qua est illic formosior, inuidet illi.
  sed nondum manifesta sibi est nullumque sub illo
465 igne facit uotum, uerumtamen aestuat intus.
  iam dominum appellat, iam nomina sanguinis odit,
  Byblida iam mauult quam se uocet ille sororem.
  spes tamen obscenas animo demittere non est
  ausa suo uigilans; placida resoluta quiete
470 saepe uidet quod amat, uisa est quoque iungere fratri
  corpus et erubuit, quamuis sopita iacebat.
  somnus abit; silet illa diu repetitque quietis
  ipsa suae speciem, dubiaque ita mente profatur:
  'me miseram! tacitae quid uult sibi noctis imago?
475 quam nolim rata sit! cur haec ego somnia uidi?
  ille quidem est oculis quamuis formosus iniquis
  et placet et possim, si non sit frater, amare,
  et me dignus erat; uerum nocet esse sororem.
  dummodo tale nihil uigilans committere temptem,
480 saepe licet simili redeat sub imagine somnus;
  testis abest somno nec abest imitata uoluptas.
  pro Venus et tenera uolucer cum matre Cupido,
  gaudia quanta tuli! quam me manifesta libido
  contigit! ut iacui totis resoluta medullis!
485 ut meminisse iuuat! quamuis breuis illa uoluptas
  noxque fuit praeceps et coeptis inuida nostris.
  o ego, si liceat mutato nomine iungi,
  quam bene, Caune, tuo poteram nurus esse parenti!
  quam bene, Caune, meo poteras gener esse parenti!
490 omnia, di facerent, essent communia nobis,
  praeter auos; tu me uellem generosior esses.
  nescioquam facies igitur, pulcherrime, matrem;
  at mihi, quae male sum quos tu sortita parentes,
  nil nisi frater eris; quod obest, id habebimus unum.

frightened him, and, though he believed he was rising up against his kingdom,   445
yet he dared not exclude him from his ancestral penates.
It was of your own accord, Miletus, that you fled, measuring the Aegean
waters with your swift ship and, on Asian land,
you established walls that bear the name of their builder.
    Here, while Meander's daughter, Cyanee, was following the windings   450
of her father's bank as it returned so many times to the same place,
she was known by you; and children of surpassing beauty,
Byblis and Caunus, twin offspring, were borne by her.
Byblis is a warning that girls should love what is permitted,
Byblis was seized with desire for her Apolline brother.   455
[She was loving, not as a sister towards a brother, nor as she ought.]
At first, indeed, she did not understand the fires within her,
and did not think it was a sin that she joined kisses too often,
that she put her arms around her brother's neck,
and for a long time she was deceived by a false semblance of piety.   460
Little by little her love changed, when she was to see
her brother she went dressed up wanting too much to seem beautiful,
and, if any girl there was more beautiful, she envied her.
But she was not yet revealed to herself, and had no longings
beneath that fire; but still she seethed within.   465
Now she called him her lord, now she hates the words for blood-ties,
Byblis now she prefers him to call her, not sister.
Still she did not dare to admit lewd hopes
into her mind when awake; but, when relaxed in peaceful rest,
she often saw the object of her love and seemed even to join her body   470
to her brother's, and she blushed, although she lay in slumber.
Sleep left her; for a long time she was silent repeating for herself
the vision of her rest, and thus, with hesitating mind, she spoke:
'Unhappy me!' What is the meaning of this image of the silent night?
How much I would not want it to come to pass! Why have I seen these dreams?   475
He is beautiful indeed, even to prejudiced eyes,
and I like him, and I could, if he were not my brother, love him,
and he was worthy of me, but it hurts that I am his sister.
Provided only that I try to commit no such thing when awake,
let sleep often come back with that same image;   480
there is no witness in sleep, but there is the semblance of pleasure.
Oh Venus and swift Cupid with your gentle mother,
what great joys I knew! How clear was the desire
that touched me! How I lay there dissolved right to my marrow!
What a delight it is to remember! Brief though that pleasure was,   485
as the night rushed by begrudging what we had begun.
Oh me, if I could be joined with that word changed,
how happily, Caunus, could I have been your father's daughter-in-law!
How happily, Caunus, could you have been my father's son-in-law!
We would, were the gods to make it so, have everything in common   490
except our grandparents; would that you were higher-born than me.
As it is, most handsome one, you will make some girl a mother;
but to me, who was unhappily allotted the same parents as you were,
you will be nothing but a brother; the one thing that we have is what stands in our way.

495   quid mihi significant ergo mea uisa? quod autem
         somnia pondus habent? an habent et somnia pondus?
         di melius! —di nempe suas habuere sorores;
         sic Saturnus Opem iunctam sibi sanguine duxit,
         Oceanus Tethyn, Iunonem rector Olympi.
500   sunt superis sua iura; quid ad caelestia ritus
         exigere humanos diuersaque foedera tempto?
         aut nostro uetitus de corde fugabitur ardor
         aut, hoc si nequeo, peream, precor, ante toroque
         mortua componar positaeque det oscula frater.
505   et tamen arbitrium quaerit res ista duorum.
         finge placere mihi; scelus esse uidebitur illi.
         at non Aeolidae thalamos timuere sororum.
         unde sed hos noui? cur haec exempla paraui?
         quo feror? obscenae procul hinc discedite flammae,
510   nec nisi qua fas est germanae frater ametur.
         si tamen ipse mihi captus prior esset amore,
         forsitan illius possem indulgere furori.
         ergo ego quem fueram non reiectura petentem
         ipsa petam! poterisne loqui? poterisne fateri?
515   coget amor, potero; uel, si pudor ora tenebit,
         littera celatos arcana fatebitur ignes.'
                hoc placet, haec dubiam uicit sententia mentem.
         in latus erigitur cubitoque innixa sinistro
         'uiderit, insanos' inquit 'fateamur amores.
520   ei mihi! quo labor? quem mens mea concipit ignem?'
         et meditata manu componit uerba trementi;
         dextra tenet ferrum, uacuam tenet altera ceram.
         incipit et dubitat; scribit damnatque tabellas
         et notat et delet; mutat culpatque probatque.
525   inque uicem sumptas ponit positasque resumit;
         quid uelit ignorat; quidquid factura uidetur
         displicet; in uultu est audacia mixta pudori.
         scripta 'soror' fuerat; uisum est delere sororem
         uerbaque correctis incidere talia ceris:
530   'quam nisi tu dederis non est habitura salutem,
         hanc tibi mittit amans; pudet, a, pudet edere nomen!
         et si quid cupiam quaeris, sine nomine uellem
         posset agi mea causa meo, nec cognita Byblis
         ante forem quam spes uotorum certa fuisset.
535   esse quidem laesi poterat tibi pectoris index
         et color et macies et uultus et umida saepe
      · lumina nec causa suspiria mota patenti
         et crebri amplexus et quae, si forte notasti,
         oscula sentiri non esse sororia possent.
540   ipsa tamen, quamuis animi graue uulnus habebam,
         quamuis intus erat furor igneus, omnia feci
         (sunt mihi di testes) ut tandem sanior essem,
         pugnauique diu uiolenta Cupidinis arma
         effugere infelix, et plus quam ferre puellam

So what do my visions mean for me? What weight then   495
do my dreams have? Or do even dreams have weight?
May the gods forbid! —But Gods, as we know, have had their sisters;
Saturn married Ops, who was linked to him by blood,
Oceanus, Tethys, and the ruler of Olympus, Juno.
The gods have their own laws; why am I trying to fit   500
human ways to different, heavenly conditions.
Either I shall forbid my ardour and it will be put to flight from my heart,
or, if I cannot do that, let me die, I pray, first, and be laid out
when dead upon the couch and given kisses by my brother as I lie there.
But that requires an understanding between the two of us.   505
Suppose it pleases me; it will seem a crime to him.
But the sons of Aeolus did not fear their sisters' beds.
But how do I know of them? Why have I produced these examples?
Where am I being carried off to? Depart from here, lewd flames,
and, except as is right for a sister, don't let me love my brother.   510
But if he had been captivated by love for me first,
I could perhaps have given way to his passion.
Let me then, if I would not have rejected his advances,
make the advances myself! Will you be able to speak? Will you be able to confess?
Love will compel, I shall be able; or, if modesty restrains my mouth, 515
a discreet letter will confess my hidden fires!'
    This was her decision; this the conclusion that won over her hesitating mind.
She raised herself up onto her side and, leaning on her left elbow,
'Let him see,' she said, 'let me confess my mad love.
Ah me! What am I slipping into? What fire has caught in my mind?'   520
And she prepared her words and set them down with a trembling hand;
her right hand held the stylus, her other hand the empty wax.
She began, then hesitated; she wrote on the tablets and condemned them
she both marked and deleted; she changed, found fault and approved.   524
By turns, she took them up, put them down, and, once put down, took them up again;
she did not know what she wanted; whatever she seemed about to do
displeased her; on her face, boldness was mixed with shame.
She had written 'sister'; she decided to delete the sister
and in the wax now corrected, to cut such words as these:
'She who will not have health unless you give it to her,   530
sends it lovingly to you; I am ashamed, ah, ashamed to give my name!
And if you ask what I want, I would wish that my case
could be put without my name and that I would not be known as Byblis
before the hope of my prayers had been secured.
Indeed, you could have as evidence of my wounded heart,   535
my colour, loss of weight, expression, eyes that are often
moist, sighs brought on from no obvious cause,
frequent embraces, and kisses which, if perhaps you realized,
could not have been felt as sisterly.
Though I myself was deeply wounded in my heart,   540
though there was a fiery passion within, I did everything
(the gods are my witnesses) that I might at last be more in my right mind,
and I fought for a long time to escape Cupid's violent
weapons, but without success, and I bore hardships more

545   posse putes ego dura tuli; superata fateri
        cogor opemque tuam timidis exposcere uotis.
        tu seruare potes, tu perdere solus amantem;
        elige utrum facias. non hoc inimica precatur,
        sed quae, cum tibi sit iunctissima, iunctior esse
.550   expetit et uinclo tecum propiore ligari.
        iura senes norint et quid liceatque nefasque
        fasque sit inquirant legumque examina seruent;
        conueniens Venus est annis temeraria nostris.
        quid liceat nescimus adhuc et cuncta licere
555   credimus et sequimur magnorum exempla deorum.
        nec nos aut durus pater aut reuerentia famae
        aut timor impediet (tantum sit causa timendi!);
        dulcia fraterno sub nomine furta tegemus.
        est mihi libertas tecum secreta loquendi,
560   et damus amplexus et iungimus oscula coram;
        quantum est quod desit? miserere fatentis amorem
        et non fassurae, nisi cogeret ultimus ardor,
        neue merere meo subscribi causa sepulcro.'
              talia nequiquam perarantem plena reliquit
565   cera manum summusque in margine uersus adhaesit.
        protinus impressa signat sua crimina gemma,
        quam tinxit lacrimis (linguam defecerat umor),
        deque suis unum famulis pudibunda uocauit
        et paulum blandita 'fer has, fidissime, nostro—'
570   dixit et adiecit longo post tempore 'fratri'.
        cum daret, elapsae manibus cecidere tabellae;
        omine turbata est, misit tamen. apta minister
        tempora nactus adit traditque latentia uerba.
        attonitus subita iuuenis Maeandrius ira
575   proicit acceptas lecta sibi parte tabellas,
        uixque manus retinens trepidantis ab ore ministri
        'dum licet, o uetitae scelerate libidinis auctor,
        effuge,' ait 'qui, si nostrum tua fata pudorem
        non traherent secum, poenas mihi morte dedisses.'
580   ille fugit pauidus dominaeque ferocia Cauni
        dicta refert. palles audita, Bybli, repulsa,
        et pauet obsessum glaciali frigore corpus;
        mens tamen ut rediit, pariter rediere furores,
        linguaque mox tales icto dedit aëre uoces:
585   'et merito! quid enim temeraria uulneris huius
        indicium feci? quid quae celanda fuerunt
        tam cito commisi properatis uerba tabellis?
        ante erat ambiguis animi sententia dictis
        praetemptanda mihi. ne non sequeretur euntem,
590   parte aliqua ueli qualis foret aura notare
        debueram tutoque mari decurrere, quae nunc
        non exploratis impleui lintea uentis.
        auferor in scopulos igitur subuersaque toto
        obruor oceano, neque habent mea uela recursus.

than you would think a girl could bear; now, overcome, I am compelled 545
to confess and demand your help in timid prayers.
You can save, you alone can destroy your lover;
choose which you will do. This is the prayer not of an enemy
but of one who, though very near to you, seeks to be
nearer still and to be tied to you in a closer bond. 550
Let old men know the rules, and question what is allowed and what is wrong
and right, and let them keep their weighings of the laws.
It is rash Venus who suits our years.
Still in ignorance of what is allowed, we believe that everything
is allowed, and we follow the examples of the great gods. 555
And neither a stern father, nor respect for our reputation,
nor fear will impede us (only would that there were reason to fear!);
we shall cover our sweet furtive acts under the fraternal word.
I have the freedom to speak with you of our secrets,
and we give embraces and join kisses openly; 560
how much is left? Pity her who is confessing love
but would not confess unless compelled by the extremes of ardour,
and do not let yourself deserve to be inscribed upon my tomb as its cause.'
　　The full wax left her hand vainly
ploughing through such words, and the last line was clinging to the edge. 565
At once she sealed her confessions with the impression of her signet;
she dipped it in her tears (her tongue had lost its moisture),
and, blushing with shame, she called to one of her servants
and, coaxing him a little, 'Take these, most faithful one, to my—'
she said and, a long time after, added, 'brother'. 570
As she gave him the tablets, they slipped from her hands and fell.
She was disturbed by the omen, but sent them even so. The servant seized
an appropriate time and went and delivered the hidden words.
The young Meandrian, thunderstruck, threw the tablets down
in sudden anger after taking them and reading a part of them to himself, 575
and, scarcely keeping his hands from the trembling servant's face,
said, 'O wicked instigator of forbidden lust, flee
while you can; if your fate did not carry my shame
with it too, I would have seen you pay the penalty with your death.'
He fled terrified and brought Caunus' savage words 580
back to his mistress. On hearing, his rebuff, you went pale, Byblis,
and your body trembled beset by icy cold;
but when her mind returned her passions returned equally,
and her tongue soon struck the air giving out words such as these:
'And rightly so! For why did I so rashly bear witness 585
to this wound of mine? Why did I so quickly commit
to hurried tablets words that should have been concealed?
I should first have tried out the feeling of his mind
with ambiguous words. So that it would not fail to follow as I went,
I ought to have used a part of my sail to note 590
how the wind was, and run for home on a safe sea, but as it is
I have filled my canvas with untested winds.
And so I am being carried onto the rocks, capsized and overwhelmed
by the whole ocean, and my sails have no way back.

595
quid quod et ominibus certis prohibebar amori
indulgere meo, tum cum mihi ferre iubenti
excidit et fecit spes nostras cera caducas?
nonne uel illa dies fuerat uel tota uoluntas,
sed potius mutanda dies? deus ipse monebat

600
signaque certa dabat, si non male sana fuissem.
et tamen ipsa loqui nec me committere cerae
debueram praesensque meos aperire furores.
uidisset lacrimas, uultum uidisset amantis;
plura loqui poteram quam quae cepere tabellae;

605
inuito potui circumdare bracchia collo
et, si reicerer, potui moritura uideri
amplectique pedes adfusaque poscere uitam.
omnia fecissem, quorum si singula duram
flectere non poterant, potuissent omnia mentem.

610
forsitan et missi sit quaedam culpa ministri;
non adiit apte nec legit idonea, credo,
tempora nec petiit horamque animumque uacantem.
haec nocuere mihi; neque enim est de tigride natus
nec rigidas silices solidumue in pectore ferrum

615
aut adamanta gerit nec lac bibit ille leaenae.
uincetur! repetendus erit, nec taedia coepti
ulla mei capiam, dum spiritus iste manebit.
nam primum, si facta mihi reuocare liceret,
non coepisse fuit; coepta expugnare secundum est.

620
quippe nec ille potest, ut iam mea uota relinquam,
non tamen ausorum semper memor esse meorum;
et quia desierim leuiter uoluisse uidebor,
aut etiam temptasse illum insidiisque petisse;
uel certe non hoc qui plurimus urget et urit

625
pectora nostra deo, sed uicta libidine credar.
denique iam nequeo nil commisisse nefandum;
et scripsi et petii; temerata est nostra uoluntas.
ut nihil adiciam, non possum innoxia dici.
quod superest multum est in uota, in crimina paruum.'

630
    dixit et (incertae tanta est discordia mentis)
cum pigeat temptasse, libet temptare; modumque
exit et infelix committit saepe repelli.
mox ubi finis abest, patriam fugit ille nefasque
inque peregrina ponit noua moenia terra.

635
tum uero maestam tota Miletida mente
defecisse ferunt, tum uero a pectore uestem
deripuit planxitque suos furibunda lacertos.
iamque palam est demens inconcessaeque fatetur
spem Veneris, siquidem patriam inuisosque penates

640
deserit et profugi sequitur uestigia fratris.
utque tuo motae, proles Semeleïa, thyrso
Ismariae celebrant repetita triennia Bacchae,
Byblida non aliter latos ululasse per agros
Bubasides uidere nurus; quibus illa relictis

What of the fact that sure omens were trying to restrain me from indulging   595
my love then when I was ordering him to carry it
and the wax fell from me and made my hopes fall too?
Was it not, surely, the day, or the whole idea,
no, rather the day, that should have been changed. The god himself was warning
and giving sure signs, if I had not been out of my mind.   600
And, in any case, I ought to have spoken myself, and not committed myself
to the wax, but revealed my passions in person.
He would have seen my tears, he would have seen the face of his lover;
I could have said more than tablets could take;
I could have put my arms around his unwilling neck   605
and, if I were rejected, I could have seemed about to die,
embraced his feet and, prostrate, begged for life.
I would have done everything; if any one thing could not
have swayed his stern mind, they all might have together.
Perhaps the servant that I sent is in some way to blame;   610
he did not come to him appropriately, nor pick, I think, a suitable
time, nor seek a free hour for me.
These are the things that hurt me; for he was not born from a tigress
nor does he carry solid rocks or hard iron in his breast
or adamant, nor does he drink lioness's milk.   615
He will be conquered! I must return to him and I shall not weary
in any way of what I have begun while breath remains in me.
For my first choice, if I were allowed to revoke my deeds,
was not to have begun; second best is to push on with what I have begun to victory.
For he cannot, even supposing I were to give up my hopes,   620
not be ever mindful of the things that I have dared;
and, because I had stopped, I shall seem to have had fickle wants,
or even to have been testing him or attacking him with snares;
and certainly he will believe that I have been conquered not by this mighty god
who assails and burns my heart, but by lust.   625
For now, of course, it is impossible for me to have committed no abomination;
I did write and I did ask; my will has been defiled.
Though I add nothing more, I cannot be said to be blameless.
As for the future, there is much to hope for and little more that is wrong.'
　　She spoke, and (so great was the conflict in her uncertain mind),   630
though she was sorry to have tried, she wanted to try; and she gave up
self-control and unhappily brought frequent rebuff upon herself.
Soon, when there was no end to it, he fled his fatherland and wickedness
and set up new walls in a distant land.
Then indeed it was, they say, that Miletus' grieving daughter completely   635
lost her mind, then indeed she tore the clothing
from her breast and beat her arms frenziedly.
And now she was obviously insane and confessed she had hoped
for illicit love, by deserting her fatherland and her hated
penates and by following the tracks of her exiled brother.   640
And as, offspring of Semele, moved by your thyrsus
the Ismenian Bacchae throng the return of their triennial,
just so was Byblis seen by the Bubasian young women
screaming through the wild fields; and when she had left them

645   Caras et armiferos Lelegas Lyciamque pererrat.
        iam Cragon et Limyren Xanthique reliquerat undas,
        quoque Chimaera iugo mediis in partibus ignem,
        pectus et ora leae, caudam serpentis habebat.
        deficiunt siluae, cum tu lassata sequendo,
650   concidis et dura positis tellure capillis,
        Bybli, iaces frondesque tuo premis ore caducas.
        saepe illam nymphae teneris Lelegeïdes ulnis
        tollere conantur, saepe ut medeatur amori
        praecipiunt surdaeque adhibent solacia menti.
655   muta iacet uiridesque suis tenet unguibus herbas
        Byblis et umectat lacrimarum gramina riuo.
        Naïdas his uenam, quae numquam arescere posset,
        supposuisse ferunt; quid enim dare maius habebant?
        protinus, ut secto piceae de cortice guttae
660   utue tenax grauida manat tellure bitumen,
        utque sub aduentu spirantis lene Fauoni
        sole remollescit quae frigore constitit unda,
        sic lacrimis consumpta suis Phoebeïa Byblis
        uertitur in fontem, quae nunc quoque uallibus illis
665   nomen habet dominae nigraque sub ilice manat.
                fama noui centum Cretaeas forsitan urbes
        implesset monstri, si non miracula nuper
        Iphide mutata Crete propiora tulisset.
        proxima Cnosiaco nam quondam Phaestia regno
670   progenuit tellus ignotum nomine Ligdum,
        ingenua de plebe uirum; nec census in illo
        nobilitate sua maior, sed uita fidesque
        inculpata fuit. grauidae qui coniugis aures
        uocibus his monuit, cum iam prope partus adesset:
675   'quae uoueam duo sunt: minimo ut releuere dolore
        utque marem parias. onerosior altera sors est
        et uires fortuna negat; quod abominor, ergo,
        edita forte tuo fuerit si femina partu
        (inuitus mando; Pietas, ignosce), necetur.'
680   dixerat, et lacrimis uultum lauere profusis
        tam qui mandabat quam cui mandata dabantur.
        sed tamen usque suum uanis Telethusa maritum
        sollicitat precibus, ne spem sibi ponat in arto;
        certa sua est Ligdo sententia. iamque ferendo
685   uix erat illa grauem maturo pondere uentrem,
        cum medio noctis spatio sub imagine somni
        Inachis ante torum pompa comitata sacrorum
        aut stetit aut uisa est; inerant lunaria fronti
        cornua cum spicis nitido flauentibus auro
690   et regale decus; cum qua latrator Anubis
        sanctaque Bubastis uariusque coloribus Apis,
        quique premit uocem digitoque silentia suadet;
        sistraque erant numquamque satis quaesitus Osiris
        plenaque somniferis serpens peregrina uenenis.

she wandered through the Carians, the armed Leleges and Lycia. 645
Now she had left Cragos and Limyre and the waters of Xanthus
and the ridge where the Chimera had fire in its middle parts,
the breast and face of a lioness, and the tail of a snake.
The woods had given out when you, Byblis, wearied from following,
collapsed, and, with your hair strewn on the hard earth, 650
lay there with your face pressed into fallen leaves.
Often did the Lelegeian nymphs try to raise her
in their tender arms, often did they instruct her how to heal
her love, bringing their solace to her deaf mind.
Byblis lay there mute, holding the green herbs with her 655
finger-nails and moistening the grass with a stream of tears.
They say that under these the Naiads put a channel which could
never run dry; for what greater thing did they have to give?
At once, as is the flow of pitchy drops when the bark is cut,
or of clinging bitumen from abundant earth, 660
and as, on the arrival of Favonius' gentle breath,
water, which had frozen in the cold, melts in the sun,
so was Phoebean Byblis consumed by her own tears
and turned into a spring which even now in those valleys
keeps its mistress' name and flows under a dark holm-oak. 665
    The story of this strange marvel would perhaps have filled the hundred
Cretan cities, if Crete had not recently,
with Iphis' transformation, borne miracles closer to home.
For the Phaestian land, very close to the kingdom of Cnossus,
was the birthplace of an obscure man, Ligdus by name, 670
from the free-born plebs; and his fortune
was no greater than his rank, but he was a reliable man
of blameless life. When his wife was pregnant, he filled
her ears with these warning words when she was already close to giving birth:
'There are two things I would pray for: that you be delivered with the least pain 675
and that you give birth to a male. The other kind is more burdensome
and fortune denies me the resources; so, and I detest this,
if you chance to give birth to a girl
(unwillingly do I command you; O Piety, forgive me), let her be killed.'
He had spoken, and their faces were washed by streaming tears, 680
as much his who was commanding as hers to whom the commands were being given.
But still Telethusa beset her husband all the time
with vain prayers not to confine her hopes;
but Ligdus was fixed in his decision. And now she was
scarcely able to bear a belly heavy with its ripe load, 685
when, in the middle span of the night, in the visions of her sleep,
Inachus' daughter, accompanied by a procession of her sacred attendants
either stood, or seemed to stand, before her bed; lunar horns were
on her forehead and yellow ears of corn in gleaming gold
and a royal ornament; and with her was Anubis the barker, 690
and holy Bubastis, and Apis of various colours,
and the one who checks his voice and urges silence with his finger;
and there were sistra, and Osiris, never sought for enough,
and the wandering snake, full of sleep-bringing poisons.

695   tum uelut excussam somno et manifesta uidentem
         sic adfata dea est: 'pars o Telethusa mearum,
         pone graues curas mandataque falle mariti;
         nec dubita, cum te partu Lucina leuarit,
         tollere quidquid erit. dea sum auxiliaris opemque
700   exorata fero, nec te coluisse quereris
         ingratum numen.' monuit thalamoque recessit.
         laeta toro surgit purasque ad sidera supplex
         Cressa manus tollens rata sint sua uisa precatur.
         ut dolor increuit seque ipsum pondus in auras
705   expulit et nata est ignaro femina patre,
         iussit ali mater puerum mentita; fidemque
         res habuit, neque erat ficti nisi conscia nutrix.
         uota pater soluit nomenque imponit auitum;
         Iphis auus fuerat. gauisa est nomine mater,
710   quod commune foret nec quemquam falleret illo.
         indecepta pia mendacia fraude latebant.
         cultus erat pueri; facies, quam siue puellae
         siue dares puero, fieret formosus uterque.
         tertius interea decimo successerat annus,
715   cum pater, Iphi, tibi flauam despondit Ianthen,
         inter Phaestiadas quae laudatissima formae
         dote fuit uirgo, Dictaeo nata Teleste.
         par aetas, par forma fuit, primasque magistris
         accepere artes, elementa aetatis, ab isdem.
720   hinc amor ambarum tetigit rude pectus et aequum
         uulnus utrique dedit, sed erat fiducia dispar.
         coniugium pactaeque exspectat tempora taedae,
         quamque uirum putat esse, uirum fore credit Ianthe;
         Iphis amat qua posse frui desperat, et auget
725   hoc ipsum flammas ardetque in uirgine uirgo.
         uixque tenens lacrimas 'quis me manet exitus,' inquit
         'cognita quam nulli, quam prodigiosa nouaeque
         cura tenet Veneris? si di me [parcere uellent,
         parcere debuerant; si non, et] perdere uellent,
730   naturale malum saltem et de more dedissent.
         nec uaccam uaccae nec equas amor urit equarum;
         urit oues aries, sequitur sua femina ceruum;
         sic et aues coeunt, interque animalia cuncta
         femina femineo correpta cupidine nulla est.
735   uellem nulla forem! ne non tamen omnia Crete
         monstra ferat, taurum dilexit filia Solis,
         femina nempe marem; meus est furiosior illo,
         si uerum profitemur, amor. tamen illa secuta est
         spem Veneris, tamen illa dolis et imagine uaccae
740   passa bouem est, et erat qui deciperetur adulter.
         huc licet e toto sollertia confluat orbe,   .
         ipse licet reuolet ceratis Daedalus alis,
         quid faciet? num me puerum de uirgine doctis
         artibus efficiet? num te mutabit, Ianthe?

Then, as if she had been shaken from sleep and was seeing plainly,   695
the goddess spoke to her so: 'O Telethusa, one of my own,
lay your heavy cares aside and disobey your husband's commands;
do not hesitate, when Lucina has delivered your child,
to raise it up, whatever it is. I am a goddess of succour, bringing
help when called upon, and you will not complain that you have worshipped   700
an ungrateful god.' She gave her advice and withdrew from the bedroom.
Joyfully the Cretan woman rose from her bed and, lifting her pure
hands to the stars in supplication, prayed that what she had seen might come true.
      And, when her pain increased and her load had driven itself out
into the air and a girl was born, though the father did not know it,   705
the mother, lying, said it was a boy and ordered it to be fed; the facts
made for credence, and no one was aware of the fiction except for the nurse.
The father paid his vows and gave it the name of its grandfather;
Iphis had been its grandfather. The mother was delighted with the name
because it was common to either sex and she did not deceive anyone with it.   710
The lies, undetected through a pious deceit, lay hidden.
Her dress was a boy's; her face one which, whether you gave
it to a girl or to a boy, was beautiful in either case.
      Meanwhile, a third year had succeeded the tenth
when the father betrothed you, Iphis, to the fair-haired Ianthe   715
who was, among the Phaestian women, the most praised
maiden for her dowry of beauty, and the daughter of Dictaean Telestes.
They were like in age and like in beauty, they received their first
skills of childhood and their elements from the same teachers.
From this, love touched the simple breast of both of them and gave   720
each an equal wound, but their expectations were unlike.
Ianthe was looking out for marriage and the time of her promised wedding;
and she believed that the girl she thought was a man would be her man;
Iphis loved a girl she despaired of enjoying, and this
very thing increased the flames and maiden was on fire for maiden.   725
Scarcely holding back the tears, 'What outcome is awaiting me,' she said,
'while I am held by a monstrous passion, known
to no one, for a strange Venus? If the gods wanted [to spare me,
they ought to have spared me; if not, and they wanted] to destroy me,
they would at least have given me an evil that was natural and normal.   730
A cow's love does not burn for a cow nor that of mares for mares;
the ram burns for ewes, it is his own mate that pursues the stag;
even so do birds unite and amongst all animals
no female is seized by desire for a female.
Would that I were not one! But so that Crete would not fail to bear   735
all the monsters, the daughter of the Sun loved a bull,
but that was, after all, female and male; my love is madder
than hers, if we tell the truth. And she was, at least, pursuing
a hope of Venus, she, at least, through trickery and the model of a cow,
experienced her bull, and there was an adulterer to be deceived.   740
Let the ingenuity from the whole world flow together here,
let Daedalus himself fly back on his waxed wings,
what will he do? Surely he will not with his learned skills
make me a boy from a maiden? Surely he will not change you, Ianthe?

745 quin animum firmas teque ipsa recolligis, Iphi,
consiliique inopes et stultos excutis ignes?
quid sis nata uides (nisi te quoque decipis ipsam);
et pete quod fas est et ama quod femina debes.
spes est quae capiat, spes est quae pascat amorem;
750 hanc tibi res adimit. non te custodia caro
arcet ab amplexu nec cauti cura mariti,
non patris asperitas, non se negat ipsa roganti;
nec tamen est potiunda tibi, nec, ut omnia fiant,
esse potes felix, ut dique hominesque laborent.
755 [nunc quoque uotorum nulla est pars uana meorum,
dique mihi faciles quidquid ualuere dederunt.]
quod uolo uult genitor, uult ipsa socerque futurus;
at non uult natura, potentior omnibus istis,
quae mihi sola nocet. uenit ecce optabile tempus
760 luxque iugalis adest et iam mea fiet Ianthe—
nec mihi continget; mediis sitiemus in undis.
pronuba quid Iuno, quid ad haec, Hymenaee, uenitis
sacra, quibus qui ducat abest, ubi nubimus ambae?'
pressit ab his uocem. nec lenius altera uirgo
765 aestuat utque celer uenias, Hymenaee, precatur.
quod petit haec Telethusa timens modo tempora differt,
nunc ficto languore moram trahit, omina saepe
uisaque causatur. sed iam consumpserat omnem
materiam ficti dilataque tempora taedae
770 institerant unusque dies restabat. at illa
crinalem capiti uittam nataeque sibique
detrahit et passis aram complexa capillis
'Isi, Paraetonium Mareoticaque arua Pharonque
quae colis et septem digestum in cornua Nilum,
775 fer, precor,' inquit 'opem nostroque medere timori.
te, dea, te, quondam tuaque haec insignia uidi
cunctaque cognoui, sonitum comitesque facesque
sacrorum, memorique animo tua iussa notaui.
quod uidet haec lucem, quod non *ego punior, ecce*
780 consilium munusque tuum est; miserere duarum
auxilioque iuua.' lacrimae sunt uerba secutae.
uisa dea est mouisse suas (et mouerat) aras,
et templi tremuere fores imitataque lunam
cornua fulserunt crepuitque sonabile sistrum.
785 non secura quidem, fausto tamen omine laeta
mater abit templo. sequitur comes Iphis euntem
quam solita est maiore gradu; nec candor in ore
permanet et uires augentur et acrior ipse est
uultus et incomptis breuior mensura capillis,
790 plusque uigoris adest habuit quam femina. nam quae
femina nuper eras, puer es. date munera templis,
nec timida gaudete fide. dant munera templis,
addunt et titulum; titulus breue carmen habebat:
DONA•PVER•SOLVIT•QVAE•FEMINA•VOVERAT•IPHIS.

Why not make up your mind, Iphis, and gather yourself together,   745
and shake off these pointless, stupid fires?
You see what you were born (unless you are deceiving your own self too);
seek what is right and love what, as a woman, you should.
It is hope that causes love, it is hope that feeds it;
and this is what the situation takes from you. It is no guard that keeps you   750
from her dear embrace, no cautious husband's care,
no father's severity, not she herself refusing when you ask;
yet she is not to be won by you nor, though everything be done,
can you be happy, though both gods and men were to strive.
[Now too no part of my prayers is in vain,   755
and the favourable gods have given me whatever was in their power.]
What I want, my father wants, she too wants and my father-in-law to be;
but nature, more powerful than all of them, does not want it,
and is the only one that hurts me. Look, the longed for time is coming
and the wedding morn is at hand and now Ianthe will be mine—   760
but she will not be given to me; we shall be thirsty in the middle of the waters.
Why, *pronuba* Juno, why, Hymenaeos, do you come to these
rites from which the groom is absent and where both of us are brides?'
    With this, she checked her voice. And the other maiden was on fire
no more gently and she prayed, Hymenaeos, that you would quickly come.   765
What she sought, Telethusa feared, and sometimes she postponed the time,
now she dragged out the delay by feigning sickness, often she blamed
omens and visions. But now she had used up all
material for deceit, and the postponed wedding date
loomed, and there was one day left. But she   770
tore off the hair-bands from the head of her daughter
and of herself, and, with her hair flowing loose, she embraced the altar and said,
'Isis, you who dwell at Paraetonium, and in the Mareotic fields,
and at Pharos, and on the Nile divided into seven branches,
bring, I pray, help and cure our fear.   775
You, goddess, you I once saw and these your symbols
and I knew them all, the sound, the companions and the torches
of the rites, and I have heeded your orders in my mindful memory.
That she sees the light, that *I am not punished, look,*
is from your advice and gift; pity two women   780
and assist us with your help.' Tears followed her words.
The goddess seemed to have moved her altars (and she had moved them),
and the temple door trembled and her moon-like
horns flashed and the soundable sistrum rattled.
Not free of care, indeed, yet happy with this glad omen,   785
the mother left the temple. As she went, Iphis followed closely
with a bigger step than she was used to; and the bloom in her face
did not remain, her strength increased, her very expression was
sharper, her hair was disordered but of shorter length,
and there was more vigour present than she had as a girl. For you,   790
till recently a girl, are now a boy. Give offerings to the temples
and rejoice with no timid faith. They gave offerings to the temples
and added an inscription; the inscription consisted of a brief poem:
THESE•GIFTS•WHICH•IPHIS•VOWED•AS•A•GIRL•HE•PAID•AS•A•BOY.

795   postera lux radiis latum patefecerat orbem,
         cum Venus et Iuno sociosque Hymenaeos ad ignes
         conueniunt, potiturque sua puer Iphis Ianthe.

The next dawn had with its rays reealed the wide world,   795
when Venus and Juno and Hymenaeos assembled for the marriage
fires, and the boy, Iphis, won his Ianthe.

LIBER X

Inde per immensum croceo uelatus amictu
aethera digreditur Ciconumque Hymenaeos ad oras
tendit et Orphea nequiquam uoce uocatur.
adfuit ille quidem, sed nec sollemnia uerba
5   nec laetos uultus nec felix attulit omen;
fax quoque quam tenuit lacrimoso stridula fumo
usque fuit nullosque inuenit motibus ignes.
exitus auspicio grauior; nam nupta per herbas
dum noua Naïadum turba comitata uagatur,
10   occidit in talum serpentis dente recepto.
quam satis ad superas postquam Rhodopeïus auras
defleuit uates, ne non temptaret et umbras,
ad Styga Taenaria est ausus descendere porta;
perque leues populos simulacraque functa sepulcro
15   Persephonen adiit inamoenaque regna tenentem
umbrarum dominum, pulsisque ad carmina neruis
sic ait: 'o positi sub terra numina mundi,
in quem reccidimus, quidquid mortale creamur,
si licet et falsi positis ambagibus oris
20   uera loqui sinitis, non huc ut opaca uiderem
Tartara descendi, nec uti uillosa colubris
terna Medusaei uincirem guttura monstri;
causa uiae est coniunx, in quam calcata uenenum
uipera diffudit crescentesque abstulit annos.
25   posse pati uolui nec me temptasse negabo;
uicit Amor. supera deus hic bene notus in ora est;
an sit et hic dubito. sed et hic tamen auguror esse,
famaque si ueteris non est mentita rapinae,
uos quoque iunxit Amor. per ego haec loca plena timoris,
30   per Chaos hoc ingens uastique silentia regni,
Eurydices, oro, properata retexite fata.
omnia debemur uobis, paulumque morati
serius aut citius sedem properamus ad unam.
tendimus huc omnes, haec est domus ultima, uosque
35   humani generis longissima regna tenetis.
haec quoque, cum iustos matura peregerit annos,
iuris erit uestri; pro munere poscimus usum.
quod si fata negant ueniam pro coniuge, certum est
nolle redire mihi; leto gaudete duorum.'
40   talia dicentem neruosque ad uerba mouentem
exsangues flebant animae; nec Tantalus undam
captauit refugam, stupuitque Ixionis orbis,
nec carpsere iecur uolucres, urnisque uacarunt
Belides, inque tuo sedisti, Sisyphe, saxo.
45   tum primum lacrimis uictarum carmine fama est

BOOK 10

From there, clad in his saffron robe, Hymenaeos departed
through the immeasurable ether and pressed on to the lands
of the Cicones, and was called on in vain by Orpheus' voice.
He was there indeed, but he brought neither the ceremonial
words, nor a joyful face, nor a happy omen;   5
and the torch too which he held hissed all the time with smoke
that made tears flow and did not catch fire at all when shaken.
The outcome was worse than the auspice; for, while the new bride,
accompanied by a throng of Naiads, was roaming through the grass,
she fell dead from a snake's tooth entering her ankle.   10
And when the Rhodopeian bard had wept his fill for her
to the heavens above, lest he fail to try even the shades,
he dared to descend to the Styx by the Taenarian gate;
and through the weightless peoples and the ghosts who had experienced the tomb
he approached Persephone and the one who rules the uncharming realms,   15
the lord of the shades, and, striking his strings to the music,
he sang thus: 'O worlds placed beneath the earth,
into which we sink back whatever we are, born mortal,
if it is permitted and you allow the telling of the truth with the ramblings
of a lying mouth put aside, I did not come down here to see   20
dark Tartarus, nor to bind the three
necks of the Medusan monster bristling with snakes;
the reason for my journey is my wife who trod upon a snake which poured
its poison into her and took away her growing years.
I wanted to be able to endure it, and I shall not deny that I tried to;   25
Love has conquered. He is a god well known in the upper world;
whether he is here too, I am uncertain. But still, I divine that he is here too,
and if the story of that old rape is not a lie,
you too were joined by Love. Through these fearful places,
through this huge Chaos and the silence of this vast realm,   30
unweave, I beg you, the hurried fate of Eurydice.
We are all owed to you, and, after we delay a little,
we hurry, sooner or later, to one resting place.
We are all making for here, this is our last home, and you
have the longest reign over human kind.   35
She too, when ripe in age she has completed her fair share of years,
will be subject to you; we ask not for a gift, but for a loan.
But if the fates refuse this mercy for my wife, I am determined
that I will not go back; rejoice in the death of two.'
As he sang thus, moving the strings to his words,   40
the bloodless spirits wept for him; and Tantalus did not snatch
at the fleeing water, Ixion's wheel stopped,
the birds were not tearing at the liver, the Belides rested
from their urns, and, Sisyphus, you sat upon your rock.
The story is that the Eumenides were conquered by the song and that it was then,   45

Eumenidum maduisse genas; nec regia coniunx
sustinet oranti nec qui regit ima negare,
Eurydicenque uocant. umbras erat illa recentes
inter et incessit passu de uulnere tardo.
50 hanc simul et legem Rhodopeïus accipit Orpheus,
ne flectat retro sua lumina, donec Auernas
exierit ualles; aut irrita dona futura.
  carpitur adcliuis per muta silentia trames,
arduus, obscurus, caligine densus opaca.
55 nec procul abfuerunt telluris margine summae;
hic ne deficeret metuens auidusque uidendi
flexit amans oculos, et protinus illa relapsa est;
bracchiaque intendens prendique et prendere certans
nil nisi cedentes infelix adripit auras.
60 iamque iterum moriens non est de coniuge quidquam
questa suo (quid enim nisi se quereretur amatam?)
supremumque 'uale', quod iam uix auribus ille
acciperet, dixit reuolutaque rursus eodem est.
  non aliter stupuit gemina nece coniugis Orpheus
65 quam tria qui Stygii, medio portante catenas,
colla canis uidit, quem non pauor ante reliquit
quam natura prior, saxo per corpus oborto;
quique in se crimen traxit uoluitque uideri
Olenos esse nocens, tuque, o confisa figurae,
70 infelix Lethaea, tuae, iunctissima quondam
pectora, nunc lapides, quos umida sustinet Ide.
orantem frustraque iterum transire uolentem
portitor arcuerat. septem tamen ille diebus
squalidus in ripa Cereris sine munere sedit;
75 cura dolorque animi lacrimaeque alimenta fuere.
esse deos Erebi crudeles questus in altam
se recipit Rhodopen pulsumque Aquilonibus Haemum.
tertius aequoreis inclusum Piscibus annum
finierat Titan, omnemque refugerat Orpheus
80 femineam Venerem, seu quod male cesserat illi,
siue fidem dederat; multas tamen ardor habebat
iungere se uati; multae doluere repulsae.
ille etiam Thracum populis fuit auctor amorem
in teneros transferre mares citraque iuuentam
85 aetatis breue uer et primos carpere flores.
  collis erat collemque super planissima campi
area, quam uiridem faciebant graminis herbae.
umbra loco deerat; qua postquam parte resedit
dis genitus uates et fila sonantia mouit,
90 umbra loco uenit. non Chaonis abfuit arbor,
non nemus Heliadum, non frondibus aesculus altis,
nec tiliae molles,nec fagus et innuba laurus,
et coryli fragiles, et fraxinus utilis hastis
enodisque abies curuataque glandibus ilex
95 et platanus genialis acerque coloribus impar

for the first time, that their cheeks grew wet with tears; the ruler's wife could not
bear to refuse his prayer nor could he who rules the depths,
and they called Eurydice. She was among the recent
shades and advanced at a slow pace because of her wound.
Rhodopeian Orpheus accepted her and, at the same time, the condition   50
that he should not turn his eyes back until he had left
Avernus' valleys; or the gift would be annulled.
    The sloping path up which they picked their way in hushed silence
was steep and dark and thick with a dense mist.
And they were not far from the edge of the upper earth;   55
here, afraid that she would give up, and eager to see her,
he turned his eyes back lovingly, and at once she slipped back;
stretching her arms out, striving to be grasped and to grasp,
the unhappy woman seized onto nothing but yielding air.
And now, dying once more, she did not complain at all   60
about her husband (for what could she complain of except that she was loved?),
and she spoke her last 'farewell' which now scarcely
reached his ears, and turned back to the same place again.
    Orpheus was stunned at the double death of his wife, just as was
the one who saw the three heads of the Stygian dog   65
and the chains worn by its middle one, and his fear did not leave him
until his former nature had, when rock grew over his body,
or as was Olenos who took the blame upon himself
and wanted to seem to be guilty, or as were you, unhappy Lethaea,
who trusted in your beauty, once two hearts closely   70
joined, now stones which watery Ida holds.
Though he begged and vainly wanted to cross again,
the ferryman had refused him. Yet for seven days
he sat in filth on the bank without the gift of Ceres;
care, heartache and tears were his nourishment.   75
After complaining of the existence of Erebus' cruel gods, he returned
to high Rhodope and to Haemus buffeted by the Aquilo.
    The third Titan had finished its year bounded
by watery *Pisces*, and Orpheus had shunned all
Venus with women, either because it had turned out ill for him,   80
or because he had given a pledge. Yet many women were gripped by a burning desire
to join themselves with the bard; many grieved when rebuffed.
He was even the instigator among the peoples of Thrace of transferring
love to tender males and of plucking the first
flowers of the brief age of spring before young manhood.   85
    There was a hill, and at the top of the hill a most level
plain which was made green by blades of grass.
Shade was missing from the place; but, after the god-born bard
sat down there and moved his sounding strings,
shade came to the place. The Chaonian tree was not absent,   90
nor was a copse of Heliades, nor the durmast with its tall foliage,
nor the soft linden trees, nor the beech and the unmarried laurel,
and the fragile hazels, and the ash useful for spears,
and the knotty fir-tree, and the holm-oak bent with acorns,
and the kindly plane-tree, and the maple tree with its varied colours,   95

amnicolaeque simul salices et aquatica lotos
perpetuoque uirens buxum tenuesque myricae
et bicolor myrtus et bacis caerula tinus.
uos quoque, flexipedes hederae, uenistis et una
100 pampineae uites et amictae uitibus ulmi
ornique et piceae pomoque onerata rubenti
arbutus et lentae, uictoris praemia, palmae
et succincta comas hirsutaque uertice pinus,
grata deum Matri; siquidem Cybeleius Attis
105 exuit hac hominem truncoque induruit alto.
    adfuit huic turbae metas imitata cypressus,
nunc arbor, puer ante deo dilectus ab illo,
qui citharam neruis et neruis temperat arcum.
namque sacer nymphis Carthaea tenentibus arua
110 ingens ceruus erat lateque patentibus altas
ipse suo capiti praebebat cornibus umbras.
cornua fulgebant auro, demissaque in armos
pendebant tereti gemmata monilia collo;
bulla super frontem paruis argentea loris
115 uincta mouebatur, parilique decore nitebant
auribus e geminis circum caua tempora bacae.
isque metu uacuus naturalique pauore
deposito celebrare domos mulcendaque colla
quamlibet ignotis manibus praebere solebat.
120 sed tamen ante alios, Ceae pulcherrime gentis,
gratus erat, Cyparisse, tibi; tu pabula ceruum
ad noua, tu liquidi ducebas fontis ad undam,
tu modo texebas uarios per cornua flores,
nunc eques in tergo residens huc laetus et illuc
125 mollia purpureis frenabas ora capistris.
aestus erat mediusque dies, solisque uapore
concaua litorei feruebant bracchia Cancri;
fessus in herbosa posuit sua corpora terra
ceruus et arborea frigus ducebat ab umbra.
130 hunc puer imprudens iaculo Cyparissus acuto
fixit et, ut saeuo morientem uulnere uidit,
uelle mori statuit. quae non solacia Phoebus
dixit? ut hunc leuiter pro materiaque doleret
admonuit! gemit ille tamen munusque supremum
135 hoc petit a superis, ut tempore lugeret omni.
iamque per immensos egesto sanguine fletus
in uiridem uerti coeperunt membra colorem,
et modo qui niuea pendebant fronte capilli
horrida caesaries fieri sumptoque rigore
140 sidereum gracili spectare cacumine caelum.
ingemuit tristisque deus 'lugebere nobis
lugebisque alios aderisque dolentibus' inquit.
    tale nemus uates attraxerat inque ferarum
concilio medius turba uolucrumque sedebat.
145 ut satis impulsas temptauit pollice chordas

and also the river-dwelling willows, and the water-lotus,
and the box-tree always green, and the fine tamarisk,
and the myrtles of both colours, and the laurustinus with its blue berries.
You too, pliant-footed ivies, came and, together with you,
grape-vines and elms clad in vines,   100
and mountain ash, and spruce, and arbutus weighed down by reddening
fruit, and pliant palms, the victor's reward,
and the pine with foliage girt up and shaggy head,
dear to the Mother of the gods; since indeed Cybele's Attis
cast off his humanity for this and hardened into a tall trunk.   105
    There was present among this throng the cone-shaped cypressus,
now a tree, before a boy adored by that god
who controls his lyre with strings and his bow with strings.
For, sacred to the nymphs who owned the Carthaean fields,
there was a huge stag who provided his own head   110
with deep shade from his widely spreading antlers.
His antlers shone with gold, and, hanging down to his shoulders,
there was a bejewelled necklace suspended from his smooth neck;
a silver boss bound by light straps moved
high on his forehead, and, just as decoratively, pearls   115
gleamed from both his ears, around his hollow temples.
And, free from fear, with his natural timidity
laid aside, he used to frequent their homes and offer
his neck to be petted by men's hands, however unfamiliar they were.
But still, Cyparissus, most handsome of the Cean race, he was   120
above any others dear to you; you used to lead the stag
to new pastures, you led him to the waters of the clear spring,
sometimes you would weave various flowers through his antlers,
now, as a horseman sitting on his back, you would joyfully guide
his soft mouth this way and that with his purple harness.   125
It was hot, and the middle of the day, and the curved arms
of shore-dwelling *Cancer* were boiling from the warmth of the sun;
weary, the stag lay his body on the grassy
earth and was drawing in the cool from the shade of the trees.
Unwittingly, the boy, Cyparissus, pierced him with his sharp   130
javelin and, as he saw him dying from the cruel wound,
decided that he would die himself. What words of consolation did Phoebus not
say to him? How he urged him to grieve slightly
and proportionately! But still he groaned and asked the gods
for this last favour, that he should grieve for all time.   135
And now, as his blood was drained by immeasurable weeping,
his limbs began to be turned to a green colour,
and his hair, which just now had hung from his snowy brow,
became bristling locks and, becoming stiff,
gazed at the starry sky from its slender tree-top.   140
With a groan, the god sadly said, 'You will be mourned by us
and you will mourn for others and be present for them as they grieve.'
    Such was the copse the bard had attracted and he was sitting
in the middle of a council of wild beasts and a throng of birds.
When he had sufficiently tried the strings he had struck with his thumb, 145

et sensit uarios, quamuis diuersa sonarent,
concordare modos, hoc uocem carmine mouit:
     'ab Ioue, Musa parens, (cedunt Iouis omnia regno)
carmina nostra moue. Iouis est mihi saepe potestas
150   dicta prius: cecini plectro grauiore Gigantas
sparsaque Phlegraeis uictricia fulmina campis.
nunc opus est leuiore lyra; puerosque canamus
dilectos superis inconcessisque puellas
ignibus attonitas meruisse libidine poenam.
155   rex superum Phrygii quondam Ganymedis amore
arsit, et inuentum est aliquid quod Iuppiter esse
quam quod erat mallet. nulla tamen alite uerti
dignatur, nisi quae posset sua fulmina ferre.
nec mora, percusso mendacibus aëre pennis
160   abripit Iliaden, qui nunc quoque pocula miscet
inuitaque Ioui nectar Iunone ministrat.
     te quoque, Amyclide, posuisset in aethera Phoebus,
tristia si spatium ponendi fata dedissent.
qua licet, aeternus tamen es, quotiensque repellit
165   uer hiemem Piscique Aries succedit aquoso,
tu totiens oreris uiridique in caespite flores.
te meus ante omnes genitor dilexit, et orbe
in medio positi caruerunt praeside Delphi,
dum deus Eurotan immunitamque frequentat
170   Sparten. nec citharae nec sunt in honore sagittae;
immemor ipse sui non retia ferre recusat,
non tenuisse canes, non per iuga montis iniqui
ire comes, longaque alit adsuetudine flammas.
iamque fere medius Titan uenientis et actae
175   noctis erat spatioque pari distabat utrimque;
corpora ueste leuant et suco pinguis oliui
splendescunt latique ineunt certamine disci,
quem prius aërias libratum Phoebus in auras
misit et oppositas disiecit pondere nubes;
180   reccidit in solidam longo post tempore terram
pondus et exhibuit iunctam cum uiribus artem.
protinus imprudens actusque cupidine lusus
tollere Taenarides orbem properabat; at illum
dura repercusso subiecit pondere tellus
185   in uultus, Hyacinthe, tuos. (expalluit aeque
quam puer ipse deus conlapsosque excipit artus.)
et modo te refouet, modo tristia uulnera siccat,
nunc animam admotis fugientem sustinet herbis.
nil prosunt artes; erat immedicabile uulnus.
190   ut, si quis uiolas riguoque papauera in horto
liliaque infringat fuluis horrentia linguis,
marcida demittant subito caput illa grauatum
nec se sustineant spectentque cacumine terram,
sic uultus moriens iacet, et defecta uigore
195   ipsa sibi est oneri ceruix umeroque recumbit.

and sensed that the various notes harmonized, although
they sounded different, he gave voice to this song:
    From Jove, mother Muse, (all things yield to Jove's rule)
start up our song. Often before have I told
of Jove's power: with a heavier plectrum I sang of the Giants   150
and the victorious thunderbolts scattered on the Phlegraean plains.
Now there is need for a lighter lyre; and let us sing of boys
loved by the gods, and how girls, crazed
by illicit fires, deserved punishment for their lust.
    The king of the gods was once burning with love   155
for Ganymede, and something was found which Jupiter would rather
be than what he was. But there was no bird he deigned
to be turned into unless it could carry his thunderbolts.
And without delay, he struck through the air with his false wings
and snatched away Iliades who even now mixes drinks   160
and serves nectar to Jove, though Juno disapproves.
    You too, Amyclides, Phoebus would have placed in the ether,
if the sad fates had given him the time to place you there.
Yet you are, as far as is allowed, immortal, and, as often as the spring
pushes winter back, and *Aries* succeeds the watery *Pisces*,   165
so often do you arise and flower in the green turf.
It was you above all that my father loved, and Delphi,
set in the middle of the world, lacked its guardian
while the god resorted to the Eurotas and undefended
Sparta. He had no regard for either lyres or arrows;   170
unmindful of himself, he did not refuse to carry nets,
nor to hold back the dogs, nor to go as a companion over the rough
mountain ridges, and he fed the flames with long association.
And already Titan was about half way between the night that was coming
and the one that was done, and was an equal distance from both;   175
they freed their bodies from their clothes, and shone with rich olive
oil, and entered into a contest with the broad discus
which Phoebus first balanced and the threw into the airy
breeze, and it dispersed the facing clouds with its weight;
a long time after, the weight fell back onto the solid   180
earth, showing skill joined with strength.
At once, Taenarides, incautious and driven by enthusiasm
for the sport, was hurrying to pick up the disk; but it
was thrown up by the hard earth, as its weight rebounded
into your face, Hyacinthus. (As the boy grew pale,   185
so did the god himself, and he picked the body up from where it had collapsed.)
And now he caressed you, now he dried your sad wounds,
now he held back your fleeing soul by applying herbs.
His skills were of no help; the wound was incurable.
Just as, if one were to break off violets in a well-watered garden,   190
or poppies or lilies bristling with yellow tongues,
suddenly they would droop and let their burdened head fall
and would not support themselves and would gaze at the earth from their tops,
so the dying face lay and, deprived of its strength,
the very neck was a burden to itself and rested on his shoulders.   195

"laberis, Oebalide, prima fraudate iuuenta,"
Phoebus ait "uideoque tuum, mea crimina, uulnus.
tu dolor es facinusque meum; mea dextera leto
inscribenda tuo est; ego sum tibi funeris auctor.
200 quae mea culpa tamen? nisi si lusisse uocari
culpa potest, nisi culpa potest et amasse uocari.
atque utinam pro te uitam tecumue liceret
reddere! quod quoniam fatali lege tenemur,
semper eris mecum memorique haerebis in ore.
205 [te lyra pulsa manu, te carmina nostra sonabunt,
flosque nouus scripto gemitus imitabere nostros.
tempus et illud erit, quo se fortissimus heros
addat in hunc florem folioque legatur eodem.]"
talia dum uero memorantur Apollinis ore,
210 ecce cruor, qui fusus humo signauerat herbas,
desinit esse cruor, Tyrioque nitentior ostro
flos oritur formamque capit quam lilia, si non
purpureus color his, argenteus esset in illis.
non satis hoc Phoebo est (is enim fuit auctor honoris);
215 ipse suos gemitus foliis inscribit et AI AI
flos habet inscriptum funestaque littera ducta est.
nec genuisse pudet Sparten Hyacinthon honorque
durat in hoc aeui celebrandaque more priorum
annua praelata redeunt Hyacinthia pompa.
220   at si forte roges fecundam Amathunta metallis
an genuisse uelit Propoetidas, abnuat aeque
atque illos, gemino quondam quibus aspera cornu
frons erat; unde etiam nomen traxere Cerastae.
ante fores horum stabat Iouis Hospitis ara,
225 ignarus sceleris quam si quis sanguine tinctam
aduena uenisset, mactatos crederet illic
lactantes uitulos Amathusiacasque bidentes;
hospes erat caesus. sacris offensa nefandis
ipsa suas urbes Ophiusiaque arua parabat
230 deserere alma Venus. "sed quid loca grata, quid urbes
peccauere meae? quod" dixit "crimen in illis?
exilio poenam potius gens impia pendat
uel nece uel si quid medium est mortisque fugaeque.
idque quid esse potest, nisi uersae poena figurae?"
235 dum dubitat quo mutat eos, ad cornua uultum
flexit et admonita est haec illis posse relinqui;
grandiaque in toruos transformat membra iuuencos.
    sunt tamen obscenae Venerem Propoetides ausae
esse negare deam; pro quo sua, numinis ira,
240 corpora cum forma primae uulgasse feruntur;
utque pudor cessit sanguisque induruit oris,
in rigidum paruo silicem discrimine uersae.
    quas quia Pygmalíon aeuum per crimen agentes
uiderat, offensus uitiis quae plurima menti
245 femineae natura dedit, sine coniuge caelebs

"You are sinking, Oebalides, cheated of the prime of youth,"
said Phoebus, "and I see your wound as my fault.
You are my grief and crime; my right hand should be
branded for your fate; I am the cause of your death.
Yet, what sin is mine? Unless to play can be   200
called a sin, unless it can be called a sin to love too.
And would that I were allowed to give up my life for you
or with you! But since we are bound by the law of fate
you will always be with me and you will stay on my mindful lips.
[Of you will the lyre, struck by my hand, sound, of you will my songs,   205
and, as a new flower, you will imitate our groans in writing.
And that time will be when a most mighty hero adds
himself to this flower and is read on the same petal.]"
While such things were being spoken by Apollo's truthful lips,
look, the blood which had poured onto the ground and stained the grass   210
stopped being blood and, brighter than Tyrian purple,
a flower arose and took the form that lilies take, except that
in these there is a purple colour, but a silver one in those.
This was not enough for Phoebus (for he was the author of the honour);
he himself wrote his groans on the petals and AI AI   215
was written on the flower and the symbol of woe was drawn.
Sparta is not ashamed to have given birth to Hyacinthus, and his honour
endures to this age, and the Hyacinthia return to be celebrated
every year led by a procession in the manner of those before us.
But, in case you should ask whether Amathus, prolific   220
in metals, wanted to have given birth to the Propoetides, she would deny it
of them and equally of those who once had a forehead bristling
with a double horn, from which they derived the name Cerastae.
In front of their door, there stood an altar of Hospitable Jupiter,
and if a stranger, ignorant of its crime, had seen the altar   225
stained with blood, he would believe that suckling calves
had been sacrificed there or Amathusiac lambs;
it was a guest that had been killed. Offended by these unspeakable rites,
kind Venus herself was preparing to abandon her own cities
and the Ophiusian fields. "But how have my favourite places, how have   230
my cities sinned? What fault," she said, "is there in them?
Let the impious tribe rather pay the penalty with exile
or with execution or with anything there may be between death and banishment.
And what could that be, except the penalty of altered appearance?
While she hesitated on what she should change them to, she turned to face   235
their horns, and this suggested to her that they could be left with those.
And she transformed their large bodies into grim bullocks.
But the lewd Propoetides dared to deny
that Venus was a goddess; for which, as a result of her divine anger,
they are said to have been the first to prostitute their bodies and their beauty; 240
and when their shame had gone, and the blood had hardened in their faces,
it was with little change that they were turned into solid stone.
And because Pygmalion had seen them spend their life
in wickedness, offended by the very many faults nature
has given to the female mind, he was living celibately   245

uiuebat thalamique diu consorte carebat.
interea niueum mira feliciter arte
sculpsit ebur formamque dedit, qua femina nasci
nulla potest, operisque sui concepit amorem.
250 uirginis est uerae facies, quam uiuere credas
et, si non obstet reuerentia, uelle moueri;
ars adeo latet arte sua. miratur et haurit
pectore Pygmalion simulati corporis ignes.
saepe manus operi temptantes admouet, an sit
255 corpus an illud ebur, nec adhuc ebur esse fatetur.
[oscula dat reddique putat loquiturque tenetque;]
et credit tactis digitos insidere membris
et metuit, pressos ueniat ne liuor in artus.
et modo blanditias adhibet, modo grata puellis
260 munera fert illi conchas teretesque lapillos
et paruas uolucres et flores mille colorum
liliaque pictasque pilas et ab arbore lapsas
Heliadum lacrimas. ornat quoque uestibus artus;
dat digitis gemmas, dat longa monilia collo;
265 aure leues bacae, redimicula pectore pendent.
cuncta decent; nec nuda minus formosa uidetur.
conlocat hanc stratis concha Sidonide tinctis
appellatque tori sociam acclinataque colla
mollibus in plumis tamquam sensura reponit.
270   festa dies Veneris tota celeberrima Cypro
uenerat, et pandis inductae cornibus aurum
conciderant ictae niuea ceruice iuuencae,
turaque fumabant, cum munere functus ad aras
constitit et timide "si, di, dare cuncta potestis,
275 sit coniunx, opto," (non ausus "eburnea uirgo")"
dicere) Pygmalion "similis mea" dixit "eburnae."
sensit, ut ipsa suis aderat Venus aurea festis,
uota quid illa uelint, et, amici numinis omen,
flamma ter accensa est apicemque per aëra duxit.
280 ut rediit, simulacra suae petit ille puellae
incumbensque toro dedit oscula; uisa tepere est.
admouet os iterum, manibus quoque pectora temptat;
temptatum mollescit ebur positoque rigore
subsidit digitis ceditque, ut Hymettia sole
285 cera remollescit tractataque pollice multas
flectitur in facies ipsoque fit utilis usu.
dum stupet et dubie gaudet fallique ueretur,
rursus amans rursusque manu sua uota retractat.
corpus erat; saliunt temptatae pollice uenae.
290 tum uero Paphius plenissima concipit heros
uerba, quibus Veneri grates agit, oraque tandem
ore suo non falsa premit; dataque oscula uirgo
sensit et erubuit, timidumque ad lumina lumen
attollens pariter cum caelo uidit amantem.
295 coniugio, quod fecit, adest dea, iamque coactis

without a wife, and for a long time lacked a partner in his bed.
Meanwhile, with wondrous and felicitous artistry, he carved
snowy ivory and gave it a beauty with which no woman
could be born, and he fell in love with his own work.
It had the face of a real maiden who, you would have thought, was living   250
and, if self respect were not stopping her, wanted to move;
his art was so hidden by his art. Pygmalion, in wonder,
drew into his breast fires for the imitation body.
Often he moved his hands onto his work to test whether it was
a body or ivory, and did not admit that it was still ivory.   255
[He gave it kisses and thought they were returned, and he spoke to it and held it.]
And he believed that his fingers sunk into its limbs as he touched them
and he was afraid that a bruise would come to its body after he pressed it.
And sometimes he plied it with endearments, sometimes he brought it
gifts pleasing to girls, shells and polished pebbles   260
and small birds and flowers of a thousand colours
and lilies and coloured balls and the tears of the Heliades
dropped from their tree. He also dressed its body in clothes;
he gave gems for the fingers, he gave long necklaces for the neck;
small pearls hung from the ear, ribbons from the breast.   265
They were all becoming; but naked she seemed no less beautiful.
He placed her on coverlets dyed by the Sidonian shell-fish.
He called her the companion of his bed and set her neck
leaning on soft feathers as if she would feel them.
　　The feast day of Venus, the most celebrated in all of Cyprus,   270
had come, and heifers, their spreading horns trimmed with gold,
had fallen, struck on their snowy neck,
and the incense was smoking, when Pygmalion, his duty performed,
stood at the altars and nervously said, "If, O gods, you can
give all things, I pray that my wife will be" (he did not dare   275
to say "the ivory maiden") "like," he said, "the ivory girl."
As she was present herself at her own feast, golden Venus sensed
what those prayers meant, and, an omen of a well-disposed divinity,
her flame blazed up three times and drew its point up through the air.
When he returned, he sought the image of his girl   280
and, leaning over the couch, he gave her kisses; she seemed to grow warm.
He moved his mouth to her again, he touched her breasts with his hands too;
where it was touched, the ivory softened and lost its hardness
and sank beneath his fingers and yielded, as Hymettian wax
melts in the sun and, if worked on by the thumb, is moulded   285
into many shapes and becomes useful from use itself.
While still stunned and hesitatingly rejoicing and fearing that he was deceived,
again with love and again he tries out his hopes with his hand.
She was flesh; her veins leapt when worked on by his thumb.
Then indeed did the Paphian hero offer up the fullest   290
words with which he gave thanks to Venus, and he pressed lips
at last not false, to his own lips; and the maiden felt the kisses
he had given and blushed, and, raising her timid eyes
to the light, saw the sky and her lover together.
The goddess was present at the marriage she had made and, now the lunar   295

cornibus in plenum nouiens lunaribus orbem
illa Paphon genuit, de qua tenet insula nomen.
    editus hac ille est, qui, si sine prole fuisset,
inter felices Cinyras potuisset haberi.

300   dira canam; procul hinc natae, procul este parentes!
aut, mea si uestras mulcebunt carmina mentes,
desit in hac mihi parte fides, nec credite factum;
uel, si credetis, facti quoque credite poenam.
si tamen admissum sinit hoc natura uideri,

305   gentibus Ismariis et nostro gratulor orbi,
gratulor huic terrae, quod abest regionibus illis
quae tantum genuere nefas. sit diues amomo,
cinnamaque costumque suum sudataque ligno
tura ferat floresque alios Panchaïa tellus,

310   dum ferat et murram; tanti noua non fuit arbor.
ipse negat nocuisse tibi sua tela Cupido,
Myrrha, facesque suas a crimine uindicat isto;
stipite te Stygio tumidisque adflauit echidnis
e tribus una soror. scelus est odisse parentem;

315   hic amor est odio maius scelus.
                             undique lecti
te cupiunt proceres, totoque oriente iuuentus
ad thalami certamen adest. ex omnibus unum
elige, Myrrha, uirum—dum ne sit in omnibus unus!
illa quidem sentit foedoque repugnat amori,

320   et secum "quo mente feror? quid molior?" inquit
"di, precor, et pietas sacrataque iura parentum,
hoc prohibete nefas scelerique resistite nostro,
si tamen hoc scelus est. sed enim damnare negatur
hanc Venerem Pietas, coeuntque animalia nullo

325   cetera dilectu, nec habetur turpe iuuencae
ferre patrem tergo; fit equo sua filia coniunx,
quasque creauit init pecudes caper, ipsaque, cuius
semine concepta est, ex illo concipit ales.
felices, quibus ista licent! humana malignas

330   cura dedit leges, et quod natura remittit
inuida iura negant. gentes tamen esse feruntur,
in quibus et nato genetrix et nata parenti
iungitur, ut pietas geminato crescat amore.
me miseram, quod non nasci mihi contigit illic

335   fortunaque loci laedor! quid in ista reuoluor?
spes interdictae, discedite! dignus amari
ille, sed ut pater, est. ergo si filia magni
non essem Cinyrae, Cinyrae concumbere possem.
nunc, quia iam meus est, non est meus, ipsaque damno

340   est mihi proximitas; aliena potentior essem.
ire libet procul hinc patriaeque relinquere fines,
dum scelus effugiam; retinet malus ardor amantem,
ut praesens spectem Cinyran tangamque loquarque
osculaque admoueam, si nil conceditur ultra.

horns had come together nine times into a full disk,
she bore Paphos from whom the island took its name.

From her was born that Cinyras who, if he had been without
offspring could have been held to be amongst the fortunate.
I shall sing of dreadful things; far from here, O daughters, be far away, O parents!   300
Or, if my songs beguile your minds,
in this part let there be no trust in me, and do not believe what happened;
or, if you do believe, believe also in the punishment for what happened.
But, if nature allows this crime to be seen,
I congratulate the Ismarian tribes and our world,   305
I congratulate this land, because it is far from those regions
which have given birth to so great a wickedness. Let her be rich in unguent,
and let cinnamon and her *costum* and incense that is sweated out
from wood be grown by the Panchaïan land, and other flowers,
provided she grows myrrh too; the new tree was not worth so much.   310
Cupid himself denies that it was his shafts that hurt you,
Myrrha, and he absolves his torches from that charge;
it was one of the three sisters that blighted you with a Stygian
brand and swollen vipers. It is a crime to hate a parent;
this love is a greater crime than hatred.
                                              Nobles chosen   315
from everywhere wanted you, the young men from all the east
were present at the competition for your wedding couch. From all of them, Myrrha,
choose one to be your husband, provided that there is one not amongst them all!
She did indeed understand and she fought back against her disgusting love,
and said to herself, "Where is my mind leading me? What am I striving for?   320
O gods, I pray, and piety and the sanctified rights of parents,
prevent this wickedness and resist my crime,
if, indeed, this is a crime. And yet Piety is said
not to condemn this sort of love, and the other animals couple
with no discrimination, and it is not held shameful for a heifer   325
to take her father on her back; the stallion has his own daughter for his wife,
the goat enters the flocks he has sired, and the bird conceives
from him by whose seed she was herself conceived.
Fortunate are those to whom these things are allowed. Human care
has given spiteful laws, and, what nature permits,   330
jealous rules refuse. They say that there are tribes
among whom mother is joined to son, and daughter
to father, so that piety may grow from doubled love.
Unhappy me, that I did not happen to be born there,
and am hurt by the chance of my birth-place! Why do I go over these things again?   335
Forbidden hopes, depart! He is worthy
to be loved, but as a father. So if I were not
the daughter of great Cinyras, with Cinyras I could lie.
Now, because he is mine already, he is not mine and my very closeness
is my curse; as a stranger, I would be better off.   340
I want to go far from here and to leave the borders of my fatherland,
provided I escape the crime; but an evil ardour keeps the lover here
to gaze on Cinyras in person, and to touch him, and speak to him,
and plant kisses on him, if nothing further is permitted.

345   ultra autem sperare aliquid potes, impia uirgo,
nec quot confundas et iura et nomina sentis?
tune eris et matris paelex et adultera patris?
tune soror nati genetrixque uocabere fratris?
nec metues atro crinitas angue sorores,
350   quas facibus saeuis oculos atque ora petentes
noxia corda uident? at tu, dum corpore non es
passa nefas, animo ne concipe, neue potentis
concubitu uetito naturae pollue foedus.
uelle puta; res ipsa uetat. pius ille memorque est
355   moris—et o uellem similis furor esset in illo!"
     dixerat. at Cinyras, quem copia digna procorum
quid faciat dubitare facit, scitatur ab ipsa,
nominibus dictis, cuius uelit esse mariti.
illa silet primo patriisque in uultibus haerens
360   aestuat et tepido suffundit lumina rore.
uirginei Cinyras haec credens esse timoris
flere uetat siccatque genas atque oscula iungit.
Myrrha datis nimium gaudet consultaque, qualem
optet habere uirum, "similem tibi" dixit, at ille
365   non intellectam uocem conlaudat et "esto
tam pia semper" ait. pietatis nomine dicto
demisit uultus sceleris sibi conscia uirgo.
     noctis erat medium, curasque et corpora somnus
soluerat; at uirgo Cinyreïa peruigil igni
370   carpitur indomito furiosaque uota retractat.
et modo desperat, modo uult temptare, pudetque
et cupit, et quid agat non inuenit; utque securi
saucia trabs ingens, ubi plaga nouissima restat,
quo cadat in dubio est omnique a parte timetur,
375   sic animus uario labefactus uulnere nutat
huc leuis atque illuc momentaque sumit utroque.
nec modus et requies, nisi mors, reperitur amoris;
mors placet. erigitur laqueoque innectere fauces
destinat, et zona summo de poste reuincta
380   "care uale Cinyra; causam te intellege mortis"
dixit et aptabat pallenti uincula collo.
     murmura uerborum fidas nutricis ad aures
peruenisse ferunt limen seruantis alumnae;
surgit anus reseratque fores mortisque paratae
385   instrumenta uidens spatio conclamat eodem
seque ferit scinditque sinus ereptaque collo
uincula dilaniat. tum denique flere uacauit,
tum dare complexus laqueique requirere causam.
muta silet uirgo terramque immota tuetur
390   et deprensa dolet tardae conamina mortis.
instat anus canosque suos et inania nudans
ubera per cunas alimentaque prima precatur
ut sibi committat quidquid dolet. illa rogantem
auersata gemit; certa est exquirere nutrix

But can you, impious girl, hope for something further,   345
and not understand how many rights and names you are confounding?
Will you be both the supplanter of your mother and an adulteress with your father?
Will you be called the sister of your son and mother of your brother?
And will you not be afraid of the sisters with black snakes for hair,
whom guilty hearts see aiming at their faces and their eyes   350
with cruel torches? But you, while you have not allowed
wickedness in your body, do not conceive it in your mind, and do not pollute
powerful nature's order with forbidden intercourse.
Suppose you want to; the facts themselves forbid it. He is pious and mindful
of morality—and oh I wish he had a like passion!"   355
    She had spoken. But Cinyras, who was being made to hesitate
about what to do by the abundance of worthy suitors, questioned her herself,
after mentioning some names, on which husband she wanted to belong to.
At first, she was silent and, with her eyes fixed upon her father's face,
she fretted and moistened her eyes with a warm dew.   360
Cinyras, believing these things to be the marks of a maiden's fear,
told her not to weep, and he dried her eyes and kissed her.
Myrrha enjoyed too much what she was given and, when asked what sort
of husband she would choose to have, "One like you," she said; but he
praised the words he had not understood and said,   365
"May you always be as pious." At the mention of piety,
the maiden cast her eyes down from guilt at her crime.
    It was the middle of the night, sleep had relaxed cares
and bodies; but the unsleeping Cinyreïan maiden was consumed
by an uncontrollable fire and was recollecting her mad hopes.   370
And now she was despairing, now wanting to try, she is both ashamed
and she desires, and is at a loss to know what she should do; and as a huge
tree-trunk, injured by an axe, when only the last blow remains,
is in doubt which way to fall and is feared on every side,
so her mind, weakened by a variety of wounds, wavered   375
easily this way and that, and started movements in both directions.
And no limit or respite is to be found for her love, except death;
she decides on death. She gets up and determines to bind her throat
in a noose, and, with her girdle bound to the top of a door-post,
"Farewell, dear Cinyras; understand that you were the reason for my death,"   380
she said, and began to fit the binding to her pale neck.
    They say that her mumbled words came to the ears
of her faithful nurse who was guarding the threshold of her foster-child;
the old woman rose up and unbarred the doors and, seeing the instruments
of deliberate death, at the same instant screamed out   385
and struck herself and tore at her bosom and snatched the bindings
from the neck and tore them apart. Then at last she was free to weep,
to give her an embrace and to ask the reason for the noose.
The maiden was hushed and silent and gazed unmoving at the ground,
grieving that her slow attempts at death had been detected.   390
The old woman pressed her and, baring her white hair and empty
breasts, begged her by her cradle and her first feeds
that she confide in her whatever was grieving her. She turned away from her
as she asked, and groaned; the nurse was determined to find out

395   nec solam spondere fidem. "dic" inquit "opemque
me sine ferre tibi; non est mea pigra senectus.
seu furor est, habeo quae carmine sanet et herbis;
siue aliquis nocuit, magico lustrabere ritu;
ira deum siue est, sacris placabilis ira.
400   quid rear ulterius? certe fortuna domusque
sospes et in cursu est; uiuit genetrixque paterque."
Myrrha patre audito suspiria duxit ab imo
pectore. nec nutrix etiamnum concipit ullum
mente nefas, aliquemque tamen praesensit amorem;
405   propositique tenax quodcumque est orat ut ipsi
indicet, et gremio lacrimantem tollit anili
atque ita complectens infirmis membra lacertis
"sensimus;" inquit "amas. sed et hic mea (pone timorem)
sedulitas erit apta tibi, nec sentiet umquam
410   hoc pater." exsiluit gremio furibunda torumque
ore premens "discede, precor, miseroque pudori
parce" ait; instanti "discede, aut desine" dixit
"quaerere quid doleam; scelus est quod scire laboras."
horret anus tremulasque manus annisque metuque
415   tendit et ante pedes supplex procumbit alumnae;
et modo blanditur, modo, si non conscia fiat,
terret et indicium laquei coeptaeque minatur
mortis, et officium commisso spondet amori.
extulit illa caput lacrimisque impleuit obortis
420   pectora nutricis conataque saepe fateri
saepe tenet uocem pudibundaque uestibus ora
texit et "o" dixit "felicem coniuge matrem!"
hactenus, et gemuit. gelidus nutricis in artus
ossaque (sensit enim) penetrat tremor, albaque toto
425   uertice canities rigidis stetit hirta capillis.
multaque ut excuteret diros, si posset, amores
addidit, at uirgo scit se non falsa moneri,
certa mori tamen est, si non potiatur amore.
"uiue," ait haec "potiere tuo"—et non ausa "parente"
430   dicere conticuit promissaque numine firmat.
     festa piae Cereris celebrabant annua matres
illa, quibus niuea uelatae corpora ueste
primitias frugum dant spicea serta suarum,
perque nouem noctes Venerem tactusque uiriles
435   in uetitis numerant. turba Cenchreis in illa
regis adest coniunx arcanaque sacra frequentat.
ergo legitima uacuus dum coniuge lectus,
nacta grauem uino Cinyran male sedula nutrix
nomine mentito ueros exponit amores
440   et faciem laudat; quaesitis uirginis annis
"par" ait "est Myrrhae." quam postquam adducere iussa est
utque domum rediit, "gaude, mea" dixit "alumna;
uicimus!" infelix non toto pectore sentit
laetitiam uirgo, praesagaque pectora maerent,

and to pledge not just loyalty. "Tell me," she said, "and let me   395
bring you help; my old age is not sluggish.
If it is passion, I know a woman who can cure it with a charm and herbs;
if someone has wronged you, you will be purified with a magic rite;
or if it is the anger of the gods, there are ceremonies to appease their anger.
How much further am I to think? Your wealth and home are   400
certainly safe and on course; your mother is alive, so too is your father."
At the mention of her father, Myrrha sighed from the bottom
of her heart. But the nurse did not even then conceive there was any
wickedness in her mind, though she already sensed some love affair;
and, tenacious of her purpose, begged her, whatever it was,   405
to tell her, and she raised the weeping girl to her old woman's lap
and embracing her body there in her frail arms,
"I understand;" she said, "you are in love. But in this too (put fear aside)
my diligence is what you need, and this will never be known
by your father." She leapt up from her lap in a frenzy and, pushing   410
her face upon the couch, "Go away, I beg you, and spare my unhappy
shame," she said, and, when she pressed her, "Go away, or stop," she replied,
"asking what is grieving me; what you are striving to know is a crime."
The old woman shuddered and stretched out hands trembling from fear
and age, and fell down in supplication at the feet of her foster-child;   415
and now she was coaxing her, now, if she were not made privy,
terrifying her by threats to tell of the noose and of the death
she had set out on, and pledged her service if she would tell of her love.
She raised her head and filled the nurse's breast
with her tears as they welled up, and often she tried to speak,   420
often she held the words back and, in her shame, covered her face
with her clothes and, "Oh," she said, "how fortunate was my mother in her husband!"
She got so far, and groaned. A chill tremor (for she understood)
passed through the nurse's body and her bones, and, on all of her head,
her hoary grey hair stood stiffly up on end.   425
And she added many things to shake, if she could, the dreadful love
out of her; but the maiden knew that the warnings were not false,
yet she was determined to die if she were not to win her love.
"Live," said the nurse, "you will win your"—and, not daring to say
"father," she fell silent and confirmed her promises with an oath.   430
        The pious mothers were celebrating Ceres' annual festival,
the one at which they veil their bodies in a snowy robe
and give, as the first-fruits of their crops, garlands of corn stalks,
and for nine nights they count amongst forbidden things
Venus and the touch of men. There was present in that throng   435
Cenchreis, the king's wife, celebrating the holy mysteries.
So, while his bed was empty of his lawful wife,
the perversely diligent nurse found Cinyras overcome by wine
and explained a true love to him under a false name
and praised her looks; when he asked about the maiden's age,   440
"Equal," she said "to Myrrha's." When she had been told to bring her
and had returned home, "Rejoice," she said, "my child;
we have won!" The unhappy maiden did not in all her heart
feel joy, and her foreboding heart grieved,

445 sed tamen et gaudet; tanta est discordia mentis.
    tempus erat quo cuncta silent, interque Triones
    flexerat obliquo Plaustrum temone Boötes;
    ad facinus uenit illa suum. fugit aurea caelo
    luna, tegunt nigrae latitantia sidera nubes,
450 nox caret igne suo; primus tegis, Icare, uultus
    Erigoneque pio sacrata parentis amore.
    ter pedis offensi signo est reuocata, ter omen
    funereus bubo letali carmine fecit;
    it tamen, et tenebrae minuunt noxque atra pudorem,
455 nutricisque manum laeua tenet, altera motu
    caecum iter explorat. thalami iam limina tangit,
    iamque fores aperit, iam ducitur intus, at illi
    poplite succiduo genua intremuere fugitque
    et color et sanguis animusque relinquit euntem.
460 quoque suo propior sceleri est, magis horret et ausi
    paenitet et uellet non cognita posse reuerti.
    cunctantem longaeua manu deducit et alto
    admotam lecto cum traderet "accipe," dixit
    "ista tua est, Cinyra" deuotaque corpora iunxit.
465   accipit obsceno genitor sua uiscera lecto
    uirgineosque metus leuat hortaturque timentem.
    forsitan aetatis quoque nomine "filia" dixit,
    dixit et illa "pater", sceleri ne nomina desint.
    plena patris thalamis excedit et impia diro
470 semina fert utero conceptaque crimina portat.
    postera nox facinus geminat, nec finis in illa est,
    cum tandem Cinyras, auidus cognoscere amantem
    post tot concubitus, inlato lumine uidit
    et scelus et natam; uerbisque dolore retentis
475 pendenti nitidum uagina deripit ensem.
    Myrrha fugit tenebrisque et caecae munere noctis
    intercepta neci est, latosque uagata per agros
    palmiferos Arabas Panchaeaque rura relinquit.
    perque nouem errauit redeuntis cornua lunae,
480 cum tandem terra requieuit fessa Sabaea;
    uixque uteri portabat onus. tum nescia uoti
    atque inter mortisque metus et taedia uitae
    est tales complexa preces: "o si qua patetis
    numina confessis, merui nec triste recuso
485 supplicium. sed ne uiolem uiuosque superstes
    mortuaque extinctos, ambobus pellite regnis
    mutataeque mihi uitamque necemque negate."
    numen confessis aliquod patet; ultima certe
    uota suos habuere deos. nam crura loquentis
490 terra superuenit, ruptosque obliqua per ungues
    porrigitur radix, longi firmamina trunci,
    ossaque robur agunt, mediaque manente medulla
    sanguis it in sucos, in magnos bracchia ramos,
    in paruos digiti, duratur cortice pellis.

and yet she rejoiced too; so great was the conflict in her mind.   445
    It was the time when all is silent, and Boötes
had turned his Wain with its slanting yoke between the Oxen;
she was coming to her crime. The golden moon fled
from the sky, black clouds were covering the hidden stars,
the night was without its fires; you were the first, Icarus, to cover your face,   450
and you, Erigone, sanctified for your pious love for your father.
Three times she was held back by the omen of a stumbling foot, three times
the funereal owl gave a portent with his fateful song;
yet she goes, and the shadows and black night lessen her shame,
and with her left hand she holds the nurse, and the other   455
feels her way in the dark. Now she is touching the threshold of the bedroom,
and now she opens the doors, now she is led inside; but her
knees shook as the sinews gave way, and both colour
and blood left her as she went, and her spirit fled.
And the closer she gets to her crime, the more she shudders and regrets   460
what she is daring to do, and would wish she could turn back unknown.
As she hesitates, the old woman led her by the hand and, having brought her
to the high bed, as she hands her over, "Take her," she said,
"she is yours, Cinyras," and she joined their doomed bodies.
    The father takes his own flesh in his lewd bed   465
and relieves her maiden's fright and urges her fears away.
Perhaps too he said "Daughter", a word to suit her age,
and she said "Father", so that the words would not be missing from the crime.
Full of her father, she withdrew from his bedroom bearing his impious
seed in her dread womb, and carrying the wickedness she had conceived.   470
The following night, she repeated her sin, and it did not end then,
till at last Cinyras, eager to know his lover
after so many nights together, brought in a lamp and saw
both the crime and his daughter; and, with words held back by grief,
he snatched down his gleaming sword from his scabbard hanging there.   475
Myrrha fled and was kept from death by the shadows
and the favour of the dark night, and, having roamed through broad fields,
she left the palm-bearing Arabs and the Panchaean country.
And for nine horns of the returning moon, she wandered,
when at last, tired out, she rested in the Sabaean land;   480
she could scarcely carry the burden in her womb. Then, not knowing what to pray for,
and, between fear of death and weariness of life,
she summed up her prayers thus: "Oh, if any of you divinities
are accessible to those who have confessed, I have deserved and do not refuse harsh
punishment. So that, surviving, I may not defile the living   485
nor when dead, the deceased, drive me from both realms
and, having changed me, refuse me both life and death."
Some divinity is accessible to those who have confessed; her last prayers,
at least, did find their gods. For, as she spoke, earth
came over her legs, and a slanting root spread   490
through her toes, a support for her tall trunk,
and her bones put on wood, and the marrow remained within her bones,
and her blood turned into sap, her arms into great branches,
her fingers into small ones, and her skin hardened into bark.

495   iamque grauem crescens uterum praestrinxerat arbor
               pectoraque obruerat collumque operire parabat;
               non tulit illa moram uenientique obuia ligno
               subsedit mersitque suos in cortice uultus.
               quae quamquam amisit ueteres cum corpore sensus,
500   flet tamen, et tepidae manant ex arbore guttae.
               est honor et lacrimis, stillataque robore murra
               nomen erile tenet nulloque tacebitur aeuo.
                  at male conceptus sub robore creuerat infans
               quaerebatque uiam qua se genetrice relicta
505   exseret; media grauidus tumet arbore uenter.
               tendit onus matrem, neque habent sua uerba dolores,
               nec Lucina potest parientis uoce uocari.
               nitenti tamen est similis curuataque crebros
               dat gemitus arbor lacrimisque cadentibus umet.
510   constitit ad ramos mitis Lucina dolentes
               admouitque manus et uerba puerpera dixit;
               arbor agit rimas et fissa cortice uiuum
               reddit onus, uagitque puer, quem mollibus herbis
               Naïdes impositum lacrimis unxere parentis.
515   laudaret faciem Liuor quoque; qualia namque
               corpora nudorum tabula pinguntur Amorum,
               talis erat—sed, ne faciat discrimina cultus,
               aut huic adde leues aut illis deme pharetras.
                  labitur occulte fallitque uolatilis aetas,
520   et nihil est annis uelocius; ille sorore
               natus auoque suo, qui conditus arbore nuper,
               nuper erat genitus, modo formosissimus infans,
               iam iuuenis, iam uir, iam se formosior ipso est;
               iam placet et Veneri matrisque ulciscitur ignes.
525   namque pharetratus dum dat puer oscula matri,
               inscius exstanti destrinxit harundine pectus.
               laesa manu natum dea reppulit; altius actum
               uulnus erat specie primoque fefellerat ipsam.
               capta uiri forma non iam Cythereïa curat
530   litora, non alto repetit Paphon aequore cinctam
               piscosamque Cnidon grauidamque Amathunta metallis.
               abstinet et caelo; caelo praefertur Adonis.
               hunc tenet, huic comes est, adsuetaque semper in umbra
               indulgere sibi formamque augere colendo
535   per iuga, per siluas dumosaque saxa uagatur
               fine genus uestem ritu succincta Dianae.
               hortaturque canes tutaeque animalia praedae
               aut pronos lepores aut celsum in cornua ceruum
               aut agitat dammas; a fortibus abstinet apris
540   raptoresque lupos armatosque unguibus ursos
               uitat et armenti saturatos caede leones.
               te quoque, ut hos timeas, si quid prodesse monendo
               possit, Adoni, monet "fortis" que "fugacibus esto;"
               inquit "in audaces non est audacia tuta.

And now the growing tree had enclosed her pregnant womb   495
and covered up her breast and was getting ready to conceal her neck;
she could not bear to wait, and sank down to meet the wood
as it came, and plunged her face in the bark.
And, although she had lost her former senses with her body,
yet she weeps, and warm drops flow from the tree.   500
There is honour even for her tears, and the myrrh dripping from the tree
keeps its mistress's name and will not go unmentioned in any age.
      But the ill-conceived infant had grown beneath the wood
and was looking for a way by which to leave his mother
and reveal himself; the pregnant belly was swelling in the middle of the tree.   505
The burden stretched its mother, but her pains had no words,
nor could Lucina be called on by her voice as she gave birth.
Yet, the tree was like a woman in labour, and bent over
giving frequent groans and becoming wet with falling tears.
Gentle Lucina stood beside the suffering branches   510
and placed her hands upon them and spoke the words of child-birth;
the tree developed cracks, the bark split and gave out
its living burden, and the baby boy wailed; the Naiads laid him down
on the soft grass and anointed him with his mother's tears.
Even Spite would praise his looks; for, like   515
the bodies of naked Loves painted on a panel,
so was he —but, in case their trappings should distinguish them,
either give him a light quiver or take theirs away.
      Fleeting time glides by unnoticed and deceives us,
and nothing is swifter than the years; the son   520
of his sister and his grandfather, he had only recently been hidden in a tree,
recently he had been born, then he was a most beautiful infant,
now a youth, now a man, now more beautiful than himself before;
now he was pleasing to Venus too and avenging his mother's fires.
For while the quivered boy was giving kisses to his mother,   525
he unwittingly grazed her breast with a protruding shaft.
The injured goddess pushed her son away with her hand; the wound went
deeper than appearances and at first had gone unnoticed even by herself.
Captivated by the man's beauty, she no longer cared for Cythera's
shores, she did not return to Paphos girt by the deep sea,   530
or to Cnidos rich in fish, or to Amathus prolific in metals.
She even stayed away from heaven; heaven was not preferred to her Adonis.
It is him she holds, his companion that she is, and she who was used to indulging
herself in the shade and to increasing her beauty by tending it,
was roaming through ridges, through woods and scrubby rocks   535
with her dress girt up to her knee in the style of Diana.
She was urging on the dogs and chasing animals safe to hunt,
either hares that run close to the ground, or a stag tall with his antlers,
or deer; she stayed away from strong boars
and avoided ravaging wolves and bears armed with claws   540
and lions dripping from the slaughter of the herd.
You too, Adonis, she warns to fear them, if only she could be
of any help by warning you, and, "Be brave with those that flee,"
she said, "it is not safe to be bold against the bold.

545   parce meo, iuuenis, temerarius esse periclo,
    neue feras quibus arma dedit natura lacesse,
    stet mihi ne magno tua gloria. non mouet aetas
    nec facies nec quae Venerem mouere leones
    saetigerosque sues oculosque animosque ferarum.
550   fulmen habent acres in aduncis dentibus apri,
    impetus est fuluis et uasta leonibus ira,
    inuisumque mihi genus est." quae causa roganti
    "dicam" ait "et ueteris monstrum mirabere culpae.
    sed labor insolitus iam me lassauit, et ecce
555   opportuna sua blanditur populus umbra
    datque torum caespes; libet hac requiescere tecum"
    (et requieuit) "humo" pressitque et gramen et ipsum.
    inque sinu iuuenis posita ceruice reclinis
    sic ait ac mediis interserit oscula uerbis:
560   "forsitan audieris aliquam certamine cursus
    ueloces superasse uiros; non fabula rumor
    ille fuit (superabat enim), nec dicere posses,
    laude pedum formaene bono praestantior esset.
    scitanti deus huic de coniuge '"coniuge"' dixit
565   '"nil opus est, Atalanta, tibi; fuge coniugis usum.
    nec tamen effugies teque ipsa uiua carebis."'
    territa sorte dei per opacas innuba siluas
    uiuit et instantem turbam uiolenta procorum
    condicione fugat, '"nec sum potienda nisi"' inquit
570   '"uicta prius cursu. pedibus contendite mecum;
    praemia ueloci coniunx thalamique dabuntur,
    mors pretium tardis. ea lex certaminis esto."'
    illa quidem immitis; sed (tanta potentia formae est)
    uenit ad hanc legem temeraria turba procorum.
575   sederat Hippomenes cursus spectator iniqui
    et '"petitur cuiquam per tanta pericula coniunx?"'
    dixerat ac nimios iuuenum damnarat amores;
    ut faciem et posito corpus uelamine uidit,
    quale meum, uel quale tuum, si femina fias,
580   obstipuit tollensque manus '"ignoscite,"' dixit
    '"quos modo culpaui; nondum mihi praemia nota,
    quae peteretis, erant."' laudando concipit ignes
    et ne quis iuuenum currat uelocius optat
    inuidiamque timet. '"sed cur certaminis huius
585   intemptata mihi fortuna relinquitur?"' inquit
    '"audentes deus ipse iuuat."' dum talia secum
    exigit Hippomenes, passu uolat alite uirgo.
    quae quamquam Scythica non setius ire sagitta
    Aonio uisa est iuueni, tamen ille decorem
590   miratur magis; et cursus facit ipse decorem.
    aura refert ablata citis talaria plantis,
    tergaque iactantur crines per eburnea, quaeque
    poplitibus suberant picto genualia limbo;
    inque puellari corpus candore ruborem

Refrain, young man, from being rash at my cost,   545
and do not provoke wild beasts that nature has given arms to,
lest I am the one who has to pay dearly for your glory. Not your age,
nor your looks, nor the things that have moved Venus, move lions,
or bristle-bearing pigs, or the eyes and hearts of wild beasts.
Fierce boars have lightning in their curved tusks,   550
there is aggression and huge anger in tawny lions,
and the race is hated by me." When he asked what was the cause,
"I shall tell you," she said, "and you will wonder at a prodigy of ancient guilt.
But now the unusual toil has tired me out, and look,
by happy chance, a poplar is enticing us with its shade   555
and the turf will give us a couch; I want to lie down with you at this"
(and she did lie down) "spot", and she pressed against the grass and him.
And, putting her neck on the young man's lap, she lay back
and spoke thus, interlacing kisses in the midst of her words:
      "Perhaps you have heard of a girl who overcame swift   560
men in a running contest; the story was
no fable (for she did overcome them), and yet you could not say whether
she stood out more for the renown of her feet or for the excellence of her beauty.
When she consulted the god about a husband, "'For a husband,'" he said,
"'you have, Atalanta, no need; avoid the experience of a husband.   565
But you will not avoid it and, though alive, you will lose yourself.'"
Terrified by the god's oracle, she lived unmarried in the dark
woods, and savagely put the insistent throng of her suitors
to flight with this stipulation, and "'I am not to be won unless,'" she said,
"'I am first conquered in a race. Compete with me in a foot-race;   570
the prize given to the swift man will be a wife and marriage,
death will be the reward for the slow. Let these be the conditions of the contest.'"
She was pitiless indeed; but (so great is the power of beauty)
a throng of suitors did rashly come under these conditions.
Hippomenes had sat down, a spectator at this unequal race,   575
and, "'Does any man go through such dangers to seek a wife?'"
he had said, and he had condemned the young men's excessive love;
when he saw her face and, once her clothes were removed, her body,
like mine, or like yours if you were a woman,
he was dumbfounded and, raising his arms, "'Forgive me,'" he said,   580
"'you whom I found fault with just now; I did not yet know
what sort of prize you were seeking.'" In praising her he took fire
and wanted none of the young men to run more swiftly
and he feared envy. "'But why is the luck
of this contest left untried by me?'" he said,   585
"'God himself helps those who dare.'" While Hippomenes was going over
such things with himself, the maiden flew by with the speed of a bird.
And although she seemed to the Aonian young man to go
no more slowly than a Scythian arrow, yet it was her beauty
he admired more; and her very running gave her beauty.   590
A breeze was blowing her ankle ribbons back from her rapid feet,
and down her ivory-coloured back her hair was tossed
as were, below her knees, their bands with the painted borders;
and her body had taken a blush on the girlish

595 traxerat, haud aliter quam cum super atria uelum
candida purpureum simulatas inficit umbras.
dum notat haec hospes, decursa nouissima meta est
et tegitur festa uictrix Atalanta corona;
dant gemitum uicti penduntque ex foedere poenas.
600 non tamen euentu iuuenis deterritus horum
constitit in medio uultuque in uirgine fixo
'"quid facilem titulum superando quaeris inertes?
mecum confer'" ait. '"seu me fortuna potentem
fecerit, a tanto non indignabere uinci;
605 (namque mihi genitor Megareus Onchestius, illi
est Neptunus auus, pronepos ego regis aquarum,
nec uirtus citra genus est), seu uincar habebis
Hippomene uicto magnum et memorabile nomen.'"
talia dicentem molli Schoeneïa uultu
610 aspicit et dubitat, superari an uincere malit.
atque ita, '"quis deus hunc formosis,'" inquit, '"iniquus
perdere uult caraeque iubet discrimine uitae
coniugium petere hoc? non sum me iudice tanti.
nec forma tangor (poteram tamen hec quoque tangi),
615 sed quod adhuc puer est; non me mouet ipse, sed aetas.
quid quod inest uirtus et mens interrita leti?
quid quod ab aequorea numeratur origine quartus?
quid quod amat tantique putat conubia nostra
ut pereat, si me fors illi dura negarit?
620 dum licet, hospes, abi thalamosque relinque cruentos.
coniugium crudele meum est; tibi nubere nulla
nolet, et optari potes a sapiente puella.
cur tamen est mihi cura tui tot iam ante peremptis?
uiderit! intereat, quoniam tot caede procorum
625 admonitus non est agiturque in taedia uitae.
occidet hic igitur, uoluit quia uiuere mecum,
indignamque necem pretium patietur amoris?
non erit inuidiae uictoria nostra ferendae.
sed non culpa mea est. utinam desistere uelles,
630 aut, quoniam es demens, utinam uelocior esses!
at quam uirgineus puerili uultus in ore est!
a, miser Hippomene, nollem tibi uisa fuissem!
uiuere dignus eras. quod si felicior essem
nec mihi coniugium fata importuna negarent,
635 unus eras cum quo sociare cubilia uellem.'"
dixerat, utque rudis primoque cupidine tacta,
quod facit ignorans amat et non sentit amorem.
iam solitos poscunt cursus populusque paterque,
cum me sollicita proles Neptunia uoce
640 inuocat Hippomenes '"Cytherea'" que '"comprecor ausis
adsit'" ait '"nostris et quos dedit adiuuet ignes.'"
detulit aura preces ad me non inuida blandas;
motaque sum, fateor, nec opis mora longa dabatur.
est ager, indigenae Tamasenum nomine dicunt,

whiteness of her skin, just as when a purple awning throws   595
an artificial shadow down on the white *atrium*.
While the stranger was noticing these things, the final turning-point had been passed
and the victorious Atalanta was being crowned with the festive garland;
the vanquished gave a groan and paid the penalty, according to their agreement.
But the young man, undeterred by how it had turned out for them,   600
stood forth and, with his gaze fixed on the maiden,
"'Why seek an easy glory by overcoming sluggards?
Compete with me,'" he said. "'If luck makes me
the winner, you will not resent being vanquished by one so great;
(for my father is Onchestian Megareus, and his   605
grandfather is Neptune, I am the great-grandson of the king of the waters.
Nor is my courage less than my breeding), or, if I am vanquished, you will have,
with a victory over Hippomenes, a great name and a memorable one.'"
As he said such things, Schoeneus' daughter looked at him with a mild
expression, and doubted whether she preferred to be overcome or to be victorious.   610
And thus she spoke: "'Who is the god who, disliking the handsome, wants
to destroy this man and tells him to seek this marriage
at the risk of his life? If I am the judge, I am not worth so much.
It is not his beauty that I am touched by (yet I could have been touched by that too),
but because he is still a boy; it is not he himself that moves me, but his age.   615
What that there is courage in him and a mind unterrified by death?
What that he is counted third in line from the sea's foundation?
What that he loves me and thinks marriage with me is worth so much
that he would die if harsh fate denied me to him?
Go away, while you can, stranger, and leave my blood-stained marriage couch.   620
Marriage with me is cruel; there is no girl who will refuse to marry
you, and you could be wanted by a wise girl.
But why do I care for you when so many have been destroyed before?
Let him see to it! Let him perish, since the slaughter of so many suitors
has not warned him, and he is being driven into weariness of life.   625
So will he die, because he wanted to live with me,
and will he suffer an undeserved death as the reward for his love?
My victory will cost unbearable ill will.
But it is not my fault. Would that you were willing to give up,
or, since you are insane, would that you were swifter!   630
But how virginal is the look in your boyish face!
Ah, unhappy Hippomenes, would that I had not been seen by you!
You deserved to live. But if I were more fortunate
and the relentless fates were not refusing marriage to me,
you were the only one with whom I would have been willing to share my bed.'"   635
She had spoken, and, like a simple girl touched by her first love,
not knowing the thing she was doing, she loves but does not realize that it is love.
Now both the people and her father were demanding the customary race,
when the Neptunian offspring, Hippomenes, called upon me
with anxious voice and said, "'I pray that Cytherea   640
be with me in my exploits and help the fires that she has started.'"
The ungrudging breeze took his coaxing prayers to me;
I was moved, I admit it, and there was no delay in my giving help.
There is a territory, the inhabitants call it Tamasos,

645   telluris Cypriae pars optima, quem mihi prisci
                sacrauere senes templisque accedere dotem
                hanc iussere meis; medio nitet arbor in aruo,
                fulua comas, fuluo ramis crepitantibus auro.
                hinc tria forte mea ueniens decerpta ferebam
650   aurea poma manu; nullique uidenda nisi ipsi
                Hippomenen adii docuique quis usus in illis.
                signa tubae dederant, cum carcere pronus uterque
                emicat et summam celeri pede libat harenam;
                posse putes illos sicco freta radere passu
655   et segetis canae stantes percurrere aristas.
                adiciunt animos iuueni clamorque fauorque
                uerbaque dicentum '"nunc, nunc incumbere tempus;
                Hippomene, propera! nunc uiribus utere totis;
                pelle moram, uinces!'" dubium Megareïus heros
660   gaudeat an uirgo magis his Schoeneïa dictis.
                o quotiens, cum iam posset transire, morata est
                spectatosque diu uultus inuita reliquit!
                aridus e lasso ueniebat anhelitus ore,
                metaque erat longe; tum denique de tribus unum
665   fetibus arboreis proles Neptunia misit.
                obstipuit uirgo nitidique cupidine pomi
                declinat cursus aurumque uolubile tollit.
                praeterit Hippomenes; resonant spectacula plausu.
                illa moram celeri cessataque tempora cursu
670   corrigit atque iterum iuuenem post terga relinquit;
                et rursus pomi iactu remorata secundi
                consequitur transitque uirum. pars ultima cursus
                restabat; '"nunc"' inquit '"ades, dea muneris auctor!"'
                inque latus campi, quo tardius illa rediret,
675   iecit ab obliquo nitidum iuuenaliter aurum.
                an peteret, uirgo uisa est dubitare; coegi
                tollere et adieci sublato pondera malo
                impediique oneris pariter grauitate moraque.
                neue meus sermo cursu sit tardior ipso:
680   praeterita est uirgo, duxit sua praemia uictor.
                   dignane cui grates ageret, cui turis honorem
                ferret, Adoni, fui? nec grates immemor egit
                nec mihi tura dedit. subitam conuertor in iram
                contemptuque dolens ne sim spernanda futuris
685   exemplo caueo meque ipsa exhortor in ambos.
                templa deum Matri quae quondam clarus Echion
                fecerat ex uoto, nemorosis abdita siluis,
                transibant, et iter longum requiescere suasit.
                illic concubitus intempestiua cupido
690   occupat Hippomenen, a numine concita nostro,
                luminis exigui fuerat prope templa recessus,
                speluncae similis, natiuo pumice tectus,
                religione sacer prisca, quo multa sacerdos
                lignea contulerat ueterum simulacra deorum;

the best part of the land of Cyprus, and which old men from long ago   645
had sanctified for me and had ordered that it be added
to my temples as a gift; in the middle of its grounds there gleamed a tree
with yellow foliage and with branches rustling with yellow gold.
It chanced that I was coming from there carrying in my hand three ·
golden apples I had picked; and, visible to no one except to him,   650
I went to Hippomenes and taught him how to use them.
The bugles had given the call, when they both sprang flat out
from the starting-gate and ran over the surface of the sand with swift feet;
you would have thought that they could skim the seas with dry tread,
and speed over standing ears of white grain.   655
The young man's spirits were being boosted by the shouts and support
and words of those saying, "'Now, now is the time to push ahead;
hurry up, Hippomenes! Now use all your strength;
do not delay, you will win!'" It is doubtful whether the Megareïan hero
or the Schoeneïan maiden rejoiced more at these words.   660
Oh how often, when she could go by him, she delayed
and, after a long gaze at his face, unwillingly left it behind!
A harsh gasping was coming from his tired mouth,
and the turning-point was far away; then at last the Neptunian offspring
dropped one of the three fruits of the tree.   665
The maiden was dumbfounded and, from desire for the gleaming apple,
veered from her course and picked up the rolling gold;
Hippomenes passed by her; the stands resounded with applause.
With swift running, she put the delay right and the wasted
time, and again left the young man behind her;   670
and once more delayed, by his throwing of the second apple,
she caught the man up and went by him. The last part of the race
remained. "'Now,'" he said, "'be with me, goddess, source of my gift.'"
And, with his youthful strength, he threw the gleaming gold obliquely
to the side of the plain so that she would return more slowly.   675
The maiden seemed to hesitate whether to go after it; I forced her
to pick it up and I added weight to the apple she had picked up
and impeded her equally with the heaviness of her load and the delay.
And in case my tale should be slower than the race itself:
the maiden was passed by; the victor led off his prize.   680
      And did I deserve that he thank me, that he bring me
an offering, Adonis, of incense? Unmindful, he neither thanked me
nor gave me incense. I was changed to sudden anger
and, pained by his insult, I was using this example to take care
not to be scorned in the future, and I was urging myself against them both.   685
They were going past a temple hidden in thick woods, which famous
Echion once had built to fulfil a vow to the Mother
of the gods, and their long journey persuaded them to rest.
It was there that an untimely desire for intercourse,
provoked by my divine power, took hold of Hippomenes.   690
Near to the temple there was a dimly lit secluded place,
like a cave, covered by native pumice stone,
and sanctified by ancient religion, where the priest had brought
many wooden images of the old gods;

695   hunc init et uetito temerat sacraria probro.
         sacra retorserunt oculos, turritaque Mater
         an Stygia sontes dubitauit mergeret unda;
         poena leuis uisa est. ergo modo leuia fuluae
         colla iubae uelant, digiti curuantur in ungues,
700   ex umeris armi fiunt, in pectora totum
         pondus abit, summae cauda uerruntur harenae;
         iram uultus habet, pro uerbis murmura reddunt,
         pro thalamis celebrant siluas aliisque timendi
         dente premunt domito Cybeleïa frena leones.
705   hos tu, care mihi, cumque his genus omne ferarum,
         quod non terga fugae, sed pugnae pectora praebet,
         effuge, ne uirtus tua sit damnosa duobus."
           illa quidem monuit iunctisque per aëra cycnis
         carpit iter, sed stat monitis contraria uirtus.
710   forte suem latebris uestigia certa secuti
         exciuere canes, siluisque exire parantem
         fixerat obliquo iuuenis Cinyreïus ictu;
         protinus excussit pando uenabula rostro
         sanguine tincta suo trepidumque et tuta petentem
715   trux aper insequitur totosque sub inguine dentes
         abdidit et fulua moribundum strauit harena.
         uecta leui curru medias Cytherea per auras
         Cypron olorinis nondum peruenerat alis;
         agnouit longe gemitum morientis et albas
720   flexit aues illuc, utque aethere uidit ab alto
         exanimem inque suo iactantem sanguine corpus,
         desiluit pariterque sinum pariterque capillos
         rupit et indignis percussit pectora palmis.
         questaque cum fatis "at non tamen omnia uestri
725   iuris erunt" dixit; "luctus monimenta manebunt
         semper, Adoni, mei, repetitaque mortis imago
         annua plangoris peraget simulamina nostri.
         at cruor in florem mutabitur. an tibi quondam
         femineos artus in olentes uertere mentas,
730   Persephone, licuit, nobis Cinyreïus heros
         inuidiae mutatus erit?" sic fata cruorem
         nectare odorato sparsit, qui tactus ab illo
         intumuit sic, ut fuluo perlucida caeno
         surgere bulla solet; nec plena longior hora
735   facta mora est, cum flos de sanguine concolor ortus,
         qualem, quae lento celant sub cortice granum,
         punica ferre solent. breuis est tamen usus in illo;
         namque male haerentem et nimia leuitate caducum
         excutiunt idem, qui praestant nomina, uenti.'

he went inside and defiled the shrine with forbidden debauchery.   695
The sacred images averted their eyes, and the turret-crowned Mother
hesitated whether to plunge the guilty ones in the Stygian waters;
the punishment seemed light. So, a tawny mane
clothed their once smooth necks, their fingers were bent into claws,
out of their shoulders forequarters were made, all their weight   700
went to their chests and the surface of the sand was swept by their tails;
their look was one of anger, they replied with growls instead of words,
instead of bedrooms they frequented woods and, though fearsome to others,
they pressed with tamed teeth the Cybelean bits as lions.
These, for you are dear to me, and with them every breed of wild beast   705
that does not turn its back in flight, but its breast towards the fray,
you must flee, in case your courage is ruinous to us both."
         She warned him indeed, and with her swans yoked made her way
through the air; but courage is opposed to warnings.
It happened that his dogs, pursuing clear tracks, had disturbed   710
a pig in its lair and, as it prepared to go out of the woods,
the Cinyreïan young man pierced it with a sidelong shot;
at once the fierce boar shook out, with the help of its round
snout, the hunting spears, stained with its own blood, and pursued him,
now terrified and seeking safety, and buried all its tusk   715
in his groin and sent him sprawling on the yellow sand in his death throes.
Cytherea was driving in her light chariot through the intervening air
and had not yet reached Cyprus with her swans' wings;
from afar she recognized his groan as he lay dying, and she turned
her white birds round to go back there and when, from the high ether, she saw him   720
senseless and his body writhing in his own blood,
she dismounted and tore equally at her bosom and equally
at her hair and beat her breast with her guiltless palms.
And when she had complained to the fates, "But not all things will be
subject to you," she said; "there will always remain,   725
Adonis, a memorial to my grief, and a repeated portrayal of your death
will bring an annual imitation of my grieving.
But his blood will be changed into a flower. Were you once,
Persephone, allowed to change a woman's body
into fragrant mint, and will the changing of the Cinyreïan   730
hero be grudged to me?" With these words, she sprinkled
perfumed nectar on the blood which, when touched by it,
swelled up just as a clear bubble will
rise in yellow mud; and there was a delay of not more
than a full hour, when a flower, the colour of the blood, rose from it   735
like the one which is borne by pomegranates, which hide
their seeds under their tough rind. But its stay is brief;
for it scarcely clings on and, from its excessive lightness, it is likely to fall,
and the same winds that shake it down also provide it with its name.'

LIBER XI

Carmine dum tali siluas animosque ferarum
Threïcius uates et saxa sequentia ducit,
ecce nurus Ciconum tectae lymphata ferinis
pectora uelleribus tumuli de uertice cernunt
5   Orphea percussis sociantem carmina neruis.
e quibus una leues iactato crine per auras
'en,' ait, 'en, hic est nostri contemptor!' et hastam
uatis Apollinei uocalia misit in ora,
quae foliis praesuta notam sine uulnere fecit;
10   alterius telum lapis est, qui missus in ipso
aëre concentu uictus uocisque lyraeque est
ac ueluti supplex pro tam furialibus ausis
ante pedes iacuit. sed enim temeraria crescunt
bella modusque abiit insanaque regnat Erinys.
15   cunctaque tela forent cantu mollita, sed ingens
clamor et infracto Berecyntia tibia cornu
tympanaque et plausus et Bacchei ululatus
obstrepuere sono citharae; tum denique saxa
non exauditi rubuerunt sanguine uatis.
20   ac primum attonitas etiamnum uoce canentis
innumeras uolucres anguesque agmenque ferarum
Maenades Orphei titulum rapuere theatri;
inde cruentatis uertuntur in Orphea dextris
et coeunt, ut aues, si quando luce uagantem
25   noctis auem cernunt, structoque utrimque theatro
ceu matutina ceruus periturus harena
praeda canum est; uatemque petunt et fronde uirentes
coniciunt thyrsos non haec in munera factos.
hae glaebas, illae dereptos arbore ramos,
30   pars torquent silices; neu desint tela furori,
forte boues presso subigebant uomere terram,
nec procul hinc multo fructum sudore parantes
dura lacertosi fodiebant arua coloni,
agmine qui uiso fugiunt operisque relinquunt
35   arma sui, uacuosque iacent dispersa per agros
sarculaque rastrique graues longique ligones.
quae postquam rapuere ferae cornuque minaci
diuulsere boues, ad uatis fata recurrunt
tendentemque manus atque illo tempore primum
40   inrita dicentem nec quidquam uoce mouentem
sacrilegae perimunt, perque os (pro Iuppiter!) illud
auditum saxis intellectumque ferarum
sensibus in uentos anima exhalata recessit.
te maestae uolucres, Orpheu, te turba ferarum,
45   te rigidi silices, tua carmina saepe secutae

BOOK 11

While, with such a song, the Thracian bard was leading
the woods and the hearts of wild beasts and the rocks that followed him,
look, the Ciconian young women, their frenzied breasts covered
by the skins of wild beasts, saw from the top of a hill
Orpheus fitting his songs to the strings as he struck them.   5
One of them, her hair tossed by the light breeze,
was saying, 'Look, look, here is the one who despises us.' And she threw
a spear into the singing mouth of Apollo's bard,
but it was sewn over by foliage, and made its mark without wounding him;
another's weapon was a stone, which, when she threw it, was conquered   10
in the very air by the harmony of his voice and lyre
and, like a suppliant for such mad daring,
fell at his feet. And yet the reckless warfare
grew and restraint was gone and mad Erinys reigned.
And all the weapons would have been softened by his song, but an enormous   15
shout, and the Berecyntian pipe with its bent horn,
and the drums and applause and Bacchic howlings
drowned out the sound of the lyre; then at last the rocks
grew red from the blood of the bard who could no longer be heard.
And first, countless birds, even now spell-bound   20
by the singer's voice, and snakes and a column of wild beasts,
Orpheus' glory and his audience, were seized by the Maenads;
from them, they turned with their bloodied hands against Orpheus himself
and came together, like birds, if ever they see the bird
of night wandering by day, or, as in the amphitheatre,   25
like a stag who is to perish in the morning's sand,
the spoil of the dogs; and they attacked the bard and flung
their thyrsi, green with foliage, and not made for this task.
Some hurled clods, others branches torn
from a tree, others stones; and, that their madness might not lack for weapons,   30
some oxen happened to be working the land with the ploughshare pressed down,
and, not far from them, some muscular farmers were preparing for their crops
with much sweat by digging over their hard ground,
and, when they saw the column, they fled leaving behind the tools
of their work, and there lay, scattered throughout the empty fields,   35
hoes and heavy rakes and long mattocks.
And when the wild women had snatched them up, and torn the oxen
from their threatening horns, they ran back to the fate of the bard,
and, as he was stretching out his hands and then, for the first time,
speaking vainly and moving nothing with his voice,   40
the sacrilegious women struck him down, and through that mouth (O Jupiter),
that had been heard by rocks and understood by the senses
of wild beasts, his soul was breathed out and withdrew into the winds.
For you, Orpheus, the grieving birds wept, for you the throng of wild beasts,
for you the solid stones and the woods that had so often   45

fleuerunt siluae, positis te frondibus arbor
tonsa comas luxit; lacrimis quoque flumina dicunt
increuisse suis, obstrusaque carbasa pullo
Naïdes et Dryades passosque habuere capillos.
50 membra iacent diuersa locis; caput, Hebre, lyramque
excipis et (mirum!) medio dum labitur amne,
flebile nescioquid queritur lyra, flebile lingua
murmurat exanimis, respondent flebile ripae,
iamque mare inuectae flumen populare relinquunt
55 et Methymnaeae potiuntur litore Lesbi.
hic ferus expositum peregrinis anguis harenis
os petit et sparsos stillanti rore capillos.
tandem Phoebus adest morsusque inferre parantem
[arcet et in lapidem rictus serpentis apertos]
60 congelat et patulos, ut erant, indurat hiatus.
umbra subit terras et quae loca uiderat ante
cuncta recognoscit quaerensque per arua piorum
inuenit Eurydicen cupidisque amplectitur ulnis.
hic modo coniunctis spatiantur passibus ambo,
65 nunc praecedentem sequitur, nunc praeuius anteit
Eurydicenque suam iam tuto respicit Orpheus.
    non impune tamen scelus hoc sinit esse Lyaeus
amissoque dolens sacrorum uate suorum
protinus in siluis matres Edonidas omnes,
70 quae uidere nefas, torta radice ligauit.
quippe pedum digitos, in quantum est quaeque secuta,
traxit et in solidam detrusit acumina terram;
utque suum laqueis, quos callidus abdidit auceps,
crus ubi commisit uolucris sensitque teneri,
75 plangitur ac trepidans astringit uincula motu,
sic, ut quaeque solo defixa cohaeserat harum,
exsternata fugam frustra temptabat; at illam
lenta tenet radix exsultantemque coercet.
dumque ubi sint digiti, dum pes ubi quaerit et ungues,
80 aspicit in teretes lignum succedere suras
et conata femur maerenti plangere dextra
robora percussit; pectus quoque robora fiunt,
robora sunt umeri, porrectaque bracchia ueros
esse putes ramos—et non fallare putando.
85   nec satis hoc Baccho est: ipsos quoque deserit agros
cumque choro meliore sui uineta Timoli
Pactolonque petit, quamuis non aureus illo
tempore nec caris erat inuidiosus harenis.
hunc adsueta cohors Satyri Bacchaeque frequentant,
90 at Silenus abest; titubantem annisque meroque
ruricolae cepere Phryges uinctumque coronis
ad regem duxere Midan, cui Thracius Orpheus
orgia tradiderat cum Cecropio Eumolpo.
qui simul agnouit socium comitemque sacrorum,
95 hospitis aduentu festum genialiter egit

followed your songs, and the tree dropped its leaves and mourned
for you with its hair shorn; they say too that the rivers grew
with their tears, and that the Naiads and the Dryads wore
their clothes edged with black and their hair flowing loose.
His body parts lay in various places; his head, Hebrus, and his lyre   50
you received and (a wonder!), as it glided on in the middle of the river,
the lyre gave out some doleful complaint, the lifeless tongue
murmured dolefully, the banks replied dolefully,
and now, carried down to the sea, they left the river of his people
and reached the shore of Lesbos at Methymna.   55
Here a fierce snake attacked his face, as it lay washed up
on distant sands, and his hair, all sprinkled with dripping dew.
At last Phoebus was present and, as it was preparing to inflict a bite,
[he held it back and into stone the serpent's open jaws]
he froze and hardened its gaping mouth, just as it was.   60
His shade went under the earth, and he recognized all the places
he had seen before and, seeking her through the fields of the pious,
he found Eurydice and embraced her with eager arms.
Here they both stroll, sometimes side by side,
or he follows as she goes ahead, or he goes in front to lead the way,   65
and Orpheus, safely now, looks back on his Eurydice.
      But Lyaeus did not allow this crime to go unpunished
and, grieving for the lost priest of his rites,
immediately, in the woods, bound with a twisted root
all the Edonian mothers who had seen the wicked act.   70
At the point where each was in her pursuit, he stretched their toes
and pushed the tips of them down into the solid earth;
and just as when a bird has put its leg into a snare
hidden by a skilful fowler and realizes that it is caught,
it flaps and trembles and with its movements tightens its bonds,   75
so, as each of the women had become stuck fast in the ground,
in consternation she vainly tried to flee; but a supple
root was holding her and restraining her from leaping up.
And while she was asking where her toes were, where her foot was and her toe-nails,
she saw wood moving up her smooth calves,   80
and as she tried to beat her thigh with her grieving right hand,
she struck oak. Her breast too was becoming oak,
oaken were her shoulders, and you would have thought that her stretched out arms
were really branches—and you would not have been mistaken to think so.
      And this was not enough for Bacchus: he left the very territory itself too   85
and, with a better chorus, sought the vineyards on his own Timolus,
also the Pactolos, although it was not golden
at that time, nor was it envied for its costly sands.
His familiar band, Satyrs and Bacchae were crowding round him,
but Silenus was absent; country-dwelling Phrygians had caught him   90
staggering from his years and from neat wine, and had led him bound
with garlands to king Midas, to whom Thracian Orpheus,
together with Cecropian Eumolpus, had given the orgies.
As soon as he recognized his comrade and companion in the rites,
in his delight at the arrival of his guest, he made a feast   95

per bis quinque dies et iunctas ordine noctes;
et iam stellarum sublime coegerat agmen
Lucifer undecimus, Lydos cum laetus in agros
rex uenit et iuueni Silenum reddit alumno.
100   huic deus optandi gratum, sed inutile, fecit
muneris arbitrium gaudens altore recepto.
ille male usurus donis ait: 'effice quidquid
corpore contigero fuluum uertatur in aurum.'
adnuit optatis nocituraque munera soluit
105   Liber et indoluit quod non meliora petisset.
     laetus abit gaudetque malo Berecyntius heros
pollicitique fidem tangendo singula temptat.
[uixque sibi credens, non alta fronde uirentem]
ilice detraxit uirgam: uirga aurea facta est;
110   tollit humo saxum: saxum quoque palluit auro;
contigit et glaebam: contactu glaeba potenti
massa fit; arentes Cereris decerpsit aristas:
aurea messis erat; demptum tenet arbore pomum:
Hesperidas donasse putes; si postibus altis
115   admouit digitos, postes radiare uidentur,
ille etiam liquidis palmas ubi lauerat undis,
unda fluens palmis Danaën eludere posset.
uix spes ipse suas animo capit aurea fingens
omnia. gaudenti mensas posuere ministri
120   exstructas dapibus nec tostae frugis egentes.
tum uero, siue ille sua Cerealia dextra
munera contigerat, Cerealia dona rigebant;
siue dapes auido conuellere dente parabat,
lammina fulua dapes admoto dente premebat;
125   miscuerat puris auctorem muneris undis:
fusile per rictus aurum fluitare uideres.
attonitus nouitate mali diuesque miserque
effugere optat opes et quae modo uouerat odit.
copia nulla famem releuat, sitis arida guttur
130   urit, et inuiso meritus torquetur ab auro.
ad caelumque manus et splendida bracchia tollens
'da ueniam, Lenaee pater! peccauimus,' inquit
'sed miserere, precor, speciosoque eripe damno.'
mite deum numen: Bacchus peccasse fatentem
135   restituit pactique fide data munera soluit.
'neue male optato maneas circumlitus auro,
uade' ait 'ad magnis uicinum Sardibus amnem
perque iugum ripae labentibus obuius undis
carpe uiam, donec uenias ad fluminis ortus,
140   spumigeroque tuum fonti, qua plurimus exit,
subde caput corpusque simul, simul elue crimen.'
rex iussae succedit aquae; uis aurea tinxit
flumen et humano de corpore cessit in amnem.
nunc quoque iam ueteris percepto semine uenae
145   arua rigent auro madidis pallentia glaebis.

for twice five days and the nights that followed them in order;
and now the eleventh Lucifer had rounded up the column
of the stars on high, when the happy king went
to the Lydian fields and returned Silenus to his foster-son.
In his joy at the return of his foster-father, the god gave him the welcome,   100
but useless, right to decide on the gift he should choose.
He, fated to make ill use of the gift, said, 'Make whatever
I touch with my body turn to yellow gold.'
Liber assented to what he had chosen and granted him the gift
that was to harm him, and was pained that he had not sought a better one.   105
     The Berecyntian hero went away rejoicing in an evil thing,
and he tested the reliability of the promise by touching things one by one.
[And scarcely trusting in himself, from not high in the foliage,] He tore from
a holm-oak a [green] twig: the twig became golden;
he picked up from the ground a stone: the stone too turned pale with gold;   110
and he touched a clod: at his potent touch, the clod
became a lump of gold; he plucked the dry ears of Ceres:
the harvest was of gold; he took an apple from a tree and held it:
you would have thought that the Hesperides had given it; if, on the high door-posts
he put his fingers, the door-posts seemed radiant;   115
even when he washed his hands in clear water,
the water flowing from his hands could have deluded Danaë.
He could scarcely grasp his hopes with his mind, imagining everything
made gold. As he rejoiced, his servants put before him tables
piled high with food and with no lack of baked meal.   120
Then indeed, if he touched the rewards of Ceres
with his right hand, the gifts of Ceres began to grow hard;
or if he prepared to tear at the food with his eager teeth,
a sheet of yellow metal was the food he pressed against as he touched it with his teeth;
he had mixed the source of his gift with pure water: 125
you could have seen liquid gold flowing down his open mouth.
Thunder-struck by the strangeness of this evil, being both rich and pitiable,
he wanted to escape his wealth and hated what he had just prayed for.
No abundance could relieve his hunger, a dry thirst was burning
his throat, and he was being deservedly tormented by the gold he now hated.   130
And, raising his hands and shining arms to heaven,
'Give pardon, Lenaean father! I have sinned,' he said,
'but have mercy, I pray, and snatch me from this fair-seeming curse.'
The spirit of the gods is gentle: when he admitted he had sinned, Bacchus   134
restored him and freed him from the reward given by the pledge of their agreement.
'And, that you may not remain coated in the gold you wrongly chose,
go,' he said, 'to the river near great Sardis,
and pick your way along the ridge of the bank,
and up the gliding waters, until you come to the river's source,
and put under the foaming spring, where it most comes out,   140
your head and body, and at the very same time, wash away your crime.'
The king approached the waters he had been ordered to; the golden power tinged
the river, passing from the human body into the stream.
Even now, receiving the seed of the old vein,
the fields, pale with dripping clods, grow hard with gold.   145

ille perosus opes siluas et rura colebat
Panaque montanis habitantem semper in antris;
pingue sed ingenium mansit nocituraque, ut ante,
rursus erant domino stultae praecordia mentis.
150   nam freta prospiciens late riget arduus alto
Tmolus in ascensu cliuoque extensus utroque
Sardibus hinc, illinc paruis finitur Hypaepis.
Pan ibi dum teneris iactat sua carmina nymphis
et leue cerata modulatur harundine carmen,
155   ausus Apollineos prae se contemnere cantus
iudice sub Tmolo certamen uenit ad impar.
monte suo senior iudex consedit et aures
liberat arboribus; quercu coma caerula tantum
cingitur, et pendent circum caua tempora glandes.
160   isque deum pecoris spectans 'in iudice' dixit
'nulla mora est.' calamis agrestibus insonat ille
barbaricoque Midan (aderat nam forte canenti)
carmine delenit. post hunc sacer ora retorsit
Tmolus ad os Phoebi; uultum sua silua secuta est.
165   ille caput flauum lauro Parnaside uinctus
uerrit humum Tyrio saturata murice palla,
distinctamque fidem gemmis et dentibus Indis
sustinet a laeua, tenuit manus altera plectrum;
artificis status ipse fuit. tum stamina docto
170   pollice sollicitat, quorum dulcedine captus
Pana iubet Tmolus citharae submittere cannas.
iudicium sanctique placet sententia montis
omnibus; arguitur tamen atque iniusta uocatur
unius sermone Midae. nec Delius aures
175   humanam stolidas patitur retinere figuram,
sed trahit in spatium uillisque albentibus implet
instabilesque imas facit et dat posse moueri.
cetera sunt hominis; partem damnatur in unam
induiturque aures lente gradientis aselli.
180   ille quidem celare cupit turpique pudore
tempora purpureis temptat uelare tiaris;
sed solitus longos ferro resecare capillos
uiderat haec famulus, qui cum nec prodere uisum
dedecus auderet, cupiens efferre sub auras,
185   nec posset reticere tamen, secedit humumque
effodit et domini quales aspexerit aures
uoce refert parua terraeque immurmurat haustae;
indiciumque suae uocis tellure regesta
obruit et scrobibus tacitus discedit opertis.
190   creber harundinibus tremulis ibi surgere lucus
coepit et, ut primum pleno maturuit anno,
prodidit agricolam; leni nam motus ab austro
obruta uerba refert dominique coarguit aures.
ultus abit Tmolo liquidumque per aëra uectus
195   angustum citra pontum Nepheleidos Helles

Hating wealth, he began to dwell in the woods and the country,
worshipping Pan who lives for ever in mountain caves;
but his stolid nature remained, and the foolish mind in his heart
was about to harm its master again as before.
For Tmolus, looking widely over the sea, is hard and steep   150
and high to climb, and, stretched out on both slopes,
is bounded on this side by Sardis and on that by small Hypaepa.
While Pan was plying the tender nymphs there with his songs,
and performing a light song on his waxed reeds,
he dared to disparage Apollo's singing beside his own,   155
and to come to an unequal contest under Tmolus as judge.
The old judge sat on his own mountain and freed
his ears from his trees; his green hair was bound only
by an oak, and acorns hung around his hollow temples.
He looked at the god of the flock and, 'From the judge,' he said,   160
'there will be no delay.' He played on his rustic reeds
and soothed Midas with his barbarous song (for he happened
to be present for him as he sang). After him, sacred Tmolus turned
his face round towards Phoebus' face; his wood followed his head.
He, his fair head bound with laurel from Parnassus,   165
swept his cloak, dyed with Tyrian murex, across the ground,
and in his left hand he was supporting a lyre embellished with gems
and Indian ivory, and his other hand held the plectrum;
he was the very image of an artist. Then he plucked the strings
with his learned thumb, and Tmolus, captivated   170
by their sweetness, ordered Pan to lower his pipes to the lyre.
The judgement and sentence of the holy mountain pleased
everyone; and it was condemned and called unjust
only by Midas' voice. The Delian did not let
his stupid ears keep their human shape,   175
but he stretched them out in length and filled them with white bristles
and loosened them at their base and gave them the ability to move.
The rest of him was human; he was condemned in one part only:
he put on the ears of a slow moving ass.
Of course he wanted to conceal them and in abject shame   180
he tried to cover his temples with a purple turban;
but the servant who usually cut his long hair with a blade
had seen these things and, since he neither dared to betray
the disgrace he had seen, though wanting to bring it out into the open,
nor yet could keep silent, he went away and dug a hole   185
in the ground and told in a low voice what sort
of ears he had seen on his master and murmured it to the scooped out earth;
he put the soil back, and the evidence of his voice
was buried, and he covered up his trench and departed.
A bed thick with trembling reeds began to grow   190
there and, as soon as its crop had ripened in the fulness of the year,
it betrayed the farmer; for, as it moved in the light south wind,
it brought the buried words back and revealed his master's ears.
Avenged, Leto's son went away from Tmolus and, riding through the clear air
to this side of the narrow sea of Helle, Nephele's daughter,   195

Laomedonteis Latoius astitit aruis.
dextera Sigei, Rhoetei laeua profundi
ara Panomphaeo uetus est sacrata Tonanti;
inde nouae primum moliri moenia Troiae

200 Laomedonta uidet susceptaque magna labore
crescere difficili nec opes exposcere paruas,
cumque tridentigero tumidi genitore profundi
mortalem induitur formam Phrygiaeque tyranno
aedificat muros pactus pro moenibus aurum.

205 stabat opus; pretium rex infitiatur et addit,
perfidiae cumulum, falsis periuria uerbis.
'non impune feres' rector maris inquit et omnes
inclinauit aquas ad auarae litora Troiae
inque freti formam terras conuertit opesque

210 abstulit agricolis et fluctibus obruit agros.
poena neque haec satis est: regis quoque filia monstro
poscitur aequoreo, quam dura ad saxa reuinctam
uindicat Alcides promissaque munera dictos
poscit equos, tantique operis mercede negata

215 bis periura capit superatae moenia Troiae.
nec, pars militiae, Telamon sine honore recessit
Hesioneque data potitur. nam coniuge Peleus
clarus erat diua nec aui magis ille superbit
nomine quam soceri, siquidem Iouis esse nepoti

220 contigit haud uni, coniunx dea contigit uni.
    namque senex Thetidi Proteus 'dea' dixerat 'undae,
concipe; mater eris iuuenis, qui fortibus actis
acta patris uincet maiorque uocabitur illo.'
ergo, ne quidquam mundus Ioue maius haberet,

225 quamuis haud tepidos sub pectore senserat ignes,
Iuppiter aequoreae Thetidis conubia fugit
in suaque Aeaciden succedere uota nepotem
iussit et amplexus in uirginis ire marinae.
    est sinus Haemoniae curuos falcatus in arcus;

230 bracchia procurrunt ubi, si foret altior unda,
portus erat; summis inductum est aequor harenis.
litus habet solidum, quod nec uestigia seruet
nec remoretur iter nec opertum pendeat alga.
myrtea silua subest bicoloribus obsita bacis;

235 est specus in medio (natura factus an arte
ambiguum, magis arte tamen), quo saepe uenire
frenato delphine sedens, Theti, nuda solebas.
illic te Peleus, ut somno uincta iacebas,
occupat et, quoniam precibus temptata repugnas,

240 uim parat innectens ambobus colla lacertis;
quod nisi uenisses uariatis saepe figuris
ad solitas artes, auso foret ille potitus.
sed modo tu uolucris (uolucrem tamen ille tenebat),
nunc grauis arbor eras (haerebat in arbore Peleus);

245 tertia forma fuit maculosae tigridis; illa

stood on the fields of Laomedon.
To the right of the Sigean deep and to the left of the Rhoetean,
is an old altar sacred to the Panomphean Thunderer;
from there he saw Laomedon first labour at the walls
of Troy when it was new, and that the great undertaking was growing   200
with toilsome work and was demanding no small help
and, together with the trident-wielding father of the swollen deep,
he put on mortal form and built the walls
for the king of Phrygia, having agreed gold for the walls.
The work was standing: the king refused the reward and added,   205
the pinnacle of his faithlessness, perjuries to his false words.
'You will not get away unpunished,' said the ruler of the sea and he diverted
all his waters to the shores of greedy Troy
and changed the lands to look like sea and took away
the farmers' wealth and overwhelmed their fields with floods.   210
And this punishment was not enough: the king's daughter was demanded
for a monster from the sea, and she was bound to the hard rocks
and Alcides rescued her and demanded the horses mentioned
as his promised gift, and when he was refused the reward for so great a deed,
he conquered Troy and took her twice perjured walls.   215
Nor did Telamon, a participant in the campaign, leave without a reward,
but he was given Hesione to possess. For Peleus was
famous for his divine wife and he was no more proud of the name
of his grandfather than of his father-in-law, since it has happened not just to one
to be Jove's grandson, but a goddess wife has happened just to one.   220
        For old Proteus had said to Thetis, 'Goddess of the waves,
conceive; you will be the mother of a young man who with his brave deeds
will surpass the deeds of his father and will be called greater than him.'
And so, that the world might not have anything greater than Jupiter,
though they were not cool fires he had felt in his breast,   225
Jupiter shunned marriage with Thetis, the sea goddess,
and ordered his grandson Aeacides to succeed him
in his wishes and to enter into the embrace of the maiden of the sea.
        There is a bay in Haemonia bent like a sickle into curved bow shapes;
its arms run out where, if the water were deeper,   230
it would be a harbour; the sea comes up to the top of the sands.
It has a hard shore of the kind that neither preserves footprints,
nor slows a journey down, nor gives way under a covering of seaweed.
There is a myrtle wood nearby covered with berries of both colours;
there is a grotto in the middle of it (whether made by nature or by art   235
is uncertain, but more probably by art) where, Thetis, you often
used to go sitting naked on a bridled dolphin.
There Peleus, as you lay bound by sleep,
took hold of you and, since you fought back when he plied you with entreaties,
he prepared to act violently, binding both his arms around your neck;   240
but if you had not resorted to your customary skills
with frequent changes of your form, he would have achieved what he was daring.
But now you were a bird (and yet a bird that he was holding),
now you were a sturdy tree (Peleus was clinging to the tree);
your third form was of a striped tiger; by that   245

territus Aeacides a corpore bracchia soluit.
isque deos pelagi uino super aequora fuso
et pecoris fibris et fumo turis adorat,
donec Carpathius medio de gurgite uates
250 'Aeacida,' dixit 'thalamis potiere petitis;
tu modo, cum rigido sopita quiescit in antro,
ignaram laqueis uincloque innecte tenaci.
nec te decipiat centum mentita figuras,
sed preme quidquid erit, dum quod fuit ante reformet.'
255 dixerat haec Proteus et condidit aequore uultum
admisitque suos in uerba nouissima fluctus.
pronus erat Titan inclinatoque tenebat
Hesperium temone fretum, cum pulchra relicto
Nereis ingreditur consueta cubilia ponto.
260 uix bene uirgineos Peleus inuaserat artus;
illa nouat formas, donec sua membra teneri
sentit et in partes diuersas bracchia tendi;
tum demum ingemuit, 'neque' ait 'sine numine uincis'
exhibita estque Thetis. confessam amplectitur heros
265 et potitur uotis ingentique implet Achille.

       felix et nato, felix et coniuge Peleus,
et cui, si demas iugulati crimina Phoci,
omnia contigerant. fraterno sanguine sontem
expulsumque domo patria Trachinia tellus
270 accipit. hic regnum sine ui, sine caede regebat
Lucifero genitore satus patriumque nitorem
ore ferens Ceyx, illo qui tempore maestus
dissimilisque sui fratrem lugebat ademptum.
quo postquam Aeacides fessus curaque uiaque
275 uenit et intrauit paucis comitantibus urbem,
quosque greges pecorum et quae secum armenta trahebat
haud procul a muris sub opaca ualle reliquit.
copia cum facta est adeundi tecta tyranni,
uelamenta manu praetendens supplice qui sit
280 quoque satus memorat, tantum sua crimina celat
mentiturque fugae causam; petit urbe uel agro
se iuuet. hunc contra placido Trachinius ore
talibus adloquitur: 'mediae quoque commoda plebi
nostra patent, Peleu, nec inhospita regna tenemus.
285 adicis huic animo momenta potentia, clarum
nomen auumque Iouem. ne tempora perde precando;
quod petis omne feres tuaque haec pro parte uocato,
qualiacumque uides. utinam meliora uideres!'
et flebat. moueat tantos quae causa dolores
290 Peleusque comitesque rogant, quibus ille profatur:
       'forsitan hanc uolucrem, rapto qui uiuit et omnes
terret aues, semper pennas habuisse putetis;
uir fuit et (tanta est animi constantia) iam tum
acer erat belloque ferox ad uimque paratus,
295 nomine Daedalion, illo genitore creatus,

Aeacides was terrified and released his arms from its body.
And he was worshipping the gods of the sea by pouring wine
over the water, and with the entrails from the flock and with the smoke of incense,
until the Carpathian seer, from the middle of the flood,
said, 'Aeacides, you will achieve the marriage that you seek;　　　　　250
only, do you, when she is quietly sleeping in the rugged cave,
bind her unawares with a noose and a tight rope.
And let her not deceive you with a hundred lying shapes,
but hold her down whatever she becomes, until she reshapes into what she was before.'
Proteus had spoken thus, and he hid his face beneath the sea　　　　　255
and let his waters flood over his last words.
Titan was setting and was reaching the western
sea under his descending yoke, when the beautiful Nereid
left the sea and approached her accustomed couch.
Scarcely had Peleus gained a good hold on her virginal body;　　　　　260
she was changing her shapes, until she felt her limbs
being held and her arms being stretched in different directions;
then at last she groaned and said, 'It is not without a deity that you conquer,'
and she was revealed as Thetis. She confessed it and the hero embraced her
and achieved his desires and filled her with the great Achilles.　　　　　265
　　　　Peleus was both fortunate in his son and fortunate in his wife,
and one for whom, if you take away the crime of slaying Phocus,
all things had turned out well. Though he was guilty of his brother's blood
and expelled from his father's home, the land of Trachis
took him in. Here there ruled over a kingdom without violence, without murder,　　　　　270
from the seed of father Lucifer, Ceyx, who bore
his father's radiance in his face, but was at that time grieving
and different from himself and mourning his brother taken from him.
And after Aeacides, tired both from cares and from the journey,
had come and entered the city with his few companions,　　　　　275
he left both the flocks of sheep and the cattle he was bringing with him
not far from the walls but down in a shady valley.
When he had been given leave to enter the king's house,
holding out an olive-branch in his suppliant's hand, he stated
who he was and to whom he had been born, only he concealed his crime　　　　　280
and lied about the reason for his flight; he asked if he would help him in the city
or the country. The Trachinian in gracious tones spoke
back to him so: 'Our resources are open even to the common
people, Peleus, and we do not live in an inhospitable kingdom.
To this our nature, you add powerful inducements, a famous　　　　　285
name, and Jupiter as grandfather. Do not waste time in asking;
you will have everything you seek, and you must claim your share of these things,
whatever sort of things you see. Would that you were seeing better things!'
And he began to weep. Both Peleus and his companions asked what cause
brought on such sorrows, and he told them:　　　　　290
　　　　'Perhaps you think that this bird, which lives on what it catches
and terrifies every other bird, has always had feathers;
it was a man and (so great is the consistency of character) even then
he was fierce and savage in war and primed for violence;
his name was Daedalion, born to that father　　　　　295

qui uocat Auroram caeloque nouissimus exit.
cura mihi pax est, pacis mihi cura tenendae
coniugiique fuit; fratri fera bella placebant.
illius uirtus reges gentesque subegit,
300 quae nunc Thisbaeas agitat mutata columbas.
nata erat huic Chione, quae dotatissima forma
mille procos habuit bis septem nubilis annis.
forte reuertentes Phoebus Maiaque creatus,
ille suis Delphis, hic uertice Cyllenaeo,
305 uidere hanc pariter, pariter traxere calorem.
spem Veneris differt in tempora noctis Apollo;
non fert ille moras uirgaque mouente soporem
uirginis os tangit: tactu iacet illa potenti
uimque dei patitur. nox caelum sparserat astris:
310 Phoebus anum simulat praereptaque gaudia sumit.
ut sua maturus compleuit tempora uenter,
alipedis de stirpe dei uersuta propago
nascitur Autolycus, furtum ingeniosus ad omne,
candida de nigris et de candentibus atra
315 qui facere adsuerat, patriae non degener artis;
nascitur e Phoebo (namque est enixa gemellos)
carmine uocali clarus citharaque Philammon.
quid peperisse duos et dis placuisse duobus,
et forti genitore et progenitore nitenti
320 esse satam prodest?' an obest quoque gloria multis?
obfuit huic certe! quae se praeferre Dianae
sustinuit faciemque deae culpauit. at illi
ira ferox mota est "factis" que "placebimus" inquit.
nec mora, curuauit cornu neruoque sagittam
325 impulit et meritam traiecit harundine linguam.
lingua tacet, nec uox temptataque uerba sequuntur,
conantemque loqui cum sanguine uita reliquit.
quam miser amplexans ego tum patriumque dolorem
corde tuli fratrique pio solacia dixi!
330 quae pater haud aliter quam cautes murmura ponti
accipit et natam delamentatur ademptam.
ut uero ardentem uidit, quater impetus illi
in medios fuit ire rogos; quater inde repulsus
concita membra fugae mandat similisque iuuenco
335 spicula crabronum pressa ceruice gerenti,
qua uia nulla, ruit. iam tum mihi currere uisus
plus homine est, alasque pedes sumpsisse putares.
effugit ergo omnes ueloxque cupidine leti
uertice Parnasi potitur; miseratus Apollo,
340 cum se Daedalion saxo misisset ab alto,
fecit auem et subitis pendentem sustulit alis
oraque adunca dedit, curuos dedit unguibus hamos,
uirtutem antiquam, maiores corpore uires.
et nunc accipiter, nulli satis aequus, in omnes
345 saeuit aues aliisque dolens fit causa dolendi.'

who summons the dawn and is the last to go from the sky.
My care was for peace, my care was for the keeping of the peace
and for my marriage; my brother's pleasure was in cruel wars.
His courage subdued kings and their tribes,
but now it is changed and chases after Thisbaean doves.   300
Chione was born to him, and she, most well endowed with beauty,
and, at twice seven years, ready for marriage, had a thousand suitors.
It happened that Phoebus and Maia's son were returning,
one from his Delphi, the other from the Cyllenaean peak,
and they saw her together, and together were on fire.   305
Apollo put off his hopes of love until the night time;
the other could not bear delay and, with his staff that brings sleep,
he touched the maiden's face: at its powerful touch, she lay down
and suffered the god's violence. Night had sprinkled the sky with stars:
Phoebus made himself like an old woman and took his forestalled joys.   310
When her ripe belly had completed its turn,
from the stock of the wing-footed god, a guileful offspring
was born, Autolycus, skilful at every theft
and used to making white from black
and dark from bright, a not unworthy heir to his father's skills.   315
There was born from Phoebus (for she gave birth to twins)
Philammon, famous for his singing voice and for his lyre.
What good was it to have borne two sons and to have pleased two gods
and to have come from the seed of a brave father
and a radiant grandfather? Or is glory indeed harmful to many?   320
To her it certainly was harmful! She dared to prefer herself
to Diana and to find fault with the goddess' face. But in her
a fierce anger was aroused and, "With my deeds I shall please you," she said.
And without delay, she bent her bow and shot an arrow
from the string and with the shaft transfixed the guilty tongue.   325
The tongue was silent, and no voice or words she had attempted followed,
and as she tried to speak, life along with her blood left her.
How miserably I embraced her then and bore both a father's
grief in my heart and spoke words of consolation to my pious brother;
the father heard them no more than do the cliffs the murmurings   330
of the sea, and he gave himself up to lamentation for the daughter taken from him.
But when he saw her burning, four times he had an impulse
to go into the middle of the pyre; four times he was driven back from there
and gave his chafing body to flight, and like a bullock
with hornets' stings in its lowered neck,   335
rushed where there was no path. Even then he seemed to me to be running
better than a man, and you would have thought that his feet had grown wings.
So, he escaped us all and, swift in his desire for death,
reached Parnassus' peak; Apollo took pity
when Daedalion had thrown himself from the high rock,   340
and made him into a bird, and held him as he hung from sudden wings,
and gave him a hooked beak, and gave him curved hooks for his toe-nails,
his courage as before, but greater strength in his body.
And now, a hawk, quite fair to none, he rages
against all birds, and in his grieving becomes a cause of others' grief.   345

quae dum Lucifero genitus miracula narrat
de consorte suo, cursu festinus anhelo
aduolat armenti custos Phoceus Onetor
et 'Peleu, Peleu! magnae tibi nuntius adsum
350 cladis' ait. quodcumque ferat, iubet edere Peleus[;
pendet et ipse metu trepidi Trachinius oris].
ille refert: 'fessos ad litora curua iuuencos
adpuleram, medio cum Sol altissimus orbe
tantum respiceret, quantum superesse uideret;
355 parsque boum fuluis genua inclinarat harenis
latarumque iacens campos spectabat aquarum,
pars gradibus tardis illuc errabat et illuc,
nant alii celsoque exstant super aequora collo.
templa mari subsunt nec marmore clara neque auro,
360 sed trabibus densis lucoque umbrosa uetusto;
Nereides Nereusque tenent (hos nauita ponti
edidit esse deos, dum retia litore siccat).
iuncta palus huic est, densis obsessa salictis,
quam restagnantis fecit maris unda paludem.
365 inde fragore graui strepitans loca proxima terret
belua uasta lupus uluisque palustribus exit,
oblitus et spumis et crasso sanguine rictus
fulmineos, rubra suffusus lumina flamma.
qui quamquam saeuit pariter rabieque fameque,
370 acrior est rabie; neque enim ieiunia curat
caede boum diramque famem finire, sed omne
uulnerat armentum sternitque hostiliter omne.
pars quoque de nobis funesto saucia morsu,
dum defensamus, leto est data; sanguine litus
375 undaque prima rubet demugitaeque paludes.
sed mora damnosa est, nec res dubitare remittit;
dum superest aliquid, cuncti coeamus et arma,
arma capessamus coniunctaque tela feramus.'
dixerat agrestis; nec Pelea damna mouebant,
380 sed memor admissi Nereida conligit orbam
damna sua inferias extincto mittere Phoco.
induere arma uiros uiolentaque sumere tela
rex iubet Oetaeus, cum quis simul ipse parabat
ire; sed Alcyone coniunx excita tumultu
385 prosilit et, nondum totos ornata capillos
disicit hos ipsos colloque infusa mariti,
mittat ut auxilium sine se, uerbisque precatur
et lacrimis, animasque duas ut seruet in una.
Aeacides illi: 'pulchros, regina, piosque
390 pone metus; plena est promissi gratia uestri.
non placet arma mihi contra noua monstra moueri;
numen adorandum pelagi est.' erat ardua turris,
arce focus summa, fessis loca grata carinis.
ascendunt illuc stratosque in litore tauros
395 cum gemitu aspiciunt uastatoremque cruenti

While Lucifer's son was telling these marvels
about his brother, there flew hurrying towards them
at a panting run Onetor, the Phocian herdsman
and, 'Peleus, Peleus! I am here, the messenger of a great
disaster,' he said. Peleus ordered him to tell whatever news he was bringing[;   350
the Trachinian too, of trembling face, was in suspense from fear].
He replied: 'I had driven the weary bullocks to the curved
shore, when the Sun at his height in the middle of his course
was looking back at as much of it as he was seeing there was left;
some of the cattle had bent their knees on the yellow sand   355
and were lying there gazing at the wide expanse of the waters,
some were wandering with slow steps this way and that,
others swam with lofty neck standing out above the sea.
Beside the sea there stood a temple, not gleaming with either marble or gold,
but made from heavy beams and shaded by an ancient grove;   360
it belonged to the Nereïds and Nereus (a sailor drying his nets
on the shore told me that these were gods of the sea).
Next to it was a marsh, thickly hemmed in by willows,
and this marsh was made by the water of the overflowing sea.
Then, resounding with a mighty crash, there terrified the area closest by   365
a huge monster, a wolf, and he came out from the marshy sedge,
with both foam and thick blood smeared on his flashing
jaws, his eyes filled with a reddish fire.
And, although he was raging just as much from fury as from hunger,
he was fiercer from the fury; for he did not trouble to use his slaughter   370
of the cattle to end his emptiness and grim hunger, but he wounded
all the herd and angrily laid them all low.
While trying to protect them, some of us too were wounded
by his deadly bite and sent to our death; the shore and the water's edge
were red with blood, so too the moo-filled marshes.   375
But delay is ruinous, and the situation does not let us hesitate;
while something is left, let us all join together and take up
arms, arms and carry our weapons out conjointly.'
      The rustic had spoken; and Peleus, unmoved by his losses
but mindful of his crime, assumed that the bereaved Nereïd   380
was sending him the losses as a funeral offering for the dead Phocus.
The Oetaean king told his men to put their armour on
and to take up their violent weapons, and he was preparing to go together with them
himself; but Alcyone, his wife, disturbed by the commotion,
leapt up and, with her hair still not fully dressed,   385
made it all dishevelled and threw herself upon her husband's neck
and begged him with words and with tears to send help
without himself, and so to preserve their two lives in one.
Aeacides spoke to her: 'Lay aside, O queen, your noble
and pious fears; I am full of thanks for what you both have promised,   390
but I have decided that arms are not to be taken up against this strange monster;
we must pray to the god of the sea.' There was a lofty tower,
with a light at its top, a place welcome to weary ships.
They climbed up there and groaned as they saw the bulls
strewn on the shore and their cruel ravager with   395

ore ferum longos infectum sanguine uillos.
inde manus tendens in aperti litora ponti
caeruleam Peleus Psamathen ut finiat iram
orat opemque ferat. nec uocibus illa rogantis
400 flectitur Aeacidae; Thetis hanc pro coniuge supplex
accepit ueniam. sed enim reuocatus ab acri
caede lupus perstat dulcedine sanguinis asper,
donec inhaerentem lacerae ceruice iuuencae
marmore mutauit. corpus praeterque colorem
405 omnia seruauit; lapidis color indicat illum
iam non esse lupum, iam non debere timeri.
nec tamen hac profugum consistere Pelea terra
fata sinunt; Magnetas adit uagus exul et illic
sumit ab Haemonio purgamina caedis Acasto.
410   interea fratrisque sui fratremque secutis
anxia prodigiis turbatus pectora Ceyx,
consulat ut sacras, hominum oblectamina, sortes,
ad Clarium parat ire deum; nam templa profanus
inuia cum Phlegyis faciebat Delphica Phorbas.
415 consilii tamen ante sui, fidissima, certam
te facit, Alcyone; cui protinus intima frigus
ossa receperunt buxoque simillimus ora
pallor obit lacrimisque genae maduere profusis.
ter conata loqui ter fletibus ora rigauit
420 singultuque pias interrumpente querelas
'quae mea culpa tuam,' dixit 'carissime, mentem
uertit? ubi est quae cura mei prior esse solebat?
iam potes Alcyone securus abesse relicta?
iam uia longa placet? iam sum tibi carior absens?
425 at, puto, per terras iter est, tantumque dolebo,
non etiam metuam, curaeque timore carebunt.
aequora me terrent et ponti tristis imago;
et laceras nuper tabulas in litore uidi
et saepe in tumulis sine corpore nomina legi.
430 neue tuum fallax animum fiducia tangat,
quod socer Hippotades tibi sit, qui carcere fortes
contineat uentos, et cum uelit, aequora placet.
cum semel emissi tenuerunt aequora uenti,
nil illis uetitum est, incommendataque tellus
435 omnis et omne fretum est; caeli quoque nubila uexant
excutiuntque feris rutilos concursibus ignes.
quo magis hos noui (nam noui et saepe paterna
parua domo uidi), magis hos reor esse timendos.
quod tua si flecti precibus sententia nullis,
440 care, potest, coniunx, nimiumque es certus eundi,
me quoque tolle simul. certe iactabimur una,
nec nisi quae patiar metuam; pariterque feremus
quidquid erit, pariter super aequora lata feremur.'
      talibus Aeolidis dictis lacrimisque mouetur
445 sidereus coniunx; neque enim minor ignis in ipso est.

gory mouth and long bristles stained with blood.
Then, stretching his hands towards the shore of the open sea,
Peleus prayed to aquamarine Psamathe that she would end
her anger and bring him help. She was not swayed by Aeacides'
words of entreaty; but Thetis supplicated for her husband and received   400
her pardon. But still the wolf, though called back from his
fierce slaughter, persisted, savage with the sweetness of the blood
until, as he bit into the neck of a mangled heifer,
she changed him into marble. She preserved his body and everything
except his colour; the stone's colour showed that he   405
no longer was a wolf, no longer should be feared.
And yet the fates did not allow the fugitive Peleus to stay
in this land; he went, a wandering exile, to the Magnesians, and there
received purification for murder from Haemonian Acastus.
Meanwhile, Ceyx, disturbed in his troubled breast   410
by the portentous stories of his brother and those that came after his brother's,
so that he might consult the sacred oracles, the delight of men,
was preparing to go to the Clarian god; for the sacrilegious Phorbas,
together with the Phlegyans, was making the way to Delphi impassable.
But first, most faithful Alcyone, he told you   415
of his plan; at once, her innermost bones
took cold, and a pallor, just like boxwood,
came over her face, and her cheeks were wet with streaming tears.
Three times she tried to speak, three times she flooded her face with weeping
and, with sobs breaking into her pious complaints,   420
'What fault of mine,' she said, 'dearest one, has altered
your mind? Where is that former care for me there used to be?
Can you now leave Alcyone behind and be away from her without a care?
Is it a long journey that pleases you now? Does my absence make me dearer to you?
But your journey is by land, I assume, and I shall only grieve,   425
not fear as well, and my caring will be free from fear.
It is the sea that terrifies me, and the grim appearance of the waters;
only recently, I saw broken timbers on the beach
and I have often read the names on burial-mounds without a body.
And let no false confidence affect your mind   430
because your father-in-law is Hippotades, who keeps the strong
winds in a prison and, when he wants to, calms the sea.
When once the winds have been sent out and have possessed the sea,
nothing is forbidden them, and the land is unprotected,
all of it, and all the sea; they also harry the clouds in the sky   435
and strike ruddy fires from their wild collisions.
The more I know them (for I know them from seeing them often
when I was small in my father's house) the more I think they are to be feared.
But, if your decision can be changed, dear
husband, by no prayers, and your course is too set on going,   440
take me with you as well. We shall, of course, be storm-tossed,
but I shall fear nothing except what I am suffering; and together we shall bear
whatever happens, together across the wide sea we shall be borne.
Such words and tears from Aeolis moved
her star-like husband; for there was no less a fire in him.   445

sed neque propositos pelagi dimittere cursus
nec uult Alcyonen in partem adhibere pericli,
multaque respondit timidum solantia pectus.
non tamen idcirco causam probat; addidit illis
450   hoc quoque lenimen, quo solo flexit amantem;
'longa quidem est nobis omnis mora; sed tibi iuro
per patrios ignes, si me modo fata remittent,
ante reuersurum quam luna bis impleat orbem.'
his ubi promissis spes est admota recursus,
455   protinus eductam naualibus aequore tingi
aptarique suis pinum iubet armamentis.
qua rursus uisa, ueluti praesaga futuri,
horruit Alcyone lacrimasque emisit obortas
amplexusque dedit tristique miserrima tandem
460   ore 'uale' dixit conlapsaque corpore toto est.
ast iuuenes, quaerente moras Ceyce, reducunt
ordinibus geminis ad fortia pectora remos
aequalique ictu scindunt freta. sustulit illa
umentes oculos stantemque in puppe recurua
465   concussaque manu dantem sibi signa maritum
prima uidet redditque notas, ubi terra recessit
longius atque oculi nequeunt cognoscere uultus,
dum licet insequitur fugientem lumine pinum;
haec quoque ut haud poterat spatio summota uideri,
470   uela tamen spectat summo fluitantia malo;
ut nec uela uidet, uacuum petit anxia lectum
seque toro ponit: renouat lectusque torusque
Alcyones lacrimas et quae pars admonet absit.
      portibus exierant, et mouerat aura rudentes;
475   obuertit lateri pendentes nauita remos
cornuaque in summa locat arbore totaque malo
carbasa deducit uenientesque accipit auras.
aut minus aut certe medium non amplius aequor
puppe secabatur, longeque erat utraque tellus,
480   cum mare sub noctem tumidis albescere coepit
fluctibus et praeceps spirare ualentius Eurus.
'ardua iamdudum demittite cornua' rector
clamat 'et antemnis totum subnectite uelum.'
hic iubet: impediunt aduersae iussa procellae,
485   nec sinit audiri uocem fragor aequoris ullam.
sponte tamen properant alii subducere remos,
pars munire latus, pars uentis uela negare;
egerit hic fluctus aequorque refundit in aequor,
hic rapit antemnas; quas dum sine lege geruntur,
490   aspera crescit hiemps omnique ex parte feroces
bella gerunt uenti fretaque indignantia miscent.
ipse pauet nec se, qui sit status, ipse fatetur
scire ratis rector nec quid iubeatue uetetue:
tanta mali moles tantoque potentior arte est.
495   quippe sonant clamore uiri, stridore rudentes,

But he was willing neither to give up the sea voyage
he had planned, nor to expose Alcyone to a share of the danger,
and he answered her with many things to console a timid breast.
Yet, even so, he did not win his case with her; to those words he added
this consolation too by which alone he swayed her loving heart: 450
'Any delay for us is long, of course; yet I swear to you
by my father's fires, if only the fates release me,
I shall come back before the moon has twice filled her orb.'
When, with this promise, he had given her hope of his return,
immediately, he ordered his boat to be taken from the dockyard,   455
launched on the sea, and fitted out with its rigging.
And when she saw it, as if foreknowing the future, Alcyone
shuddered again, and shed tears as they welled up,
and gave him her embrace, and at last, with her sad lips
said most miserably 'Farewell', and collapsed completely.   460
But the young men, in their twin rows, though Ceyx sought delay,
were drawing the oars back to their strong breasts
and cleaving the waters with a balanced stroke. She raised
her moist eyes and, as her husband stood on the curved
stern and waved his hand to signal to her,   465
she first saw and returned his gestures; when the land had sunk
too far, and her eyes could not make out his face,
while it was possible, she followed the fleeing boat with her eye;
when, with the distance it had moved away, this too could not be seen,
she still made out the sails streaming from the top of the mast;   470
and, when she could not see the sails, she uneasily sought her empty bed
and laid herself down on its pillow; bed and pillow renewed
Alcyone's tears, and brought to mind what part of her was absent.
      They had left the port and a breeze had set the sheets in motion;
the sailors turned their oars to hang from the side,   475
and they put the sailyard to the top of the mast, and unfurled all
the sails down the mast, and took up the following breeze.
Either at less than half-way across or, certainly, no further, the sea
was being cut through by the ship, and the land both ways was far off,
when, towards night, the sea began to grow white with swelling   480
waves, and Eurus suddenly began to blow more strongly.
'Bring down the high sailyards now,' the captain
shouted, 'and furl the whole sail under the yard-arm.'
He ordered: the adverse squalls stopped his orders,
and not a word did the crash of the sea allow to be heard.   485
Yet, of their own accord, some hastened to ship their oars,
others to protect the side, others to deny the sails to the winds;
one man was baling out the water and pouring the sea back into the sea,
another snatched the yard-arms; and, while these things were being done randomly,
the harsh storm grew and from every side fierce   490
winds were waging war and stirring up the resentful waters.
The ship's captain himself was afraid, and himself admitted that he did not know
what the situation was nor what he should order or forbid:
so great was the mass of this evil, and so much more powerful than their skill.
There was the sound of men shouting, of ropes screeching,   495

undarum incursu grauis unda, tonitribus aether.
fluctibus erigitur caelumque aequare uidetur
pontus et inductas aspergine tangere nubes;
et modo, cum fuluas ex imo uertit harenas,
500   concolor est illis, Stygia modo nigrior unda,
sternitur interdum spumisque sonantibus albet.
ipsa quoque his agitur uicibus Trachinia puppis
et nunc sublimis ueluti de uertice montis
despicere in ualles imumque Acheronta uidetur,
505   nunc, ubi demissam curuum circumstetit aequor,
suspicere inferno summum de gurgite caelum.
saepe dat ingentem fluctu latus icta fragorem
nec leuius pulsata sonat quam ferreus olim
cum laceras aries ballistaue concutit arces[;
510   utque solent sumptis incursu uiribus ire
pectore in arma feri protentaque tela leones,
sic, ubi se uentis admiserat unda coortis,
ibat in alta ratis multoque erat altior illis].
iamque labant cunei, spoliataque tegmine cerae
515   rima patet praebetque uiam letalibus undis.
ecce cadunt largi resolutis nubibus imbres,
inque fretum credas totum descendere caelum
inque plagas caeli tumefactum ascendere pontum.
uela madent nimbis, et cum caelestibus undis
520   aequoreae miscentur aquae. caret ignibus aether,
caecaque nox premitur tenebris hiemisque suisque;
discutiunt tamen has praebentque micantia lumen
fulmina; fulmineis ardescunt ignibus ignes.
dat quoque iam saltus intra caua texta carinae
525   fluctus; et ut miles, numero praestantior omni,
cum saepe adsiluit defensae moenibus urbis,
spe potitur tandem laudisque accensus amore
inter mille uiros murum tamen occupat unus,
sic, ubi pulsarunt nouiens latera ardua fluctus,
530   uastius insurgens decimae ruit impetus undae,
nec prius absistit fessam oppugnare carinam
quam uelut in captae descendat moenia nauis.
pars igitur temptabat adhuc inuadere pinum,
pars maris intus erat; trepidant haud setius omnes,
535   quam solet urbs aliis murum fodientibus extra
atque aliis murum trepidare tenentibus intus.
deficit ars animique cadunt totidemque uidentur,
quot ueniunt fluctus, ruere atque inrumpere mortes.
non tenet hic lacrimas, stupet hic, uocat ille beatos,
540   funera quos maneant, hic uotis numen adorat
bracchiaque ad caelum, quod non uidet, inrita tollens
poscit opem; subeunt illi fraterque parensque,
huic cum pignoribus domus et quod cuique relictum est.
Alcyone Ceyca mouet, Ceycis in ore
545   nulla nisi Alcyone est et, cum desideret unam,

of a wave heavy with the onrush of waves, of the ether with its thunderclaps.
The sea was lifted up by the surge and seemed to meet
the sky and to touch the clouds and smear them in foam.
And sometimes, when it had stirred the yellow sands up from the bottom,   499
it was the same colour as they were, sometimes it was blacker than the Stygian stream,
from time to time it was stilled and grew white with sounding spray.
The Trachinian ship herself was also affected by these chances,
and now, as if from high up on a mountain peak,
she seemed to be looking down onto valleys and the depths of Acheron,
now, when she was brought down and the curved sea stood around her,   505
she seemed to be looking up at the top of the sky from the infernal flood.
When struck on the side by a billow, she often gave out an enormous crash
and, when pounded, made a sound no lighter than when an iron
battering-ram or catapult shakes citadels and shatters them[;
and as when wild lions will gather up their strength for the charge and go   510
with their breast against arms and weapons drawn against them,
so, when the winds had picked up and the wave had let itself go,
the ship went into the heights and was much higher than they were].
And now the wedges slipped, and a crack, stripped of its covering
of wax, lay open and provided a way for lethal waters.   515
Look, the clouds opened and heavy rains fell,
and you would have believed that the whole sky was coming down onto the waters,
and that the swelling sea was rising up into the regions of the sky.
The sails were wet from the showers, and with the waves of the sky
were mingled the waters of the sea.. The ether was without its fires,   520
and the dark night was buried in the storm's shadows and its own;
but flashing thunderbolts scattered these and provided
light; from the thunderbolts' fires, fires began to burn.
And now too the billows leapt within the bound hollows
of the hull; and as a soldier, outstanding in his whole company,   525
after he has often leapt at the walls of a defended city,
at last achieves his hopes and, fired up with the love of praise,
though among a thousand men, captures the wall alone,
so, when the billows had pounded the high sides nine times,
the force of the tenth wave, rising up more hugely, rushed on   530
and did not cease from attacking the weary vessel
until it descended, as if upon the walls of a captured ship.
So, part of the sea was still trying to invade the boat,
part was already within; they all trembled no less
than a city does when some are digging under the wall from outside,   535
and others are already holding the walls inside.
Their skill deserted them, their courage collapsed, and for every wave
that came there seemed to be as many deaths that rushed and burst upon them.
One man could not hold back his tears, another froze, another called them blessed
for whom funerals awaited, another worshipped god with vows,   540
vainly raising his arms to a sky, which he could not see,
and demanding help; to one man there came thoughts of brother and of parent,
to another, of his home and children, and to all of what they had left behind.
It was Alcyone that moved Ceyx, on Ceyx' lips
there was no one except Alcyone and, though he longed only for her,   545

gaudet abesse tamen. patriae quoque uellet ad oras
respicere inque domum supremos uertere uultus,
uerum ubi sit nescit: tanta uertigine pontus
feruet, et inducta piceis e nubibus umbra
550   omne latet caelum, duplicataque noctis imago est.
frangitur incursu nimbosi turbinis arbor,
frangitur et regimen, spoliisque animosa superstes
unda uelut uictrix sinuataque despicit undas;
nec leuius, quam si quis Athon Pindumue reuulsos
555   sede sua totos in apertum euerterit aequor,
praecipitata cadit pariterque et pondere et ictu
mergit in ima ratem; cum qua pars magna uirorum
gurgite pressa graui neque in aëra reddita fato
functa suo est. alii partes et membra carinae
560   trunca tenent; tenet ipse manu, qua sceptra solebat,
fragmina nauigii Ceyx socerumque patremque
inuocat (heu!) frustra. sed plurima nantis in ore est
Alcyone coniunx; illam meminitque refertque,
illius ante oculos ut agant sua corpora fluctus
565   optat et exanimis manibus tumuletur amicis;
dum natat absentem, quotiens sinit hiscere fluctus,
nominat Alcyonen ipsisque immurmurat undis.
ecce super medios fluctus niger arcus aquarum
frangitur et rupta mersum caput obruit unda.
570   Lucifer obscurus nec quem cognoscere posses
illa luce fuit, quoniamque excedere caelo
non licuit, densis texit sua nubibus ora.
    Aeolis interea tantorum ignara malorum
dinumerat noctes et iam, quas induat ille,
575   festinat uestes, iam quas, ubi uenerit ille,
ipsa gerat, reditusque sibi promittit inanes.
omnibus illa quidem superis pia tura ferebat,
ante tamen cunctos Iunonis templa colebat
proque uiro, qui nullus erat, ueniebat ad aras,
580   utque foret sospes coniunx suus utque rediret
optabat, nullamque sibi praeferret; at illi
hoc de tot uotis poterat contingere solum.
    at dea non ultra pro functo morte rogari
sustinet, utque manus funestas arceat aris,
585   'Iri, meae' dixit 'fidissima nuntia uocis,
uise soporiferam Somni uelociter aulam
exstinctique iube Ceycis imagine mittat
somnia ad Alcyonen ueros narrantia casus.'
dixerat; induitur uelamina mille colorum
590   Iris et arcuato caelum curuamine signans
tecta petit iussi sub nube latentia regis.
    est prope Cimmerios longo spelunca recessu,
mons cauus, ignaui domus et penetralia Somni,
quo numquam radiis oriens mediusue cadensue
595   Phoebus adire potest; nebulae caligine mixtae

yet he rejoiced she was not there; he would have wanted too to look back to the shores
of his fatherland and to turn a last gaze towards home,
but he did not know where it was: the sea was boiling with so great
a whirlpool and, in the shadow brought on by the pitchy clouds,
the whole sky was hidden and the image of night was doubled.   550
Smashed was the mast by the onrush of the rainy whirlwinds,
smashed too the tiller, and, encouraged by its spoils, a curling
wave stood looking down over the waves, like a conqueror;
and no more gently, than if someone were to wrench the whole of Athos
or Pindus from their place and overturn them into the open sea,   555
did it fall headlong and, just as much from its weight as from its impetus,
it plunged the boat into the depths; and with her, a great part of the crew
were driven down by the weight of the flood, and, without returning to the air, they met
their fate. Others were holding on to parts of the ship
and shattered pieces; Ceyx himself, with the hand that used to hold the sceptre,   560
was holding on to fragments of the boat, and he called upon his father-in-law
and his father (alas!) in vain. But most of all on his lips, as he swam, was
his wife, Alcyone; she it was he remembered and returned to,
she it was before whose eyes he wanted the billows to drive his body
and he wanted, when lifeless, his burial mound to be built by her loving hands;   565
while he was swimming, whenever the billow allowed him to gasp, he called the name
of the absent Alcyone, and murmured it to the very waves.
Look, over the middle of the billows, a black arch of water
broke and plunged his head down burying it in the burst wave.
Lucifer was dark that day so that you could not   570
recognize him, and, since he was not allowed
to leave the sky, he covered his face with thick clouds.
      Aeolis, meanwhile, unaware of such great ills,
was counting the nights and hurrying, now to make the clothes
which he would put on, now to make those which she would wear   575
herself, when he came, and she was promising herself his return in vain.
Though she was piously offering incense to all the gods,
yet, above all, she was worshipping at Juno's temple
and going to her altars on behalf of a man who was no more,
and she was praying that her husband might be safe and that he might   580
return and prefer no other woman to herself; but to her,
out of all these prayers, this was the only one that could be granted.
      But the goddess could no longer endure petitions for a man who had met
his death and, so that she might keep polluted hands from her altars,
'Iris,' she said, 'most faithful messenger of my word,   585
go quickly to visit the sleep-bringing halls of Sleep
and order him to send Alcyone dreams in the form
of dead Ceyx to tell her the truth about his disaster.'
She had spoken; Iris put on her cloak of a thousand
colours and, marking the sky with her bow-shaped arc   590
she sought, as ordered, the house of the king, hidden under the clouds.
There is, near the Cimmerians, a cave with a deep recess,
a hollow mountain, the house and home of lazy Sleep,
which Phoebus can never approach with his rays
either when rising, or at midday, or when setting; clouds mixed with fog   595

exhalantur humo dubiaeque crepuscula lucis.
non uigil ales ibi cristati cantibus oris
euocat Auroram, nec uoce silentia rumpunt
sollicitiue canes canibusue sagacior anser;
600 [non fera, non pecudes, non moti flamine rami
humanaeue sonum reddunt conuicia linguae;]
muta quies habitat. saxo tamen exit ab imo
riuus aquae Lethes, per quem cum murmure labens
inuitat somnos crepitantibus unda lapillis.
605 ante fores antri fecunda papauera florent
innumeraeque herbae, quarum de lacte soporem
Nox legit et spargit per opacas umida terras.
ianua ne uerso stridorem cardine reddat,
nulla domo tota est, custos in limine nullus.
610 at medio torus est ebeno sublimis in antro,
plumeus, atricolor, pullo uelamine tectus,
quo cubat ipse deus membris languore solutis.
hunc circa passim uarias imitantia formas
somnia uana iacent totidem quot messis aristas,
615 silua gerit frondes, eiectas litus harenas.
        quo simul intrauit manibusque obstantia uirgo
somnia dimouit, uestis fulgore reluxit
sacra domus, tardaque deus grauitate iacentes
uix oculos tollens iterumque iterumque relabens
620 summaque percutiens nutanti pectora mento
excussit tandem sibi se cubitoque leuatus,
quid ueniat (cognouit enim) scitatur; at illa:
'Somne, quies rerum, placidissime, Somne, deorum,
pax animi, quem cura fugit, qui corpora duris
625 fessa ministeriis mulces reparasque labori,
somnia quae ueras aequent imitamine formas
Herculea Trachine iube sub imagine regis
Alcyonen adeant simulacraque naufraga fingant.
imperat hoc Iuno.' postquam mandata peregit,
630 Iris abit; neque enim ulterius tolerare soporis
uim poterat, labique ut somnum sensit in artus,
effugit et remeat per quos modo uenerat arcus.
        at pater e populo natorum mille suorum
excitat artificem simulatoremque figurae
635 Morphea. non illo quisquam sollertius alter
exprimit incessus uultumque sonumque loquendi;
adicit et uestes et consuetissima cuique
uerba. sed hic solos homines imitatur, at alter
fit fera, fit uolucris, fit longo corpore serpens:
640 hunc Icelon superi, mortale Phobetora uulgus
nominat. est etiam diuersae tertius artis
Phantasos: ille in humum saxumque undamque trabemque,
quaeque uacant anima, fallaciter omnia transit.
regibus hi ducibusque suos ostendere uultus
645 nocte solent, populos alii plebemque pererrant.

are breathed out by the earth and so too is the murk of uncertain twilight.
No watchful bird with crested head is there summoning
Dawn with his songs, nor is the silence broken by the sound
of alarmed dogs, or of a goose, shrewder than dogs;
[no wild beast, no flocks, no branches moving in the breeze   600
or the clamourings of human tongue gave out a sound;]
hushed quiet lives there. But from the bottom of the rock comes
the stream of Lethe's water, whose gliding flow
summons sleep with the murmur of rustling pebbles.
Before the entrance to the cave, fertile poppies flourish   605
and countless other herbs from whose juice damp
Night gathers sleep and sprinkles it over the darkened lands.
In case a door gives out a creak when it is turned in its socket,
there is none in all the house, and no guard at the threshold.
But, in the middle of the cave, there is a high ebony bed,   610
feather-filled, dark in colour, and covered by a dusky bedspread
where the god himself lies, his limbs languorously relaxed.
All around him, lie empty dreams
imitating various forms, as many as the ears of corn at harvest,
or as the leaves borne by the trees, or as the sands cast up on the shore.   615
    As soon as the virgin had entered there and used her hands to push aside
the dreams that were in her way, the sacred house shone out
with the radiance of her clothing, and the god, scarcely raising his slow
and heavy eyes from their rest, and again and again slipping back,
and knocking against the top of his breast with his nodding chin,   620
at last shook himself from himself and, propped up on his elbow,
asked her (for he knew her) why she had come; but she replied:
'O Sleep, quiet of all things, Sleep, most gentle of the gods,
peace of the mind, from whom care flees, who soothes bodies
weary from hard tasks, and refreshes them for work,   625
tell dreams which match the likeness of true forms,
to go to Alcyone at Herculean Trachis
in the guise of its king, and to make up a shipwreck image.
This is what Juno commands.' When she had carried out her instructions,
Iris left; for she could no longer endure   630
the power of drowsiness and, as she felt sleep gliding into her limbs,
she fled away, returning by the arc through which she had just come.
    But, from his tribe of a thousand sons, the father
woke up the artist and imitator of shape,
Morpheus. No one else catches more skilfully   635
than he does a man's walk, his expression, or the sound of his voice;
he adds to each both his clothes and his most usual
words. But he imitates only humans, it is another one
that becomes a wild beast, becomes a bird, becomes a long-bodied snake:
gods name him Icelos, mortal folk   640
Phobetor. There is also a third, with a different skill,
Phantasos: he turns into earth, or rock, or wave, or timber,
or anything that is without life, all done deceitfully.
These are used to showing their faces at night
to kings and leaders, others wander among the masses and the plebs.   645

praeterit hos senior cunctisque e fratribus unum
Morphea, qui peragat Thaumantidos edita, Somnus
eligit et rursus molli languore solutus
deposuitque caput stratoque recondidit alto.
650 ille uolat nullos strepitus facientibus alis
per tenebras intraque morae breue tempus in urbem
peruenit Haemoniam, positisque e corpore pennis
in faciem Ceycis abit sumptaque figura
luridus, exanimi similis, sine uestibus ullis
655 coniugis ante torum miserae stetit; uda uidetur
barba uiri madidisque grauis fluere unda capillis.
tum lecto incumbens, fletu super ora profuso,
haec ait: 'agnoscis Ceyca, miserrima coniunx?
an mea mutata est facies nece? respice: nosces
660 inueniesque tuo pro coniuge coniugis umbram.
nil opis, Alcyone, nobis tua uota tulerunt:
occidimus. falso tibi me promittere noli.
nubilus Aegaeo deprendit in aequore nauem
Auster et ingenti iactatam flamine soluit,
665 oraque nostra tuum frustra clamantia nomen
implerunt fluctus. non haec tibi nuntiat auctor
ambiguus, non ista uagis rumoribus audis;
ipse ego fata tibi praesens mea naufragus edo.
surge, age, da lacrimas lugubriaque indue nec me
670 indeploratum sub inania Tartara mitte.'
adicit his uocem Morpheus, quam coniugis illa
crederet esse sui; fletus quoque fundere ueros
uisus erat, gestumque manus Ceycis habebat.
ingemit Alcyone lacrimans mouet atque lacertos
675 per somnum corpusque petens amplectitur auras
exclamatque 'mane! quo te rapis? ibimus una.'
uoce sua specieque uiri turbata soporem
excutit et primo si sit circumspicit illic
qui modo uisus erat (nam moti uoce ministri
680 intulerant lumen). postquam non inuenit usquam,
percutit ora manu laniatque a pectore uestes
pectoraque ipsa ferit; nec crines soluere curat:
scindit et altrici quae luctus causa roganti
'nulla est Alcyone, nulla est;' ait 'occidit una
685 cum Ceyce suo. solantia tollite uerba;
naufragus interiit. uidi agnouique manusque
ad discedentem cupiens retinere tetendi.
umbra fuit, sed et umbra tamen manifesta uirique
uera mihi. non ille quidem, si quaeris, habebat
690 adsuetos uultus nec quo prius ore nitebat;
pallentem nudumque et adhuc umente capillo
infelix uidi. stetit hoc miserabilis ipso,
ecce, loco' (et quaerit, uestigia si qua supersint).
'hoc erat, hoc, animo quod diuinante timebam,
695 et ne me fugiens uentos sequerere rogabam.

Old Sleep passed these by and, from all the brothers,
chose Morpheus alone to carry out Thaumantis'
instructions, and, relaxed into gentle languor again,
he put his head down and settled it again on the deep coverlets.
He flew through the shadows on wings that made   650
no sound and, within a brief space of time, came
to the Haemonian city, and, after removing the wings from his body,
he changed into the likeness of Ceyx and, in his assumed appearance,
ghastly, like a dead man, without any clothes,
he stood before the bed of his unhappy wife; it looked as if his beard   655
was wet and that a heavy stream was flowing from his dripping locks.
Then, leaning over the couch, and with tears running over his cheeks,
he spoke thus: 'Do you recognize Ceyx, most unhappy wife?
Or has my appearance been changed by death? Look at me: you will know me,
but, you will find, instead of your husband, your husband's shade.   660
Your prayers, Alcyone, brought me no help:
I have died: do not falsely promise me to yourself.
Cloudy Auster seized my ship in the Aegean
sea, tossed it in a huge blast and destroyed it,
and as my mouth vainly cried out your name,   665
it was filled by the waters. No unreliable source brings you these
tidings, you do not learn these things from wandering rumours;
I myself, shipwrecked and in person, am telling you of my fate.
Come, get up, shed tears, put mourning dress on, and do not send me
down to empty Tartarus unwept for.'   670
Morpheus added to these words a voice which she would believe
was her husband's; and he seemed also to be weeping
real tears, and he had Ceyx' gestures.
Alcyone groaned and wept and moved her arms
in sleep and, seeking his body, embraced the air   675
and cried out, 'Wait! Where are you rushing off to? We shall go together.'
Disturbed by her own voice and by the vision of her husband, she shook
sleep off and, at first, looked round to see if he was still there,
the one who had appeared to her just now (for slaves, aroused by her voice,
had brought a light in). When she did not find him anywhere,   680
she struck her face with her hand and tore the clothing from her breast
and beat the breasts themselves; and, without pausing to let it down,
she tore her hair and, when her nurse asked what was the reason for her grief,
'Alcyone is no more, she is no more;' she said to her, 'she has died
together with her Ceyx. Away with consoling words;   685
he has died shipwrecked. I have seen him and recognized him and, as he left,
stretched my hands out to him in my desire to keep him.
He was a shade, but, even so, a clear shade and truly
of my husband. He did not indeed, in case you ask, have
the looks I was used to nor his former radiance in the face;   690
he was pale and naked and with his hair still wet
when he appeared to unhappy me. He stood, pitiable, look, on this
very spot' (and she looked to see if any traces were left).
'It was this, this that I was afraid of in my foreboding mind,
and I asked you not to leave me to follow the winds.   695

at certe uellem, quoniam periturus abibas,
me quoque duxisses tecum! fuit utile tecum
ire mihi; neque enim de uitae tempore quidquam
non simul egissem, nec mors discreta fuisset.
700　nunc absens perii, iactor quoque fluctibus absens,
et sine me me pontus habet. crudelior ipso
sit mihi mens pelago, si uitam ducere nitar
longius et tanto pugnem superesse dolori.
sed neque pugnabo nec te, miserande, relinquam,
705　et tibi nunc saltem ueniam comes, inque sepulcro
si non urna, tamen iunget nos littera; si non
ossibus ossa meis, at nomen nomine tangam.'
plura dolor prohibet uerboque interuenit omni
plangor et attonito gemitus a corde trahuntur.
710　　mane erat: egreditur tectis ad litus et illum
maesta locum repetit, de quo spectarat euntem;
dumque moratur ibi dumque 'hic retinacula soluit,
hoc mihi discedens dedit oscula litore' dicit
dumque notata locis reminiscitur acta fretumque
715　prospicit, in liquida spatio distante tuetur
nescioquid quasi corpus aqua, primoque quid illud
esset erat dubium; postquam paulum adpulit unda,
et, quamuis aberat, corpus tamen esse liquebat,
qui foret ignorans, quia naufragus, omine mota est
720　et, tamquam ignoto lacrimam daret, 'heu! miser,' inquit,
'quisquis es, et si qua es coniunx tibi.' fluctibus actum
fit propius corpus; quod quo magis illa tuetur,
hoc minus et minus est mentis sua. iamque propinquae
admotum terrae, iam quod cognoscere posset,
725　cernit: erat coniunx. 'ille est!' exclamat et una
ora, comas, uestem lacerat tendensque trementes
ad Ceyca manus 'sic, o carissime coniunx,
sic ad me, miserande, redis?' ait. adiacet undis
facta manu moles, quae primas aequoris undas
730　frangit et incursus quae praedelassat aquarum.
insilit huc (mirumque fuit potuisse); uolabat
percutiensque leuem modo natis aëra pennis
stringebat summas ales miserabilis undas;
dumque uolat, maesto similem plenumque querelae
735　ora dedere sonum tenui crepitantia rostro.
ut uero tetigit mutum et sine sanguine corpus,
dilectos artus amplexa recentibus alis
frigida nequiquam duro dedit oscula rostro.
senserit hoc Ceyx an uultum motibus undae
740　tollere sit uisus, populus dubitabat; at ille
senserat, et, tandem superis miserantibus, ambo
alite mutantur. fatis obnoxius isdem
tunc quoque mansit amor, nec coniugale solutum est
foedus in alitibus; coeunt fiuntque parentes,
745　perque dies placidos hiberno tempore septem

But truly, since you were going off to die, would that
you had taken me too with you! The right thing was for me
to go with you; for neither would I have done anything in my life time
not with you, nor would we have been apart in death.
Now I have died, though not there; I too am tossed by the waves, though not there,   700
and the sea, though without me, holds me. My mind would be
crueller to me than the sea itself, if I strove to lead my life
any longer and if I fought to survive so great a grief.
But neither shall I fight so nor, piteous one, shall I leave you,
and now at least I shall come and be your companion, and the lettering   705
on the tomb, if not the urn, will still unite us. If not
bones to bones, yet I shall touch you name to name.'
Grief prevented any more, and every word was interrupted
by a wail, and groans were forced out from her stricken heart.
      It was morning: she came out from the house to the shore, and sought again   710
mournfully that place from which she had seen him go;
and while she lingered there, and while she was saying, 'Here he untied
his moorings, on this shore he gave me kisses as he left,'
and while she was remembering what they had done and where, and, looking out
to sea, she saw in the clear water at some distance   715
something like a body, and at first it was doubtful
what it was; when a wave had driven it in a little,
and, although far off, it was clearly a body,
she, not knowing who it was, because it was a shipwreck, was troubled by the omen
and, as if she were shedding a tear for a stranger, 'Alas, poor man,' she said,   720
'whoever you are, and alas for your wife, if you have one.' Driven by the waves,
the body became closer; and the more she looked at it,
the less and less was she in her right mind. And now it had moved
to the land nearby, now she was seeing what she could
recognize: it was her husband. 'It is he,' she cried out, and at once   725
she tore at her face, her hair, her clothes and, stretching her trembling
hands towards Ceyx, 'Is it like this, O dearest husband,
is it like this, piteous one, you return to me,' she said. Nearby in the waves there lay
a man-made mole which broke the first waves
of the sea and which pre-exhausted the onrush of the waters.   730
She jumped up there (and it was a wonder that she could); she was flying
and, striking the light air with wings just formed,
she was skimming the top of the waves, a pitiable bird.
And, as she flew, her mouth croaking with its narrow beak
gave out a sound like one in mourning and full of complaint.   735
And, as she touched the mute and bloodless body,
she embraced his beloved limbs with her new wings
and vainly gave them cold kisses with her hard beak.
Whether Ceyx felt this or just seemed to raise his face
with the movement of the waves was what the people wondered; but he   740
had felt it, and at last the gods pitied them, and they were both
changed into birds. Then too their love
remained, subject to the same fate, and not even when they were birds
was their marriage bond dissolved; they couple and become parents,
and, for seven calm days in winter time,   745

incubat Alcyone pendentibus aequore nidis.
tunc iacet unda maris; uentos custodit et arcet
Aeolos egressu praestatque nepotibus aequor.
　　hos aliquis senior iunctim freta lata uolantes
750　spectat et ad finem seruatos laudat amores.
proximus, aut idem, si fors tulit, 'hic quoque,' dixit
'quem mare carpentem substrictaque crura gerentem
aspicis,' (ostendens spatiosum in guttura mergum)
'regia progenies; et si descendere ad ipsum
755　ordine perpetuo quaeris, sunt huius origo
Ilus et Assaracus raptusque Ioui Ganymedes
Laomedonque senex Priamusque nouissima Troiae
tempora sortitus. frater fuit Hectoris iste;
qui nisi sensisset prima noua fata iuuenta,
760　forsitan inferius non Hectore nomen haberet,
quamuis est illum proles enixa Dymantis,
Aesacon umbrosa furtim peperisse sub Ida
fertur Alexirhoë, Granico nata bicorni.
oderat hic urbes nitidaque remotus ab aula
765　secretos montes et inambitiosa colebat
rura nec Iliacos coetus nisi rarus adibat.
non agreste tamen nec inexpugnabile amori
pectus habens, siluas captatam saepe per omnes
aspicit Hesperien patria Cebrenida ripa
770　iniectos umeris siccantem sole capillos.
uisa fugit nymphe, ueluti perterrita fuluum
cerua lupum longeque lacu deprensa relicto
accipitrem fluuialis anas; quam Troius heros
insequitur celeremque metu celer urget amore.
775　ecce latens herba coluber fugientis adunco
dente pedem strinxit uirusque in corpore liquit;
cum uita suppressa fuga est. amplectitur amens
exanimem clamatque "piget, piget esse secutum!
sed non hoc timui, neque erat mihi uincere tanti.
780　perdidimus miseram nos te duo: uulnus ab angue,
a me causa data est. ego sum sceleratior illo,
qui tibi morte mea mortis solacia mittam."
dixit et e scopulo, quem rauca subederat unda,
decidit in pontum; Tethys miserata cadentem
785　molliter excepit nantemque per aequora pennis
texit, et optatae non est data copia mortis.
indignatur amans inuitum uiuere cogi
obstarique animae misera de sede uolenti
exire, utque nouas umeris adsumpserat alas,
790　subuolat atque iterum corpus super aequora mittit.
pluma leuat casus; furit Aesacos inque profundum
pronus abit letique uiam sine fine retemptat.
fecit amor maciem; longa internodia crurum,
longa manet ceruix, caput est a corpore longe.
795　aequor amat, nomenque tenet, quia mergitur illo.'

Alcyone sits on her nest as it floats on the calm sea.
Then does the ocean swell lie still; Aeolos locks up the winds,
and keeps them from getting out, and provides a calm sea for his grandchildren.
    An old man was watching them as they flew together over the wide
sea, and he praised the love they had kept to the end.   750
The man next to him, or perhaps the same man, said, 'This one too
that you are looking at as it skims the sea with legs
drawn under; (and he pointed out a long-throated diver)
'is of royal lineage; and if you seek to trace right down
to him in an unbroken order, his origins were   755
Ilus and Assaracus and Ganymede, who was seized by Jupiter,
and old Laomedon and Priam whose lot was Troy's
last days. The one over there was Hector's brother;
and, if he had not endured a strange fate in early youth,
he would perhaps have had no less a name than Hector's,   760
although Dymas' daughter bore him,
and Aesacos is said to have been born secretly under cloudy
Ida to Alexirhoë, the daughter of two-horned Granicus.
He hated cities and, far from his gleaming halls,
dwelt in secluded mountains and the unambitious   765
countryside and he attended the councils of Ilium only rarely.
And yet he had no boorish heart nor one unconquerable
by love, and, after often trying to catch her through all the woods,
he noticed Hesperie, Cebren's daughter, on her father's bank
drying her hair in the sun as it lay strewn over her shoulders.   770
On being seen, the nymph fled, like a terrified doe
from a tawny wolf, or like a waterfowl from a hawk when
she is caught far from the lake she has left behind; the Trojan hero
pursued and chased after her, he swift from love, she swift from fear.
Look, lying hidden in the grass a snake with crooked fang   775
grazed her foot as she fled, and left its poison in her body;
her flight was stopped together with her life. Out of his mind, he embraced
the lifeless body and cried out, "I am sorry, I am sorry that I chased you!
But this I did not fear, and winning you was not worth so much to me.
We two have destroyed you, unhappy one: the wound was from the serpent,   780
the real cause came from me. I am more wicked than he is,
and with my death I shall send you a consolation for your death."
He spoke, and, from a rock a raucous wave had eaten at below,
he fell down into the sea; Tethys pitied him and caught him
gently as he fell, and covered him with feathers as he swam   785
through the waters, and he was given no opportunity for the death that he wanted.
The lover resented being compelled to live against his will
and that his soul's wish to leave its unhappy seat
was being thwarted, and, as he had acquired new wings on his shoulders,
he flew down and, once again, threw his body over the waters.   790
His plumage softened his fall; Aesacos was enraged and went off
straight down into the deep, and endlessly tried again for a way to death.
Love made him thin; his legs between the joints are long,
his neck remains long, his head is far from his body.
He loves the sea and takes his name from diving into it.'   795

LIBER XII

Nescius adsumptis Priamus pater Aesacon alis
uiuere lugebat; tumulo quoque nomen habenti
inferias dederat cum fratribus Hector inani.
defuit officio Paridis praesentia tristi,
5   postmodo qui rapta longum cum coniuge bellum
attulit in patriam; coniurataeque sequuntur
mille rates gentisque simul commune Pelasgae.
nec dilata foret uindicta nisi aequora saeui
inuia fecissent uenti Boeotaque tellus
10   Aulide piscosa puppes tenuisset ituras.
hic patrio de more Ioui cum sacra parassent,
ut uetus accensis incanduit ignibus ara,
serpere caeruleum Danai uidere draconem
in platanum, coeptis qui stabat proxima sacris.
15   nidus erat uolucrum bis quattuor arbore summa;
quas simul et matrem circum sua damna uolantem
corripuit serpens auidaque recondidit aluo.
obstipuere omnes, at ueri prouidus augur
Thestorides 'uincemus,' ait 'gaudete, Pelasgi!
20   Troia cadet, sed erit nostri mora longa laboris,'
atque nouem uolucres in belli digerit annos.
ille, ut erat, uirides amplexus in arbore ramos
fit lapis et seruat serpentis imagine saxum.
    permanet Aoniis Nereus uiolentus in undis
25   bellaque non transfert; et sunt qui parcere Troiae
Neptunum credant, quia moenia fecerat urbi.
at non Thestorides; nec enim nescitue tacetue
sanguine uirgineo placandam uirginis iram
esse deae. postquam pietatem publica causa
30   rexque patrem uicit castumque datura cruorem
flentibus ante aram stetit Iphigenia ministris,
uicta dea est nubemque oculis obiecit et inter
officium turbamque sacri uocesque precantum
supposita fertur mutasse Mycenida cerua.
35   ergo ubi qua decuit lenita est caede Diana
et pariter Phoebes, pariter maris ira recessit,
accipiunt uentos a tergo mille carinae
multaque perpessae Phrygia potiuntur harena.
    orbe locus medio est inter terrasque fretumque
40   caelestesque plagas, triplicis confinia mundi;
unde quod est usquam, quamuis regionibus absit,
inspicitur, penetratque cauas uox omnis ad aures.
Fama tenet summaque domum sibi legit in arce,
innumerosque aditus ac mille foramina tectis
45   addidit et nullis inclusit limina portis;

BOOK 12

His father, Priam, not knowing that Aesacos had acquired wings
and lived, was mourning him; and also Hector, with his brothers,
had given funeral offerings to a burial mound bearing his name, but empty.
The sad ceremony lacked the presence of Paris
who later brought a long war together with a snatched   5
wife to his fatherland; and a thousand ships
in alliance followed her together with the commonwealth of the Pelasgian race.
And the retribution would not have been delayed if savage winds had not
made the seas impassable, and the Boeotian land had not
held the boats back when they were about to go from fish-teeming Aulis.   10
Here, when they had prepared sacrifices to Jupiter in the manner of their fatherland,
as the old altar became white hot from the lighted fires,
the Danaäns saw a blue-green snake crawl
onto a plane-tree which stood next to the sacrifices they had begun.
There was a nest of twice four birds at the top of the tree;   15
these, together with their mother as she flew around what she had lost,
the serpent seized and stuffed into his greedy belly.
All were dumbfounded, but the augur, who foresaw the truth,
Thestorides, said, 'We shall conquer, rejoice, Pelasgians!
Troy will fall, but there will be a long toilsome delay for us,'   20
and he interpreted the nine birds as the years of the war.
The snake, coiled as he was around the green branches of the tree
became stone, and remains a rock in the image of a serpent.
    Nereus remained violent among the Aonian waves
and did not carry the war across; and there were those who believed that Neptune   25
was sparing Troy because he had made the walls for the city.
But Thestorides did not; for he was neither ignorant nor silent
that a virgin's blood was needed to placate the anger
of the virgin goddess. When the public interest had conquered
piety, and kingship fatherhood, and Iphigenia, about to give her chaste   30
blood, was standing before the altar with the weeping attendants,
the goddess was conquered, and cast a cloud before their eyes, and, during
the ceremony and the confusion of the sacrifice and the words of prayer,
it is said that she replaced Mycene's daughter by substituting a doe.
So, when Diana had been appeased by a killing that was seemly,   35
and, just as Phoebe's anger had passed away, just so had the sea's,
the thousand ships took the winds from astern
and, after enduring many things, reached the Phrygian sand.
    There is a place in the middle of the world, between the lands and the sea
and the heavenly regions, the boundaries of the three-fold cosmos;   40
and from there, whatever is anywhere, however many regions apart,
is watched, and every word penetrates its hollow ears.
Rumour lives there and has chosen a home for herself at the top of a citadel,
and has provided countless ways in and a thousand apertures
for the house, and has sealed none of the thresholds with doors;   45

nocte dieque patet. tota est ex aere sonanti,
tota fremit uocesque refert iteratque quod audit.
nulla quies intus nullaque silentia parte,
nec tamen est clamor, sed paruae murmura uocis,
50 qualia de pelagi, si quis procul audiat, undis
esse solent, qualemue sonum, cum Iuppiter atras
increpuit nubes, extrema tonitrua reddunt.
atria turba tenet; ueniunt, leue uulgus, euntque
mixtaque cum ueris passim commenta uagantur
55 milia rumorum confusaque uerba uolutant.
e quibus hi uacuas implent sermonibus aures,
hi narrata ferunt alio, mensuraque ficti
crescit, et auditis aliquid nouus adicit auctor.
illic Credulitas, illic temerarius Error
60 uanaque Laetitia est consternatique Timores
Seditioque repens dubioque auctore Susurri.
ipsa quid in caelo rerum pelagoque geratur
et tellure uidet totumque inquirit in orbem.
    fecerat haec notum Graias cum milite forti
65 aduentare rates, neque inexspectatus in armis
hostis adest. prohibent aditus litusque tuentur
Troes, et Hectorea primus fataliter hasta,
Protesilaë, cadis, commissaque proelia magno
stant Danais, fortisque animae nece cognitus Hector;
70 nec Phryges exiguo quid Achaica dextera posset
sanguine senserunt. et iam Sigea rubebant
litora, iam leto proles Neptunia Cycnus
mille uiros dederat, iam curru instabat Achilles
totaque Peliacae sternebat cuspidis ictu
75 agmina; perque acies aut Cycnum aut Hectora quaerens
congreditur Cycno (decimum dilatus in annum
Hector erat). tum colla iugo canentia pressos
exhortatus equos currum derexit in hostem
concutiensque suis uibrantia tela lacertis
80 'quisquis es, o iuuenis,' dixit 'solamen habeto
mortis, ab Haemonio quod sis iugulatus Achille.'
hactenus Aeacides; uocem grauis hasta secuta est.
sed quamquam certa nullus fuit error in hasta,
nil tamen emissi profecit acumine ferri.
85 utque hebeti pectus tantummodo contudit ictu,
'nate dea, nam te fama praenouimus,' inquit
ille 'quid a nobis uulnus miraris abesse?'
(mirabatur enim) 'non haec, quam cernis, equinis
fulua iubis cassis neque onus caua parma sinistrae
90 auxilio mihi sunt; decor est quaesitus ab istis.
Mars quoque ob hoc capere arma solet. remouebitur omne
tegminis officium, tamen indestrictus abibo.
est aliquid non esse satum Nereïde, sed qui
Nereaque et natas et totum temperat aequor.'
95 dixit et haesurum clipei curuamine telum

night and day it is open. It is all made of sounding bronze,
it all mutters, it carries words back and repeats what it hears.
There is no quiet within, and silence is nowhere there,
and yet there is no shouting, but the murmurings of a low voice,
just like those that come from the waves of the sea if one   50
hears them from afar, or like the sound the final thunder gives
when Jupiter has made the dark clouds clash.
A throng occupies the *atrium*; they come, an insubstantial crowd, and go,
and thousands of rumours, false ones mixed with true,
wander here and there and toss their confused words around.   55
Of these, some fill empty ears with talk,
some take their stories elsewhere, and the scale of the fiction
grows, and the new teller adds something to things he has heard.
There is Credulity, there reckless Error
and empty Joy and frantic Fears   60
and sudden Revolt and Whispers from a doubtful source.
She herself sees what things are being done in heaven
and on the sea and on the land, and enquires about the whole world.
        She had made it known that the Greek ships were approaching
with a strong force, and it was no unexpected enemy   65
that was there under arms. The approaches were defended and the shore watched
by the Trojans, and the first to fall by fate to Hector's
spear was you, Protesilaüs, and the joining of the battle cost
the Danaäns greatly, and it was from killing that Hector was known as brave in spirit,
but the Phrygians too realized from no slight bloodshed what an Achaean   70
right hand could do. And already the Sigean shores
were growing red, already Cycnus, the Neptunian offspring, had sent
a thousand men to their doom, already Achilles was standing in his chariot
and laying troops low with a blow from his Pelian
speartip; and, as he sought throughout the battle lines for either Cycnus or Hector,   75
he met with Cycnus (for Hector had been postponed
to the tenth year). Then he urged his horses on, their white necks
pressed beneath the yoke, and steered his chariot against his enemy,
and, brandishing his flashing weapon with those strong arms of his,
'Whoever you are, young man,' he said, 'have as a solace   80
for your death the fact that you were slain by Haemonian Achilles.'
Aeacides got so far; his heavy spear followed after his speech.
But, although there was no deviation in that sure spear,
even so, when dispatched, it achieved nothing with its iron point.
And when it had only bruised his breast with a feeble blow,   85
'Son of a goddess,' he said, 'for we already knew of you
from rumour, why are you surprised that I am not wounded?'
(For he was surprised.) 'Neither this helmet that you can see
with its tawny horse-mane, nor the hollow shield that burdens my left hand
are of help to me: adornment is what I seek from them.   90
That is why Mars too puts armour on. Remove all
their protective function, and I shall still go away unscratched.
It is something not to have been born to a Nereïd, but to him who
controls Nereus and his daughters and the whole sea.'
He spoke and threw his weapon at Aeacides to make it stick in   95

misit in Aeaciden, quod et aes et proxima rupit
terga nouena boum, decimo tamen orbe moratum est.
excutit hoc heros rursusque trementia forti
tela manu torsit; rursus sine uulnere corpus
100   sincerumque fuit. nec tertia cuspis apertum
et se praebentem ualuit destringere Cycnum.
    haud secus exarsit quam circo taurus aperto,
cum sua terribili petit inritamina cornu,
poeniceas uestes, elusaque uulnera sentit.
105   num tamen exciderit ferrum considerat hastae:
haerebat ligno. 'manus est mea debilis ergo,
quasque' ait 'ante habuit uires, effudit in uno?
nam certe ualuit, uel cum Lyrnesia primum
moenia deieci, uel cum Tenedonque suoque
110   Eëtioneas impleui sanguine Thebas,
uel cum purpureus populari caede Caïcus
fluxit opusque meae bis sensit Telephus hastae.
hic quoque tot caesis, quorum per litus aceruos
et feci et uideo, ualuit mea dextra ualetque.'
115   dixit et, ante actis ueluti male crederet, hastam
misit in aduersum Lycia de plebe Menoeten
loricamque simul subiectaque pectora rupit.
quo plangente grauem moribundo pectore terram
extrahit illud idem calido de uulnere telum
120   atque ait: haec manus est, haec qua modo uicimus, hasta.
utar in hoc isdem; sit in hoc, precor, exitus idem!'
sic fatus Cycnum repetit, nec fraxinus errat
inque umero sonuit non euitata sinistro;
inde uelut muro solidaque a caute repulsa est.
125   qua tamen ictus erat, signatum sanguine Cycnum
uiderat et frustra fuerat gauisus Achilles;
uulnus erat nullum, sanguis fuit ille Menoetae.
    tum uero praeceps curru fremebundus ab alto
desilit et nitido securum comminus hostem
130   ense petens parmam gladio galeamque cauari
cernit, at in duro laedi quoque corpore ferrum.
haud tulit ulterius clipeoque aduersa reducto
ter quater ora uiri, capulo caua tempora pulsat
cedentique sequens instat turbatque ruitque
135   attonitoque negat requiem; pauor occupat illum,
ante oculosque natant tenebrae retroque ferenti
auersos passus medio lapis obstitit aruo.
quem super impulsum resupino corpore Cycnum
ui multa uertit terraeque adflixit Achilles.
140   tum clipeo genibusque premens praecordia duris
uincla trahit galeae, quae pressa subdita mento
elidunt fauces et respiramen iterque
eripiunt animae. uictum spoliare parabat:
arma relicta uidet. corpus deus aequoris albam
145   contulit in uolucrem, cuius modo nomen habebat.

the curve of his shield, and it burst through both the bronze and the nine
round oxhides next to it, but was stopped by the tenth.
The hero shook it out and again hurled his quivering
weapon with his strong hand; his body was again unwounded
and whole. Nor was a third speartip able   100
to scratch Cycnus even though he offered himself unprotected.
  Not otherwise did he flare up than a bull does in an open arena
When, with its terrible horn, it goes for the red rags
that torment it and realizes its attacks have been eluded.
He wondered whether the iron tip had fallen from the spear: 105
it was fixed to the shaft. 'Then is my hand weak,'
he said, 'and has it spent on one man the strength it had before?
For surely it was strong when first I threw down the walls
of Lyrnesos, or when I filled both Tenedos
and Eëtionian Thebes with their own blood,   110
or when the Caïcus flowed red with its people's
slaughter and Telephus twice experienced the work of my spear.
Here also, when so many were slaughtered, and I both made and can see
heaps of them throughout the shore, my right hand was strong and is strong.'
He spoke and, as if he disbelieved what he had done before, he threw   115
his spear towards the approaching Menoetes, one of the Lycian plebs,
and it burst through his breastplate together with his chest underneath.
And as, in his death throes, he struck the hard earth with his chest,
he drew that same weapon from the warm wound
and said, 'This is the hand, this the spear with which I have just conquered.   120
I shall use the same ones on him; on him, I pray, may the outcome be the same!'
Thus he spoke and aimed at Cycnus again, and the ash spear did not stray
but rang inescapably against his left shoulder;
from there it bounced off as if from a wall or a solid cliff.
But where Cycnus had been struck, Achilles saw   125
that he was stained with blood, and he rejoiced in vain;
there was no wound, the blood was Menoetes'.
  Then indeed, roaring, he leapt headlong from his high
chariot and, attacking his untroubled enemy from close up
with his gleaming blade, he saw the shield and head-piece pierced   130
by the sword, but the blade itself damaged by the hard body.
He could bear it no longer and, drawing the man's shield back, pounded him
three or four times with his sword-hilt full in the face and in the hollow temples,
and, as he gave way, he followed up and pressed upon him, confusing and rushing him
and denying the stunned man any rest; fear took hold of him,   135
shadows swam before his eyes and, as he took retreating
steps back, a stone stopped him in the middle of the field.
Achilles pushed Cycnus down over it with great violence,
turned him face up and dashed him to the ground.
Then, pressing down on his breast with his shield and his hard knees,   140
he pulled on the ties of his head-piece which, pressed underneath his chin,
squeezed his throat and took his respiration from him
and the pathway for his breath. He was preparing to despoil his conquest:
he saw that the armour was left behind. The sea god had changed the body
into a white bird, whose name he had just now been bearing.   145

    hic labor, haec requiem multorum pugna dierum
    attulit et positis pars utraque substitit armis.
    dumque uigil Phrygios seruat custodia muros
    et uigil Argolicas seruat custodia fossas,
150 festa dies aderat, qua Cycni uictor Achilles
    Pallada mactatae placabat sanguine uaccae;
    cuius ut imposuit prosecta calentibus aris
    et dis acceptus penetrauit in aethera nidor,
    sacra tulere suam, pars est data cetera mensis.
155 discubuere toris proceres et corpora tosta
    carne replent uinoque leuant curasque sitimque.
    non illos citharae, non illos carmina uocum
    longaue multifori delectat tibia buxi,
    sed noctem sermone trahunt, uirtusque loquendi
160 materia est; pugnam referunt hostisque suamque,
    inque uices adita atque exhausta pericula saepe
    commemorare iuuat. quid enim loqueretur Achilles,
    aut quid apud magnum potius loquerentur Achillem?
    proxima praecipue domito uictoria Cycno
165 in sermone fuit; uisum mirabile cunctis,
    quod iuuenis corpus nullo penetrabile telo
    inuictumque a uulnere erat ferrumque terebat.
     hoc ipse Aeacides, hoc mirabantur Achiui,
    cum sic Nestor ait: 'uestro fuit unicus aeuo
170 contemptor ferri nulloque forabilis ictu
    Cycnus. at ipse olim patientem uulnera mille
    corpore non laeso Perrhaebum Caenea uidi,
    Caenea Perrhaebum, qui factis inclitus Othryn
    incoluit; quoque id mirum magis esset in illo,
175 femina natus erat.' monstri nouitate mouentur,
    quisquis adest, narretque rogant; quos inter Achilles:
    'dic age, nam cunctis eadem est audire uoluntas,
    o facunde senex, aeui prudentia nostri,
    quis fuerit Caeneus, cur in contraria uersus,
180 qua tibi militia, cuius certamine pugnae
    cognitus, a quo sit uictus, si uictus ab ullo est.'
    tum senior: 'quamuis obstet mihi tarda uetustas
    multaque me fugiant primis spectata sub annis
    plura tamen memini; nec quae magis haereat ulla
185 pectore res nostro est inter bellique domique
    acta tot, ac si quem potuit spatiosa senectus
    spectatorem operum multorum reddere, uixi
    annos bis centum; nunc tertia uiuitur aetas.
     clara decore fuit proles Elateïa Caenis,
190 Thessalidum uirgo pulcherrima, perque propinquas
    perque tuas urbes (tibi enim popularis, Achille)
    multorum frustra uotis optata procorum.
    temptasset Peleus thalamos quoque forsitan illos,
    sed iam aut contigerant illi conubia matris,
195 aut fuerant promissa, tuae. nec Caenis in ullos

This toil, this fight brought on a rest of many
days, and both sides laid down their arms and stood fast.
And while a watchful guard was protecting the Phrygian walls
and a watchful guard was protecting the Argive ditches,
there came a festive day on which Achilles, the victor over Cycnus,   150
was placating Pallas with the blood of a heifer he had sacrificed;
and when he had placed her entrails on the hot altar,
and the odour, welcome to the gods, had penetrated into the ether,
the sacred rites took their part, the rest was given for the banquet.
The nobles reclined on their couches and filled their bodies   155
with cooked meat, and with wine relieved their cares and thirst.
It was not the songs of the lyre or of voices that entertained them,
or the long boxwood pipe with many holes,
but they drew out the night with conversation, and courage was
the subject of their talk; they related the fights both of the enemy and their own,   160
and they took delight in recalling, in turn, again and again,
the dangers they had met and overcome. For what else would Achilles
talk of, or what else would they talk of in the presence of Achilles?
The very recent victory in which Cycnus had been defeated was
prominent in their conversation; it seemed amazing to them all   165
that the young man's body could be penetrated by no weapon,
that it was unconquered by wounds and that it wore iron down.
    At this, Aeacides himself, at this the Achaeans were marvelling,
when Nestor spoke thus, 'In your lifetime there was a single
despiser of the sword, pierceable by no blow,   170
Cycnus. But I myself long ago saw Perrhaebian Caeneus
suffering a thousand wounds in an uninjured body,
Caeneus of Perrhaebia who, famed for his deeds, lived
on Othrys; and, so that that might be more amazing in him,
he was born a woman.' They were excited by the strangeness of the miracle,   175
all who were present, and they asked him to tell of it; and among them, Achilles said,
'Come, speak, for we all have the same wish to hear,
O eloquent old man, the wisdom of our age,
who Caeneus was, why he was turned into his opposite,
in what campaign, in the contest of what fight   180
you got to know him, by whom he was conquered, if conquered he was by anyone.
Then said the older man, 'though the slowness of age impedes me
and many things seen in my earliest years escape me,
there are, even so, more that I do remember; and there is not anything
among so many deeds of war and peace that sticks more   185
in my heart, and if there is anyone that lengthy old age could
have made a spectator of many works, I have lived
for twice a hundred years; now I am living in my third age.
    Famous for her beauty was Caenis, the Elateïan offspring,
the fairest maiden of the daughters of Thessaly and, throughout the neighbouring   190
cities and throughout your own (for she was your compatriot, Achilles),
vainly desired in the prayers of many suitors.
Peleus too would perhaps have tried for that marriage,
but either the wedding with your mother had already fallen to his lot
or it had been promised. And Caenis did not enter into   195

denupsit thalamos secretaque litora carpens
aequorei uim passa dei (ita fama ferebat);
utque nouae Veneris Neptunus gaudia cepit,
"sint tua uota licet" dixit "secura repulsae:
200   elige quid uoueas!" (eadem hoc quoque fama ferebat.)
"magnum" Caenis ait "facit haec iniuria uotum,
tale pati iam posse nihil. da femina ne sim:
omnia praestiteris." grauiore nouissima dixit
uerba sono poteratque uiri uox illa uideri,
205   sicut erat; nam iam uoto deus aequoris alti
adnuerat dederatque super, ne saucius ullis
uulneribus fieri ferroue occumbere posset.
munere laetus abit studiisque uirilibus aeuum
exigit Atracides Peneïaque arua pererrat.
210   duxerat Hippodamen audaci Ixione natus
nubigenasque feros positis ex ordine mensis
arboribus tecto discumbere iusserat antro.
Haemonii proceres aderant, aderamus et ipsi,
festaque confusa resonabat regia turba.
215   ecce canunt Hymenaeon, et ignibus atria fumant,
cinctaque adest uirgo matrum nuruumque caterua,
praesignis facie. felicem diximus illa
coniuge Pirithoüm; quod paene fefellimus omen.
nam tibi, saeuorum saeuissime Centaurorum,
220   Euryte, quam uino pectus tam uirgine uisa
ardet, et ebrietas geminata libidine regnat.
protinus euersae turbant conuiuia mensae,
raptaturque comis per uim noua nupta prehensis.
Eurytus Hippodamen, alii quam quisque probabant
225   aut poterant rapiunt, captaeque erat urbis imago.
femineo clamore sonat domus; ocius omnes
surgimus, et primus "quae te uecordia," Theseus
"Euryte, pulsat," ait "qui me uiuente lacessas
Pirithoüm uiolesque duos ignarus in uno?"
230   [neue ea magnanimus frustra memorauerit heros,
submouet instantes raptamque furentibus aufert.]
ille nihil contra (neque enim defendere uerbis
talia facta potest), sed uindicis ora proteruis
insequitur manibus generosaque pectora pulsat.
235   forte fuit iuxta signis exstantibus asper
antiquus crater, quem uastum uastior ipse
şustulit Aegides aduersaque misit in ora;
sanguinis ille globos pariter cerebrumque merumque
uulnere et ore uomens madida resupinus harena
240   calcitrat. ardescunt germani caede bimembres
certatimque omnes uno ore "arma, arma" loquuntur.
uina dabant animos, et prima pocula pugna
missa uolant fragilesque cadi curuique lebetes,
res epulis quondam, tum bello et caedibus aptae.
245   primus Ophionides Amycus penetralia donis

any marriage, but, as she picked her way along a secluded beach,
she suffered the violence of the sea god (so the rumour told it);
and when Neptune had taken the joys of this new passion,
"Your prayers shall be," he said, "safe from rejection:
choose what you would pray for!" (the same rumour told this too).   200
"This wrong," said Caenis, "makes for a great prayer
that from now I can suffer no such thing. Grant that I be not a woman,
and you will have provided me with everything." She spoke the last words
at a lower pitch, and her voice could seem to be a man's,
as it was; for the god of the deep sea had already assented   205
to the prayer and had granted besides that he could not be
hurt by any wounds or fall to the sword.
Happy with this gift, Atrax' son left, and he spends his life
in manly pursuits and he wanders through the Peneïan fields.
        Bold Ixion's son had married Hippodame   210
and had told the cloudborn beasts to recline at tables
set in order in his tree protected cave.
The Haemonian nobles were present, present was I myself too,
and the festive palace rang with the disordered throng.
Look, they are singing the Hymenaeos, and the *atrium* is smoky from the fires,   215
and the maiden is present, surrounded by a company of mothers and young wives,
and pre-eminent in beauty. We called Pirithoüs fortunate
in that wife; and we almost nullified the omen.
For your heart, most savage of the savage Centaurs,
O Eurytus, was on fire as much from wine as from the sight   220
of the maiden, and drunkenness doubled by lust prevailed.
At once, overturned tables disrupted the banquet,
and the new bride was grasped violently by the hair and snatched away.
Eurytus seized Hippodame, the others each the one
they admired or could, and it was the image of a captured city.   225
The house rang with women's shrieks; quickly we were all
standing up, and Theseus was the first to say, "What madness,
Eurytus, is driving you that, while I live, you would provoke
Pirithoüs and in your ignorance attack two in one?"
[And, so that the high-spirited hero might not have spoken these things in vain,   230
he pushed their attack aside, and, as they raged, took back the woman they had seized.]
He said nothing in reply (for he could not defend
such deeds with words), but he went after the face of her defender
with violent hands and pounded his noble breast.
It happened that there was nearby an ancient mixing-bowl encrusted   235
with high-relief figures, and this, though vast, vaster himself
Aegides lifted up and threw full into his face;
he, spewing equally clots of blood and brains
and wine from his wound and from his mouth lay face up on the soaking sand
and kicked. His bi-limbed brothers were incensed by his killing   240
and outdid one another in all saying with one voice, "To arms, to arms."
Wine gave them courage, and from the beginning of the fight thrown
cups and fragile jars and round cauldrons flew,
things once useful for feasts, but then for war and slaughter.
        Ophion's son, Amycus, was the first not to fear   245

haud timuit spoliare suis et primus ab aede
lampadibus densum rapuit funale coruscis,
elatumque alte, ueluti qui candida tauri
rumpere sacrifica molitur colla securi,
250 illisit fronti Lapithae Celadontis et ossa
non cognoscendo confusa reliquit in ore.
exsiluere oculi, disiectisque ossibus oris
acta retro naris medioque est fixa palato.
hunc pede conuulso mensae Pellaeus acernae
255 strauit humi Pelates deiecto in pectora mento
cumque atro mixtos sputantem sanguine dentes
uulnere Tartareas geminato mittit ad umbras.
    proximus ut steterat spectans altaria uultu
fumida terribili "cur non" ait "utimur istis?"
260 cumque suis Gryneus immanem sustulit aram
ignibus et medium Lapitharum iecit in agmen
depressitque duos, Brotean et Orion; Orio
mater erat Mycale, quam deduxisse canendo
saepe reluctanti constabat cornua lunae.
265 "non impune feres, teli modo copia detur"
dixerat Exadius telique habet instar, in alta
quae fuerant pinu uotiui cornua cerui.
figitur hinc duplici Gryneus in lumina ramo
eruiturque oculos, quorum pars cornibus haeret,
270 pars fluit in barbam concretaque sanguine pendet.
    ecce rapit mediis flagrantem Rhoetus ab aris
pruniceum torrem dextraque a parte Charaxi
tempora perfringit fuluo protecta capillo.
correpti rapida, ueluti seges arida, flamma
275 arserunt crines, et uulnere sanguis inustus
terribilem stridore sonum dedit, ut dare ferrum
igne rubens plerumque solet, quod forcipe curua
cum faber eduxit lacubus demittit; at illud
stridet et in tepida submersum sibilat unda.
280 saucius hirsutis auidum de crinibus ignem
excutit inque umeros limen tellure reuulsum
tollit, onus plaustri, quod ne permittat in hostem,
ipsa facit grauitas; socium quoque saxea moles
oppressit spatio stantem propiore Cometen.
285 gaudia nec retinet Rhoetus: "sic, comprecor," inquit
"cetera sit fortis castrorum turba tuorum!"
semicremoque nouat repetitum stipite uulnus
terque quaterque graui iuncturas uerticis ictu
rupit, et in liquido sederunt ossa cerebro.
290   uictor ad Euagrum Corythumque Dryantaque transit.
e quibus ut prima tectus lanugine malas
procubuit Corythus, "puero quae gloria fuso
parta tibi est?" Euagrus ait; nec dicere Rhoetus
plura sinit rutilasque ferox in aperta loquentis
295 condidit ora uiri perque os in pectora flammas.

to despoil the inner rooms of their gifts, and the first to seize
from the house a chandelier thick with gleaming lamps,
and raising it up high, like one who is poised to break
the white neck of a bull with the sacrificial axe,
he smashed it into the forehead of the Lapith, Celadon, and left   250
the bones mangled in an unrecognizable face.
His eyes jumped out, and, with his facial bones displaced,
his nose was pushed back and lodged in the middle of his palate.
Pellaean Pelates wrenched the leg from a maple-wood table
and used it to strike him to the ground, his chin driven down into his breast,   255
and, as he spat out teeth mixed with dark blood,
repeated the blow, sending him to the shades of Tartarus.
    Next, as he stood gazing at the smoking altar
with a terrifying look, "Why do we not use these?" said
Gryneus, and he lifted up the huge altar, fires   260
and all, and threw it into the middle of the ranks of Lapiths,
crushing two of them, Broteas and Orion; Orion's
mother was Mycale who, it was well known, often
brought down the horns of the reluctant moon with her chanting.
"You will not get away unpunished, if only I can get a weapon,"   265
said Exadius and he was took, for a weapon, what had been
the antlers of a stag, a votive offering on a tall pine-tree.
Gryneus was pierced in the eyes by its double branch,
and his eyes were dug out, and part of them clung to the antlers,
part dripped onto his beard and hung congealed with blood.   270
    Look, Rhoetus seized a blazing plum-wood brand
from the middle of the altar and shattered Charaxus' temple with it,
on the right side, covered as it was, with fair hair.
Seized, like dry crops, by a raging flame,
his hair caught alight; and his blood, scorched in the wound,   275
gave out a terrible screeching sound, as iron, red hot
from the fire often gives when the smith lifts it out
with his curved tongs and plunges it in the tank; and it
screeches and hisses when submerged in cold water.
The injured man shook the greedy fire from his shaggy   280
locks and, wrenching a doorstep from the ground, lifted it
onto his shoulders, a wagon load, whose very weight stopped him
from reaching the enemy; indeed, the stone block crushed
his comrade, Cometes, standing in a place closer by.
Rhoetus did not restrain his joy: "Thus, I pray," he said,   285
"may be the strength of the rest of the troops in your camp."
And he returned to the wound and renewed it with the halfburnt stick,
and, three times or four, he broke the seams of his skull with a heavy
blow, and the bones settled in his liquid brains.
    The victor passed on to Euagrus, Corythus and Dryas.   290
And of these, when Corythus, whose cheeks were covered by the first
down, had fallen, "What glory do you achieve
from slaying a boy?" said Euagrus; but Rhoetus did not let him
say more, as he fiercely drove the ruddy flames
into his open mouth while he was speaking and through his mouth into his chest.   295

te quoque, saeue Drya, circum caput igne rotato
insequitur, sed non in te quoque constitit idem
exitus; adsiduae successu caedis ouantem,
qua iuncta est umero ceruix, sude figis obusta.
300   ingemuit duroque sudem uix osse reuellit
Rhoetus et ipse suo madefactus sanguine fugit.
fugit et Orneüs Lycabasque et saucius armo
dexteriore Medon et cum Pisenore Thaumas,
quique pedum nuper certamine uicerat omnes
305   Mermeros (accepto tum uulnere tardius ibat),
et Pholus et Melaneus et Abas praedator aprorum,
quique suis frustra bellum dissuaderat augur
Asbolus; ille etiam metuenti uulnera Nesso
"ne fuge! ad Herculeos" inquit "seruaberis arcus."
310   at non Eurynomus Lycidasque et Areos et Imbreus
effugere necem; quos omnes dextra Dryantis
perculit aduersos. aduersum tu quoque, quamuis
terga fugae dederas, uulnus, Crenaee, tulisti;
nam graue respiciens inter duo lumina ferrum,
315   qua naris fronti committitur, accipis, imae.
       in tanto fremitu cunctis sine fine iacebat
sopitus uenis et inexperrectus Aphidas
languentique manu carchesia mixta tenebat,
fusus in Ossaeae uillosis pellibus ursae.
320   quem procul ut uidit frustra nulla arma mouentem,
inserit amento digitos "miscenda" que dixit
"cum Styge uina bibes" Phorbas; nec plura moratus
in iuuenem torsit iaculum, ferrataque collo
fraxinus, ut casu iacuit resupinus, adacta est.
325   mors caruit sensu, plenoque e gutture fluxit
inque toros inque ipsa niger carchesia sanguis.
       uidi ego Petraeum conantem tollere terra
glandiferam quercum; quam dum complexibus ambit
et quatit huc illuc labefactaque robora iactat,
330   lancea Pirithoi costis immissa Petraei
pectora cum duro luctantia robore fixit.
Pirithoi cecidisse Lycum uirtute ferebant,
Pirithoi uirtute Chromin. sed uterque minorem
uictori titulum quam Dictys Helopsque dederunt:
335   fixus Helops iaculo, quod peruia tempora fecit
et missum a dextra laeuam penetrauit ad aurem:
Dictys ab ancipiti delapsus acumine montis,
dum fugit instantem trepidans Ixione natum,
decidit in praeceps et pondere corporis ornum
340   ingentem fregit suaque induit ilia fractae.
ultor adest Aphareus saxumque e monte reuulsum
mittere conatur; mittentem stipite querno
occupat Aegides cubitique ingentia frangit
ossa. nec ulterius dare corpus inutile leto
345   aut uacat aut curat, tergoque Bienoris alti

You too, savage Dryas, he pursued, spinning the fire around
his head, but there did not await for you too the same
outcome; as he exulted in his constantly successful slaughtering,
you pierced him with a fire-hardened stake where the neck joins the shoulder.
Rhoetus groaned and struggled to wrench the stake from his hard   300
bone and, drenched himself in his own blood, fled.
Orneüs fled too and Lycabas and Medon, who was injured
in the right forequarter, and Thaumas together with Pisenor,
and the one who had recently defeated all of them in a foot-race,
Mermeros (he was going slower now, for he had received a wound),   305
and Pholus and Melaneus and Abas, the boars' predator,
and the one who had in vain urged his people against the war, the augur
Asbolus; he even said to Nessus who was afraid of being wounded,
"Do not flee! You will be saved for Hercules' bow."
But Eurynomus and Lycidas and Areos and Imbreus   310
did not escape death; they were struck by Dryas' right
hand full in the face. Full in the face, you too, Crenaeus,
bore a wound, although you had turned your back in flight;
for, as you looked back, you took a heavy speartip between your two
eyes, where the nose meets the bottom of the forehead.   315
        In all this uproar, there was lying there, with ceaseless sleep
in all his veins, and unawakened, Aphidas,
and he was holding a cup of mixed wine in his drooping hand,
while stretched out on the shaggy pelt of an Ossaean bear.
And, when from afar he saw him uselessly wielding no weapons,   320
Phorbas inserted his fingers into his throwing strap and said, "Mixed
with the Styx must be the wines that you will drink;" and, without more delay,
he hurled his javelin at the young man, and the iron-tipped ash-wood
was driven into his neck as he chanced to lie there face up.
His death was unconscious, and, from his full throat both onto   325
his couch and even into his cups, there flowed his black blood.
        I saw Petraeus trying to lift out an acorn-bearing
oak from the earth; and, while he was encircling it in his embrace
and shaking it this way and that and heaving at the loosened tree-trunk,
Pirithoüs' lance, thrust into Petraeus' ribs,   330
pierced his struggling breast together with the hard tree-trunk.
By Pirithoüs' prowess, they say it was that Lycus fell,
by Pirithoüs' prowess, Chromis too. But both gave
less glory to the victor than did Dictys and Helops:
Helops was pierced by a javelin which made a way through his temples   335
and, in its flight, penetrated from the right ear to the left;
Dictys slipped from a high mountain ridge,
while fleeing in panic from the assault of Ixion's son,
and fell headlong, breaking a huge ash-tree
with the weight of his body, and impaling his flanks on the broken tree.   340
Aphareus was there to avenge him and he tried to throw a rock
he had wrenched from the mountain; as he was throwing it, Aegides forestalled him
with a stick of oak and broke the huge bones
of his forearm. He had not either the leisure or the concern to send
the useless body further towards its doom, and he jumped on tall Bienor's   345

insilit, haud solito quemquam portare nisi ipsum,
opposuitque genu costis prensamque sinistra
caesariem retinens uultum minitantiaque ora
robore nodoso praeduraque tempora fregit.
350   robore Nedymnum iaculatoremque Lycotan
sternit et immissa protectum pectora barba
Hippason et summis exstantem Riphea siluis
Thereaque, Haemoniis qui prensos montibus ursos
ferre domum uiuos indignantesque solebat.
355   haud tulit utentem pugnae successibus ultra
Thesea Demoleon, solidoque reuellere *dumo*
annosam pinum magno molimine temptat;
quod quia non potuit, praefractam misit in hostem.
sed procul a telo Theseus ueniente recessit
360   Pallados admonitu (credi sic ipse uolebat).
non tamen arbor iners cecidit; nam Crantoris alti
abscidit iugulo pectusque umerumque sinistrum.
(armiger ille tui fuerat genitoris, Achille,
quem Dolopum rector, bello superatus Amyntor
365   Aeacidae dederat pacis pignusque fidemque.)
hunc procul ut foedo disiectum uulnere Peleus
uidit, "at inferias, iuuenum gratissime Crantor,
accipe" ait ualidoque in Demoleonta lacerto
fraxineam misit mentis quoque uiribus hastam,
370   quae laterum cratem perrupit et ossibus haerens
intremuit; trahit ille manu sine cuspide lignum
(id quoque uix sequitur), cuspis pulmone retenta est.
ipse dolor uires animo dabat; aeger in hostem
erigitur pedibusque uirum proculcat equinis.
375   excipit ille ictus galea clipeoque sonanti
defensatque umeros praetentaque sustinet arma
perque armos uno duo pectora perforat ictu.
    ante tamen leto dederat Phlegraeon et Hylen
eminus, Iphinoüm collato Marte Claninque.
380   additur his Dorylas, qui tempora tecta gerebat
pelle lupi saeuique uicem praestantia teli
cornua uara boum multo rubefacta cruore;
huic ego (nam uires animus dabat) "aspice" dixi
"quantum concedant nostro tua cornua ferro"
385   et iaculum torsi; quod cum uitare nequiret,
opposuit dextram passurae uulnera fronti.
adfixa est cum fronte manus; fit clamor, at illum
haerentem Peleus et acerbo uulnere uictum
(stabat enim propior) mediam ferit ense sub aluum.
390   prosiluit terraque ferox sua uiscera traxit
tractaque calcauit calcataque rupit et illis
crura quoque impediit et inani concidit aluo.
    nec te pugnantem tua, Cyllare, forma redemit,
si modo naturae formam concedimus illi.
395   barba erat incipiens, barbae color aureus, aurea

back, which was not used to carrying anyone except himself,
and put his knee against his ribs and, grasping his hair
and holding it in his left hand, he shattered his face and threatening
mouth and hard temples with a knotty club.
With the club, he struck Nedymnus down and the javelin-thrower,   350
Lycotas, and Hippasos, whose breast was protected by a flowing
beard, and Ripheus who stood out above the tops of the trees,
and Thereus who used to catch bears on the Haemonian
mountains and bring them home alive and resentful.
    Demoleon could not bear Theseus enjoying successes   355
in the fight any more, and with great effort he was trying
to wrench a pine tree full of years from the solid *thorn-bush*;
and because he was unable to, he broke it off short and threw it at his enemy.
But as the weapon came, Theseus withdrew far back from it
because of a warning from Pallas (so he himself wanted it to be believed).   360
But the tree did not fall without effect; for from tall Crantor's
throat it tore away the left breast and shoulder.
(He had been your father's armour-bearer, Achilles,
and Amyntor, the ruler of the Dolopes, when overcome in war,
had given him to Aeacides as a token and pledge of peace.)   365
When Peleus saw him from afar, torn apart by a disgusting
wound, "But receive, Crantor, most gracious of young men,
my funeral offerings," he said, and, with a mighty arm and strength
of purpose too, he threw an ash spear at Demoleon
which burst through the rib cage and stuck in the bones   370
trembling; his hand drew out the shaft without its tip
(even that scarcely came out), the tip was held in his lung.
The very pain gave strength to his courage; though injured, he reared up
against his enemy and trampled the man with his horse's hooves.
He took the blows on his helmet and, with his ringing shield,   375
protected his shoulders, and, holding his weapons up at full stretch before him,
with one stroke, he pierced the two breasts through the forequarters.
    But earlier he had sent to their doom Phlegraeos and Hyles
from long range, Iphinoüs and Clanis in close combat.
Added to these was Dorylas, who had a wolf's skin   380
to protect his temples and, taking the place of a cruel spear,
the branching horns of a bull reddened with much gore;
to him (for courage gave me strength), "Look," I said,
"how far your horns give way to my steel,"
and I hurled my javelin; and since he could not avoid it,   385
he put his right hand up in front of his forehead where he was about to be wounded.
His head was pierced together with his hand; there was a cry, but, as he
stuck there defeated by the bitter wound, Peleus
(for he was standing nearer) struck him under the middle of the belly with his sword.
He leapt forwards, fiercely dragging his own guts on the ground,   390
and as they dragged he trampled them, and as he trampled them he tore them and
tangled his legs in them too, and fell on his empty belly.
    And your beauty, Cyllaros, did not buy you safety in the fight,
if, indeed, we do grant beauty to that kind.
His beard was just beginning, the colour of the beard was golden, gold   395

ex umeris medios coma dependebat in armos.
gratus in ore uigor; ceruix umerique manusque
pectoraque artificum laudatis proxima signis,
et quacumque uir est. nec equi mendosa sub illo
400 deteriorque uiro facies; da colla caputque,
Castore dignus erit: sic tergum sessile, sic sunt
pectora celsa toris. totus pice nigrior atra,
candida cauda tamen; color est quoque cruribus albus.
multae illum petiere sua de gente, sed una
405 abstulit Hylonome, qua nulla decentior inter
semiferos altis habitauit femina siluis.
haec et blanditiis et amando et amare fatendo
Cyllaron una tenet; cultu quoque, quantus in illis
esse potest membris, ut sit coma pectine leuis,
410 ut modo rore maris, modo se uiolaue rosaue
implicet, interdum canentia lilia gestet,
bisque die lapsis Pagasaeae uertice siluae
fontibus ora lauet, bis flumine corpora tingat,
nec nisi quae deceant electarumque ferarum
415 aut umero aut lateri praetendat uellera laeuo.
par amor est illis; errant in montibus una,
antra simul subeunt; et tum Lapitheia tecta
intrarant pariter, pariter fera bella gerebant.
auctor in incerto est, iaculum de parte sinistra
420 uenit et inferius quam collo pectora subsunt,
Cyllare, te fixit; paruo cor uulnere laesum
corpore cum toto post tela educta refrixit.
protinus Hylonome morientes excipit artus
impositaque manu uulnus fouet oraque ad ora
425 admouet atque animae fugienti obsistere temptat;
ut uidet extinctum, dictis, quae clamor ad aures
arcuit ire meas, telo, quod inhaeserat illi,
incubuit moriensque suum complexa maritum est.
      ante oculos stat et ille meos, qui sena leonum
430 uinxerat inter se conexis uellera nodis,
Phaeocomes, hominemque simul protectus equumque;
caudice qui misso, quem uix iuga bina mouerent,
Tectaphon Oleniden a summo uertice fregit.
[fracta uolubilitas capitis latissima, perque os
435 perque cauas nares oculosque auresque cerebrum
molle fluit, ueluti concretum uimine querno
lac solet utue liquor rari sub pondere cribri
manat et exprimitur per densa foramina spissus.]
ast ego, dum parat hic armis nudare iacentem
440 (scit tuus hoc genitor), gladium spoliantis in ima
ilia demisi. Chthonius quoque Teleboasque
ense iacent nostro; ramum prior ille bifurcum
gesserat, hic iaculum. iaculo mihi uulnera fecit;
signa uides, apparet adhuc uetus inde cicatrix.
445 tunc ego debueram capienda ad Pergama mitti,

hair hung from his shoulders down to the middle of his forequarters.
There was a charming vigour in his face; his neck, shoulders, hands
and breast were very like artists' prized statues,
as was wherever he was a man. And under that, the horse's body
was unblemished and not inferior to the man's; give him a neck and a head   400
and he will be worthy of Castor; his back was so fit to be sat on, the muscles
bulged so on his chest, he was blacker than dark pitch all over,
save that his tail was white; and the colour on his legs was white too.
Many females from his race sought after him, but Hylonome
alone had carried him off, and, among the half-beasts, none   405
more graceful than her was living in the high woods.
She, with her endearments and her loving and her confessing that she loved,
alone held Cyllaros; and with her toilet too, as much as was possible
in that body, such that her hair was smoothed with a comb,
sometimes she entwined herself with rosemary, sometimes with violets   410
or roses, from time to time she wore white lilies
and twice a day she washed her face in spring water flowing down
from the top of the Pagasaean wood; twice she dipped her body in the river,
and she spread across her shoulder or her left side
only those skins which suited her and were from select wild beasts.   415
Their love was equal, they wandered on the mountains together,
they went into caves together; and at that time they had entered the Lapith
palace together, together they were waging cruel war.
The perpetrator is unclear, a javelin came from the left
side and, below where the chest comes up to the neck,   420
pierced you, Cyllaros; though hurt by a small wound, the heart,
after the weapon was taken out, grew cold together with the whole body.
At once Hylonome gathered up his dying limbs,
and put her hand upon the wound and soothed it, and brought her lips
to his, and tried to block his fleeing soul;   425
when she saw that he was dead, after saying things that the shouting kept
from getting to my ears, she fell upon the weapon that had stuck
into him and, dying, she embraced her husband.
   Before my eyes there stood also the one who had bound six
lion skins to one another with tied knots,   430
Phaeocomes, with both the human and the horse protected together;
he threw a log, which two pairs of oxen would hardly move,
and smashed Tectaphos, Olen's son, on the top of his head.
[The very broad roundness of his head was smashed, and through his mouth
and, through his hollow nostrils, eyes and ears, his soft   435
brains flowed, just as milk will when congealed
in oaken withies, or as a liquid flows under the weight of a coarse
sieve, and, thickened, is pressed out through fine holes.]
But I, while he was preparing to strip him of his arms as he lay there
(your father knows this too), plunged my blade very deep   440
into the flanks of the despoiler. Chthonius too and Teleboas
lie dead from my sword; the former had been wielding a forked
branch, the other a javelin. With the javelin he had given me a wound;
you can see the evidence; the old scar made from it still shows.
Then it was I ought to have been sent to take Pergamum,   445

tum poteram magni, si non superare, morari
Hectoris arma meis. illo sed tempore nullus
aut puer Hector erat, nunc me mea deficit aetas.
    quid tibi uictorem gemini Periphanta Pyraethi,
450 Ampyca quid referam, qui quadripedantis Echecli
fixit in aduerso cornum sine cuspide uultu?
uecte Pelethronium Macareus in pectus adacto
strauit Erigdupum; memini et uenabula condi
inguine Nesseis manibus coniecta Cymeli.
455 nec tu credideris tantum cecinisse futura
Ampyciden Mopsum; Mopso iaculante biformis
occubuit frustraque loqui temptauit Hodites
ad mentum lingua mentoque ad guttura fixo.
    quinque neci Caeneus dederat, Styphelumque Bromumque
460 Antimachumque Elymumque securiferumque Pyracmon;
uulnera non memini, numerum nomenque notaui.
prouolat Emathii spoliis armatus Halesi,
quem dederat leto, membris et corpore Latreus
maximus; huic aetas inter iuuenemque senemque
465 uis iuuenalis erat, uariabant tempora cani.
qui clipeo gladioque Macedoniaque sarisa
conspicuus faciemque obuersus in agmen utrumque
armaque concussit certumque equitauit in orbem
uerbaque tot fudit uacuas animosus in auras:
470 "et te, Caeni, feram? nam tu mihi femina semper,
tu mihi Caenis eris. nec te natalis origo
commonuit, mentemque subit, quo praemia facto
quaque uiri falsam speciem mercede pararis?
quid sis nata uide, uel quid sis passa, columque,
475 i, cape cum calathis et stamina pollice torque;
bella relinque uiris!" iactanti talia Caeneus
extentum cursu missa latus eruit hasta,
qua uir equo commissus erat. furit ille dolore
nudaque Phyllei iuuenis ferit ora sarisa;
480 non secus haec resilit, quam tecti a culmine grando,
aut si quis paruo feriat caua tympana saxo.
comminus adgreditur laterique recondere duro
luctatur gladium; gladio loca peruia non sunt.
"haud tamen effugies! medio iugulaberis ense,
485 quandoquidem mucro est hebes" inquit et in latus ensem
obliquat longaque amplectitur ilia dextra;
plaga facit gemitus in corpore marmoris icti,
fractaque dissiluit percusso lammina callo.
ut satis inlaesos miranti praebuit artus,
490 "nunc age," ait Caeneus "nostro tua corpora ferro
temptemus" capuloque tenus demisit in armos
ensem fatiferum caecamque in uiscera mouit
uersauitque manum uulnusque in uulnere fecit.
    ecce ruunt uasto rapidi clamore bimembres
495 telaque in hunc omnes unum mittuntque feruntque.

then I could have delayed, if not overcome, great
Hector's arms with mine. But, at that time, Hector
was nothing or just a boy, now my age is failing me.
    Why should I tell you of Periphas, victor over double-formed
Pyraethus, why of Ampyx who struck his cornel spear,   450
without its tip, full in the face of four-footed Echeclus?
Macareus drove a crowbar into the breast of Pelethronian
Erigdupus and struck him down; I remember too that hunting spears hurled
by Nessean hands were buried in Cymelus' groin.
And you would not have believed that singing of the future was all that was done   455
by Ampyx' son, Mopsus; when Mopsus threw his javelin, the two-formed
Hodites was laid low trying in vain to speak
with his tongue pierced to his chin and his chin to his throat.
    Caeneus had sent five to their deaths, Styphelus, Bromus,
Antimachus, Elymus and axebearing Pyracmos;   460
I do not remember the wounds, but I did make a note of the number and the name.
There rushed forward, armed with the spoils of Emathian Halesus,
whom he had sent to his doom, Latreus who was, in limbs and body,
enormous; his age was between young and old,
his strength was youthful, grey hairs flecked his temples.   465
Resplendent with his shield and sword and Macedonian
pike, and with his face turned towards both battle lines,
he brandished his weapons and rode around in a fixed circle
and proudly poured these many words into the empty air:
"Am I to endure you too, Caenis? For to me you will always be a woman,   470
to me you will always be Caenis. And has not your start at birth
reminded you, and does it not enter your mind for what act you were rewarded,
for what price you have obtained the false appearance of a man?
Consider what you were born, or what you have suffered, and go,
take your distaff together with your baskets and twist the strands with your thumb; 475
leave wars to men!" As he was uttering such things, Caeneus
threw a spear which tore out his side where man met horse,
stretched as it was from running. He went mad with pain
and struck the bare face of the Phyllean youth with his pike;
it bounced back not unlike hail from the roof of a house,   480
or if anyone beats a hollow drum with a small stone.
He attacked close up and struggled to bury a sword
in his hard side; for a sword, there was no way through.
"But you will not escape! You will be slain by the middle of my blade,
since the point is blunt," he said and, turning the blade   485
towards its side, he grasped the other's flanks with his long right hand;
the blow produced the groans of struck marble from his body,
and the blade broke on striking his hide, and split off.
As he showed off his uninjured body to the other's amazement,
"Come now," said Caeneus, "let me try your body with my   490
sword," and he plunged the fateful blade up to the hilt
into his forequarters, and he moved his hand blindly
into his guts and twisted it about and made wound on wound.
    Look, the bi-limbed ones rushed swiftly with a huge shout
all throwing and thrusting weapons into this one man.   495

tela retusa cadunt, manet imperfossus ab omni
inque cruentatus Caeneus Elateïus ictu.
fecerat attonitos noua res. "heu dedecus ingens!"
Monychus exclamat "populus superamur ab uno
500   uixque uiro; quamquam ille uir est, nos segnibus actis
quod fuit ille, sumus. quid membra immania prosunt,
quid geminae uires et quod fortissima rerum
in nobis duplex natura animalia iunxit?
nec nos matre dea nec nos Ixione natos
505   esse reor, qui tantus erat, Iunonis ut altae
spem caperet; nos semimari superamur ab hoste.
saxa trabesque super totosque inuoluite montes
uiuacemque animam missis elidite siluis!
silua premat fauces, et erit pro uulnere pondus."
510   dixit et insani deiectam uiribus Austri
forte trabem nactus ualidum coniecit in hostem
exemplumque fuit; paruoque in tempore nudus
arboris Othrys erat, nec habebat Pelion umbras.
obrutus immani cumulo sub pondere Caeneus
515   aestuat arboreo congestaque robora duris
fert umeris; sed enim postquam super ora caputque
creuit onus neque habet quas ducat spiritus auras,
deficit interdum, modo se super aëra frustra
tollere conatur iactasque euoluere siluas,
520   interdumque mouet, ueluti, quam cernimus, ecce,
ardua si terrae quatiatur motibus Ide.
exitus in dubio est. alii sub inania corpus
Tartara detrusum siluarum mole ferebant;
abnuit Ampycides medioque ex aggere fuluis
525   uidit auem pennis liquidas exire sub auras,
quae mihi tum primum, tunc est conspecta supremum.
hanc ubi lustrantem leni sua castra uolatu
Mopsus et ingenti circum clangore sonantem
aspexit pariterque animo est oculisque secutus,
530   "o salue," dixit "Lapithaeae gloria gentis,
maxime uir quondam, sed auis nunc unica, Caeneu!"
credita res auctore suo est. dolor addidit iram,
oppressumque aegre tulimus tot hostibus unum;
nec prius abstitimus ferro exercere dolorem,
535   quam data pars leto, partem fuga noxque remouit.'
        haec inter Lapithas et semihomines Centauros
proelia Tlepolemus Pylio referente dolorem
praeteriti Alcidae tacito non pertulit ore
atque ait: 'Herculeae mirum est obliuia laudis
540   acta tibi, senior. certe mihi saepe referre
nubigenas domitos a se pater esse solebat.'
tristis ad haec Pylius: 'quid me meminisse malorum
cogis et obductos annis rescindere luctus
inque tuum genitorem odium offensasque fateri?
545   ille quidem maiora fide (di!) gessit et orbem

The weapons fell blunted, Elateïan Caeneus stayed
unpierced and unbloodied from every blow.
The strange event had left them stunned. "Alas, the huge shame!"
Monychus cried out, "We, a people, are being overcome by just one,
and he scarcely a man; yet he is a man, and we, because of our slothful deeds,   500
are what he was. What use are our tremendous limbs,
what help our twinned strength and the fact that a double nature
has joined in us the strongest animals of all?
I think that we are the sons neither of a goddess mother
nor of Ixion, who was so great that he had designs   505
on lofty Juno; we are being overcome by a half-male enemy.
Roll rocks and tree-trunks and whole mountains over him,
and choke the living breath from him by throwing forests on him.
Let a forest squeeze his throat, and its weight will do the wounding."
He spoke and, happening to come across a tree-trunk thrown down   510
by the violence of wild Auster, he hurled it at his mighty enemy
which set an example; and in a short time Othrys
was bare of trees, and Pelion had no shade.
Buried by a tremendous heap, Caeneus was sweating
under the weight of trees and he was carrying piles of oaks   515
on his hard shoulders; but after the load had grown
above his face and head, and he had no air to draw breath,
at times he gave up, then he tried in vain to raise himself
up into the air and to roll away the forests they had thrown,
and at times he moved them just as if lofty Ida   520
which, look, we can see, were being shaken by tremors of the earth.
The outcome was in doubt. Some say that his body
was driven down into empty Tartarus by the mass of the forests;
Ampyx' son denies it, and he saw a bird with tawny ·
wings come out from the middle of the pile up into the clear air;   525
and I too saw it then for the first and last time.
And when Mopsus noticed it circling their camp
in smooth flight and giving a huge scream
all round, he followed it with mind and eyes equally,
saying, "O hail, glory of the Lapiths' race,   530
once a very great man, but now a unique bird, Caeneus!"
The tale was believed because of its source. Grief added anger,
and we bore it ill that one had been crushed by so many enemies;
and we did not cease from working out our grief with the sword
till some had been sent to their doom and others removed by flight or darkness.'   535
      While the Pylian was relating these battles between the Lapiths
and the half-human Centaurs, Tlepolemus could not, with silent lips,
bear his distress that Alcides had been passed over,
and he said, 'I am amazed at your forgetfulness
of Hercules' renown, old man. Certainly, my father often used   540
to relate to me how the cloudborn had been subdued by him.'
To this, the Pylian sadly replied, 'Why compel me to remember
evils and to lay bare sorrows hidden by the years
and to admit to hatred and resentments against your father?
He did indeed (O gods!) do things beyond belief and filled   545

impleuit meritis, quod mallem posse negare;
sed neque Deïphobum nec Pulydamanta nec ipsum
Hectora laudamus—quis enim laudauerit hostem?
ille tuus genitor Messenia moenia quondam
550 strauit et immeritas urbes Elinque Pylonque
diruit inque meos ferrum flammamque penatis
impulit. utque alios taceam, quos ille peremit,
bis sex Nelidae fuimus, conspecta iuuentus;
bis sex Herculeis ceciderunt me minus uno
555 uiribus. atque alios uinci potuisse ferendum est;
mira Periclymeni mors est, cui posse figuras
sumere quas uellet rursusque reponere sumptas
Neptunus dederat, Neleï sanguinis auctor.
hic ubi nequiquam est formas uariatus in omnes,
560 uertitur in faciem uolucris, quae fulmina curuis
ferre solet pedibus, diuum gratissima regi;
uiribus usus auis, pennis rostroque redunco
hamatisque uiri laniauerat unguibus ora.
tendit in hunc nimium certos Tirynthius arcus
565 atque inter nubes sublimia membra ferentem
pendentemque ferit, lateri qua iungitur ala;
nec graue uulnus erat, sed rupti uulnere nerui
deficiunt motumque negant uiresque uolandi.
decidit in terram non concipientibus auras
570 infirmis pennis, et quae leuis haeserat alae
corporis adfixi pressa est grauitate sagitta
perque latus summum iugulo est exacta sinistro.
nunc uideor debere tui praeconia rebus
Herculis, o Rhodiae rector pulcherrime classis?
575 nec tamen ulterius quam fortia facta silendo
ulciscor fratres; solida est mihi gratia tecum.'
      haec postquam dulci Neleïus edidit ore,
a sermone senis repetito munere Bacchi
surrexere toris; nox est data cetera somno.
580   at deus aequoreas qui cuspide temperat undas
in uolucrem corpus nati Phaëthontida uersum
mente dolet patria saeuumque perosus Achillem
exercet memores plus quam ciuiliter iras.
iamque fere tracto duo per quinquennia bello
585 talibus intonsum compellat Sminthea dictis:
'o mihi de fratris longe gratissime natis,
inrita qui mecum posuisti moenia Troiae,
ecquid, ubi has iamiam casuras aspicis arces,
ingemis? aut ecquid tot defendentia muros
590 milia caesa doles? ecquid, ne persequar omnes,
Hectoris umbra subit circum sua Pergama tracti?
cum tamen ille ferox belloque cruentior ipso
uiuit adhuc, operis nostri populator, Achilles,
det mihi se; faxo triplici quid cuspide possim
595 sentiat. at quoniam concurrere comminus hosti

the world with his merits, which I would prefer to be able to deny;
but we praise neither Deïphobus nor Pulydamas
nor Hector himself—for who would praise an enemy?
That father of yours once levelled the Messenian
walls and smashed the blameless cities, both Elis   550
and Pylos, and brought fire and sword to my
penates. And, to say nothing of the others he struck down,
twice six we were, the sons of Neleus, gleaming youth;
twice six they fell, less me alone, to Hercules'
strength. And that the others could be conquered had to be borne;   555
the death of Periclymenus was amazing, for the ability to take up
the shapes he wanted and put them aside once taken up
had been given him by Neptune, the founder of Neleus' blood line.
When he had in vain changed into every other form,
he turned into the appearance of the bird which is wont to carry   560
thunderbolts in its curved talons, the one most favoured by the king of the gods;
using the bird's strength, he had torn at the man's face
with his wings, hooked beak and bent claws.
The Tirynthian drew his too sure bow against him
and, as he bore his body hanging on high among   565
the clouds, struck him where the wings joined to his side;
the wound was not serious, but his sinews, torn by the wound,
failed and refused him motion and the strength to fly.
He fell to the earth, his frail wings unable
to catch the air, and the light arrow which had stuck   570
in his wing was pressed by the weight of the body it had pierced
and driven through the top of his side out of his throat from the left.
Does it seem now that I owe public praise to the actions of your
Hercules, O most noble leader of the Rhodian fleet?
But I do not avenge my brothers any further than by being silent about   575
his brave deeds; my good will towards you is firm.'
　　After the Neleïan had spoken these things from his gentle mouth,
and, with the end of the old man's speech, the gift of Bacchus had been repeated,
they rose from their couches; the rest of the night was given to sleep.
　　But the god who controls the waters of the sea with his spear   580
was grieving with a father's feelings that the body of his son
had been turned into Phaëthon's bird and, hating cruel Achilles,
he worked out his mindful anger in a less than civilized way.
And now, when the war had been dragged out for about two quinquennia,
he called out to the unshorn Smintheus with such words as these: 585
'O you, by far the most favourite of my brother's sons,
you who vainly built with me the walls of Troy,
when you see this citadel now at last about to fall, do you groan
at all? Or do you grieve at all that so many thousands
have been slain defending the walls? At all, lest I go through every one,   590
when there appears the ghost of Hector who was dragged around his own Pergamum?
And yet that fierce man, bloodier than war itself,
still lives, the despoiler of our work, Achilles.
Let him give himself to me; I will make him feel what I can do
with my trident. But, since I am not allowed to charge   595

non datur, occulta necopinum perde sagitta.'
adnuit atque animo pariter patruique suoque
Delius indulgens nebula uelatus in agmen
peruenit Iliacum mediaque in caede uirorum
600   rara per ignotos spargentem cernit Achiuos
tela Parin fassusque deum, 'quid spicula perdis
sanguine plebis?' ait 'si qua est tibi cura tuorum,
uertere in Aeaciden caesosque ulciscere fratres.'
dixit et ostendens sternentem Troïca ferro
605   corpora Peliden, arcus obuertit in illum
certaque letifera derexit spicula dextra.
quod Priamus gaudere senex post Hectora posset,
hoc fuit. ille igitur tantorum uictor, Achille,
uictus es a timido Graiae raptore maritae!
610   at si femineo fuerat tibi Marte cadendum,
Thermodontiaca malles cecidisse bipenni.
        iam timor ille Phrygum, decus et tutela Pelasgi
nominis, Aeacides, caput insuperabile bello,
arserat; armarat deus idem idemque cremarat.
615   iam cinis est, et de tam magno restat Achille
nescioquid, paruam quod non bene compleat urnam.
at uiuit totum quae gloria compleat orbem;
haec illi mensura uiro respondet et hac est
par sibi Pelides nec inania Tartara sentit.
620   ipse etiam, ut cuius fuerit cognoscere posses,
bella mouet clipeus, deque armis arma feruntur.
non ea Tydides, non audet Oileos Aiax,
non minor Atrides, non bello maior et aeuo
poscere, non alii; solis Telamone creato
625   Laërteque fuit tantae fiducia laudis.
a se Tantalides onus inuidiamque remouit
Argolicosque duces mediis considere castris
iussit et arbitrium litis traiecit in omnes.

close up to our enemy, you must destroy him unawares with a hidden arrow.
The Delian assented and, indulging equally both his uncle's
desires and his own, veiled in a cloud, he arrived at the Trojan
lines and, in the middle of the slaughter of men,
saw Paris scattering arrows sparsely among   600
unknown Achaeans, and, admitting he was a god, 'Why waste your darts
on plebeian blood?' he said. 'If you care at all for your own people
turn against Aeacides and avenge your slaughtered brothers.'
He spoke and, pointing out Pelides striking Trojan
bodies down with his sword, he turned the bow against him   605
and aimed the sure darts with his death-dealing right hand.
And the only thing, with Hector gone, that Priam could rejoice at
was this. So you, the victor over such great men, Achilles,
were vanquished by the timid ravisher of a Greek wife!
But if you had to fall in a womanish battle   610
you would have preferred to fall to the double axe of Thermodon.
     Now, that terror of the Phrygians, the glory and protection of the Pelasgian
name, Aeacides, the invincible leader in war,
had burnt; the very god that had armed him was the very one that had cremated him.
Now he is ash, and from great Achilles there remains   615
something that could not well fill an urn.
But his glory lives on to fill the whole world;
this is the measure that is worthy of that man, and with this
Pelides is equal to himself and does not experience empty Tartarus.
     Even his very shield, so that you could know whose   ·   620
it was, brought on a war, and, about his arms, arms were taken up.
Tydides did not dare to demand them, nor Ajax,
Oileus' son, nor the lesser Atrides, nor the one greater in age
and warfare, nor the others; only Telamon's son
and Laërtes' were confident of such renown.   625
Tantalides rid himself of a burden and of ill will;
he ordered the Argive leaders to sit in the middle
of the camp and transferred the judgement of the suit to them all.

COMMENTARY

Further elucidation and alternative views will often be found in Anderson's edition of books 6-10. For a detailed account of the first third of this book, see Galinsky.

BOOK IX

1-97 Achelous and Hercules

The earliest extant account is Sophocles *Trachiniae* 9-23 (Storr's translation, slightly adapted; Deïanira is speaking):

> 'For my first wooer was a river god, Achelous,
> who in triple form appeared to sue my father for my hand,   10
> now as a bull, now as a sinuous snake
> with glittering coils, and now in bulk a man
> with front of ox, while from his shaggy beard
> runnels of fountain-water spouted forth.
> In terror of so strange a wooer, I   15
> was ever praying death might end my woes,
> before I came to such a marriage bed.
> Then to my joy, though long delayed, the son
> of Zeus and Alcmena, good at need,
> grappled the monster and delivered me.   20
> The circumstance and manner of that fight
> I cannot tell, not knowing; but whoso watched it,
> indifferent to the issue, might describe it.'

However, as Easterling points out (pp. 15-19) the story is very much older. Note that Ovid seems to be fulfilling the rôle ascribed by Deïanira to 'whoso watched it, indifferent to the issue'. The ninth of Ovid's *Heroides* was Deïanira's letter to Hercules.

1 **the god's:** Achelous'; the story, as so often in this *carmen perpetuum* (see on 1.4), continues very closely from the end of the last book; see on 5.1.

1-2 **and...forehead:** the disjointed word order reflects an unusual degree of dislocation in the Latin word order.

Neptunian hero: Theseus; there were two views about Theseus' father; Ovid usually accepts the normal view that his father was Aegeus (see on 7.402-24). However, the passage from Apollod. 3.15.6-7, 16.1 (Frazer's translation) quoted there is not complete; in full, it runs:

> As no child was born to him [Aegeus], he...went to Pythia and consulted the
> oracle concerning the begetting of children. The god answered him:
> "The bulging mouth of the wineskin, O best of men,
> Loose not until thou hast reached the height of Athens."
> Not knowing what to make of the oracle, he set out on his return to Athens.
> And journeying by way of Troezen, he lodged with Pittheus, son of Pelops,
> who, understanding the oracle, made him drunk and caused him to lie with
> his daughter Aethra. But in the same night Po-
> seidon [Neptune] also had connexion with her...
> Aethra bore to Aegeus a son Theseus...

Cf. Stat. *Theb.* 12.665; for a full discussion, see Jebb on Bacchylides 16.36.

2 **the Calydonian river:** Achelous; the phrase is repeated from 8.727.

5-6 **it was not so shameful to be conquered:** here Ovid develops a topic explored at 5.315-6.

6   **glorious:** *decorum*; the whole context with its military language must put Achelous in a
ridiculous light but never more so than with this echo of Horace's *dulce et decorum est pro
patria mori* (*Odes* 3.2.13) 'It is sweet and glorious to die for the fatherland.' It is characteristic of Ovid to imitate particularly sublime passages at relatively banal moments; see on
5.605-6. See also on 1.200-6; 9.8-9, 17-18, 27, 46-9, 61, 131, 137, 170-1; 10.190-5, 199,
300, 716; 12.46.

7   **so great...great:** no such ugly jingle occurs in the Latin because the correlatives that correspond to 'great' and 'so great' (*tantus* and *magnus*) are more different from each other.

8   **If in talk...to your ears:** once again (see on 9.6), Achelous makes himself seem ridiculous
by closely imitating Virg. *Aen.* 2.81-2:

>   fando aliquod si forte tuas peruenit ad aures
>   Belidae nomen Palamedis...
>   *If it happens that in talk the name of Palamedes, son of Belus,
>   has come to your ears...*

Ovid's manuscripts read *tandem* 'at last' but Burman's emendation, *fando* 'in talk', makes
far more sense; its greater closeness to Virgil is, of course, a two-edged argument. See also
15.497.

10   **and the jealous hope of many suitors:** an exact repetition of 4.795 where I erroneously
translated *procorum* 'of suitors' as if it were *procerum* 'of nobles'. It was, of course, the
suitors who were jealous but the transferred epithet, moving the adjective from its noun to
another noun, is common in ancient poetry. It is especially common in Latin hexameters
where there was an almost overwhelming preference for sharing the adjectives in a line or
clause evenly among the nouns, regardless of strict logic; cf. e.g. 8.676.

11   **had been entered:** understand 'by me'; the ellipse is almost as strained in the Latin as in
the translation.

11-12 **father-in-law...son-in-law:** the Latin, *soceri...generum* is far less cumbersome; see on
1.145.

12   **son of Parthaon:** Oeneus was son of Parthaon (elsewhere 'Porthaon' or 'Parthaon' see
Hom. *Il.* 14.115-7) and father of Deïanira (Soph. *Trach.* 6); see also on 8.543, 544-5.

13   **Alcides:** Alceus' descendant, i.e. Hercules who was the son of Amphitryon and grandson of
Alceus; see Apollodorus 2.4.5 (Frazer's translation):

>   *Electryon married Anaxo, daughter of Alcaeus, and begat a daughter Al-
>   cmena...*

also Apollod. 2.4.8 (Frazer's translation):

>   *But before Amphitryon reached Thebes, Zeus came by night and prolonging
>   the one night threefold he assumed the likeness of Amphitryon and bedded
>   with Alcmena... But when Amphitryon arrived and saw that he was not wel-
>   comed by his wife, he inquired the cause; and when she told him that he had
>   come the night before and slept with her, he learned from Tiresias how Zeus
>   had enjoyed her. And Alcmena bore two sons, to wit, Hercules, whom she
>   had by Zeus and who was the elder by one night, and Iphicles, whom she
>   had by Amphitryon. When the child was eight months old, Hera desired the
>   destruction of the babe and sent two serpents to the bed. Alcmena called
>   Amphitryon to her help, but Hercules arose and killed the serpents by
>   strangling them with both his hands.*

See Frazer's note for other treatments; see also on 6.112; 9.14-15, 304. Ovid's account of
Hercules' birth appears at 9.281-313.

14   **Jupiter...as her father-in-law:** Hercules is described either as son of Amphitryon or as son
of Jupiter, see on 9.13.

14-15 **the fame of his labours:** for the story, see Apollod. 2.4.12 (Frazer's translation):

>   *Now it came to pass that after the battle with the Minyans Hercules was
>   driven mad by the jealousy of Hera and flung his own children, whom he
>   had had by Megara, and two children of Iphicles into the fire; wherefore he*

condemned himself to exile, and was purified by Thespius, and repairing to
Delphi he enquired of the god where he should dwell. The Pythian priestess
then first called him Hercules, for hitherto he was called Alcides. And she
told him to dwell in Tiryns, serving Eurystheus for twelve years and to per-
form the ten labours imposed on him, and so, she said, when the tasks were
accomplished, he would be immortal.

The story is alluded to even as early as Homer (*Il.* 19.121-33; *Od.* 11.621-6). Hercules lists these and others of his labours at 9.182-98.

15   **orders of his stepmother:** *suae... iussa nouercae*, i.e. the orders of Juno. Normally, both the Latin *nouerca* and the English 'stepmother' refers to a father's new wife who has replaced the children's natural mother. Here, however (and at 9.135 and 181) it is used of Juno in relation to the children of one of her husband's illicit sexual conquests and reminds us of Juno's constant anger in such situations; cf. 6.336. Stepmothers are generally ill thought of, cf. e.g. 1.147, Hor. *Epod.* 5.9. 'orders' *iussa*, is either a further reference to the Labours, seen as the indirect result of Juno's hatred (cf. 9.21-2), or an allusion to Juno's other acts of hostility towards Hercules e.g. the story to be found at Apollod. 2.4.8 (Frazer's translation):
When the child was eight months old, Hera desired the destruction of the
babe and sent two huge serpents to the bed... but Hercules arose and killed
the serpents by strangling them with both his hands.

17   **(he was not yet a god):** Ovid is very fond of these parenthetical asides; cf. 1.591, 597; 2.703; 5.280-2; 6.262-3, 359, 421, 438, 472-3; 7.219, 453-4, 567, 660; 9.53, 55-6, 242, 344, 356-7, 396, 782; 10.424, 557, 562; 11.51, 162, 235-6, 316, 361-2, 437-8, 622, 679-80, 731; 12.76-7, 88, 197 and 200. For a discussion, see Wilkinson, *Ovidiana* 235, M. v. Albrecht, *Die Parenthese in Ovids Metamorphosen und ihre dichterische Funktion*, Hildesheim, 1964.

17-18   This echoes a famous passage in the *Aeneid* where Virgil introduces us to the Tiber (*Aen.* 8.62-3, 77 with West's translation):
>   ego sum pleno quem flumine cernis
>   stringentem ripas et pinguia culta secantem
>   ...
>   corniger Hesperidum fluuius regnator aquarum...
I am that full river whom you see scouring these banks and cutting through
the rich farmland... O hornèd river, king of all the waters of Hesperia...

For the effect, see on 9.6.

19   This line echoes and contrasts with Virgil's account of Aeneas as Lavinia's suitor, e.g. *Aen.* 7.98:
*foreign [*externi*] sons-in-law [*generi*] will come.*
and *Aen.* 7.270:
*that sons-in-law [*generos*] will be here from foreign [*externis*] lands.*

Note that Achelous' credentials seem to be much better than Aeneas'. For a much fuller discussion see Galinsky 95-6.

lands: *oris*; see on 9.254-5.

20   **of your people...of your state:** *popularis...rerum... tuarum*, the language is very political and continues to underline Achelous' superior claims as a suitor to those of Hercules.

21-2   Achelous undercuts Hercules' boasts (9.14-15) that Jupiter was his father and that he has performed his famous labours, by ironically hoping that he might not be unacceptable because he had not incurred Juno's hatred (the inevitable consequence of being, like Hercules, Jupiter's illegitimate son) and had not suffered the imposition of the punishment of the labours (the indirect result, for Hercules, of Juno's hatred; see on 9.14-5). That these points also distinguish Achelous from Aeneas (Juno's particular *bête noire*, see e.g. Virg. *Aen.* 1.8-11) is obvious; for further details see Galinsky 96.

23   **son of Alcmene:** the one fact about his birth that is not in dispute.

27   **While I was speaking thus…already:** *talia dicentem iamdudum*, commentators (e.g. Galinsky 96) note that Virgil uses these same three words to start his description of Dido's angry response to Aeneas' words at a memorable point (*Aen.* 4.362). See above on 9.6.

28   **scarcely:** *non fortiter*, literally 'not strongly'; the litotes is impossible in English; cf. 4.27.

30   **in the fighting…in the speaking:** an attempt at Ovid's jingle, *pugnando…loquendo*.

31   **after boasting:** *magna locutum* (literally 'having spoken big'), a standard expression for boasting, cf. 1.751; 8.396.

32   **I threw…from my body:** it was, of course, standard practice to engage in any gymnastic activity naked; *gymnos* is the Greek for 'naked'.
    green clothing: green is a colour associated with water divinities, (cf. 2.12; 5.575) perhaps, but not necessarily, because of the verdant vegetation commonly found near rivers and lakes (cf. 2.371). See also Virg. *Aen.* 8.33-4, 712-3.

32-4   **my body…my body:** *corpore…membra*; the repetition in the English does not reflect a repetition in the Latin. *corpus* is the standard Latin word for 'body'; *membra* basically means 'limbs' but is frequently used, as here, to mean 'body', see 9.81, *OLD* s.v. 'membrum' 2. See also on 5.55-6; other examples in this volume can be found at 9.67-75, 388-91, 466-7; 10.211-3; 11.203-4, 271-2, 358-9, 467-8, 476-7, 650-2; 12.130-1, 273-5, 587-90.

33   **half-clenched:** *uaras*; a rare word meaning, basically, in the words of *OLD*, 'Bent outwards in different directions but with converging extremities'; it seems to be the technical term for the position of the hands or arms at the beginning of a wrestling match, cf. Stat. *Theb.* 6.851.

34   **at the ready:** *in statione*; a technical military term (cf. *OLD* s.v. 'statio' 5) and a further (see on 9.6) example of Ovid's use of such language in this context. For similar examples, see 1.627; 2.115.

35-6   It was the custom for wrestlers to anoint themselves with oil and then sprinkle themselves or one another with dust so as to improve their grip.

36   **was yellowed…yellow:** *fuluae…flauescit*; the two Latin adjectives, *fuluus* and *flauus* (from which the verb *flauescit* derives) are ultimately cognate and both mean essentially 'yellow'; it is hard to see any differences in Ovid's treatment in the *Metamorphoses*. He uses *flauus* (and *flaueo* and *flauesco*) of 'blond people or gods' (2.749; 3.617; 6.118, 130, 718; 8.275; 9.307, 715; 11.165), 'ears of wheat' (9.689), 'gold' (8.701), 'honey' (1.112), 'a horse' (13.848), 'pigs' (14.97), 'a river' (2.245), 'sand' (9.56; 14.448; 15.722), 'wax' (3.487; 8.275, 670), 'wings' (5.560). He uses *fuluus* of 'ash-wood' (7.678), 'cloud' (3.273), 'gold' (1.115; 10.648; 11.103, 124; 14.345, 395), 'human hair' (12. 273), 'lilies' (10.191), 'a lion' (1.304; 10.551, 698), 'mud' (10.733), 'myrrh' (15.399), 'sand' (2.865; 9.36; 10.716; 11.355, 499), 'wings' (5.546; 6.707; 8.146; 12.524), 'a wolf' (11.771).

37   **flashing:** *micantia*; this word has been much doubted by editors but has attracted no plausible correction. Tarrant has suggested to me that the word might be (or perhaps conceals) a technical term from wrestling, like *uarus* (9.33) and *nexus* (9.58).

40-1   **just like a rock…pound:** Anderson points out the humour of a river god being likened to a rock attacked by pounding waters.

44   **toe to toe:** *cum pede pes* (cf. e.g. Virg. *Aen.* 10.361); literally 'foot to foot', but that is not the English idiom. This device where two forms of a word are put near to one another is known as polyptoton. It is common throughout Latin literature and is a special favourite of Ovid's. I list many examples from book 1-8 in my notes on 1.33 and 5.52. Here should be added 9.45, 74, 80-1, 167, 195-6, 215-6, 250, 260-1, 407, 525, 549-50, 608-9, 725, 731-4, 757, 793; 10.121, 282-3, 286, 293-4, 338, 532, 544; 11.109-117, 125, 222-3, 243-4, 297, 308, 325-6, 435, 523, 559-60, 599, 621, 660, 701, 707; 12.213, 219, 236, 262, 312, 390-1, 395, 443, 456, 482-3, 493, 621. See also Kenney, 460-1.

45   **fingers to fingers and brow to brow:** *digitos digitis et frontem fronte*; the polyptoton continues from the previous line.

46-9 Fighting bull similes are common in Greek and Latin literature, and Bömer collects many. Perhaps the most interesting here is at Virg. *Aen.* 12.715-22 (West's translation):

> *Just as two enemy bulls on the great mountain of Sila or on top of Taburnus bring their horns to bear and charge into battle; the herdsmen stand back in terror, the herd stands silent and afraid, and the heifers low quietly together waiting to see who is to rule the grove, who is to be the leader of the whole herd; meanwhile the bulls are locked together exchanging blow upon blow, gouging horn into hide till their necks and shoulders are awash with blood and all the grove rings with their lowing and groaning.*

See also Skutsch on Ennius *Ann.* pp. 222-3. For the deliberately inappropriate echoing of a famous epic simile, see on 9.6. Ovid had earlier adapted the same simile at *Amores* 2.12.25-6.

47 **wife:** *coniunx*; Ovid seems to have been the first to use *coniunx* for animals (see Bömer); the usage is clearly tinged with humour and may be in imitation of earlier similar uses of *maritus* (husband), see Nisbet-Hubbard on Hor. *Od.* 1.17.7.

49 **victory of so great a realm:** *tanti uictoria regni*; both in the Latin and the English, the expressions are slightly strained, but with a clear meaning. Ovid is alluding to Ennius' account of the competition between Romulus and Remus for the control of Rome: *utri magni uictoria sit data regni* ('to which of them should be given the victory of the great realm') *Annales* 1.83 (Skutsch), 1.88 (Vahlen), 1.91 (Warmington) (= Cic. *de Diu.* 1.107-8); Skutsch (p. 231) comments:

> *a most unusual expression... Ov. Met. 9.49* tanti uictoria regni *is the only other example and conclusively proves Ovid's indebtedness to Ennius.*

Achelous' style continues to be very pompous.

53-7 **(I am determined...the truth)...(for I do not...falsehoods):** see on 9.17.

57 **streaming:** *fluentia*; a suitable metaphor for a river-god.

58 **hold:** *nexus*; another technical term from wrestling, cf. 6.242, see on 9.33, 37.

60-1 **my knee was forced to the ground:** *tellus pressa genu nostro*: literally 'the ground was pressed down by my knee'; there is a similar expression but in a wholly non-violent context at 6.346-7.

61 **bit upon the sand:** an echo of Virgil's *humum... ore momordit* (*Aen.* 11.418) itself an echo of Hom. *Il.* 2.418. Ovid borrows an epic formula for violent death (English 'bit the dust') for this more trivial sense and this far from epic context; see on 9.6.

62 **my own skills:** mutability was a common characteristic of water divinities as early as Homer's Proteus (*Od.* 4.394-461); see on 2.9. For Achelous in particular, see Easterling on Sophocles *Trach.* 10-14, 12-14.

63-4 **manly strength...man:** Anderson observes:

> *...to exploit the basic sense of* uir-tus *['man-liness'] and suggest that Achelous, not a man of course, is less than manly in his godhood...* elaborque uiro *['and <I> slipped away from the man'] 63: god escapes from man only by utilizing his subhuman ability and becoming a snake!*

66 **the Tirynthian:** Hercules, whose parents, Amphitryon and Alcmene, had been expelled from Tiryns before going as exiles to Thebes (Apollod. 2.4.6; see also on 9.304); Hercules was also indelibly associated with Eurystheus of Tiryns; see on 9.14-15; 7.410. The first extant Latin examples of this usage appear to be Virg. *Aen.* 7.662, 8.228; but see e.g. Callim. *Hymn* 3.146 where Heracles is referred to as the 'Tirynthian anvil'.

67 **the labour of my cradle:** *cunarum labor*; for the story, see Apollod. 2.4.8 quoted in the note on 9.13. This was not, of course, one of the Labours of Hercules (see on 9.14-15), but I have followed Ovid in using the word normally associated with them.

67-75 **snakes...serpents...snake...hydra...snakes...snake:** *angues ... dracones ... serpens ... echidnae ... colubris ... anguem*; Latin has a much richer vocabulary for 'snakes' than English does. See on 9.32-4.

69 **Lernaean hydra:** to kill the Lernaean hydra was the second of the labours imposed on Hercules by Eurystheus (see on 9.14-15); for its point here, cf. Apollod. 2.5.2 (Frazer's translation):

> As a second labour he ordered him to kill the Lernaean hydra. That crea-
> ture, bred in the swamp of Lerna, used to go forth into the plain and ravage
> both the cattle and the country. Now the hydra had a huge body, with nine
> heads, eight mortal, but the middle one immortal...Nor could he effect
> anything by smashing its heads with his club, for as fast as one head was
> smashed there grew up two...he...called for help on Iolaus who, by setting
> fire to a piece of the neighbouring wood and burning the roots of the heads
> with the brands, prevented them from sprouting. Having thus got the better
> of the sprouting heads, he chopped off the immortal head, and buried it, and
> put a heavy rock on it...But the body of the Hydra he slit up and dipped his
> arrows in the gall. However, Eurystheus said that this labour should not be
> reckoned among the ten because he had not got the better of the hydra by
> himself, but with the help of Iolaus.

As will emerge, that version is far less glorious than Hercules' account here.

71 **out of the number of its companions:** *de comitum numero*; some manuscripts read a much less plausible *centum* 'one hundred' for *comitum* 'of its companions'. The reading lies behind many translations from Golding's on, as well as Frazer on Apollod. 2.5.2.

74 **subdued...was subdued:** for the polyptoton, see on 9.44.

dispatched: *peremi*; most manuscripts read *reduxi* 'led back', but the sense required is 'killed'. Suggestions more palaeographically plausible have been made, but none that gives a satisfactory sense. *peremi* has slight manuscript support and was adopted by Heinsius. I adopt it as the best stopgap available.

76 **borrowed:** *precaria*; so Golding. This is the only example of the word in Ovid. Its basic sense is 'obtained by prayer' but it is generally used to mean 'That is given as a favour, that is held or used on sufferance, that depends on the pleasure or mercy of others' (*OLD* s.v. 1); *OLD* offers a developed sense (s.v. 1b) 'not properly one's own, borrowed', and assigns it to this passage. While Anderson is surely wrong to claim 'It suggests...that Achelous secured this snake form by praying to an external power' (for the narrative excludes that), he is surely right to detect a sense of instability inherent in the situation, so that Achelous' tenure of the snake form is no more secure than it would have been if he had won it by prayer from a capricious divinity.

78 **of my neck:** note the enjambment, the emphatic effect produced by placing the last word of a sentence as the first word of a line, which is how I use the term. Some, however, define the term 'enjambment' less strictly and will include examples where the sentence ends with the second or even third word of a line. Ovid has put *inicit* ('he clapped') into the enjambment, but to do so in the translation would have produced an intolerably awkward sentence. See also on 5.420. Cf. 9.211, 319, 325; 10.181; 11.350; 12.240, 289, 298, 346, 371, 379, 431, 464.

81 **bull...bull's:** *tauri...tauro* (80-1); for the polyptoton, see on 9.44.

body: *membra*; see on 9.32-4.

82 **muscles:** *toris*; the normal meaning of *torus* in Ovid is 'bed' (e.g. 9.702), especially 'marriage bed' (e.g. 10.268) or 'funeral couch' (e.g. 9.503). This meaning seems to arise from the similarity between the bolster of a bed and the ridge of muscle behind a bull's neck (see 2.854).

86 **from my mutilated forehead:** *truncaque a fronte*; the phrase is repeated from and explains 9.2.

mutilated: *trunca*; the adjective is used proleptically (i.e. in anticipation), the forehead was mutilated when the horn had been torn from it. The usage is less common in English, but consider, 'Dig a deep hole'.

Note that Achelous passes over the fact that his defeat entailed the loss of Deïanira. When Ovid himself resumes as narrator (9.89ff.), the focus soon changes to Hercules and Deïanira.

88   *Bona Copia*; the Cornucopia, see Hor. *Carm. Saec.* 60.

90   **girt-up in Diana's style:** cf. 1.695.

92   **autumn, that is glad fruits:** *autumnum et...felicia poma*; it is very daring of Ovid to use *autumnus* ('autumn') to mean 'the autumnal fruits' (see *OLD* s.v. 2), and he softens the effect by explaining it immediately; for this use of *et*, see *OLD* s.v. 11.

94   **the young men:** Theseus, Pirithous, Lelex, and 'the others deemed worthy of a like honour' (8.566-9).

94-6   **they did not wait...for...the waters to subside:** they were, presumably, too impatient or too embarrassed to follow Achelous' advice at 8.550-9.

98-133 *Hercules, Deïanira and Nessus*

The earliest extant account is Sophocles *Trachiniae* 555-77 (Storr's translation, slightly adapted; Deïanira is speaking):

> *'Stored in an urn of brass I long have kept a keepsake*   555
> *of the old-world monster; this the shaggy-breasted Nessus gave*
> *to me while yet a girl, and from his wounded side*
> *I took it as he lay at point of death;*
> *Nessus who ferried wayfarers for hire*
> *across the deep Evenus in his arms,*   560
> *without the help of oar or sail. I too*
> *when first I met with Heracles, a bride*
> *assigned him by my sire, I too was borne*
> *on his broad shoulders, and in mid-stream he*
> *touched me with wanton hands. I shrieked aloud,*   565
> *he turned, the son of Zeus, and straight let fly*
> *a winged shaft that, whizzing in the air,*
> *pierced to the lungs. Faint with approaching death*
> *the Centaur spake: "Daughter of Oeneus old,*
> *this profit of my ferrying at least, as last of all I've ferried,*   570
> *shall be thine, if thou wilt heed me. Gather with thy hands*
> *the clotted gore that curdles round my wound,*
> *just where the Hydra, Lerna's monstrous breed,*
> *has tinged the barbèd arrow with her gall.*
> *Thus shalt thou have a charm to bind the heart*   575
> *of Heracles, and never shall he look*
> *on wife or maid to love her more than thee." '*

See also on 9.1-97.

100   **bulrushes:** *harundine*; cf. 9.3.

101   **but you, fierce Nessus:** This type of apostrophe is discussed by Fränkel (214). It was a favourite Hellenistic device, sometimes to heighten the pathos; here, perhaps, its function is slightly ironical. For other examples, see 5.111ff., 242-7, 8.128, 9.229, 447, 581, 649-51, 715, 790-1; 10.69, 120-5, 162, 185, 318, 542-3; 11.236-44, 415; 12.296, 312, 393, 421, 610. Austin has good discussions in his notes on Virg. *Aen.* 2.429 and 4.27.

103   **native walls:** *patrios...muros*, literally 'his father's or fatherland's walls', and so either Tiryns (see on 9.66) or Thebes (see on 9.13, 304).

104   **Jove's son:** Hercules, see on 9.14.
           Euenus: this river is only a few miles east of the Achelous.

109   **and...he said:** the slightly awkward placing is an attempt to reflect something of Ovid's idiosyncratic trick of joining direct speech to narrative by attaching the connective *-que* not to the verb of speaking, but to the first word of the speech. See on 1.456; 5.195.

he: Nessus.

112 **the...Calydonian:** Deïanira; her father was Oeneus (see Soph. *Trach.* 569 quoted in the note on 9.98-133; see also on 8.543); for Oeneus ruling in Calydon, see 8.270-5, itself a close imitation of Hom. *Il.* 9.529-35.

the Aonian: Hercules; only Ovid refers to him so. Aonia was another name for Boeotia, and it was in Boeotian Thebes that Hercules was born, see on 9.13, 304.

113-4 **lion skin...club...bow:** Hercules' traditional accoutrements found both in literature and in art.

115 This line is even more elliptical in the Latin. Hercules' point is that since he has made such a good start with Achelous, he expects to encounter no difficulty with this new river.

117 Golding's paraphrase of the line brings out its implication:
   But through the roughest of the streame he cuts his way apace.

120 **breach his trust:** *fallere depositum*; a technical banking phrase; for a similar use of the term in an unlikely context, see 5.480.

121 **two-formed:** *biformis*, used of a centaur also at 2.664.

123 **your father's wheel:** Ixion's wheel; for the story see Apollod. *Epit.* 1.20 (Frazer's translation):

   Ixion fell in love with Hera and attempted to force her; and when Hera reported it, Zeus, wishing to know if the thing were so, made a cloud [Nephele] in the likeness of Hera and laid it beside him; and when Ixion boasted that he had enjoyed the favours of Hera, Zeus bound him to a wheel, on which he is whirled by winds through the air; such is the penalty he pays. And the cloud, impregnated by Ixion, gave birth to Centaurus.

For other details, see on 4.461 and Austin on Virg. *Aen.* 6.601.

126 **with a wounding:** *uulnere*; literally, 'with a wound', i.e. 'with a wound-causing weapon', see on 5.141; 7.782, *OLD* s.v. 1c.

129-30 **mixed with foul Lernaean poison:** for the Lernaean poison on Hercules' arrows, see on 9.69.

131 **But I shall not die unavenged:** *neque enim moriemur inulti*; another pastiche of Virgil (see on 9.6): at *Aen.* 2.670, a particularly defiant speech by Aeneas as Troy falls ends with the words: *numquam omnes hodie moriemur inulti* ('But we shall not all die unavenged'); at *Aen.* 4.659, almost the last words of Dido are: *moriemur inultae, sed moriamur* ('I shall die unavenged, but let me die'); Muecke (on Hor. *Sat.* 2.8.34) reminds us that Ovid was not the first to parody these lines.

134-272 *The death and deification of Hercules*

This story is the subject of Sophocles *Trachiniae*. Where appropriate, reference will be made to the details of the play. However, the outline is told conveniently at Apollod. 2.7.7 (Frazer's translation):

   On his [Hercules'] arrival at Trachis he mustered an army to attack Oechalia, wishing to punish Eurytus [see also on 9.356]...he slew Eurytus and his sons and took the city. After burying those of his own side who had fallen...he pillaged the city and led Iole captive. And having put in at Cenaeum, a headland of Euboea, he built an altar of Cenaean Zeus. Intending to offer sacrifice, he sent the herald Lichas to Trachis to fetch fine raiment. From him Deianira learned about Iole, and fearing that Hercules might love that damsel more than herself, she supposed that the spilt blood of Nessus was in truth a love-charm, and with it she smeared the tunic. So Hercules put it on and proceeded to offer sacrifice. But no sooner was the tunic warmed than the poison of the hydra began to corrode his skin; and on that he lifted Lichas by the feet, hurled him down from the headland, and tore off the tunic, which clung to his body, so that his flesh was torn away with it. In such a sad plight he was carried on shipboard to Trachis: and

> *Deianira, on learning what had happened, hanged herself. But Hercules,*
> *after charging Hyllus his elder son by Deianira, to marry Iole when he*
> *came of age, proceeded to Mount Oeta, in the Trachinian territory, and*
> *there constructed a pyre, mounted it, and gave orders to kindle it... While*
> *the pyre was burning, it is said that a cloud passed under Hercules and with*
> *a peal of thunder wafted him up to heaven. Thereafter he obtained immor-*
> *tality...*

Ovid's treatment of this story has given rise to much controversy; some have seen it as a more or less incompetent attempt at sublimity; others see it as a deliberately humorous undercutting of a famous theme. Galinsky (99-105) gives a characteristically robust exposition of the second view, but he also pays due attention to other opinions.

135 had filled the lands and the hatred: an especially striking syllepsis which warns us not to take the passage too seriously. In context, 'had filled the hatred' must be made to mean 'had satisfied the hatred', a sense only slightly easier to extract from *implerant* than from 'had filled', but see *OLD* s.v. 10a. Fränkel (197) discusses Ovid's use of syllepsis; see also on 2.312-3; 6.476-7; 9.279, 409, 612, 633; 10.50, 474; 10.557; 11.146-7, 12.5-6, 156. Gregory takes *odium* as nominative so that it is Hercules' acts and Juno's hatred that filled the lands, but this gives a much more feeble point.

stepmother: *nouercae*, Juno, see on 9.15.

136-7 Oechalia...Cenaean Jove: when, in the *Trachiniae*, Deïanira asks Lichas where Hercules is, he replies (237-8, Storr's translation, slightly adapted):

> *Upon a headland in Euboea, where he marks out*
> *altars to Cenaean Zeus, and dedicates the fertile lands around.*

And when she asks him why, he replies (240-1):

> *'Tis for a vow he made when he went forth to conquer*
> *and despoil Oechalia of these women whom thou see'st.*

Lichas suppresses the reason why which had emerged a little earlier (351-5):

> *'Twas for this maiden's* [Iole's] *sake (I heard the man,*
> *and many witnesses were by, declare it)*
> *that Heracles laid prostrate in the dust*
> *Oechalia's battlements and Eurytus.*
> *Love was his leader, love alone inspired*
> *this doughty deed.*

In Ovid's version it is Rumour and not Lichas who brings the story to Deïanira.

137 Rumour: *Fama*; in a celebrated Virgilian passage (*Aen.* 4.173-97), a personified *Fama* brings to Iarbas the explosive news that Dido is becoming deeply involved with Aeneas. Once again, Ovid cannot resist a pastiche of a predecessor (see on 9.6); for the details, see on 9.138-9. For a further development, see 12.39-63.

138-9 adding falsehood to truth is her delight: *quae uersis addere falsa gaudet*; cf. Virg. *Aen.* 4.188: *tam ficti prauique tenax quam nuntia ueri* 'holding fast to her lies and distortions as often as she tells the truth' (West's translation); also *Aen.* 4.190: *gaudens et pariter facta atque infecta canebat* 'she was taking delight...in fact and fiction mixed in equal parts' (West's translation). Most modern editors place a comma after Virgil's *gaudens* and take it with what precedes; that is also how West takes it, a fact I have concealed by quoting him only in part. The Ovidian imitation, however, may suggest that Ovid, at least, interpreted Virgil the other way. Ovid returns to the same idea at 12.54. For a discussion, see Austin on *Aen.* 4.190.

140 Amphitryoniades: i.e. Amphitryon's son, Hercules, see on 9.13.

141 She loved him, but believed it: *credit amans*; the contrast is implicit in the Latin, explicit in the English.

of a new passion: *Venerisque nouae*; literally, 'of a new Venus'; but this sort of metonymy is much rarer in English than in Latin; cf. 2.68; 3.123, 323, 437, 540; 4.258; 6.460, 488;

7.104, 140, 450; 8.7, 292; 9.251, 263, 283-4, 639, 728 (where the same phrase is used rather differently), 739; 10.74, 78, 80, 324; 11.112, 304, 784, 12.24, 198, 379, 578, 610.

144   **wench:** this is the word I have generally used for *paelex*, whose basic meaning, to quote *OLD*, is: 'A mistress installed as a rival or in addition to a wife'. In Ovid, however, the word seems frequently to have a jocular connotation, cf. 1.622, 7.524, only sometimes a pejorative one, as here and at 4.235, 277. While 'wench' does not necessarily carry the connotation of 'mistress', it does cover the range from cheerful ribaldry to moral disapprobation. For a different solution, see on 6.606.

149   **Meleager:** Oeneus was father both of Meleager (Hom. *Il.* 9.543) and of Deïanira (Soph. *Trach.* 6). Was she one of the Meleagrides (8.526-46)? Here, she is remembering Meleager's violent conduct on behalf of Atalanta (8.437-44).

155   **she gave...her own grief:** *luctus...suos tradit*: the meaning is clear but the expression stretches both languages; hence Miller explains with: 'she commits the cause of her future woe.' At 1.654-5, there is a similar but less arresting example. The other passages quoted by *OLD* (s.v. 2b) are even less remarkable.

155-7   **ignorant...not knowing...unwitting:** *ignaroque...nescia...inscius*; Ovid goes out of his way to stress the innocence of both Deïanira and Lichas.

159   **He:** i.e. Hercules; see on 9.279. In both the Latin and the English it gradually becomes plain that the story has suddenly moved on in typically Ovidian fashion, and that the scene has moved back to Cenaeum.

161-4   **evil...sufferings:** *mali...malis*; the repetition of this very common word in two of its senses is without significance; see on 10.443-4.

162   **Herculean:** *Herculeus*; for a discussion of this use of adjectives derived from proper names, see Fordyce on *Aen.* 7.1.

163   **with his usual virtue:** *solita...uirtute*; there was a long tradition of the deepest respect for Hercules as a semi-divine human saviour. The word *uirtus*, literally 'manliness' and therefore often meaning no more than 'courage', can and often does have a deep spiritual resonance unattainable by its English derivative or by any other single word. Accordingly, there is something irreverent about this line, particularly its allusion to Hercules' 'usual virtue'; the point is further brought out by the obvious allusion to Virgil's description of Hercules at a particularly poignant moment (*Aen.* 10.464-5, Harrison's translation; his note is also helpful):

> *Hercules heard the youth, and held back a great groan in the depths of his heart* [*magnumque sub imo corde* premit gemitum].

165   **Oeta:** see on 9.134-272.

167   **it was pulled, it pulled:** *trahitur, trahit*; for the polyptoton, see on 9.44.

170-1   Editors compare Homer's simile to describe the boiling of Polyphemus' eye when Odysseus and his men plunged the burning stake into it (*Od.* 9.391-4, Lattimore's translation):

> *As when a man who works as a blacksmith plunges a screaming*
> *great ax blade or plane into cold water, treating it*
> *for temper, since this is the way steel is made strong, even*
> *so Cyclops' eye sizzled...*

See on 9.6. The simile returns at 12.276-9.

175   **raising...stars:** *tollens...palmas*; cf. 6.368.

176   **Saturnia:** Juno, Saturn's daughter; cf. e.g. Hom. *Il.* 16.431. For the history of *Saturnia* for 'Juno', see Skutsch on Ennius *Annales* 1.53.

176-8   These lines are taken largely from 6.280-2 and 276.

179   **sick as it is:** sc. 'my life'. The Latin is almost as awkward as the English. The question is whether it is too awkward and jejune to be Ovidian. The translation is intended to work with or without this disputed line.

180   **labours:** *laboribus*; both in the sense of 'toil', 'suffering' and an allusion to his famous Labours, cf. 9.14, 22, 67.

181 stepmother: *nouercam,* Juno, see on 9.15.

182-98 Hercules, in his agony, contrasts this defeat with many of his previous triumphs much as he did at Sophocles *Trachiniae* 1058-61, 1091-1102. For a sensitive analysis of the differences between Sophocles' treatment and Ovid's, see Galinsky 100ff.

182-4 Busiris...Antaeus: the stories are told by Apollodorus, but in the reverse order (2.5.11, Frazer's translation):

> he *[*Hercules*] traversed Libya. That country was then ruled by Antaeus, son of Poseidon, who used to kill strangers by forcing them to wrestle. Being forced to wrestle with him, Hercules hugged him, lifted him aloft, broke and killed him; for when he touched earth so it was that he waxed stronger, wherefore some said that he was a son of Earth.*
>
> *After Libya he traversed Egypt. That country was then ruled by Busiris... This Busiris used to sacrifice strangers on an altar of Zeus in accordance with a certain oracle. For Egypt was visited with dearth for nine years, and Phrasius, a learned seer who had come from Cyprus, said that the dearth would cease if they slaughtered a stranger man in honour of Zeus every year. Busiris began by slaughtering the seer himself and continued to slaughter the strangers who landed. So Hercules also was seized and haled to the altars, but he burst his bonds and slew both Busiris and his son Amphidamas.*

Frazer's notes give full histories of both myths.

183 his mother's nourishment: the support he was thought to gain from his mother, Earth. Note the arresting image of snatching the earth from Antaeus instead of the more obvious image of snatching Antaeus from the earth.

184-5 the triple form of the Spanish shepherd: Geryon; according to Apollod. 2.5.10, Hercules' tenth labour (see on 9.14-5) was to fetch Geryon's cattle. The story is alluded to as early as Hesiod (*Theog.* 287-94, Evelyn-White's translation):

> But Chrysaor was joined in love to Callirhoë, the daughter of glorious Ocean, and begot three-headed Geryones. Him mighty Heracles slew in sea-girt Erythea by his shambling oxen on that day when he drove the wide-browed oxen to holy Tiryns, and had crossed the ford of Ocean and killed Orthus and Eurytion the herdsman in the dim stead out beyond glorious Ocean.

Note that the triple form and the setting in the extreme west are already established.

185 your triple form, Cerberus: also alluded to in Sophocles' account of this speech (*Trach.* 1097-9 and see Easterling's note). Hercules' twelfth labour was to bring the three-headed dog up from Hades. The story is alluded to as early as Homer (*Il.* 8.368, *Od.* 11.622-6) and is told in detail by Apollodorus (2.5.12 and see Frazer's notes). Hesiod (*Theog.* 304-11) is the earliest extant source for the name, but he gives him fifty heads whereas Virgil (*Aen.* 6.417-25) offers the more usual three. For further details, see on 4.450; 7.414.

186 the mighty bull: see Apollod. 2.5.7 (Frazer's translation):

> The seventh labour he enjoined on him *[see on 9.14-5] was to bring the Cretan Bull. Acusilaus says that this was the bull that ferried across Europa for 'Zeus [see 2.843-75]; but some say that it was the bull that Poseidon sent up from the sea when Minos promised to sacrifice to Poseidon what should appear out of the sea. And they say that when he saw the beauty of the bull he sent it away to the herds and sacrificed another to Poseidon; at which the god was angry and made the bull savage.*

For a fuller version, see Apollod. 3.1.3-4 quoted in my note on 8.131.

187 Elis: see Apollod. 2.5.5 (Frazer's translation):

> The fifth labour he laid on him was to carry out the dung of the cattle of Augeas in a single day. Now Augeas was king of Elis...

Augeas was known as a horseman as early as Hom. *Il.* 11.695-701; there, however, there is no allusion to this story.

the Stymphalian waters: see Apollod. 2.5.6 (Frazer's translation):

> *The sixth labour he enjoined on him was to chase away the Stymphalian birds. Now at the city of Stymphalus in Arcadia was the lake called Stymphalian, embosomed in a deep wood. To it countless birds had flocked for refuge, fearing to be preyed upon by the wolves...*

188   **the Parthenian copse:** see Apollod. 2.5.3 (Frazer's translation):

> *As a third labour he ordered him to bring the Cerynitian hind alive to Mycenae. Now the hind was at Oenoë; it had golden horns and was sacred to Artemis; so wishing neither to kill nor wound it, Hercules hunted it a whole year. But when, weary with the chase, the beast took refuge on the mountain called Artemisius, and then passed to the river Ladon, Hercules shot it just as it was about to cross the stream...*

Oenoë was a small town a little to the west of Argos, Artemisius was a mountain a little further south, while the Parthenian mountain was in the same region but further south still. The river Ladon was considerably further west in Arcadia.

virtue: *uirtute*, see on 9.163.

189   **baldric...Thermodon:** see Apollod. 2.5.9 (Frazer's translation):

> *The ninth labour he enjoined on Hercules was to bring the belt of Hippolyte. She was queen of the Amazons, who dwelt about the river Thermodon...*

For the Amazons and the Thermodon, see also 12.611, Virg. *Aen.* 11.659-60.

190   **the apples...snake:** also alluded to in Sophocles' account of this speech (*Trach.* 1099-1100, where see Easterling). The apples of the Hesperides appear as early as Hesiod (*Theog.* 215-6), and are alluded to at 4.631-62. In particular, the fulfilment of the prophecy at 4.644-5 is referred to at 9.198. There were two stories neatly presented by Euripides (*H.F.* 394-407, Barlow's translation):

> *Then he travelled to the gardens of the West with their singing maidens to pluck the golden apples from the fruit-bearing boughs, having killed the fiery-backed dragon which guarded it with its monstrous spiralling coils. He penetrated the remotest parts of the high seas and made them safe to the ships of men.*
>
> *Coming to the house of Atlas, he stretched out his arms beneath the zenith of the sky and with his strength held firm the gods' starry palaces.*

Note that, like Ovid, Euripides seems not to connect the two stories. Ovid alludes to the first here and to the second at 198. Bömer (on 9.198) gives further details. The version which connects the two stories is to be found at Apollod. 2.5.11 (Frazer's translation):

> *When the labours had been performed in eight years and a month, Eurystheus ordered Hercules, as an eleventh labour, to fetch golden apples from the Hesperides, for he did not acknowledge the labour of the cattle of Augeas nor that of the hydra... They were... guarded by an immortal dragon with a hundred heads... with it the Hesperides also were on guard... Now Prometheus had told Hercules not to go himself after the apples but to send Atlas, first relieving him of the burden of the sphere...*

191   **Nor could the Centaurs...nor could the boar that ravaged Arcadia:** the Latin repeats the word for 'me', *mihi...mi*, but there is no way of doing that neatly in the translation, so this repetition of 'could' has been substituted. It joins the story of the killing of the centaurs to that of the Erymanthian Boar just as they were joined by Sophocles in his account of Hercules' speech (*Trach.* 1095-7, Storr's translation):

> *...overcame that twy-form multitude, half man, half horse,*
> *rude, lawless, savage, unapproachable,*
> *unmatched in fight; and the Erymanthian Boar.*

For the full story, see Apollod. 2.5.4 (Frazer's translation):

> As a fourth labour he ordered him to bring the Erymanthian Boar alive;
> now that animal ravaged Psophis, sallying from a mountain which they call
> Erymanthus. So passing through Pholoe he was entertained by the centaur
> Pholus... He set roast meat before Hercules, while he himself ate his meat
> raw. When Hercules called for wine, he said he feared to open the jar which
> belonged to the centaurs in common. But Hercules... opened it, and not long
> afterwards, scenting the smell, the centaurs arrived at the cave of Pholus,
> armed with rocks and firs. The first who dared to enter... were repelled by
> Hercules with a shower of brands, and the rest of them he shot and pursued
> as far as Malea... And when he had chased the boar with shouts from a
> certain thicket, he drove the exhausted animal into deep snow, trapped it
> and brought it to Mycenae.

Erymanthus and Psophis were both in Arcadia; Malea was the promontory at the end of the
south-east corner of the Peloponnese.

192   **hydra:** the Lernaean hydra, also alluded to in Sophocles' version of this speech (*Trach.* 1094); the story is told at 9.70-4, see also the note on 9.69.

           twinned strength: *geminas... uires*; cf. 'twin heirs' *gemino... herede* (9.72).

194   **the Thracian's horses:** for the story, see Apollod. 2.5.8 (Frazer's translation):

> The eighth labour he enjoined on him was to bring the mares of Diomedes
> the Thracian to Mycenae. Now this Diomedes was a son of Ares and
> Cyrene, and he was king of the Bistones, a very war-like Thracian people,
> and he owned man-eating mares...

Apollodorus continues with a version far more complex than Ovid's; Frazer's notes discuss
the various forms the story took.

195-6 **I saw and, having seen:** *uidi uisaque*; for the polyptoton, see on 9.44; here, it emphasises
how instantaneous was Hercules' action once he had seen the revolting spectacle.

197   **the Nemean monster:** The Nemean lion first appears at Hesiod *Theog.* 327; for this story,
traditionally the first of Hercules' labours and also alluded to in Sophocles' account of this
speech (*Trach.* 1092-4 with Easterling's note), see Apollod. 2.5.1 (Frazer's translation):

> First Eurystheus ordered him to bring the skin of the Nemean lion; now that
> was an invulnerable beast begotten by Typhon... And having come to Nemea
> and tracked the lion, he first shot an arrow at him, but when he perceived
> that the beast was invulnerable, he heaved up his club and made after him.
> And when the lion took refuge in a cave with two mouths, Hercules built up
> the one entrance and came in upon the beast from the other, and putting his
> arm around its neck held it tight till he had choked it...

Nemea is a valley in the Argolis about half way between Corinth and Argos.

198   **on this neck did I carry the sky:** see on 9.190.

201   **manly strength:** *uirtute*; see on 9.163.

208   **trying again:** *retemptantem*; cf. 9.166-7.

210   **stretching out his arms:** the standard gesture of supplication often, though not here, exploited by Ovid for pathetic, humorous or grotesque effect; cf. e.g. 1.635-6; 2.487; 3.240-1, 723-4; 11.39, 83, 131. For a full discussion, see my note on 2.487.

211-29 Lichas' metamorphosis into a reef is probably not (*pace* Galinsky 102) an Ovidian invention, see Forbes Irving 294.

211   **caught sight of:** *aspicit*; the translation has not been able fully to reproduce the effect of
Ovid's enjambment (see on 9.78) of the word; but an enjambment of sorts has been produced with 'crag'.

215   **words of excuse:** *uerba excusantia*; Anderson's comment is apt:

> Ovid lets this phrase stand for the conventional speech which could be produced for the situation.

215-6 **spoke…spoke:** *dicit; dicentem*, for the polyptoton, see on 9.44. Its effect (cf. 9.195-6) is to dramatize the narrative; Hercules did not wait to hear what Lichas had to say.

216 **put hands to knees:** i.e. 'put Lichas' hands to Hercules' knees'; Latin is much more tolerant of this sort of ambiguity than English is. This is the supreme gesture of supplication; the most famous Homeric examples, are, perhaps, when Thetis supplicates Zeus (*Il.* 1.500-1) or Priam supplicates Achilles (*Il.* 24.478).

217 **spun him three or four times round:** *terque quaterque rotatum*, the ultimate origin of this phrase is Hom. *Od.* 5.306 where Odysseus, in the expectation of immediate drowning, claims that those Greeks who fell before Troy were '*three times and four* more happy' than he was; Virgil (*Aen.* 1.94) picks it up and puts it into Aeneas' mouth when he too thinks he is about to drown. These elevated associations clearly add to the humour here. For similar uses of the phrase, cf. 2.49; 6.133; 12.133, 288, Hor. *Od.* 1.31.13, Virg. *G.* 1.410. At 4.517-8, Ovid's language is very similar in his description of Athamas dashing his baby son Learchus against a rock; there, however, the child is spun *bis terque* 'two or three times'.

218 **catapult:** the word *tormentum* is a general term for war engines, such as the *ballista*, which projected missiles at an enemy, especially at cities under siege.

219-22 The passage plays with Lucretius' descriptions of the formation of snow and hail (6.494-7, 527-9):

> nunc age, quo pacto pluuius <u>concrescat</u> in altis
> nubibus umor in terras demissus ut imber
> decidat, expediam…
> cetera quae sursum crescunt sursum creantur,
> et quae <u>concrescunt</u> in nubibus, omnia, prorsum
> omnia, <u>nix</u> uenti <u>grando</u> <u>gelidae</u>que pruinae…

or (in Bailey's translation):

> *Come now, in what manner the rainy moisture gathers together in the high clouds, and how the shower falls shot down upon the earth, I will unfold…*
> *All other things which grow above and are brought to being above, and which gather together in the clouds, all, yes all of them, snow, winds, hail, chill hoar-frosts…*

Anderson (on 9.219) makes the interesting point that normally a missile sent through the air would be expected to heat up, not cool down; he compares 14.825-6, itself based on Lucr. 6.306-8. He makes the further point that *pendens* 'hanging' is hardly appropriate for a missile travelling at speed; instead it takes us from the speeding Lichas to the still petrified figure, about to fall to earth like frozen snow. Characteristically, Ovid explores the physics of metamorphosis in some detail.

221 **swirled around:** *rotatis*; the translation conceals the echo of *rotatum* at 9.217, there rendered 'spun…round'. English has no word suitable for both contexts.

223 **through the void:** *per inane*, a term which maintains the Epicurean flavour of this passage, cf. e.g. Lucr. 1.330.

229 **But you, famed offspring of Jupiter:** Hercules, of course; for the apostrophe, see on 9.101.

232 **again:** Hercules himself had sacked Troy on an earlier occasion; cf. 11.211-20 and the note on 11.194-220.

234 **put beneath:** i.e. 'beneath the pyre'; the word is more easily supplied in the Latin because Ovid is relying on a specialised use of *subdo*; cf. e.g. Lucr. 6.1285, also a description of igniting a funeral pyre.

pile: *agger*; the pyre, of course, but Ovid has chosen a less specific word.

233 **Poeas' son:** Philoctetes (see Soph. *Phil.* 5); his story is most familiar from Sophocles' play. After putting the torch to Hercules' pyre and being rewarded with Hercules' arms (Soph. *Phil.* 670, 801-3), he joined the expedition against Troy but was left on Lemnos before they arrived (Hom. *Il.* 2.716-25); later, as even Homer hints (*Il.* 2.725), the Greeks rescued him and took him back to Troy because of a prophecy that only his arms could bring them victory.

235-6 strewed...reclined: *sternis...recumbis*; the standard terms for strewing the coverlets over the *triclinium* and for reclining on it at a Roman dinner.

Nemean skin...club: see on 9.113-4, 197.

241 the earth's defender: *uindice terrae*; ancient notions of Hercules were very varied from the earliest times. Here we have the sublime saviour of mankind, the divine man, much admired in Stoic thought. See Reid pp. 515-6.

242 (for he had noticed it): see on 9.17.

Saturnian: Jupiter (Zeus) was the son of Saturn (Kronos), see on 5.368, 8.703.

245 ruler and father of a grateful people: the 'people' here is the population of heaven, the gods; cf. 2.848. The formula comes from Homeric usage, e.g. *Il.* 1.544, by way of Ennius, e.g. *Ann.* 203 (Skutsch), and Virgil, e.g. *Aen.* 1.65.

247 this: i.e. 'their favour'.

250 has conquered...will conquer: *uicit uincet*; for the polyptoton, see on 9.44.

251 Vulcan: i.e. 'fire' see on 9.141.

251-2 except in his mother's part: Hercules has a divine inheritance from Jupiter, his father, and a mortal one from Alcmene, his mother.

254-5 heavenly domains: *caelestibus oris*; translators tend to render *oris* as 'shores', but, though the word can have that meaning (e.g. at 3.597, *OLD* s.v. 2) it also regularly means 'region', 'district' (e.g. at 8.788; 9.19; 10.2, *OLD* s.v. 3), or 'rim', 'border' (e.g. at 3.480, *OLD* s.v. 1), or 'a division of the world or universe' (e.g. at 10.26, *OLD* s.v. 4). 'The shores of heaven' is not a concept that would have been recognized at Ovid's time.

256-8 anyone...anyone...he...he: the Latin too firmly identifies the hypothetical objector as male; Juno, however is correctly in no doubt that she is the target of these remarks (9.260-1 and see on 9.14-5); the gender is a fig-leaf only.

259 the king's wife: *regia coniunx*; here, of course, Juno, wife of the king of heaven. Both in Latin and English, the phrase would more naturally refer to a human queen as it does at 13.483 and Virg. *Aen.* 7.56. Twice elsewhere (6.332, 14.592), Ovid uses it of Juno; at 10.46 he uses the phrase of Proserpina.

259-6 seemed...seemed: the repetition is not Ovid's but is required for the sake of clarity in the translation.

260-1 without a morose...morosely: *non duro, duro*; this is not a polyptoton, because the repeated word is in exactly the same grammatical form; however, the effect is not dissimilar to that produced by polyptoton, see on 9.44.

262 ravageable: *populabile*, a made-up word to represent an Ovidian coinage; for *populari* ('to ravage') in a fire context, cf. 2.319. Ovid has a great penchant for inventing new words, cf. e.g. 1.16, 30, 223, 289, 732; 2.544, 757; 3.15, 358, 407, 531; 4.12, 251; 5.426, 487; 6.315, 339, 478; 7.123, 212, 259, 356, 611; 8.564, 845, 871; 9. 285, 295, 399, 784; 10.15, 96, 99, 162; 11.202, 375, 434, 670, 730, 766; 12.170, 287, 317, 460, 497.

263 Mulciber: the 'Softener', one of Vulcan's titles (cf. 2.5, Virg. *Aen* 8.724) used here as a metonymy for 'fire', see on 9.141.

266 For the idea, cf. 7.237, Lucr. 3.612-4, Virg. *G.* 3.437-8, *Aen.* 2.471-5.

268 the Tirynthian: Hercules, see on 9.66.

270 august solemnity: *augusta...grauitate*; the irreverent allusion to Augustus is inescapable; see on 1.200-6; 6.73. *grauitas* most commonly means either literal 'weight' (*OLD* s.v. 1) or it is used metaphorically, as here, to mean 'solemnity', 'seriousness' etc. (*OLD* s.v. 6), one of the most admired qualities amongst Romans. When, accordingly, Ovid alludes again to Hercules with the word *pondus* (9.273), a word that basically means 'weight' and cannot be used in the metaphorical sense of *grauitas*, it is tempting to suspect undercutting humour. Such suspicions are surely heightened at 9.287, where *grauitas* is again used for Hercules, but in its literal sense, of the way his weight stretches his mother's womb before he is born, and they are finally confirmed upon meeting *pondus* once more (9.289), again of the unborn

Hercules; cf. also 9.685, 704 where also *pondus* is used of a foetus but not, perhaps, with the humour signalled here.

273-323 *The birth of Hercules and the story of Galanthis*

For the origin of Juno's Hatred for Hercules, see on 9.13. The story of his delayed birth appears first in Homer (*Il.* 19.95-133), as an illustration of the fact that even Zeus could be deceived, but more fully in Apollodorus (2.4.5, Frazer's translation):

> ...*when Hercules was about to be born, Zeus declared among the gods that the descendant of Perseus then about to be born would reign over Mycenae, and Hera out of jealousy persuaded the Ilithyias to retard Alcmena's delivery, and contrived that Eurys-theus, son of Sthenelus, should be born a seven-month child.*

The story of Galanthis is much less common; it appeared in the fourth book of Nicander's *Heteroeumena* according to Antoninus Liberalis (29); his version differs from Ovid's in a number of respects. He calls the girl Galinthias, a friend, not a servant, of Alcmene; in his version it is the Moirai (Fates) and Eileithyia (Ilithyia), acting on Hera's instructions, who delayed Alcmene's delivery. In both versions, the girl falsely announces the birth of Hercules, and in both versions, those attempting to delay the birth (Lucina, or the Moirai and Eileithyia) relaxed their grip and allowed the baby to be born. According to Antoninus, the Moirai punished her by changing her into a weasel doomed to live in dark corners, to become pregnant through her ears and to give birth through her mouth. Subsequently she received various honours from Hecate and Hercules and continued to be venerated at Thebes. For more details, see Forbes Irving 205-7.

273   Atlas felt his weight: Atlas notices the extra weight on his shoulders when Hercules goes to heaven; he is, of course, carrying heaven as his normal task. That gods are heavier than mortals is an idea familiar from Hom.*Il.*5.838-9 where the extra weight of Athene makes the axle of Diomedes' chariot groan. Cf. also 15.693-4. See also on 9.270.

Stheneleian: see on 9.272-323.

273-5   See Apollodorus 2.8.1 (Frazer's translation):

> *When Hercules had been translated to the gods, his sons fled from Eurystheus and came to Ceyx. But when Eurystheus demanded their surrender and threatened war, they were afraid, and, quitting Trachis, fled through Greece. Being pursued, they came to Athens, and sitting down on the altar of Mercy, claimed protection. Refusing to surrender them, the Athenians bore the brunt of war with Eurystheus and slew his sons...Eurystheus himself fled in a chariot and was pursued and slain by Hyllus.*

Ever after, this was a source of great patriotic pride for Athenians; it was also the subject of Euripides' *Heraclidae*.

276   Argive Alcmene: she was the daughter of Electryon (see on 9.16), and he was king of Mycenae (Apollod. 2.4.6), a city in the Argolid.

276-9   For **Iole** and **Hyllus**, see on 9.134-272; see also Soph. *Trach.* 1216ff. and the remarks of Easterling pp. 10-11.

279   her: Iole; the inflected nature of the language and Latin's richer store of pronouns means that the ambiguity in the English is absent in the Latin, cf. 10.429; 11.165, 322; 12.22.

in the marriage bed and in his heart: for the syllepsis, see on 9.135.

282   due: *matura*; both words can be used either of the foetus (7.127) or, as here, of the mother.

283-4   Ilithyia...who was made difficult: here, *Ilithyia* slides from being a Greek goddess of childbirth to a metonymy for 'childbirth' itself; see on 9.141.

284   by the grace of Juno: *Iunonis gratia*; this has normally been taken ironically: 'by the favour' (*OLD* s.v. 1), i.e. 'disfavour of Juno towards me.' Anderson, however, wants to take it to mean 'influence' (*OLD* s.v. 5c), i.e. 'Juno's influence with Ilithyia'. This seems to have less point.

285   labour-enduring: *laboriferi*; apparently an Ovidian coinage; see on 9.262.

286 **the tenth sign:** i.e. the tenth sign of the zodiac. In the course of a year the sun appears to travel along a path, the zodiac, through the stars. The path is divided into twelve signs and so the sun spends one calendar month in each. (See also on 2.70-5). Alcmene's pregnancy began with the first of these ten; now that the sun is pursuing the tenth, she has been in labour for nine calendar months and is therefore due.

287-9 **weight...of...the load:** *grauitas...ponderis*; see on 9.270.

294 **Lucina:** the Roman goddess of childbirth; see on 9.314.

and...the Nixus: there were thought to be three *Nixus* who assisted at childbirth by kneeling down as if to help at the delivery; the evidence for this is most conveniently available in *OLD* s.v. 'Nixi'; the word derives ultimately from *nitor* 'I strain, or strive'. Petersmann has argued for the form *Nixus* (fourth declension) as found in the manuscripts against Heinsius' *Nixos*.

295 **She:** *illa*; Lucina; see on 9.279.

precorrupted: *praecorrupta*, apparently an Ovidian coinage; see on 9.262.

299 **in a comb:** *pectine*; the word is used as a technical term for a number of things, including this particular formation of the fingers; see *OLD* s.v. 3c.

304 **Cadmeian:** *Cadmeides*; i.e. 'Theban', cf. 3.127-31; 6.177. Amphitryon and Alcmene were in Thebes at the time; see Hom. *Il.* 14.323-4; 19.98-9; Hesiod *Aspis*. 1-3, 79ff.; *Hom. Hymn* 15. 1-2; Eur. *Heracles* 13.

306 **Galanthis:** for her story, see on 9.273-323.

307 **plebs:** Ovid, like Virgil before him, was very fond of introducing Roman terms and concepts into alien contexts. Perhaps the most familiar Virgilian examples are in *Aeneid* 4 (where Dido's foundation of her city is constantly described in Roman terms) and at *Aeneid* 8.337-69 (where Evander's tour of his primitive settlement is clearly intended to evoke the Rome that it is to become). In both cases, there is a serious point behind Virgil's choice of language; Ovid's practice is more self-indulgent. See also 1.92 (and the note), 170-6 (quoted in the note on 6.73), 382, 576; 2.538-9; 3.111-4, 531 (and the note), 539, 583; 4.122; 5.128, 155 (and the note) 207-8, 210, 382, 496, 640, 650; 6.10, 73, 283, 428ff.; 7.101, 701 (and the note), 739 (and the note); 8.91, 154 (and the note), 331, 562, 564, 566, 632, 637, 660, 846; 9.446, 640, 671, 762, 771, 793-4; 10.8, 27 (and the note), 106, 595-6 (and the note), 652-3 (and the note); 11.25-7, 599; 12.102-4, 116, 149, 155, 215, 552, 602. Henderson on 3.111-4 is instructive though, perhaps, unsympathetic:

> *Ovid has chosen an anachronistic comparison, a favourite trick of his, and one of the ways in which he prevents the reader from practising for long that willing suspension of disbelief which most epic poets are careful to foster.*

310 **the goddess:** Lucina; see on 9.314.

314 **the powerful goddess of the womb:** *diua potens uteri*; technically, no doubt, *potens* is to be taken with *uteri* 'she who has power over the womb', but that is awkward in English. For a Miltonic precedent, see N.-H. on Hor. *Odes* 1.5.15. Lucina is called *potens* (but without *uteri*) also at 5.303.

316 **the divinity:** *numen*, a word frequently used by Ovid as a variant on the basic words, *deus*, 'god' and *dea*, 'goddess', e.g. 9.281. Since *numen* is neuter it, like the translation 'divinity', cannot distinguish between gods and goddesses. Here, it probably refers to Lucina, but see on 9.317.

317 **the cruel goddess:** *dea saeua*; possibly Lucina still but, as Anderson argues in detail, more probably Juno who was the real victim of Galanthis' actions and who would be expected to be angry at a trick played on a *numen* working for her; the actions here closely resemble Juno's actions at 2.476ff., and Juno is regularly described as *saeua* (2.470; 4.547; 9.199).

318 **to lift up:** *releuare*; *leuare* can mean either 'lift up' (*OLD* s.v. 1, 2) or 'relieve' (*OLD* s.v. 3), as at 9.312 and 315 where it was used of Alcmene giving birth and translated 'delivered'. *releuare* also has both meanings (*OLD* s.v. 4, 2); it is very characteristic of

Ovid to represent Galanthis prevented from *releuare* because she has assisted in Alcmene's *leuare*. The point cannot, however, survive in translation.

319 **she prevented her:** *arcuit*; i.e. 'the goddess prevented her'; there is no ambiguity in the Latin. For the enjambment and its effect, see on 9.78.

320 **zeal:** *strenuitas*; this refers back to *strenua*, 'zealous' at 9.307.
as before: *antiqua*; see 6.145 for an exact parallel. See also on 11.343.

320-1 **her hide did not lose its colour:** as Bömer suggests, this must refer to Galanthis' fair hair (9.306); to suggest, as Anderson does, that the point is that 'the hide of some weasels has the color of human skin' is absurd. It is very common for an Ovidian metamorphosis to preserve, or even enhance, some, at least, of the characteristics of the victim, see on 6.97. The whole matter is treated at greater length by Hollis (xx) and in my note on 1.234; cf. 10.242; 11.293, 343.

324-93 Dryope

Ovid's version of this story is very different from the one attributed to the first book of Nicander's *Heteroeumena* by Antoninus Liberalis (32). In Ovid's version, Dryope's son, Amphissos, is only a baby and Dryope is taken from him as a punishment for her plucking Lotis' flower. According to Antoninus Liberalis, Amphissos was grown up; no offence was committed but Dryope was taken up to heaven after which Amphissos founded a cult for her, a feature entirely missing from Ovid's account which introduces instead the pathos of a baby separated from his mother. For further details, see Forbes Irving 263-4.

325 **she groaned:** *ingemuit*; for the enjambment and its effect, see on 9.78.

327-9 In Virgil's *Aeneid*, Aeneas uses a similar technique to introduce two books of narrative (2.10-13, West's translation):
But if you have such a great desire to know what we suffered, to hear in brief about the last agony of Troy, although my mind recoiled in anguish when you asked and I shudder to remember, I shall begin.

331 **the Oechalides:** 'the women of Oechalia', Iole's home, see on 9.136-7.

332 **the god who holds Delphi and Delos:** Apollo; cf. e.g. 1.515, 454.

333 **Andraemon:** his part of the story is also in Antoninus Liberalis 32.3.

334 **There is a lake:** *est lacus*; the typical start to an ekphrasis (though this example is unusually brief) where the poet breaks off to set a scene. It is a device as old as Homer and more usually starts 'There is a place ['city'/'cave' etc.]...', see on 1.168 and, for a much fuller discussion, on 5.385-91; see also Austin on Virg. *Aen.* 4.480ff. who compares Hom. *Il.* 6.152, *Od.* 13.32. For other examples in these books, see 10.86-8, 126-9, 644-8; 11.229-37, 359-64, 392-3, 592-615; 12.39-63.

335 **myrtle grove:** *myrteta*; not well motivated here but Ovid may have recalled it from *Aen.* 3.23 where it was well motivated since Aeneas was building an altar to Venus, and myrtle was her plant.

340 **Tyrian colours:** purple and similar dyes were produced from a shell-fish, the murex, by the Phoenicians of Tyre and Sidon; see Austin on Virg. *Aen.* 4.262.

344 **(for I was there):** see on 9.17.

344-5 This part of the story is probably Ovid's invention; for the details, he is much in debt to Virgil's description of Aeneas drawing blood apparently from a plant, but really from Polydorus' murdered body (*Aen.* 3.22-36, West's translation):
Close by there happened to be a mound on top of which [summo] there grew a thicket bristling with spears of cornel and myrtle [myrtus] wood. I had gone there and was beginning to pull green shoots out of the ground to cover the altar with leafy branches [ramis], when I saw a strange and horrible sight. As soon as I broke the roots of a tree and was pulling it out of the ground, dark gouts [guttae] of blood dripped from it and stained the earth with gore. The horror [horror] of it chilled me to the bone, I trembled and my blood congealed with fear.

It is worth noting that Virgil's story of Polydorus is itself of most uncertain origin; see Williams on *Aen.* 3.19f.

346 **too late:** *tardi*; so Golding, cf. *OLD* s.v. 2. Some modern translators have taken it to mean 'slow witted' here (as does *OLD* s.v. 5), but that seems to lack point in context.

347 **Lotis...Priapus:** their story occurs only here and at *Fasti* 1.415-40 where Priapus (a Roman god of fertility whose wooden image with its characteristic large bright red phallus was often to be found in gardens) was disappointed while trying to rape the sleeping Lotis because of an ass which woke her up so that she escaped. The story is told to explain why asses were sacrificed to Priapus. For further details, see Forbes Irving 267. Priapus is stressed on the middle syllable.

348 **this:** *hanc*; the lotus flower; see on 9.279.

351 **in a root:** *radice*; the Latin may equally mean 'by' or 'in a root'; in English it is necessary to choose but it is hard to believe that both senses are not present.

356 **Eurytus, his grandfather:** (stress the first syllable); see Apollodorus 2.6.1 (Frazer's translation):

> *Hercules...wishing himself to wed...ascertained that Eurytus, prince of Oechalia, had proposed the hand of his daughter Iole as a prize to him who should vanquish himself and his sons in archery...*

For the parenthetical aside, see on 9.17.

358 **as he sucked:** *ducentem*; see *OLD* s.v. 25b.

364 **Dryope; Dryope:** *Dryopen; Dryopen*; the juxtaposition must represent the sound as they call out her name.

366 **their:** *suae*; the obvious word if it were still 'his wife' or 'his daughter' is unashamedly grotesque both in Latin and English when it becomes 'their tree'.

370 **poured forth...thus:** an attempt to capture the antique Ennian flavour of *tales effundit* here; see Ennius *Ann.* 553 (Skutsch), 540 (Vahlen), 457 (Warmington) and Skutsch pp. 699-700.

371 See on 6.542-3.

376 **nurse:** *nutrici*; here in the basic sense: 'wet-nurse'.

383 **piety:** *pietas*; the Latin word has a resonance that far exceeds that of its English derivative; see on 1.149, 6.630. Here, the sense is that of *OLD* s.v. 1: 'An attitude of dutiful respect towards those to whom one is bound by ties of...consanguinity etc.' This translation always renders the word 'piety' so as to draw attention to the Roman sense of a single coherent quality which to us seems to be a wide range of different qualities. Cf. 6.502.

388-9 **bark...bark:** *liber...cortex*; English does not have two basic words for 'bark'; strictly speaking, *liber* is more generally used of the 'inner bark' or 'rind', (hence 'soft' *mollis*), but neither term would work well here; see on 9.32-4.

391 **without your help:** throughout antiquity, it was the duty of someone close to the deceased to close their eyes upon death. Cf. e.g. Hom. *Il.* 11.452-4 (Lattimore's translation):

> *Wretch, since now your father and your honoured mother will not be able to close your eyes in death, but the tearing birds will get you, with their wings close-beating about you.*

394-449 *Iolaüs and the sons of Callirhoë*

This section links Iole's report of the sad story of Dryope and her baby son to the dreadful story of Byblis. The theme that unites the interlude is divine interference in the aging process: Iolaüs (stress the penultimate syllable) was given back his youth, Callirhoë's sons were miraculously brought to manhood when only young. Iolaüs was Hercules' nephew and charioteer (see on 8.310 where we also encounter him as one of those involved in the Calydonian boar hunt); he had been one of Hercules' greatest helpers (see on 9.69). For the story, see the messenger's speech to Alcmene in Euripides' *Heraclidae* 849-58 (Kovacs's translation):

> *As he [Iolaüs] was passing through the sacred district of Athene Pallenis, looking toward Eurystheus' chariot he prayed to Hebe and to Zeus that he might be young again for a single day and exact retribution from his ene-*

> *mies. Now you may hear a marvel. A pair of stars stood above the chariot*
> *yoke and covered the chariot in dark cloud. Those who are wise say that it*
> *was your son Heracles and Hebe: out of this murky darkness he [Iolaüs]*
> *showed forth the youthful form of his young arms.*

It will be noted that this account differs in a number of respects from Ovid's; in particular, Euripides' Iolaüs is made young for only one day and the transformation is attributed to Hebe alone, not to Hebe and Hercules.

The story of Callirhoë (stress the antepenultimate syllable) is the final stage of the complex tale of Eriphyle, her husband, Amphiaraüs, and their son, Alcmaeon, who was Callirhoë's husband. Put at its briefest, the story was that Eriphyle, bribed by a necklace, tricked her husband, Amphiaraüs, into joining the seven against Thebes against his better judgement. Their son, Alcmaeon, who had been instructed to avenge his father by killing his mother was reinforced in that intention by the discovery that his mother had accepted another bribe (a robe) to trick him into joining the second expedition against Thebes. After Alcmaeon killed Eriphyle, he suffered a number of adventures, eventually marrying Callirhoë. She too coveted the neclace and the robe; Alcmaeon's attempt to get them for her resulted in his own violent death, a death avenged by his own infant sons miraculously brought to manhood in response to their mother's prayers. The full narrative is conveniently found in Apollodorus 3.6.2, 3.7.2, 3.7.5-6 (Frazer's translation):

> *But Amphiaraus... being a seer and foreseeing that all who joined in the ex-*
> *pedition except Adrastus were destined to perish, shrank from it himself and*
> *discouraged the rest. However, Polynices went to Iphis... and begged to*
> *know how Amphiaraus could be compelled to go to the war. He answered*
> *that it could be done if Eriphyle got the necklace. Now Amphiaraus had*
> *forbidden Eriphyle to accept gifts from Polynices; but Polynices gave her*
> *the necklace and begged her to persuade Amphiaraus to go to the war; for*
> *the decision lay with her, because once, when a difference arose between*
> *him and Adrastus, he had made it up with him and sworn to let Eriphyle de-*
> *cide any future dispute he might have with Adrastus. Accordingly, when*
> *war was to be made on Thebes, and the measure was advocated by Adras-*
> *tus and opposed by Amphiaraus, Eriphyle accepted the necklace and per-*
> *suaded him to march with Adrastus. Thus forced to go to the war, Am-*
> *phiaraus laid his commands on his sons, that, when they were grown up,*
> *they should slay their mother and march against Thebes.*
>
> *Ten years afterwards the sons of the fallen, called the Epigoni, pur-*
> *posed to march against Thebes to avenge the death of their fathers; and*
> *when they consulted the oracle, the god predicted victory under the leader-*
> *ship of Alcmaeon. So Alcmaeon joined the expedition, though he was loath*
> *to lead the army till he had punished his mother; for Eriphyle had received*
> *the robe from Thersander, son of Polynices, and had persuaded her sons*
> *also to go to the war.*
>
> *After the capture of Thebes, when Alcmaeon learned that his mother*
> *Eriphyle had been bribed to his undoing also, he was more incensed than*
> *ever, and in accordance with an oracle given to him by Apollo he killed his*
> *mother... But Alcmaeon was visited by the Fury of his mother's murder, and*
> *going mad he... repaired... to Phegeus at Psophis. And having been purified*
> *by him he married Arsinoe, daughter of Phegeus, and gave her the necklace*
> *and the robe. But afterwards... the god bade him in an oracle to depart to*
> *Achelous and to stand another trial on the river bank... finally he went to*
> *the springs of Achelous, and was purified by him, and received Callirrhoe,*
> *his daughter, to wife... But afterwards Callirrhoe coveted the necklace and*
> *robe, and said she would not live with him if she did not get them. So away*
> *Alcmaeon hied to Psophis and told Phegeus how it had been predicted that*
> *he should be rid of his madness when he had brought the necklace and the*

robe to Delphi and dedicated them to him. But a servant having let out that he was taking the things to Callirrhoe, Phegeus commanded his sons, and they lay in wait and killed him... Being apprized of Alcmaeon's untimely end and courted by Zeus, Callirrhoe requested that the sons she had by Alcmaeon might be full-grown in order to avenge their father's murder.

396 **Eurytus' daughter:** Iole, see on 9.356.

(and yet she wept herself): see on 9.17.

398 **a boy almost:** i.e. 'almost as young as a boy'.

with a hint of down covering his cheeks: Homer (*Il.* 24.348) is our earliest source for the commonplace that this was the most attractive time in a young man's life; see also on 12.291-2 and cf. 12.395-6.

399 **reshaped:** *reformatus*; apparently another Ovidian coinage (see on 9.262); as Anderson hints, it is another way of latinizing the Greek 'metamorphosis'.

Iolaüs: as a glance at the text will show, the translation slightly exaggerates Ovid's delay in presenting the name.

400-1 **Juno's Hebe...her husband's:** Hebe was normally regarded as the daughter of Jupiter and Juno (see on 3.269-70), but note that Ovid refers only to Hebe's mother, and, at 9.416, he describes Hebe as Jupiter's stepdaughter; she was given in marriage to Hercules after he entered heaven; cf. Hom. *Od.* 11.601-4 (Lattimore's translation):

After him I was aware of powerful Herakles...
married to sweet stepping
Hebe, child of great Zeus and Hera of the golden sandals.

Note that according to Apollodorus (quoted in the note on 394-449) the request originated with Iolaüs himself, not with Hercules, and was addressed to Hebe and Jupiter; also, according to Apollodorus, the transformation was effected by both Hercules and Hebe.

403 **Themis:** in Homer (*Il.* 20.4, *Od.* 2.68), Themis was seen as the goddess who summoned the divine assembly and was, accordingly, responsible for good order. She was also associated with oracles and prophecy (see on 1.321). It is, accordingly, natural that she would be most concerned at the prospect of gods swearing not to intervene in human affairs, especially when she can foresee so much trouble to come. Themis' account of the future is very allusive and hard to follow, but that was characteristic of oracular utterances.

403-4 **Thebes...wars:** this war was the subject of Aeschylus' tragedy, *Septem contra Thebas*.

404 **Capaneus:** for the story of this notorious hero, see e.g. Aesch. *Sept.* 440-6 (Weir Smyth's translation):

...and Capaneus utters threats, well prepared to act, dishonouring the gods; and in vain glee plying his tongue to its full strength, sends up to heaven— mortal that he is—his surging boasts to be heard of Zeus. But right sure am I that upon him, as he well deserves, will come that fire-bearer, the thunderer's bolt, no whit changed into the likeness of the sun's hot rays at midday...

405 **the brothers:** Eteocles and Polynices; for the story, see e.g. Aesch. *Sept.* 804-19.

406 **the seer:** Amphiaraüs; for this part of his story, see Eur. *Suppl.* 925-7 (Kovacs's translation):

As regards the noble son of Oecles [Amphiaraüs], the gods by snatching him away alive, chariot and all, into the depths of the earth openly praise him.

407 **shade:** *manes*, the word refers to weak disembodied spirits believed to be all that survives of humans after death. I have consistently rendered the word 'shade' to avoid confusion with other more familiar views about the afterlife.

taking vengeance on a parent for a parent: Alcmaeon, taking vengeance on one parent, his mother, Eriphyle, for his other parent, his father, Amphiaraüs; for the story, see on 9.394-449. For the polyptoton, see on 9.44.

408 **pious and wicked:** Ovid likes this sort of conceit; for an exact parallel, see 3.5; for similar passages, see 6.635; 7.339-40; 9.711. For 'pious', see on 9.382.

409 **an exile from his mind and from his home:** for the syllepsis, see on 9.135.

410 **Eumenides:** (stress the second syllable); 'the Kindly Ones', the standard Greek euphemism for the Furies, whose special task it was to avenge those murdered by their children. For an understanding of their nature, see Aeschylus' tragedy, *Eumenides*. For further details, see on 10.313-4, 349.

411 **his wife:** Callirhoë; for her story, see on 9.394-449.

412 **kinsman:** Alcmaeon, who had previously been married to Phegeus' daughter (see Apollod. 3.7.5 quoted above on 9.394-449). Apollodorus' version is fuller and easier to understand than Themis'. In particular, since Themis omits the fact that Alcmaeon had tricked the necklace ('the fatal gold' *fatale...aurum*) out of Phegeus, she offers no motive for Phegeus to kill Alcmaeon.

414-6 those years...the gifts: i.e. the years taken from Iolaüs by Hebe at 9.397-401.

415 Heinsius regarded this line as spurious. There are various difficulties with it but the overwhelming reason for rejecting it is that the phrase 'moved by these words' (*his motus*) from the next line must refer to the passage culminating in line 414, a connexion which is badly disturbed if 415 is allowed to stand.

416-7 his stepdaughter and daughter-in-law: i.e. Hebe, see on 9.400-1.

421 **Pallantias:** i.e. Aurora (Dawn); the normal view was that Aurora was the daughter of Hyperion (Hes. *Theog.* 371-4). Ovid, however, favours an alternative view that she was the daughter of Hyperion's brother, Pallas (see also 15.191, 700, *Fasti* 4.373, 6.567). It may be worth observing that, whereas Hesiod believes Selene (the Moon) to have been Hyperion's daughter, she was Pallas' daughter according to *Hom. Hymn* 4.99-100.

her husband's old years: Tithonus, a mortal who married the immortal Aurora; she asked Jupiter to make him immortal but forgot to ask for eternal youth. As a result, he lived for ever as a useless, shrunken, babbling shell. The story is to be found at *Hom. Hymn* 5.218-28. The complaint is indeed, therefore, that his 'years' are 'old', not that they are 'many'.

423 **Iasion:** Homer's version of the story is quite different (*Od.* 5.125-8, Lattimore's translation):

> *and so it was when Demeter [Ceres] of the lovely hair, yielding*
> *to her desire, lay down with Iasion and loved him*
> *in a thrice-turned field, it was not long before this was made known*
> *to Zeus, who struck him down with the cast of a shining thunderbolt.*

Hesiod (*Theog.* 969-74 tells a similar story, including the thrice-turned field) but adds that she gave birth to Plutus and omits Zeus' intervention and Iasion's death. Ovid may well have adapted the story to fit the context.

424 **Erichthonius:** Mulciber (i.e. Vulcan, see on 9.263) was his father (for the story of how that happened see on 2.553). The story that Vulcan asked for his life to be repeated is found only here.

425 **Anchises:** Venus' involvement with Anchises and the consequential birth of Aeneas was, of course, familiar as early as Homer (*Il.* 2.820 etc.). According to Virgil, Anchises lived to so great an age that he needed to be carried out of Troy on his son's back; he was, however, a figure of great dignity (*Aeneid* 2 and 6 *passim*). It is characteristic of Ovid that he seems to be alluding to a much less dignified story to be found in Hyginus (*Fab.* 94):

> *Venus is said to have loved Anchises..., slept with him, produced Aeneas*
> *from him and told him not to announce the fact among mankind. But An-*
> *chises, in his cups, spoke about it to his friends. Because of this he was*
> *struck with a thunderbolt by Jupiter. Some say that he committed suicide.*

432 **campaigning:** *ambitione*, a very unpoetical word for what Romans saw as the degrading practice of politicians going around (the literal meaning of the word) to solicit political support.

435-6 my Aeacus (stress the first syllable)...**Rhadamanthus** (stress the penultimate syllable)...**my Minos:** cf. Achilles' words (Hom. *Il.* 21.188-9, Lattimore's translation):

> *The man is my father who is lord over many Myrmidons,*
> *Peleus, Aiakos' son, but Zeus was the father of Aiakos.*

and Zeus' words listing his many conquests (Hom. *Il.* 14.321-2):

> *nor when I loved the daughter of far-renowned Phoinix, Europa*
> *who bore Minos to me, and Rhadamanthys the godlike.*

All three, according to Plato (*Apology* 41a and *Gorgias* 523e, see also Dodds's note) were judges of the dead. Ovid has already treated Aeacus briefly (7.490-522) and Minos, in earlier days, at some length (7.453-89 and 8.1-182).

441 he: Minos. There is no ambiguity in the Latin; see on 9.279.

443 Deïone's (stress the '-i-') **son Miletus** (stress the '-e-'): a quite different story about Minos and Miletus, apparently set much earlier, appears in Apollodorus (3.1.2, Frazer's translation):

> *But when they [Minos and Sarpedon] were grown up, they quarrelled with*
> *each other; for they loved a boy called Miletus, son of Apollo by Aria,*
> *daughter of Cleochus. As the boy was more friendly to Sarpedon, Minos*
> *went to war and had the better of it, and the others fled. Miletus landed in*
> *Caria and there founded a city which he called Miletus after himself...*

Antoninus Liberalis (30.1), also introducing the Byblis story and citing as his source the second book of Nicander's *Heteroeumena,* tells a similar tale but calls Miletus' mother 'Acacallis, daughter of Minos'; according to him, Miletus, though originally exposed to avoid Minos' anger, did in fact grow up to be a handsome boy whom Minos wished to ravish. He accordingly escaped to Caria and founded Miletus. Ovid's version is not otherwise known, nor is his Deïone; it is, furthermore, not entirely coherent. It does, however, help to link the story of Miletus' daughter, Byblis, to what precedes it.

444 Phoebus: the standard epithet of Apollo throughout antiquity, see e.g. Hom. *Il.* 1.43.

445-6 him...he...he...his...he...him: Minos...Minos...Miletus...Minos'...Mi-nos...Miletus. There is no ambiguity in the Latin.

446 from his ancestral penates: probably 'from Minos' penates', but it may mean 'from Miletus' penates in Crete where his ancestors had long lived.' 'penates', is a very Roman concept (see on 9.307), the household gods, but comes naturally to mean 'home'.

447-53 For the apostrophe, see on 9.101.

450-665 Byblis

This story was very popular in the Hellenistic age. It was treated by a number of poets including Nikainetos, Parthenius, Apollonius Rhodius and Nicander, whose version appears in Antoninus Liberalis (30); there too, Miletus was the father of Caunus and Byblis. In all versions, Caunus and Byblis are brother and sister, but the similarities end there. Sometimes, it is Caunus who initiates the affair, only to be rebuffed by Byblis; sometimes Byblis is the rebuffed suitor and sometimes she kills herself, as in Hyginus (*Fab.* 243.6), or is turned by the nymphs into a spring only after a failed attempt at suicide by throwing herself from a rock, as in Antoninus Liberalis (30.4). The details are conveniently collected by Otis (1966) 386-8, (1970) 415-7. Ovid himself had already mentioned Byblis once (*Ars* 1.283-4), but in that version Byblis hanged herself.

450-3 This is one of the most convoluted sentences to be found in the *Metamorphoses*. It is presumably to represent the tortuous course of the river. For further details on the Meander, see on 2.246, 8.162.

450 Meander's daughter, Cyanee: Cyanee is known only from Ovid as a daughter of Meander and the mother of Caunus and Byblis.

452 known: *cognita*; the Latin word, like its English equivalent, can refer, as here, to sexual intercourse. In both languages, however, the usage is rare and becomes clear only as the context unfolds.

children: *pignora*; this is Shackleton Bailey's emendation for *corpore* or *corpora* which would relate the beauty to Byblis rather than to her children. The basic meaning of *pignora* is 'pledges' or 'tokens' and it comes to mean 'children' since they are 'pledges for the future' or 'tokens of love' (see e.g. 8.490). It seemed impossible, however, to sustain the deliberate ambiguity in the translation.

453 **twin:** this detail appears to be unique to Ovid.

455 **Apolline:** Apollo was the grandfather of Caunus and Byblis, see on 9.443. No doubt, there is a further implication that Caunus shared something of Apollo's famous beauty.

456 I accept Tarrant's view that this is 'an inept reworking of 510' where, as it seems to me, it is much more appropriate.

457 For this kind of naivety, cf. 7.12-14 and 10.636-7.

458-62 **too often...too much:** *saepius...nimium*: as Anderson notes:
> '*the comparative adverb* [saepius] *conveys a note of judgment which belongs to the narrator; it obviously does not represent Byblis' thinking.*'

460 **piety:** see on 9.382.

464 **she had no longings:** i.e. for sexual fulfilment.

466 **the words for blood-ties:** *nomina sanguinis*; literally. 'names of blood' i.e. 'names of blood relationships'. in this case, 'brother' or 'sister'.

466-7 **she calls...to call:** *appellat...uocet*; English does not have two basic words for 'calling'; see on 9.32-4.

467 **Byblis...sister:** *Byblida...sororem*, note that these two words are as far apart as is possible in one line.

472 **for herself:** *ipsa*; literally just 'herself'. The dream is seen as something outside her control, but her thoughts when awake are controlled by Byblis herself.

473 **the vision of her rest:** *quietis...suae speciem*: here 'sleep' might seem a more natural rendering but it has already just been used for *somnus* (472) and, more importantly, the word picks up 'quiet' (*quietis*) at 469.

474-8 Very disjointed sentences to reflect a confused mind.

476 **beautiful:** *formosus*; traditionally, in English, women are 'beautiful' and men are 'handsome'; however, the distinction is probably sufficiently eroded to permit the translation to draw attention to Ovid's echo of *formosa...formosior* at 9.462-3.

477 **and I like him:** *et placet*; in both languages this is the simplest possible formula to express approval. The nature and intensity of the approval must be gleaned from the context.

482 **your gentle mother:** Venus again, of course.

487 **with that word changed:** *mutato nomine*; i.e. 'sister', see on 9.466.

488-9 For this effect, see on 1.325-6; it is found more often in the earlier books.

488-93 **happily...happily...unhappily:** *bene...bene...male*; the matching antonyms help to point the rhetoric.

491 **except our grandparents:** *praeter auos*; if they did not share grandparents, they would not be siblings and would be free to marry.

497 **have had:** i.e. as 'wives' or 'sexual partners'; Bömer compares, e.g. Virg. *Aen.* 9.594.

498 **Ops:** see Hesiod *Theogony* 132-8, 453 (Evelyn-White's translation):
> But afterwards she [Earth] lay with Heaven and bare deep-swirling
> Oceanus...and Rhea [Ops]...and lovely Tethys. After them was born Cronos
> [Saturn] the wily, youngest and most terrible of her children.
> But Rhea was subject in love to Cronos...

499 **Oceanus, Tethys:** i.e. 'Oceanus married Tethys'; they too were siblings (see on 9.498); for their marriage, see Homer's account of Juno's speech (*Il.* 14.200-7, Lattimore's translation):
> Since I go now to the ends of the generous earth, on a visit
> to Okeanos...and Tethys our mother...
> I shall go to visit these, and resolve their division of discord,
> since now for a long time they have stayed apart from each other
> and from the bed of love...

the ruler of Olympus, Juno: i.e. 'Jupiter married Juno'; for their relationships, see on 9.176.

504 **couch:** *toroque*; the term *torus* can mean, among other things, either 'the marriage bed' (cf. e.g. 7.91; 10.268) or 'a bed to receive a corpse' (e.g. 6.289); while the latter meaning is clearly the primary one here, it is difficult, in this context, not to be reminded of the other meaning.

505 **but that:** *ista*; i.e. her desire for her brother, not, as Anderson thinks, her desire to kill herself.

understanding: *arbitrium*, a technical term of Roman law.

507 **the sons of Aeolus:** see Hom. *Od.* 10.1-7 (Lattimore's translation):

> *We came next to the Aeolian island, where Aiolos*
> *lived...*
> *...and twelve children were born to him in his palace,*
> *six of them daughters, and six sons in the pride of their youth, so*
> *he bestowed his daughters on his sons to be their consorts.*

516 **letter:** Ovid had published his *Heroides*, a collection of verse letters from female lovers to their beloved (together with a few replies from the males) many years before. Here his readers see once again the same sympathy with and understanding of women in love that he showed there.

520 Tarrant would delete this line.

522 **stylus:** *ferrum*; this line is a startling echo of *Heroides* 11.3 where Canace is writing to Macareus, her brother, and the father of her child. But the *ferrum that* Canace holds in her right hand is not a writing implement, like Byblis', but the sword with which she has been told to kill herself. *ferrum* (literally 'iron') can be used of a variety of objects made from iron, but most frequently of a sword. The same principle lies behind the English use of 'iron' for the humble tool in the laundry.

524 Tarrant would delete this line.

525 **put them down, and, once put down:** *ponit positasque*; for the polyptoton, see on 9.44.

528 **'sister'...the sister:** *'sister'...sororem*; the Latin quotes what was written first, then alludes to it, using a different case; the translation is an attempt to reproduce the effect. For why Byblis was considering using the word at all, see on 9.530.

529 **corrected:** *correctis*; the procedure to correct a wax tablet was to smooth it back to its original even surface. Some manuscripts read *correptis* ('snatched up') which gives a much less satisfactory sense.

530 **health...you wish:** *dederis...salutem*; the standard opening to a Roman letter would require, in this case: 'His sister gives health to her brother Caunus' (*soror fratri Cauno salutem dat*). *salus* basically means 'safety', 'good health' etc. (*OLD* s.v. 1-2) which is how it came to develop its rôle in conventional greetings to such an extent that in the epistolary formula it means little more than 'greetings' (*OLD* s.v. 8). The English word 'health' similarly has one function in a doctor's surgery, another, more conventional one, at a drinking party. Byblis, by introducing a complex variation on the standard formula, plays with both functions of the word. The translation offers the non-conventional interpretation at the expense of the conventional one which would substitute something like 'give greeting' for 'give health'.

532-3 **my case could be put:** *posset agi mea causa*; here, Byblis indulges in the language of the law-court.

533 **not be known as Byblis:** she seems rather to let the cat out of the bag.

549-50 **very near...nearer still:** *iunctissima, iunctior*; for the polyptoton, which here stresses the key idea, see on 9.44.

551-2 **old men...wrong and right:** *senes...nefasque fasque*; editors quote Catul. 5.1-3:

> *Let us live, my Lesbia, and let us love,*
> *and let us value all the notions*
> *of too severe old men [senum] at a single penny.*

But, as Anderson observes:

> ...*in the matter of incest, all ages share the convictions which Byblis attempts to limit prejudicially to older people. There is something absolute about* fas *and* nefas *['right' and 'wrong']...*

558 **the fraternal word:** *fraterno sub nomine*; presumably she is referring both to 'brother' (*frater*) and 'sister' (*soror*).

567 **she dipped it in her tears:** it was normal practice to dampen a signet before applying it to the wax so that it would come away cleanly without adhering to it.
  (her tongue had lost its moisture): presumably a symptom of anxiety.

574 **Meandrian:** i.e. 'Caunus, the grandson of Meander', see 9.450.

581 For the apostrophe, see on 9.101.

584 **soon:** *mox*, Tarrant's correction for the *uix* ('scarcely') of the manuscripts. *uix* would imply whispering or the like, whereas the context suggests a Byblis of suddenly renewed confidence.

596 **omens:** see 9.571-2.
  him...it: i.e. 'the servant...the wax tablet'; the Latin is even more vague than the English, perhaps to represent Byblis' confusion, but the sense is eventually clear.

608-9 **could not have...might have:** *poterant, potuissent*; for the polyptoton, see on 9.44.

611-2 **he did not approach appropriately, nor pick...a suitable time:** but we know from 9.572-3 that there was nothing wrong with the servant's approach.

612 **a free hour or mind:** *horamque animumque uacantem*; for the syllepsis, see on 9.135.

613-5 **for he was not born...lioness's milk:** the origin of this commonplace is in Homer (*Il.* 16.33-5, Lattimore's translation):

> *Pitiless: the rider Peleus was never your father*
> *nor Thetis was your mother, but it was the grey sea that bore you*
> *and the towering rocks, so sheer the heart in you is turned from us.*

See also 8.120-1. The versions apparently clearest in Ovid's mind here are Catul. 64.154-7 (Godwin's translation):

> *What lioness gave birth to you under a lonely rock?*
> *What sea conceived you and vomited you out of its foaming waters?*
> *What Syrtes, what voracious Scylla, what devouring Charybdis—*
> *seeing that you give back returns such as this for your sweet life?* .

and Virg. *Aen.* 4.365-7, (West's translation):

> *You are not the son of a goddess and Dardanus was not the first founder of*
> *your family. It was the Caucasus that fathered you on its hard rocks and*
> *Hyrcanian tigers offered you their udders.*

Pease gives an exhaustive history of the motif.

615 **adamant:** *adamanta*, a Greek word used as early as Hesiod (*Theog.* 161) for a very hard, mythical substance; literally the word means 'that cannot be overcome'. Virgil provides the first extant use of the word in Latin, see *Aen.* 6.552 and Austin. See further on 4.281.

619 **push on...to victory:** *expugnare*; as so often in Ovid, a military metaphor is used in an erotic context.

630 **(so great...mind):** cf. 10.445

633 **his fatherland and wickedness:** *patriam...nefasque*; for the syllepsis, see on 9.135.

634 **new walls in a distant land:** in fact, Caunus is about 100 miles south east from Miletus as the crow flies. However, if he went by sea he would have been involved in a meandering voyage through or around the Sporades and if he went by land there would have been much difficult mountainous terrain to cross.

635 **Miletus'...daughter:** Byblis, cf. 9.457-453 and see on 9.450-665.

637 **beat her arms:** Thisbe too did this when she found the dying Pyramus (4.138). Philomela, distressed upon discovering what has happened to her sister, is said, though in a possibly spurious line (6.532), to 'cut and beat her arms'.

639 **illicit:** *inconcessaeque*; an unusual word, possibly coined by Virgil; it must conjure up his phrase for the disastrous marriage of Paris and Helen: *inconcessosque hymenaeos* (*Aen.* 1.651) where Austin's note is instructive; cf. 10.153.
  love: *Veneris*; see on 9.141.
640 **penates:** see on 9.307, 446.
641-2 This simile owes much to Virgil's use of the same image to describe Dido when she too has been forced to acknowledge the loss of the one she loves (*Aen.* 4.300-3, West's translation):

> *Driven to distraction and burning with passion, she raged and raved around the whole city like a Bacchant stirred by the shaking of the sacred emblems and roused to fury when she hears the name of Bacchus at the biennial orgy and the shouting on Mount Cithaeron calls to her in the night.*

641 **offspring of Semele:** *proles Semeleïa*; i.e. 'Bacchus', cf. 3.259-315, 520; 5.329.
  thyrsus: a staff bound in ivy leaves and shaken by Bacchic revellers.
642 **Ismarian:** i.e. 'Thracian', Ismarus was a mountain in Thrace. Chiefly because of Euripides' *Bacchae*, Bacchic worship is usually associated with Thebes, as in the Virgilian passage above. However, Ovid has already given us a memorable picture of Thracian Bacchanalia at 6.587-600.
  their triennial: i.e. 'a festival occurring every other year'; 'triennial' because the ancients used inclusive reckoning. Virgil, in the passage quoted in the note on 9.641-2, uses *trieterica* (a Greek synonym for *triennia*) which West renders 'biennial'. However, I have thought it more important to preserve the allusion to 'three', a mystical number for most religions, than to give an immediate accurate picture of the length of this particular ritual cycle.
643 **Bubasian:** *Bubasides*; an Ovidian formation from Bubassus; Pliny (*N.H.* 5.104) knows it as *Bubassus*, a *regio* (region) of Caria; Herodotus (1.174) uses an adjective 'Bybassian'; Diodorus Siculus (5.62) records the name as 'Boubastos' as does Parthenius (*Erot. P.*11).
645 **Carians:** Caria was the country in the south-west corner of Asia Minor where Caunus (see on 9.634) was situated.
  Leleges: a prehistoric people associated with Caria (see on 7.443-4). The line is clearly based on Virg. *Aeneid* 8.725 (West's translation), but with the arming transferred from the Gelonians to the Leleges:

> *...the Lelegeians and Carians of Asia and the Gelonians from Scythia with their arrows.*

See also Hom. *Il.* 10.428-9; for further details, see Fordyce on Virg. *Aen.* 8.725.
  Lycia: the next country to the south and east of Caria. Byblis has now travelled far beyond where Caunus had settled.
646 **Cragos:** a coastal town and mountain range in central Lycia; see N.-H. on Hor. *Odes* 1.21.8 where the spelling *Gragos* is preferred.
  Limyre: (stress the first syllable) a town and mountain range in Eastern Lycia.
  Xanthus: a river and town in central Lycia, a little to the east of Cragos and not to be confused with the other river Xanthus in the Troad that was alluded to at 2.245.
647 **the Chimera had fire in its middle parts:** for the fantastic form of the Chimera and its association with Lycia, see Hom. *Il.* 6.171-3, 179-82 (Lattimore's translation, corrected):

> *But he [Bellerophontes] went to Lykia in the blameless convoy of the gods; when he came to Lykia and the running stream of Xanthos, the lord of wide Lykia tendered him full-hearted honour...*
> *...he sent him away with orders to kill the Chimaira none might approach; a thing of immortal make, not human in front a lion, and behind a snake, and in the middle, a goat snorting out the breath of the terrible flame of bright fire.*

Anderson seems to think that Ovid is making a clever point in suggesting that the middle part, the goat, is the source of the fire; however, the same is true of the Homeric account (quoted above) and of Apollodorus (2.3.1). 'Chimera' has, of course, entered English meaning 'a mere wild fancy'.

649-51 For the apostrophe, see on 9.101.

649 following: i.e. 'following Caunus', cf. 9.640.

659-62 Anderson comments:

> *...Ovid introduces a triad of brief comparisons, none of them very lovely or pathetic as a composite "naturalistic" account of how a girl could turn into a fountain. The resulting ambivalent tone is deliberate.*

The tone of this passage is certainly undercut by the grotesquely inappropriate comparisons with pitch and bitumen. However, the comparison with ice melting in the spring is perhaps more sympathetic enabling the reader to view this metamorphosis as something of a happy release, in contrast to her suicide in the version alluded to by Ovid at *Ars* 1.283-4 (see on 9.450-665). Alternatively, this may be better viewed as another example of Ovid's delight in proposing pseudo-scientific 'explanations' for his metamorphoses.

659 the bark: *cortice*; Ovid leaves it to his reader to infer from the context that this is the bark of a pitch-pine. The general idea is reminiscent of the tears of Phaethon's sisters at 2.364-6.

660 bitumen: for its natural occurrence in soil, cf. Lucr. 6.806-7.

661 Favonius: (stress the second syllable); the west wind; its character is eloquently brought out by Horace (*Odes* 1.4.1):

> *Harsh winter is dissolved by the welcome return of spring and of Favonius.*

663 Phoebean: Phoebus Apollo was Byblis' grandfather, cf. 9.455, see on 9.443.

665 flows: *manat*, picking up 'is the flow of' (*manat*) at 9.659. The translation slightly obscures the wit of this particular repetition.

a dark holm-oak: *nigra...ilice*; the *ilex* is an evergreen; as Anderson suggests, its presence in Horace's account of the spring at Bandusia (*Odes* 3.13.14) is guarantee enough that it was associated with scenes of great natural beauty. See also 1.112.

666-797 Iphis

No other version of this story is extant except that of Antoninus Liberalis (17) who tells us that he found it in book 2 of Nicander's *Heteroeumena*. Ovid has changed all the names and much of the plot. Some of these changes enable Ovid to give a more favourable view of the characters; others, especially the name changes, are unusual; Ovid does not normally make such detailed and apparently unmotivated changes so that it is tempting to speculate that Ovid had an intermediate source, now lost. The differences will be noted as they arise. For a full discussion see Otis (1966) 388-9, (1970) 417-8 and *passim*. Ovid clearly sees his version of the Iphis story as a happy and innocent contrast to that of Byblis.

666-7 the hundred Cretan cities: Ovid here reminds us that Miletus, the father of Caunus and Byblis, had originated in Crete (9.440-6) and this provides a link with Iphis. Crete was noted for its hundred cities from the earliest times, cf. 7.480-1, Hom. *Il.* 2.649.

668 Iphis: in Ant. Lib. she was called Leucippus; see also on 9.708-9.

669 the Phaestian land very close to the kingdom of Cnossus: Phaestus was at about the centre of the south coast of Crete, Cnossus a few miles north on the north coast.

670 Ligdus by name: in Ant. Lib. he was called Lampros.

671 plebs: see on 9.307. Ant. Lib's Lampros was poor but well-born.

fortune: *census*; the Latin word is a technical term for a property qualification from which it developed the sense 'fortune'; see also on 7.739, 8.846.

672-3 Ant. Lib. does not discuss Lampros' character.

675-9 Note how Ovid uses this speech to bring out the essential decency of a man trapped in a situation he hates. In Ant. Lib. the father tells his wife to produce a son, for no stated reason, and instructs her to kill the baby if it turns out to be a girl.

677 the resources: i.e. to rear and provide for a girl; she would be much less likely to contribute to a family's needs and she would also require a dowry.

679 O Piety: see on 9.382; for the personification, cf. 7.72..

682 **Telethusa:** in Ant. Lib. the mother was called Galatea and she made no attempt to dissuade her husband.

685 **load:** *pondere*: see on 9.270.

686-701 No such divine intervention is found at this stage of Ant. Lib's version, though there is mention of 'dreams and prophecies'.

687 **Inachus' daughter:** *Inachis*; this is the Egyptian goddess, Isis; we last met her at 1.568-747 where the story was told of how Io, Inachus' daughter, was seduced by Jupiter, transformed into a cow to deceive Juno and eventually rewarded by being transformed into Isis. For further details, see the passage and my notes. For Isis, see Booth on Ov. *Am.* 2.13.7, a poem much of whose material is re-used in this story; for further details see on 9.773-81.

688-9 **lunar horns were on her forehead and yellow ears of corn:** cf. Herodotus 2.41 (de Sélincourt's translation):

> *The statues of Isis show a female figure with cow's horns, like the Greek*
> *representations of Io.*

But Herodotus also associates Isis with Demeter (2.59):

> *...the assembly at Busiris—a city in the middle of the Delta, containing a*
> *vast temple devoted to Isis, the Egyptian equivalent of Demeter...*

Demeter was known to the Romans as Ceres; for her story and her association with wheat, see 5.341-661 and the notes there, especially 5.341-2:

> *Ceres was the first to part the clods with the curved plough,*
> *the first to give corn and gentle nourishment to the lands...*

For Isis' lunar association, see Diod. Sic. 1.11.1 (Oldfather's translation):

> *Now the men of Egypt... as they looked up at the firmament and were struck*
> *with both awe and wonder at the nature of the universe, conceived that two*
> *gods were both eternal and first, namely the sun and moon, whom they called*
> *respectively Osiris and Isis...*

690 **a royal ornament:** presumably a crown or diadem. Bömer collects much evidence from papyri and inscriptions for Isis as a queen; he refers also to Stat. *Silv.* 3.2.101-2 (Mozley's translation):

> *Isis, once stalled in Phoroneus' caves, now queen of Pharos.*

Anubis the barker: *latrator Anubis*; Ovid borrows the phrase from Virgil's famous description of Aeneas' shield and its portrayal of the Battle of Actium with the monstrous gods of Egypt ranged against the civilised gods of Rome (*Aen.* 8.698). Anubis was always represented with a dog's head. See also Booth on Ov. *Am.* 2.13.11.

691 **holy Bubastis:** cf. Herodotus 2.137, in a passage on flood control, (de Sélincourt's translation):

> *None of the Egyptian cities, I think, was raised so much as Bubastis, where*
> *there is a temple of Bubastis (the Greek Artemis)...*

Artemis corresponds, of course, to the Roman Diana.

Apis of various colours: cf. Herodotus 3.28 (de Sélincourt's translation):

> *The Apis-calf has distinctive marks: it is black with a white diamond on its*
> *forehead, the image of an eagle on its back, the hairs on its tail double, and*
> *a scarab under its tongue.*

692 The line refers to Harpocrates, a Hellenized version of an Egyptian divinity whose name meant 'Horus-child'; Egyptian statues represented him with his finger in his mouth to suggest childhood. The gesture was, however, misunderstood by Greeks and Romans who thought it was a call for silence; cf. Catul. 74.4 and 102.4 with Fordyce's note.

693 **sistra:** the sistron was a rattle associated with the worship of Isis, cf. Fordyce on Virg. *Aen.* 8.696 and Booth on Ov. *Am.* 2.13.11.

Osiris never sought for enough: cf. Booth's note (and her bibliography) on *pius... Osiris* (Ov. *Am.* 2.13.12):

> *brother-husband of Isis and, together with their son Horus, one of the chief*
> *figures in the cult. Re-enactment of Isis' tireless search for Osiris after his*
> *murder by another brother..., of her mourning for him and her eventual*
> *discovery of his dismembered body and revival of it took place at the Ro-*
> *man festival of the Isia...*

Plutarch *Mor*. 351c-84c gives a very full account of the worship of Isis and Osiris; see also Courtney on Juvenal 8.29.

694   **the wandering snake:** snakes were associated with Isis worship, see Booth on *Am*. 2.13.13.

695   **she...her:** the sleeping Telethusa...Isis; see on 9.279.

699   **to raise it up:** *tollere*; the verb is commonly used of the father lifting a new-born child from the ground to acknowledge paternity and, accordingly, to accept the responsibility for its nurture. The word can, however, be used, as here, of persons other than the father; see *OLD* s.v. 'tollo' 2.

whatever it is: i.e. 'of whichever sex it is'.

704   **load:** *pondus*; see on 9.270.

708   **paid his vows:** i.e. to the gods for the birth of, as he believes, the son he had prayed for.

708-9   **the grandfather's name...Iphis:** it was common for Greeks to be named after their grandfathers; in Ant. Lib. it is the mother who names the child and she chooses Leucippus which, unlike Iphis, can be only a boy's name. It is psychologically satisfying that, if the mother chooses the name, she should choose a boy's name to further the deceit, but that if the deceived father chooses the name he should, in all innocence, use a sexually neutral name. Bömer produces much material on the naming of children from which it emerges that both naming by the father and naming by the mother are attested from the earliest times.

711   **pious deceit:** *pia fraude*; the oxymoron brings out the moral issue, see on 9.408; for 'pious' see on 9.382.

714   **the third...tenth:** i.e. 'it was the thirteenth year after'; many Roman numerals are impossible or difficult to use in Latin verse; *tertius decimus* ('thirteenth') could be included in hexameters only if its two elements were separated; *tredecim* ('thirteen') would be just possible, though it would require a harsh elision, and periphrasis is so often required for numerals in verse that it seems natural even when it is strictly unnecessary; indeed, Ovid never uses *tredecim*.

715   For the apostrophe, see on 9.101.

Ianthe: there is no betrothal in Ant. Lib's version nor any other girl.

717   **Dictaean:** i.e. 'Cretan' from Mt Dicte in Crete.

718-21   **like...like...unlike:** an attempt to represent the effect of *par...par...dispar*.

719   **elements:** *elementa*; the word was, among other things, a technical term for the contents of what is still called an 'elementary' education; see *OLD* s.v. 4.

721   **wound:** *uulnus*; the use of this metaphor for 'love' has become a poetic commonplace by Ovid's time; see *OLD* s.v. 1d.

722-4   **Ianthe...Iphis:** Ovid stresses the contrast by placing Ianthe's name at the end of her sentence (and of a line) and Iphis' immediately after as the first word of hers (and of a line). The effect is impossible to reproduce in English.

723   **a man...her man:** *uirum...uirum*; Ovid is playing on the fact that *uir* can mean either 'man' or 'husband'; I have decided to keep the word-play even though it introduces, in English, a slightly colloquial and inappropriate tone.

725   **flames...on fire:** cf. 7.9ff, 8.50; for earlier examples of this very familiar image for passion, see e.g. Ap. Rhod. 3.285-98, Virg. *Aen*. 4.2 (with Pease's monumental note).

725-34   **maiden...maiden...cow's...cow...mares...mares...female...female:** *uirgine uirgo... uaccam uaccae...equas...equarum...femina femineo*; the situation lends itself to polyptoton, but Ovid exercises some restraint by introducing much variety of expression in this report of Iphis' turbulent thoughts; see further on 9.44.

728 **a strange Venus:** *nouae... Veneris* i.e. 'a strange kind of sexual pleasure', cf. 3.323. For metonymy in general, see on 9.141 where the same Latin phrase is used in a quite different way.

735 **Would that I were nothing!**: *uellem nulla forem*; a wish to die, as Bömer observes; Anderson (and others) who believe that the words could also mean 'I wish I were no woman' are stretching the Latin intolerably. Furthermore, it seems premature to hint at the solution here.

736 For the story of Pasiphaë, wife of Minos, king of Crete, her affair with a bull, and the birth of the Minotaur, see 8.131-7 and the notes.

739 **Venus:** 'a sexual experience', see on 9.141, 728.

742 **Daedalus:** he was the craftsman who made Pasiphaë's wooden cow; later he escaped from Crete back to his native Athens by flying with wings made of feathers glued together by wax; see 8.152-259 and the notes.

750 **this:** *hanc*; hope, see on 9.279.

757 **I want...wants...she too wants:** *uolo uult... uult ipsa*; for the polyptoton see on 9.44.

762 ***pronuba***: an untranslatable term for the matron who conducted the bride to the marriage chamber; cf. Virg. *Aen.* 4.166 (and Austin) and the pseudo-marriage between Aeneas and Dido. For further details, see on 6.428. Once again, Ovid is using anachronistic Roman terminology (see on 9.307).
   Hymenaeos: the marriage hymn here, as often, personified as a god; the word is as early as Homer (*Il.* 18.493); for a full discussion see Fordyce on Cat. 61.

763 **groom...brides:** *ducat... nubimus*; in Latin, there is one set of verb forms to describe a bridegroom marrying and a different set for a bride. Here, Ovid exploits the difference but, in the absence of such distinctions in English, a literal translation ('at which the one who marries is absent and where both of us are marrying') would be nonsense.

771 **hair-bands:** *crinalem... uittam*; Roman matrons, priests and sacrificial victims wore bands in their hair; see Austin on Virg. *Aen.* 2.133 (for the Roman anachronism see on 9.307); it is not clear why Iphis, who was disguised as a man, was wearing them, unless we are to suppose that this is a private moment shared only by Iphis and her mother; the bands were certainly removed for Bacchic worship, cf. 4.6-7 itself based on Virg. *Aen.* 7.401-3 (West's translation):
   *...untie the ribbons of your hair [*crinales uittas*] and take to the secret rites with me.*
Ovid is presumably likening Isis worship to Bacchic worship; in Rome, both were generally regarded as alien and dangerous.

772 **her hair flowing loose:** *passis... capillis*; the same phrase is used of Ino in the grip of Bacchic frenzy at 4.521 and of Medea supervising the most outrageous ceremonials at 7.257.

773-81 The prayer is a close reworking of Ovid's own prayer to Isis on behalf of his mistress whose life was in the balance as a result of an attempt at abortion (*Am.* 2.13.7ff.). Many of the standard features of ancient prayers are included: the invocation with a relative clause giving an 'address' (cf. 'Our Father, which art in heaven...'), the petition itself, and the reference to previous dealings. For further details, see Booth on Ov. *Am.* 2.13. By a strange coincidence, a part of both prayers has been severely corrupted in the manuscript tradition.

773 **Paraetonium:** a port on the north coast of Africa often said to be on the border between Egypt and Libya; however, that border moved so much both in ancient and modern times that it is not a helpful indication. The site seems to have been very slightly to the east of the modern Matrûh.
   the Mareotic fields: Mareotis was an inland lake just to the south of Alexandria.

774 **Pharos:** an island off the coast at Alexandria, noted for its famous lighthouse built by Ptolemy II Philadelphus.
   the Nile divided into seven branches: the reference is to the delta; seven was the traditional number of its streams; cf. 1.422, 5.188, Herod. 2.17, Catul. 11.78, Virg. *Aen.* 6.800.

777-8 777 was deleted as corrupt by Merkel; though it makes more sense than it did if we follow Tarrant in reading Shackleton Bailey's *sacrorum* ('of the rites') for *sistrorum* ('of the sistra') in 778.

779-80 These lines have long been thought of as corrupt; both text and translation should be regarded as makeshift.

782 (and she had moved them): see on 9.17.

783-4 her moon-like horns: see on 9.688-9.

784 soundable: *sonabile*; an Ovidian coinage found only here; see on 9.26?

790-1 For the apostrophe, see on 9.101.

793-4 The vow and inscription are yet another example of Ovid's taste for Roman anachronism; see on 9.307.

793 an inscription; the inscription: *titulum; titulus*; for the polyptoton see on 9.44.

796-7 marriage fires: *ignes*; the marriage torches.

BOOK X

1-11.84 *Orpheus*

Much has been written on Ovid's treatment of Orpheus. My own views, together with an outline of other opinions, are to be found in Hill (1992). To put the essential point briefly, Ovid retells Virgil's narrative, omitting his details and filling in all his omissions. I shall draw attention to individual examples as seems appropriate. From the earliest times, Orpheus was regarded as a consummate poet, musician and mystic, hence the interest shown in him by Virgil (*G.* 4.453-527), Horace (*Ars P.* 391-3) and Ovid.

1-85 *Orpheus and Eurydice*

The story of Orpheus and Eurydice (stress the '-y-') is told by Apollodorus (1.3.2, Frazer's translation):

> *Now Calliope bore to Oeagrus or, nominally, to Apollo, a son Linus, whom Hercules slew; and another son, Orpheus who practised minstrelsy and by his songs moved stones and trees. And when his wife Eurydice died, bitten by a snake, he went down to Hades, being fain to bring her up, and he persuaded Pluto to send her up. The god promised to do so, if on the way Orpheus would not turn round until he should be coming to his own house. But he disobeyed and turning round beheld his wife; so she turned back.*

It is presumably an ancient story but Virgil's version seems to be the earliest extant. In any case, it is clear that Ovid is very aware of Virgil as he writes; the verbal echoes are constant and Ovid constantly narrates what Virgil has passed over and passes over what Virgil has narrated. For the details, see Hill (1992) 124-31.

1   **From there:** *Inde*; from Phaestos in Crete (see on 9.669) where Iphis and Ianthe had just celebrated their wedding. Hymenaeos is, accordingly, travelling from an unexpectedly happy wedding to the doomed wedding of Orpheus and Eurydice.

2   **ether:** *aethera*; in Greek the word refers to the upper air, as here. I have translated it as 'ether' throughout.

      the lands: *oras*; see on 9.254-5.

3   **Cicones:** see on 11.3.

4   **he was there:** *adfuit ille*; Hymenaeus (see on 9.279) was there. But 'no Hymenaeus was there' (*non Hymenaeus adest*) at the even more ill-starred wedding of Tereus and Procne (6.429).

6-7   At the wedding of Tereus and Procne, the torches were brought by the Eumenides and 'snatched from a funeral' (6.430). This wedding torch merely fails to burn, in contrast to those of Iphis and Ianthe (9.796-7).

8   **auspice:** *auspicio*; the Roman practice (see on 9.307) of inspecting bird flight and other omens before embarking on any serious business.

11   **Rhodopeian:** Rhodope was a mountain range in western Thrace (cf. 6.87, 10.77 and the notes); here the adjective means no more than 'Thracian'; Ovid is here borrowing from Virgil's account of Orpheus' country (*G.* 4.461).

      bard: *uates*; the fundamental sense of this word is 'prophet', 'seer' which is how it is frequently used in the *Metamorphoses*: of Tiresias (3.348, 511, 527), of the Sphinx (7.761), of Amphiaraüs (9.407) and of Proteus (11.249); poets were, however, thought of as spokesmen of the gods, so that the word was also regularly used to mean 'poet', 'bard' as here, or even 'priest' (as at 11.68); indeed from here to 11.68, it is used exclusively of Orpheus.

12   **to the heavens above:** *ad...superas auras*; for the usage, see *OLD* s.v. 'aura' 4b. However, in his account of Eurydice's story, Virgil uses the phrase to refer to Eurydice's return from the Underworld to the earth above (*G.* 4.486).

13   **descend to the Styx by the Taenarian gate:** Styx was a river of the Underworld as early as Homer (*Il.* 8.367-9, Lattimore's translation):

> *when Herakles was sent down to Hades of the Gates, to hale back*
> *from the Kingdom of the Dark the hound of the grisly death god,*
> *never would he have got clear of the steep-dripping Stygian water.*

Taenarus was at the southern tip of the middle of the three peninsulas which stretch out below the Peloponnese; it was most famous for a cave reputed to be an entrance to the Underworld, and it was the route attributed to Orpheus by Virgil (*G.* 4.467). For further details, see N.-H. on Horace *Odes* 1.34.10 where too Styx and Taenarus are juxtaposed.

14   **weightless:** *leues*; Horace (*Odes* 1.10.18) uses the word in the same way; that the dead are lighter than the living is a commonplace made especially memorable by Virgil in his description of Charon ferrying Aeneas across the Styx (*Aen.* 6.412-4, West's translation):

> *In the same moment he took the huge Aeneas into the hull of his little boat.*
> *Being only sown together, it groaned under his weight...*

See also on 4.449-50.

the ghosts who had experienced the tomb: *simulacraque functa sepulcro*; the phrase is reused from 4.435, where Juno is visiting the Underworld. The whole line is something of an echo of Virg. *G.* 4.472:

> *the thin shades came and the ghosts [*simulacraque*] of those without the light*

with *functa* borrowed from *defuncta* (*G.* 4.475); the Virgilian passage is also from Orpheus' visit to the Underworld.

15-6   **Persephone...and the lord of the shades:** Persephone (the Greek form of the name 'Proserpina') and Dis, rulers of the Underworld; for their story, see 5.341-661.

15   **uncharming:** *inamoena*; a made-up word to represent an Ovidian coinage; see on 9.262.

18-39   Virgil gives no account of Orpheus' speech to Dis but passes directly from the reaction of the Underworld to Orpheus' arrival (*G.* 4.467-84) to an account of his return journey (485ff.), leaving the reader to supply the appeal and Dis' reply. This omission presents Ovid with an irresistible temptation.

21   **Tartarus:** the Underworld, the home of the dead; cf. Hom. *Il.* 8.13-16 (Lattimore's translation):

> *or I shall take him and dash him down to the murk of Tartaros,*
> *far below, where the uttermost depth of the pit lies under*
> *earth, where there are gates of iron and a brazen doorstone,*
> *as far beneath the house of Hades as from earth the sky lies.*

21-2   **nor to bind...the Medusian monster:** Cerberus, the three-headed hound of Hell, was indeed bound by Hercules, a previous visitor to the Underworld. For an account, see 7.408-15 and the notes. He is 'Medusian' only because, like Medusa (see 4.771-89 and the notes), he had snakes for hair.

24   **growing years:** *crescentes...annos*; a striking phrase both in Latin and English, though its meaning is not hard to see. Ovid used the phrase earlier (*Ars* 1.61) and probably invented it; Bömer collects examples of later imitations.

26   **Love has conquered:** *uicit Amor*; almost universally seen as a reference to Virgil's famous line (*Ecl.* 10.69): 'Love conquers all, and let us yield to Love' *omnia uincit Amor et nos cedamus Amori*.

in the upper world: *supera...in ora*; see on 9.254-5.

27   **I divine:** *auguror*, a technical term of Roman religion which humorously lends a spurious solemnity; see also on 9.307.

28   **that old rape:** for the rape of Proserpina by Dis, see on 5.341-661.

30   **Chaos:** see on 1.7.

37   **a loan:** *usum*, a technical legal term for a loan (*OLD* s.v. 4); editors compare Lucr. 3.971 (Bailey's translation):

> *and life is granted to none for freehold, to all on lease [*usu*].*

41-6   For a discussion of the relationship between this account of the Underworld's reaction to Orpheus and Virgil's version (*G.* 4.481-4), see Hill (1992) 128; briefly, Ovid omits Cerberus from Virgil's account and adds Tantalus, Tityos, the Danaïds and Sisyphus.

41   **Tantalus:** the first of a group of famous wrongdoers whose punishments are temporarily suspended, because of Orpheus' song; there is another similar list at 4.457-63. All such lists derive ultimately from Hom. *Od.* 11.576-600; cf. also Virg. *Aen.* 6.595-607, Horace *Odes* 3.11.21-4. Tantalus' punishment was never to be able to slake his thirst because the water around him always receded as he reached out for it. For the story, see 6.172-3 (and the notes).

42   **Ixion's wheel:** see on 9.124, 4.461.

43   **the birds...liver:** this alludes to Tityos whose punishment was to have his constantly re-generating liver pecked out, equally constantly, by vultures. For further details, see on 4.457.

43-4 **Belides...urns:** the Belides (stress the first syllable), i.e. 'daughters of Belus' were, in fact, Belus' granddaughters, being daughters of his son,. Danaüs. Their punishment was to fill leaking vessels for ever. For further details, see on 4.462-3.

44   **Sisyphus:** (stress the first syllable); his punishment was to roll a rock up a hill towards its summit, only to lose control of it and watch it roll to the bottom again and then to be forced to repeat the cycle for ever. For further details, see on 4.460 and 466.

45   **Eumenides:** see on 9.410. It would be very surprising to see them weep for pity.

46-7 **the king's wife...he who rules the depths:** *regia coniunx...qui regit ima*; Proserpina and her husband, Dis, see on 9.259; 10.15-16.

50-7 For a discussion on the relationship between this account of the loss of Eurydice and Vir-gil's (*G.* 4.485-95), see Hill (1992) 128-9.

50   **her and, at the same time, the condition:** *hanc simul et legem*; for the syllepsis, see on 9.135.

52   **Avernus' valleys:** Avernus here means not the lake which was one of the entrances to the Underworld (for which see Austin on Virg. *Aen.* 6.42-76) but is used to refer to the Under-world itself; see Austin on Virg. *Aen.* 6.126.

        the gift would be annulled: *irrita dona futura*; the words clearly echo Virg. *G.* 4.519-20 where Orpheus, at the end of the story, complains that Eurydice has been snatched from him and that 'the gifts of Dis had been in vain' (*irrita Ditis dona*); in Ovid's adaptation, how-ever, the words are not part of Orpheus' complaint but part of Dis' threat; the context is of contract and condition, and the legalistic sense of *irritus* (*OLD* s.v. 1a) seems to be domi-nant. This is a good example of how Ovid re-uses a word or phrase to give it a subtly differ-ent nuance.

53-4 **The sloping path...in hushed silence...dense mist:** this picture of the way up from the Underworld echoes Ovid's description of the way down to the Underworld that confronted Juno at 4.432-3:

> *There is a downward path, shaded by funereal yew;*
> *it leads through a hushed silence to the place below.*

Other echoes of that incident have already been noted at 10.14, 42, 43, 43-4, 44. For the pleonasm, 'hushed silence' *muta silentia* see on 10.389.

58-63 There is a great difference between Ovid's discussion of the last poignant moments Or-pheus had with Eurydice, with its characteristic exploration of possible psychological ex-planations, and Virgil's sublime contemplation of the poignancy of the event (*G.* 4.485-505); for a detailed analysis, see Hill (1992) 129-30.

58-9 **stretching...yielding air:** the earliest model for these lines is from Homer's description of Odysseus' encounter with his mother who has temporarily come up from the Underworld to converse with him (*Od.* 11.204-8, Lattimore's translation):

> *So she spoke, but I, pondering it in my heart, yet wished*
> *to take the soul of my dead mother in my arms. Three times*
> *I started towards her, and my heart was urgent to hold her,*
> *and three times she fluttered out of my hands like a shadow*
> *or a dream, and the sorrow sharpened at the heart within me.*

In Virgil's account of the loss of Eurydice, she cries out to Orpheus so (*G.* 4.497-8):

> '... and now farewell: I am being carried off surrounded by vast night
> and (alas no longer yours) stretching out [tendens] to you my weak hands.'

A little later, at the last moment (G. 4.499-502):

> He spoke and suddenly, like thin smoke mixed in with the air,
> she had turned and was fleeing from his eyes, and she did not see
> him grasping [prensantem] the shadows in vain and wanting
> to say much besides...

When Creusa makes her final mysterious appearance to Aeneas, she was, presumably, already dead; consider Virgil's description of this poignant moment (Aen. 2.790-3):

> When she had said these things, she left me weeping and wishing
> to say much, and she faded into thin air.
> Three times, I tried to put my arms around her neck;
> three times, her phantom, vainly grasped at [comprensa], escaped my hands.

Aen. 2.792-4 are repeated at 6.700-2 to describe Aeneas' last moments with his father in the Underworld. In all these very famous cases, it is the living man who strives to hold the dead loved one, and an expectation has been established in many translators and editors that the same must be true here; indeed, that argument is specific in Anderson; accordingly, 58-9 are attributed to Orpheus so that it is he who 'stretches out [intendens] his arms' and he who 'unhappy man, seizes on nothing but yielding air.' There is, however, no indication of change of subject either at the beginning of 58 or at the beginning of 60; and Ovid is normally scrupulous about that. Ovid's attention here is on Eurydice; there is no indication of attempted embrace at all; as editors observe, prendique et prendere would be unparalleled for an embrace; what is being described is Eurydice's desperate attempt to get Orpheus to grasp her outstretched arm, as she slips back, or to grasp his. Instead, she 'seized onto [adripit] nothing but yielding air' [cedentes...auras], quite different from Virgil's Orpheus 'grasping [prensantem] the shadows' [umbras] or Aeneas 'grasping at' [comprensa] Creusa's phantom. The one respect in which Ovid's Eurydice imitates Virgil's here is that both are 'stretching out [(in)tendens] their arms'; in the alternative interpretation, of course, one of these arm-stretchers is Orpheus and the other, Eurydice. It is, in any case, characteristic of Ovid to concentrate on the feelings of the dead character if his predecessors have concentrated on the living one.

65-7 This story of an unknown man literally petrified at the sight of Cerberus ('the Stygian dog') is otherwise unknown but is generally assumed to be a continuation of the story that Hercules carried Cerberus out of the Underworld; see 10.21-2 and the note.

67-71 he story of **Olenos** (stress the first syllable) and **Lethaea** (stress the middle syllable) is also known only from this account. Presumably, when, Lethaea was to be punished by petrification for some arrogance about her beauty, Olenos was so anxious not to be separated from her that he insisted that he shared her guilt so that he could also share her punishment.

69 **unhappy Lethaea:** infelix Lethaea; Anderson comments:

> Notice that Ovid apostrophizes Lethaea and calls her infelix, a concession
> he never made to Eurydice.

But, if 10.58-9 is attributed to Eurydice, both women are indeed called infelix. Since, as Anderson himself points out, Olenos seems to share with Orpheus a passionate desire never to be separated from his wife even by death, there is some point in drawing attention to the similarity between Eurydice and Lethaea. For apostrophe generally, see on 9.101.

71 **watery Ida:** a mountain near Troy. Homer (Il. 12.19-22) lists eight rivers that rise on its slopes. See also from Ovid's description of the destruction caused to mountains by Phaëthon's loss of control of the horses of the Sun (2.218):

> and Ida, dry then, but previously abounding in springs.

72 **he:** Orpheus.

73-85 For a discussion of the relationship between this account of Orpheus' choice of celibacy and Virgil's version (G. 4.516-20), see Hill (1992) 130-1.

73   **ferryman:** *portitor*; Virgil (*G*. 4.502, *Aen.* 6.298) also uses this word for Charon whose duty it was to ferry the souls of the dead across the Styx; see Austin on Virgil *Aen.* 6.298ff. He had also ferried a number of living visitors to the Underworld, including Aeneas (see on 10.14). Virgil too (*G*. 4.502-3) portrays Charon refusing to allow Orpheus to return to the Underworld, but neither he nor Ovid gives him a rôle in Orpheus' original descent.

74   **the gift of Ceres:** 'bread'; cf. 3.437 and the note, 5.341-2 and the notes on 5. 341-661, 341-5. For the metonymy, see on 9.141.

76   **Erebus:** the realm of the dead; cf. Hom. *Od.* 10.528.

77   **Rhodope...Haemus:** it cannot be accidental that Orpheus retreats to Mt Rhodope and Mt Haemus which, according to a legend alluded to at 6.87-9 (and see the notes), had originally been lovers before their cruel metamorphosis into mountains.
      Aquilo: the north wind, notorious as a violent wind; Dido rebukes Aeneas for contemplating sailing when the Aquilo is blowing (Virg. *Aen.* 4.310) but, in spite of Austin's comment ('The *Aquilo* was notoriously the wind of rain and storm'), it was not especially a bringer of rain to Greeks and Romans for whom it had, after all, come from over land. Here, however, we are to the north, in Thrace, where the wind might be expected still to have its full force and plenteous rain.

78   **the third Titan:** according to Hesiod (*Theog.* 371-2), the Titan, Hyperion, was the father of the Sun, the Moon and Dawn. Hence Cicero, in his translation of Aratus (589) [*de Nat. Deorum* 2.42] uses *Titan* for Sun, and he was followed by Virgil (*Aen.* 4.119), Seneca and others. See also on 1.10. Here, the Titan, Sun, (whose apparent annual motion around the earth is the basis for the year) is used as a metonymy for 'year'; see on 9.141.

78-9 **bounded by watery *Pisces*:** *aequoreis inclusum Piscibus*; literally 'bound by maritime Fish'; however, 'maritime' seems hopelessly inappropriate and, since it is the zodiac sign that is at issue, it seems best to leave *Pisces* in Latin since that is how it is still most commonly known. *Pisces* is still normally regarded as the last sign of the year, although, as a result of the precession of the equinoxes, the sun is no longer in each of its signs during the traditional dates. For an explanation of the sun's annual journey through the zodiac, see on 2.70-5.

80   **Venus with women:** *femineam Venerem* i.e. 'sex with women', cf. 3.323; 9.728. Virgil uses *Venus* in the same sense in his account of this part of the story (*G*. 4.516). For metonymy in general, see on 9.141 where V*enus* is used in rather a different way.

84-5 While it is true that, in the ancient world generally, pederasty attracted less outrage than it does today, Ovid clearly sees it here as evidence of deep neurosis in Orpheus. It is the climax of the difference between Virgil's account of Orpheus' symptoms and Ovid's. Virgil's Orpheus (*G*. 4.507-20) does not fast but grieves and is celibate for seven months; Ovid's Orpheus fasts for seven days but is celibate for three years until, finally, he gives way to pederasty; see further Hill (1992) 130-1; see also on 11.775-6.

86-142 Cyparissus

This is the first extant version of the story in literature. Possible antecedents in cult and Pompeian wall painting are discussed by Bömer.

86-8 For the ekphrasis, see on 9.334.

88   **god-born:** see on 10.1-85, N.-H. on Hor. *Odes* 1.12.9.

88-90 **shade was missing from the place...shade came to the place:** an attempt to render the echoing *umbra loco deerat...umbra loco uenit*.

90-105 The story is interrupted by a catalogue of trees. Catalogues were a feature of epic as early as Homer's Catalogue of Ships (*Il.* 2.484-759); for other examples, see 3.206-33; 8.298-328.

90   **The Chaonian tree:** the oak; there was an oak tree at Zeus' famous oracle at Dodona in the part of Epirus called Chaonia; cf. 7.623 and the note.

91   **Heliades:** *Heliadum;* 'Daughters of the Sun' i.e. Phaëthon's sisters lamenting his loss until they were changed into trees (often said to be poplars, cf. e.g. Virg. *Aen.* 10.189-90) which wept amber. See 2.340-66 and the notes, Forbes Irving 269-71.
   durmast: *aesculus;* used by modern botanists for the chestnut but in antiquity for an especially tall species of oak; see Mynors on Virg. *G.* 2.16.

92   **the unmarried laurel:** for the story of Daphne, who was determined not to be married in spite of Apollo's desire for her, and was changed into a laurel, see 1.452-567 and the notes, Forbes Irving 261-3.

93   **the ash useful for spears;** cf. 5.142; Achilles was famous for his ash spear (cf. Hom. *Il.* 16.140-4).

95   **the kindly plane-tree:** *platanus genialis;* the tree was popular in public places because it provided generous shade; see N.-H. on Hor. *Odes* 2.15.4.

96   **river-dwelling:** *amnicolae;* an Ovidian coinage (see on 9.262) which literally means 'river-dwelling' but which presumably alludes to the fact that willows live beside rivers.
   the water-lotus: *aquatica lotus;* see 9.340-5.

97   **and the fine tamarisks:** *tenuesque myricae;* according to Hessayon 54:

> You are not likely to confuse Tamarisk with any other shrub—when in
> bloom the delicate leaves combine with the plumes of tiny pink flowers to
> give a unique feathery effect. Despite its appearance it is not delicate...

98   **the myrtles of both colours:** according to Cato (*Agr.* 8.2 and 133.2) myrtle berries are indeed both black and white; cf. 11.234.

99-100   **pliant-footed...elms clad in vines:** *flexipedes* (pliant-footed) another Ovidian coinage (see on 9.262) is seen by editors (compare 3.664) to refer to the way ivy grows, though *OLD* takes it to refer to the rooting system. Anderson, however, is surely right to connect it to the pines in the following line:

> Ivy cannot come by itself, so it accompanies the tree around which it
> winds...grapevines...also climb trees with their tendrils. The Italians used
> elms to support the vines, so here elms transport the vines to Orpheus' con-
> cert.

For this use of elms, see Catul. 62.49-55 and Fordyce.

102   **the victor's reward:** the use of palms for athletic victors came to Greece from the East too late for Pindar. Livy (10.47.3) reports its adoption by Romans in 293 B.C.; see Williams on Verg. *Aen.* 5.70, N.-H. on Hor. *Odes* 1.1.5.

103   **with foliage girt up:** *succincta comas;* the image is of the tall, bare-trunked pine with its foliage at the top. The primary meaning of *coma* is 'hair' but its use for foliage is so common that it is natural to translate it as 'hair' in such contexts. Even so, the word probably does retain enough of its basic sense here to conjure up a metaphor of a woman with her unkempt hair worn high on her head.

104   **the Mother of the gods...Attis:** Cybele, whose worship probably originated in Phrygia but who was much cherished at Rome, was tragically involved with Attis who, for reasons about which there was no unanimity in antiquity, castrated himself. Their worship involved a re-enactment by Cybele's priests of Attis' emasculation. However, this story of Attis' transformation into a pine is known only from Ovid. See Lucr. 2.598-643 (and Bailey), Catul. 63 (and Fordyce and Godwin), Virg. *Aen.* 6.784-7 (and Austin).

106   **cone-shaped:** *metas imitata,* literally 'that imitated the turning posts' i.e. the conical turning-posts for the chariot racing on Rome's Circus Maximus; yet another example of Ovid's penchant for introducing anachronistic Roman concepts (see on 9.307).

107   **that god:** Apollo, whose lyre appears as early as Hom. *Il.* 1.603 and whose bow as early as Hom. *Il.* 1.43-7.

109   **Carthaean:** Carthaea was a town on the island of Ceos; for further details, see on 7.368 where Ovid uses an alternative form of the adjective.

110   **a huge stag:** *ingens ceruus;* the phrase is borrowed from Virgil *Aen.* 7.483 where the killing of Silvia's pet stag by Iulus provokes the outbreak of hostilities. The verbal echoes between the two incidents are listed by Fordyce and discussed by Anderson. As one might expect, Virgil's account is poignant, Ovid's is not. Martial (13.96) plays on the possible confusion between the two stags.

112-3 hanging down to his shoulders, there was a...necklace suspended: *demissaque in armos pendebant...monilia*; a clear echo of Virgil's description of Latinus' horses (*Aen.* 7.278): *aurea pectoribus demissa monilia pendent*).

120-5 For the apostrophe, see on 9.101.

121 to you; you: *tibi; tu*; for the polyptoton see on 9.44.

122-4 you...you...you: *tu...tu...tu*; the repetition of the second person pronoun gives a mock-hymnic tone to the passage; see on 6.177-9. The second 'you' has been maintained in the translation at the expense of adding 'led' (122) which is absent from the Latin; see on 7.433-50.

126-9 For the ekphrasis, see on 9.334.

127 shore-dwelling *Cancer*: *litorei...Cancri*, literally 'Crab'; Ovid delights in playing with the names of the signs of the zodiac by alluding to their literal meanings; see also on 10.165. Cancer was the sign through which the sun was passing in antiquity (and still does to this day in the minds of newspaper astrologers) from late June till late July. See on 10.78-9.

134 and proportionately: *pro materiaque*; the translation attempts to catch the humour of the descent by the Latin into the prosaic and banal.

138-40 Some translators assume, without justification, that the subject of this sentence suddenly changes from *capilli* ('hair') to Cyparissus; they also take *caesaries* to mean 'foliage' but, despite Bömer's best efforts, the word (unlike *coma*, see on 10.103) cannot bear that meaning, certainly not as early as Ovid.

141-2 For the widespread association of the cypressus with death and funerals, see N.-H. on Hor. *Odes* 2.14.23.

143-7 A brief interlude to introduce Orpheus' song

143 bard: *uates*; see on 10.11.

145 Calliope behaves similarly at 5.339-40.

147-9 he gave voice...start up our song: *uocem...mouit...carmina nostra moue*; the translation makes no attempt to reproduce the repetition *mouit...moue* in spite of Bömer's rather surprising claim that the former is a 'spielerische Variante' of the latter; see on 10.443-4).

148-54 Orpheus' song: introduction

148 From Jove: *ab Ioue*; a famous beginning perhaps best known from Aratus 1, Theocritus 17.1 and Virg. *Ecl.* 3.60; Anderson relates it also to the rather different *Hom. Hymn* 25.1; cf. also Statius *Theb.* 4.848; Statius indeed, in his prose preface to *Silvae* 1, interprets his beginning with Domitian as conformity to the practice, *a Ioue principium* 'From Jupiter one begins'.

150-2 a heavier plectrum...a lighter lyre: *plectro grauiore...leuiore lyra*; for a full discussion, see N.-H. on Horace *Odes* 2.1.40.

150 Giants: the story of the Giants' unsuccessful attack upon Zeus appears to be very early, but the earliest full extant account seems to be Apollodorus 1.6.1-2. For a detailed account of earlier and later allusions, both in literature and art, see N.-H. on Horace *Odes* 2.12.7 (where the myth's use as political allegory is discussed) and on 2.19.22. Horace himself (*Odes* 3.4.42-8) used the story with a clear suggestion that disobedience to Augustus is to be likened to the Giants' attack on Zeus' authority.

151 Phlegraean: cf. Apollodorus 1.6.1 (Frazer's translation):
> They [the Giants] were born, as some say, in Phlegrae, but according to others in Pallene.

According to Herodotus (7.123), Phlegra was an earlier name for Pallene, the westernmost of the three peninsulas of Chalcidice.

153 illicit: *inconcessisque*; see on 9.639.

154 fires: *ignibus*; i.e. 'fires of love', cf. 3.490, 10.253.

155-61 Orpheus' song: Ganymede

That Ganymede, Tros' son, was stolen away to be Zeus' cup-bearer because he was so beautiful
was a story known as early as Homer (*Il.* 20.230-7, Lattimore's translation):

> *Erichthonius had a son, Tros, who was lord of the Trojans,*
> *and to Tros in turn there were born three sons unfaulted,*
> *Ilos and Assarakos and godlike Ganymedes*
> *who was the loveliest born of the race of mortals, and therefore*
> *the gods caught him away to themselves, to be Zeus' wine-pourer,*
> *for the sake of his beauty, so he might be among the immortals.*
> *Ilos in turn was given a son, the blameless Laomedon,*
> *and Laomedon had sons in turn, Tithonus and Priam...*

Even by the time of the *Homeric Hymns* (5.202-5), the responsibility for the theft had passed to
Zeus himself. According to Virgil (*Aen.* 5.254-5), Jupiter used his eagle to effect the theft; there
is, however, every reason to suspect that it was Ovid who developed the idea that the eagle was
Jupiter in metamorphosis, a characteristically impudent suggestion.

155 Phrygian: Phrygia was an area in north-western Anatolia where Troy was situated; as early
  as Catullus (61.18), the adjective is used to mean 'Trojan', sometimes contemptuously (see
  Austin on Virg. *Aen.* 4.103), but not always. Homer (*Il.* 2.862) regards the Phrygians as distinct from the Trojans.

156 something: *aliquid*; i.e. a bird, to catch Ganymede and fly him to heaven.

158 That Jupiter's eagle who snatched Ganymede also carried his thunderbolt is familiar from
  Horace *Odes* 4.4.1-4; see also Williams on Virg. *Aen.* 5.254f., 255.

160 Iliades: Ovid alone introduces this Greek word to Latin; he uses it here alone to mean
  'Troy's son'; elsewhere, it means 'Ilia's son(s)' (14.781, 824; *A.* 3.4.40; *F.* 3.62, 4.23,
  5.565; *T.* 4.3.8), i.e. 'Romulus and/or Remus'.
  mixes drinks: *pocula miscet*; this refers to the ancient practice of mixing water with wine;
  it is not an anachronistic reference to cocktails.

161 though Juno disapproves: Virgil (*Aen.* 1.28) specifically cites this story as one of the
  causes of Juno's hatred of the Trojans.

162-219 Orpheus' song: Hyacinthus

It is clearly only accidental that this is the earliest extant account of the full story. For instance,
both Euripides (*Helen* 1469ff.) and Nicander (*Ther.* 902ff.) allude to it. For fuller details, see
Frazer on Apollodorus 1.3.3 and Forbes Irving 280-2 who also discusses the cult evidence.

162 For the apostrophe, see on 9.101.
  Amyclides: (another Ovidian coinage, see on 9.262) i.e. 'son of Amyclae', Hyacinthus;
  while it is true that Apollodorus (3.10.3) claims that Amyclas was the father of Hyacinthus,
  it seems easier to suggest that here Ovid is linking Ganymede (see on 10.160) and Hyacinthus by giving them 'patronymics' to allude to their places of origin; see also on 10.182. For
  Amyclae (a settlement near Sparta) as a cult centre for the worship of Hyacinthus, see
  Forbes Irving 281-2.
  ether: see on 10.2.

165 Aries...watery Pisces: *Piscique Aries...aquoso*; Ovid enjoys visualising the zodiacal signs
  literally (see also on 10.127): the Fish (*Piscis*), is 'watery' both because water is the home
  of fish and because his traditional time of the year is rainy. For a similar trick, see 10.78-9
  (and the note) where the same translation, 'watery *Pisces*', is offered for a different phrase.
  No attempt has been made to render the singular, *Piscique*, but cf. 8.854.

167 my father: i.e. Apollo; see on 10.1-85.

168 set in the middle of the world: there was a stone at Delphi thought to mark the navel, or
  centre, of the world; see e.g. Eur. *Ion.* 461-2.

169 the Eurotas: Sparta's river.

169-70 undefended Sparta: it was Sparta's proud boast that her city was never walled until the end of the third century B.C., see Livy 39.37.2-5.

171 nets: *retia*: i.e. Hyacinthus' hunting nets.

174 Titan: i.e. 'the sun'; see on 10.78.

176-7 Gymnasts competed naked (see on 9.32) and anointed with olive oil.

181 Ovid stresses *pondus* 'the weight' with the enjambment (see on 9.78); the translation substitutes 'earth' (*terram*) for the enjambment, but the effect is much the same.

182 Taenarides: 'a son of Taenarus' i.e. Hyacinthus. Here, Taenarus is being used as a rough synonym for Sparta (cf. *OLD* s.v. 'Taenars') and not with the precise geographical association discussed at 10.13.

185-7 For the apostrophe, see on 9.101.

189 At 1.521-4, Apollo laments that his medical skill cannot cure the sickness of love; here we encounter the irony that sometimes he cannot even cure the physical injuries of his beloved.

190-5 The passage is based on Virgil's simile for the death of Euryalus, one of the most poignant moments in the *Aeneid* (9.434-7, West's translation; Latin words also in the Ovidian passage are added in parentheses):

> *...his neck* (ceruix) *grew limp* (conlapsa 187) *and the head drooped* (recumbit) *on his shoulders* (umeros), *like a scarlet flower languishing and dying* (moriens) *when its stem has been cut by the plough, or like poppies* (papauera) *bowing* (demisere) *their heads* (caput) *when the rain burdens* (grauantur) *them and their necks grow weary.*

It is characteristic of Ovid to imitate particularly sublime passages at relatively banal moments; see on 5.605-6. The Virgilian simile is itself indebted to Homer (*Il.* 8.306-7) and to Catullus (11.21-4) and has generated a very considerable literature conveniently discussed by Hardie. See also on 9.6.

192-5 burdened...burden: *grauatum... oneri*; the repetition in the English is accidental.

193 would gaze at the earth: *spectentque...terram*; contrast 10.140.

196 Oebalides: 'son of Oebalus' i.e. Hyacinthus. Oebalus was the name of a legendary early king of Sparta so that *Oebalides* comes to mean no more than 'Spartan', see Fordyce on Verg. *Aen.* 7.734; however Hyginus (*Fab.* 271.1) calls Hyacinthus *Oebali filius* 'son of Oebalus'.

199 branded for: *inscribenda*; the basic sense, that Apollo's right hand should be acknowledged as guilty, is clear; the exact sense of *inscribenda*, however, is disputed: Anderson takes it to refer literally to branding (cf. *OLD* s.v. 'inscribo' 1d), presumably as thieves and fugitive slaves were branded; Miller, followed by *OLD* (s.v. 'inscribo' 5b) seem to envisage a published list of criminals and their crimes. The translation attempts to bridge the ambiguity depending on whether 'branded' is seen as metaphorical or literal. If literal, it would be better to substitute 'with' for 'for'.

I am the cause of your death: *ego sum tibi funeris auctor*; irresistibly evocative of that most poignant moment in the *Aeneid* (see also on 9.6) when Aeneas meets Dido in the Underworld and says (6.458): *funeris heu tibi causa fui?* 'Alas, was I the reason for your death?' Ovid had, in fact, alluded to that passage once before at *Heroides* 17(18) 200.

205-8 These lines seem to anticipate 10.212-6 and 13.396-8 (where we learn that the 'most mighty hero' is Ajax) in a peculiarly clumsy way; I believe them to be the work of a crude interpolator and support Merkel in excising them. For a quite different view, see Anderson.

211 Tyrian purple: the purple dye was extracted from the murex, a shellfish, and was especially associated with the Phoenicians of Tyre and Sidon; for further details, see Austin on Verg. *Aen.* 4.262.

211-3 purple...purple: *ostro...purpureus*; unfortunately, English does not have two different words for 'purple'; see on 9.32-4.

213 those...these: *his...illis*; we are taught that *hic* means 'this' and *ille* means 'that'. However, *hic* and *ille* can also mean 'the latter' and 'the former' respectively, though they do not do so here. The new plant (*his* 'these') is purple because of the blood of Hyacinthus.

215 **AI AI:** *ai* was a standard Greek cry of distress.

218 **the Hyacinthia:** the festival is, perhaps, most remembered for delaying the Spartan response to the Athenian appeal for help against the Persians in the period between the battles of Salamis and Plataea (Herod. 9.7).

220-42 Orpheus' song: the Cerastae and the Propoetides

The stories of these two groups appear nowhere else in literature; for some speculation on their origin, see Forbes Irving 220 and 298.

220-1 **Amathus, prolific in metals:** Amathus was a town at the middle of the southern coast of Cyprus; the whole island was rich in metals, especially copper, to which, indeed, the island gave its name. In view of this story, it is striking that Amathus was also the site of a temple to Venus, see Virg. *Aen.* 10.51.

221 **to have given birth to:** *genuisse*; this provides a particular link with the Hyacinthus story; at 10.217, Sparta was not ashamed 'to have given birth to' (*genuisse*) Hyacinthus; here, the same word is used in the same place in the line to convey the opposite of Amathus' attitude towards giving birth to the Propoetides and the Cerastae.

223 **Cerastae:** the Greek for 'horned'.

224 **Hospitable Jupiter:** *Iouis Hospitis*: a translation of the Greek 'Zeus Xenios', one of that god's important functions; see e.g. Hom. *Od.* 9.270-1.

228 **guest:** it is especially scandalous that a *hospes* 'guest' should be murdered at the altar of 'the Hospitable Jupiter'. Translators, starting with Golding, offer a plural here. However, we are still imagining a single visiting stranger, seeing, but not correctly interpreting, the blood of a previous visiting stranger. With the next sentence, the reader draws the conclusion that any stranger would have seen the same thing, and that, accordingly, many strangers had been sacrificed.

229 Cyprus was the birthplace of Aphrodite (Venus) and indelibly associated with her throughout antiquity (cf. Hes. *Theog.* 192-9). Any suggestion that she might abandon the island would, accordingly, be most remarkable.

230 **Ophiusian:** *Ophiusia*; an otherwise unknown word; the context demands that it means 'of Cyprus', presumably derived from an obscure name for the island.

232 **impious:** *impia*; i.e. lacking in *pietas*, see on 9.383

235-6 For a much more grotesque example of this situation, see 6.619-21.

241 Such was their shamelessness that they could no longer blush.

242 **with little change:** for the kind of metamorphosis that brings out an inherent truth, see on 11.343.

243-97 Orpheus' song: Pygmalion

We know from the 2nd to 3rd century Christian writer, Clement of Alexandria (*Protr.* 4.57.1), that the earlier version of this story had been told by the 3rd century B.C. writer, Philostephanus, a version according to which Pygmalion had succumbed to an unnatural passion for a statue. For further details, see Otis (1966) 389-90, (1970) 418-9; his account stresses how Ovid has changed what was a frankly prurient story into something approaching the sublime. The interest in this story ever since the middle ages is quite remarkable. Reid (pp. 955-62) lists 189 items devoted to Pygmalion, including poems, plays, paintings, statues, operas ranging in date from c.1275 to 1984. It is worth remembering throughout this story that ancient statues were painted with lifelike colours.

247-68 Throughout this passage, English forces the translator to choose, when alluding to the statue, between 'it' and 'she' or 'her', and between 'its' and 'her'. The Latin allows that ambiguity to remain unresolved until 266 when the femininity of the statue suddenly emerges.

251 The statue is naked (until 10.263); there is a powerful feeling that nakedness in a woman is less indecent if she does not move, a feeling that, presumably, lay behind the old rule for the London stage that female nakedness was permitted only if the subject remained motionless.

253 **fires:** *ignes*; i.e. 'fires of love', cf. 3.490, 10.154.

256 This line violently interrupts Pygmalion's otherwise gradual and subtle progress in his approach to the statue/girl.

262 **tears of the Heliades:** i.e. amber; the Heliades were the sisters of Phaëthon (1.747-2.400); they mourned his death until they were turned into trees; even then (2.364-6):

> *Their tears flowed on, and dripped from the new branches*
> *as amber which hardened in the sun and was taken off by the clear*
> *stream and sent to be admired by Latin brides.*

264 **necklaces...neck:** *monilia collo*; see on 10.233.

266 **she:** see on 10.247-68.

267 **the Sidonian shell-fish:** see on 10.211.

273 **his duty performed:** *munere functus*; the same expression is found at Verg. *Aen.* 6.885-6.

277 **golden:** *aurea*; a translation of Aphrodite's most familiar epithet, cf. e.g. Hom. *Il.* 3.64; see also Verg. *Aen.* 10.16-7 (and Harrison).

279 **her flame:** i.e. the flame on her altar.

280 **the image of his girl:** *simulacra suae...puellae*, slightly illogical for 'his image of a girl', but it rather nicely anticipates what we can all see is about to occur.

282-3 **touched...was touched:** *temptat; temptatum*; in the translation, it is impossible to juxtapose the two words to give the full effect of the polyptoton (see on 9.44).

284 **Hymettian:** Hymettus is a mountain in Attica noted for its honey, see N.-H. on Hor. *Od.* 2.6.14.

285 **worked on...worked on:** *tractataque...retractat*.

286 **useful from use:** *utilis usu*; for the polyptoton, see on 9.44.

290 **Paphian:** see on 10.297.

   offer up: *concipit*; the word can mean no more than 'devise', but it is used in religious contexts for solemn utterances as 'offer up' is in English; see *OLD* s.v. 12a where this passage is cited.

293-4 **eyes to the light:** *lumina lumen*, this polyptoton (see on 9.44) cannot survive translation since *lumen* can mean either 'light' or 'eye'. The same pun occurs at Lucr. 3.364.

296 **nine times:** *nouiens*; see on 9.286, cf. 10.479.

297 Cyprus was not called 'Paphos', Paphos was a town on the south-west coast of Cyprus, the traditional site of Aphrodite's birth (see Hom. *Od.* 8.362-3). Ovid is, in any case, toying with his readers; seven lines before he called Pygmalion 'Paphian hero' which was, if this derivation were correct, anachronistic.

298-502 Orpheus' song: Myrrha

This was a very popular story. According to Apollodorus (3.14.4), it was told by the 5th century epic poet, Panyas(s)is; Ps.-Lycophron (see *OCD* s.v. 'Lycophron') in his *Alexandra* (828-30), a poem probably written at the end of the 2nd century, makes a passing reference to Adonis' birth from the myrrh tree, and from Antoninus Liberalis (34) we learn the version of the story he attributes to Pherecydes. However, the version most famous in antiquity is also the least known to us: Catullus (95, and see Fordyce) tells us of the masterpiece written by his friend, Cinna, and entitled *Zmyrna* (Myrrha, Smyrna and Zmyrna are dialectical variants of the same name); almost nothing of that work survives, but there is a considerable modern literature devoted to providing as good a reconstruction as possible. The various earlier versions are deeply divided over the genealogy of Myrrha, but only Ovid connects her with Pygmalion. Panyas(s)is, probably, but not Nicander or Ovid, attributes Myrrha's fate to her refusal to honour Aphrodite. Nicander, but not Panyas(s)is or Ovid, suppresses the metamorphosis and substitutes a more nearly natural birth. All versions seem to include the nurse; Ovid clearly bases her significantly on Phaedra's nurse in Euripides' *Hippolytus*; it may, accordingly, be of some interest that in Pherecydes (Ant. Lib. 34.2) the nurse is called Hippolyta. Details of all these points and a full bibliography can be found in Otis (1966) 391-2, (1970) 410-1, and in Forbes Irving (274-7). See also on 10.307-10, 436.

298 **From her:** i.e. from Paphos.

Cinyras: of the extant literary accounts, only Ovid's seems to identify Myrrha's father with Cinyras. He was, however, known in his own right as early as Hom. *Il.* 11.19-23 where he is a wealthy man from Cyprus who had given Agamemnon a most elaborate corselet.

300   This line is a pastiche of the formulas used to dismiss the uninitiated from an important religious ritual; cf. e.g. Callim. *Hymn* 2.2 (Mair's translation):

> *...away, away, he that is sinful.*

Horace (*Odes* 3.1) uses a similar formula to introduce his so-called Roman odes, but the closest parallel is in Virgil (*Aen.* 6.258) where the Sibyl's ceremony to admit Aeneas to the Underworld is introduced by the words *procul, o procul este, profani.* This is another example (see on 9.6) of Ovid's habit of imitating the sublimities of his predecessors in wholly inappropriate contexts.

305   **Ismarian:** i.e. 'Thracian', see on 9.642. Orpheus is home in Thrace (10.77) singing these songs and would naturally wish to flatter his audience. However, the Thracians had an appalling reputation—one needs to look no further than 11.1-43—so that it is not hard to detect the irony here.

307-10   The argument of these lines is a little obscure. The point seems to be first that, however rich the region becomes, it should grow myrrh to remind itself of its guilty story, and then that, even so, the benefits of growing myrrh cannot match the cost. In these lines, Ovid clearly sets Cinyras' story in Arabia, although he also chooses to trace his parentage back to the Cypriot Pygmalion and his daughter Paphos. As Anderson points out (on 10.476-8), Ovid 'has linked two separate traditions'; Apollodorus makes the position clear (3.14.3-4, Frazer's translation):

> *This Cinyras in Cyprus, whither he had come with some people, founded Paphos; and having there married Metharme, daughter of Pygmalion, king of Cyprus, he begat...Adonis...Hesiod, however, affirms that he was a son of Phoenix and Alphesiboea; and Panyasis says that he was a son of Thias, king of Assyria, who had a daughter Smyrna. In consequence of the wrath of Aphrodite, for she did not honour the goddess, this Smyrna conceived a passion for her father, and with the complicity of her nurse she shared her father's bed...*

Hyginus (*Fab.* 58) also identifies Cinyras as a king of the Assyrians.

308   *costum:* obviously a spice or perfume but, since there seems to be no secure identification, it has been left untranslated.

309   **Panchaïan:** i.e. 'of Panchaïa' (stress the middle 'a'), a mythical place imagined to be a spice-bearing island in the Indian Ocean; it first appears in extant Latin literature at Lucr. 2.417. The whole section, of course, reflects the normal Greco-Roman view that the East was morally degenerate.

310-2   **myrrh...Myrrha:** *murram... Myrrha;* both in English and in Latin, the form of the proper name is nearer to the Greek than is the name of the perfume.

312   **torches:** Cupid's torch is a commonplace, cf. 1.461, Tib. 2.1.82, Prop. 3.16.16.

313-4   The scene is reminiscent of the story of Althaea and Meleager (8.451-6):

> *There was a stick* (stipes) *which, when Thestius' daughter lay in*
> *childbirth, the threefold sisters placed in the flame*
> *and, as they applied the thumb to spin the threads of fate,*
> *'The same time, ' they said, 'oh newly born, do we give to the wood*
> *and to you...'*

There, however the 'threefold sisters' were the Fates (see on 8.452); here, the 'three sisters' are the Furies whose presence had so blighted the wedding of Procne and Tereus (6.428-32):

> *No pronuba Juno,*
> *no Hymenaeos was there, no Grace attended at the bed;*
> *Eumenides held the torches, they had snatched them from a funeral,*

Eumenides spread the couch and, on the house, an accursed
owl settled perching on the roof of the bridal chamber.

In early times, the number of the Furies was uncertain; for the Romans, however, they were three, Allecto, Megaera and Tisiphone, whose names, though Greek, seem to arise first in Latin literature; see Fordyce on Virg. *Aen.* 7.324ff; see also on 10.349; 11.14.

318   **Myrrha:** For the apostrophe, see on 9.101.

321-4   **piety...Piety:** see on 9.382. The clear personification at 324 might tempt one to assume personification at 321. There, however, the non-personification of *iura* strongly suggests otherwise.

324-31   Note that, whereas at 304-10 Orpheus had congratulated his people for being morally superior to what mere nature (304) would allow, Myrrha is using precisely the opposite argument. Contrast, in particular, the treatment of nature in 304 and 330.

324   **this sort of love:** *hanc Venerem*; for the metonymy, impossible in English, see on 9.141; 10.80.

326   **wife:** *coniunx* see on 9.47.

333   **piety:** see on 9.382; duty to family clearly predominates here.

338   **Cinyras, with Cinyras:** *Cinyrae, Cinyrae*; though the forms are identical, this is still a polyptoton (see on 9.44) because the first is genitive, the second dative, cf. 10.532.

345   **impious:** *impia*; see on 9.382.

347   **supplanter:** *paelex*; I have generally translated this word 'wench' (see on 9.144); sometimes, however, a different solution seems appropriate as here and at 6.606.

349   **the sisters with...snakes for hair:** i.e. the Furies foreshadowed at 10.313; cf. also 4.495-6. Their snakes are familiar from Aeschylus (*Cho.* 1049-50), remembered by Virgil who interestingly transferred the snakes from the Furies to Clytemnestra (*Aen.* 4.471-2, West's translation):

> *...or like Orestes, son of Agamemnon, driven in flight across the stage by*
> *his own mother armed with her torches and black (atris) snakes, while the*
> *avenging Furies sat at the door.*

See also Tibullus 1.3.69-70, Austin's notes on Virg. *Aen.* 4.469ff., 469, 472f., 6.324ff., and Fordyce's note on Virg. *Aen.* 7.324ff.

black: *atro*; Aeschylus' Furies were dressed in black (*Cho.* 1048) and Virgil's snakes were also *atris*; Austin comments:

> *not merely 'black' but 'ghastly'.*

354   **pious:** see on 9.382.

357   **was being made...to do:** *faciat...facit*; for the sake of idiom and clarity it has been necessary here to reverse the order of the original, change one verb from active to passive, and conceal the fact that both verb forms are from *facio* in the original.

366   **pious...piety:** *pia...pietatis*; see on 9.382; here as at 10.333, it is the sense of duty to family that predominates.

368ff.   Cf. Hom. *Il.* 2.1ff. where all the other gods are asleep but Zeus cannot sleep. This becomes an epic cliché; Dido's inability to sleep after Aeneas' recounting of his exploits has made her fall in love with him (Virg. *Aen.* 4.1ff.) is a famous example, and Virgil repeats the motif as she approaches the end (*Aen.* 4.522ff.; see Pease and Austin). Cf. also 6.490-3 (and the note); 7.185-7, 634-5 (where there are close verbal resemblances to this passage); 8.83ff.

372   **is at a loss to know:** *non inuenit*; for the usage, see *OLD* s.v. 'inuenio' 6d.

373   **only:** for Latin's idiomatic omission of this (for us) necessary detail, cf. 3.401; 4.115; 5.520; 7.565; 8.346; 11.178, 219-20; 12.449 and see Mayer on Lucan 8.51-2.

383   **foster-child:** see on 10.442.

389   **hushed and silent:** *muta silet*; English is less tolerant of pleonasm than Latin is; this one, however, is an apparently unique development from *muta silentia* 'hushed silence' which Ovid used also at 4.433; 7.184; 10.53. In both languages, the development seems less convincing than the original.

399 anger...anger: *ira...ira*; the translation gets as close as it can to Ovid's trick of beginning and ending the line with *ira* 'anger'.

409 thoroughness: *sedulitas*; the idea recurs strikingly at 10.438.

415 foster-child: see on 10.442.

424 (for she understood): see on 9.17.

429 said the nurse: *ait haec*; throughout this section, Latin's richer fund of pronouns has made the identity of 'she' etc. more difficult in the English than in the Latin. Here, it was impossible to use the pronoun without causing an intolerable effect.

430 with an oath: *numine*; *numen* is divine power; here it is used of the invocation of divine power to guarantee a promise; see *OLD* s.v. 4b.

431 pious: *piae*; see on 9.382. Here the word may well be emphasising that Ovid is rejecting any version that blames the mother; see on 10.436.
   Ceres: for her story and her association with grain crops (hence 'cereals'), see 5.341-661.

436 Cenchreis: most versions of the story (see on 10.298-502) omit the name of the mother; Hyginus (*Fab.* 58), however, names her and blames her arrogance about her daughter's beauty ('more beautiful than Venus' she is alleged to have claimed) for the tragedy. In that version, Myrrha's passion for her father is brought on by Venus to punish her mother.

438 perversely thorough: *male sedula*; see on 10.409, 462-4.

442 home: *domum*; presumably 'to the women's quarters'.
   child: *alumna*; elsewhere (10.383, 415) translated 'foster-child'.

443-4 heart...heart: *pectore...pectora*; while Latin is less sensitive to this kind of repetition than English is (cf. 5.129-30; 6.465-6; 9.161-4; 10.147-9; 11.153-4, 164, 379-81; 12.117-8), this does seem almost intolerable.

445 so great...in her mind: cf. 9.630.

446-7 Boötes...Wain...yoke-beam...between the Oxen: *interque Triones...Plaustrum...temone ...Boötes*; an elaborate circumlocution for midnight. The references are to those constellations that are highest in the sky at midnight from the point of view of those living in the Northern hemisphere. At midnight they 'turn' from rising to sinking. Aratus is helpful here (24-7, 36-7, 40-2, 91-3, Mair's translation):

> On either side the Axis ends in two Poles, but thereof the one is not seen, whereas the other faces us in the north high above the ocean. Encompassing it two Bears wheel together—wherefore they are also called Wains...Now the one men call by name Cynosura and the other Helice...But Helice, appearing large at earliest night, is brighter and easy to mark; but the other is small...Behind Helice, like to one that drives, is borne along Arctophylax [Bear-guard] whom men also call Boötes [Ox-driver], since he seems to lay hand on the wain-like Bear.

In Latin, *Septem Triones* or *Septentriones* usually refers to *Helice*, 'The Greater Bear', *Vrsa Maior*, (*OLD* s.v. 'septentriones' 1a) but can refer to *Cynosura*, 'The Lesser Bear, *Vrsa Minor*, (*OLD* s.v. 1b). Thus, in Ovid, Boötes drives the Wain (known to Aratus as *Helice*, 'the wain-like Bear') through the Oxen (here, *Cynosura*, 'The Lesser Bear' *Vrsa Minor*).

450 fires: *igne*; 'the stars'.

450-1 Icarus...and Erigone: their story is conveniently told by Apollodorus (3.14.7, Frazer's translation):

> But Demeter was welcomed by Celeus at Eleusis, and Dionysus by Icarius, who received from him a branch of a vine and learned the process of making wine. And wishing to bestow the god's boons on men, Icarius went to some shepherds who, having tasted the beverage and quaffed it copiously without water for the pleasure of it, imagined that they were bewitched and killed him; but by day they understood how it was and buried him. When his daughter Erigone was searching for her father, a domestic dog, named Maera, which had attended Icarius, discovered his dead body to her, and she bewailed her father and hanged herself.

The same story is told by Hyginus (*Fab.* 130) where too the father is called 'Icarius' not, as in Ovid and Propertius (2.33.29), 'Icarus'.

451 **pious love for her father:** *pio...parentis amore*; see on 9.382. Note the pointed contrast between Myrrha's immoral love for her father and Erigone's pious love for hers.

452 For stumbling as a bad omen, see Austin on *Aen.* 2.242.

453 **owl:** the bird was regarded as of extremely ill omen, cf. 5.550; 6.431-2 (where it is present at the doomed marriage of Tereus and Procne); 7.269; 15.791; see also Pease (who collects numerous parallels from ancient and modern literature) and Austin on Virg. *Aen.* 4.462, D'Arcy Thompson, 56, 66-7, 476-80.

458-9 **both her colour and her blood:** this is, of course, one process; the blood rushes from her face and, with it, her colour. Latin finds such expressions (they are called 'hendiadys' that is 'one thing through two') much more natural than English does.

462 **as she hesitates:** *cunctantem*; both in Roman times and now, brides hesitate just before the ceremony to display a decent modesty; see Fordyce on Cat. 61.79 and Austin on Virg. *Aen.* 4.133 where Dido is described as *cunctantem* shortly before her supposed marriage. The introduction of the idea here underlines just how different this is from a marriage.
led: *deducit*; the word is regularly used both as a technical term for bringing a bride home and, jocularly, for introducing an illegitimate lover to the home, see *OLD* s.v. 10b

462-4 From being an unwilling accomplice, the nurse suddenly takes on the dominant rôle; 'perversely thorough' *male sedula* (10.438) indeed.

464 **yours:** *tua*; the striking ambiguity of this word ('your daughter' or 'your lover') is well discussed by Anderson.

466 **maiden's fright:** *uirgineosque metus*; at 10.361, Cinyras has already encountered such emotions in Myrrha in a much more innocent context.

469 **impious:** *impia*; see on 10.232.

472 **eager to know:** *auidus cognoscere*; note how 10.461 prepares the reader for these words.

474 **both the crime and his daughter:** *et scelus et natam*; for the syllepsis, see on 9.135. Bömer prefers to take it as a hendiadys (see on 10.458-9), paraphrasing it as '*natam scelestam*' (wicked daughter); but the context seems to demand the more arch and undercutting interpretation.

478 **palm-bearing Arabs:** *palmiferos Arabas*: elsewhere, *palmiferus* is used of places rather than peoples, see *OLD* s.v.
Panchaean: *Panchaea*, an alternative form of the adjective *Panchaïus*; see on 10.309.

479 **nine horns of the returning moon:** see on 9.286, cf. 10.296.

480 **the Sabaean land:** the Sabaeans dwelt in south-west Arabia and were noted for their wealth based significantly on spices. Their land is also familiar from the Old Testament where it is traditionally rendered 'Sheba'.

503-59 Orpheus' song: Venus and Adonis
Bion's *Lament for Adonis* seems to have been known to Ovid; it is the only earlier extant account of Ovid's version. See also Forbes Irving 279, Reid 26-40 for an incredible list of treatments of this story in literature and art from the 13th to the 20th centuries.

515 **Spite:** *Liuor*; for the personification, see on 6.129; for personification in general, see on 2.760-82.

516 **Loves:** *Amores*; the decorative figures of naked baby boys, usually equipped with bows and quivers of arrows which smite their victims with love; they are familiar in the art both of antiquity and of much more recent times. Sometimes they are called *Cupidines* 'Cupids'; see N.-H. on Horace *Odes* 1.19.1.

519 This line is repeated from *Am.* 1.8.49 and its sentiment is a commonplace often expressed with similar vocabulary. For a discussion, see N.-H. on Hor. *Odes* 2.14.1-2.

524 **avenging his mother's fires:** 'fires of passion', see 10.369-70. As Anderson points out, there may be a hint here of the alternative version that Myrrha's passion had deliberately been given to her by an angry Venus (see on 10.298-502); alternatively, this may do no more than to suggest some sort of 'poetic justice'.

525 **the quivered boy:** *pharetratus...puer*; i.e. Cupid; cf. 10.517-8.

529 **the man's:** *uiri*; i.e. Adonis'; the line refers back to 10.523.

Cythera's: Cythera (stress the middle syllable) was an island especially favoured by Venus; see on 4.190, 537-8.

530-1 **Paphos...Cnidos:** cf. Hor. *Odes* 1.30.1-2 (West's Translation):

> *Venus , queen of Cnidos and Paphos,*
> *abandon your beloved Cyprus...*

There is also a full discussion in N.-H. of the association of these places with Venus; for more on Paphos, see on 10.297. Cnidos, is off the coast of Caria, a little north of Rhodes. See also Fordyce on Catul. 36.13.

531 **rich in fish:** *piscosam*; there seems to be no other reference to Cnidos as a fishing town.

Amathus: (stress the first syllable) a town in Cyprus; for its situation and its wealth in metals, see on 10.220-1; for its association with Venus, see Catul. 36.14; 68.51.

532 **heaven; heaven:** *caelo; caelo*; for the polyptoton, see on 9.44. As at 10.338, though the forms are identical, this is still a polyptoton because the first is ablative, the second dative. Literally, the second half of the line means: 'Adonis is preferred to heaven' but here it seemed better to preserve the striking word order rather than the less obviously significant grammatical structure.

533-6 Ovid enjoys the humour inherent in Venus, the pampered goddess of sex, dressing herself to go hunting in the manner of Diana, goddess of chastity and the hunt. For a mysterious and much more subtle example of Venus disguised as Diana, see Virg. *Aen.* 1.314-34. Venus' normal preference for shade arises partly from the fact that the Romans prized fair complexions and partly because love-making characteristically takes place in the dark. For examples and further details, see Bömer.

538 **boars:** as commentators observe, this is the animal that will bring the story to its tragic end.

542-3 For the apostrophe, see on 9.101.

544 **bold against the bold:** for the near polyptoton, see on 9.44.

549 **or bristle-bearing pigs:** *saetigerosque sues*; at 8.272 and 359, Ovid uses the monosyllabic nominative form *sus* (pig), when he clearly means *aper* (boar), to produce a comic effect. For a full explanation, see the note on 8.272 and 359. Here, however, the masculine adjective makes it plain that boars are meant, and there seems no reason to suppose that the use of *sus* in cases other than the nominative singular (the only case where the word is monosyllabic) produces any particular effect; cf. 10.711, 14.286.

550 **lightning:** *fulmen*; lightning or fire are frequently used by Ovid in connexion with the boar, presumably to catch the sudden glint when the tusks are moved rapidly in sunshine; cf. 1.305 (regrettably concealed in my translation), 8.289, 339 (fire), 356; 11.367 (of a wolf).

557 **(and she did lie down)...grass and him:** the dislocation caused by the parenthesis is almost as extreme in the Latin as it is in the English; Ovid is very fond of these asides (see on 9.17); combined with the syllepsis (see on 9.135) of 'grass and him', it produces a remarkably arch effect.

560-707 Venus' song within Orpheus' song: Atalanta and Hippomenes

This is one of two legends about Atalanta; the first was part of the story of the Calydonian Boar Hunt told at 8.260-444 and presents Atalanta as a great huntress to whom Meleager grants the spoils of the hunt with tragic results. This story is conveniently told by Apollodorus (3.9.2, Frazer's translation):

> *And Iasus had a daughter Atalanta...she caused her wooers to race...and ran herself in arms; and if the wooer was caught up, his due was death on the spot, and if he was not caught up, his due was marriage. When many had already perished, Melanion came to run for love of her, bringing golden apples from Aphrodite, and being pursued he threw them down, and*

she, picking up the dropped fruit, was beaten in the race. So Melanion married her. And once on a time it is said that out hunting they entered into the precinct of Zeus, and there taking their fill of love were changed into lions. But Hesiod and some others have said that Atalanta was not a daughter of Iasus, but of Schoeneus; and Euripides says that she was a daughter of Maenalus, and that her husband was not Melanion but Hippomenes.

Apollodorus tells the story of Atalanta and the Calydonian Boar Hunt together with this story in such a way that he clearly assumes that they relate to the same woman; note, in particular, that it is when they are out hunting that the running Atalanta succumbs to disastrous temptation with her lover, a linking detail absent from Ovid's account. Indeed, it seems plausible that Ovid did regard them as different women. The name 'Atalanta' occurs six times in Ovid, only once (*Her.* 4.99) of the huntress but five times (*Met.* 10.565, 598, *Am.* 3.2.29, *Ars am..* 2.185; 3.775) of the runner. Six times, Ovid refers to the daughter of Schoeneus, five times (*Met.* 10.609, 660, *Her.* 15.265; 20.123, *Tr.* 2.399) of the racing Atalanta, once (*Am.* 1.7.13) of the huntress. It would, however, be hazardous to assume that, apart from that last passage, only the racer is described as a daughter of Schoeneus since Hyginus (*Fab.* 173, 175, 244, 246) identifies both as daughters of Schoeneus. It is, presumably, remotely possible that there were two girls called Atalanta, each the daughter of a different Schoeneus. Much more probably, as in the words of McKeown (on *Am.* 1.7.13-14): 'Since they are almost certainly local variants on the same legend, the two versions cannot be fully distinguished.' The story is as old as Ps-Hesiod *Catalogue of Women* (fr. 14, Evelyn-White) though the text breaks off too soon for us to know whether it included inappropriate love-making and the metamorphoses. For fuller accounts of the myth in literature, see Forbes Irving 201-2, Fordyce on Catul. 2b.

562 **(for she did overcome them):** for the parenthesis, see on 9.17.

564-6 This oracle appears to be Ovid's invention; it gives Atalanta some excuse for her conduct, and it distinguishes her from the standard determined virgin, such as Daphne (1.452-567) or Io (1.568-746). The oracle's response is typically obscure.

569 **and 'I am not:** '*nec sum*; for this phenomenon (where a negative such as *nec* which means 'and not' is used where the 'and' is not part of direct speech but the 'not is), see Housman (*CR* 11 (1897) 426) who notes the same use at. 11.263 and, perhaps less certainly, at 9.131-2.

575 **Hippomenes:** for the name, see on 10.560-707.

578 **once her clothes were removed:** *posito...uelamine*; ancient gymnastics were performed naked (the Greek word *gymnos* means 'naked'); women, of course, normally neither competed nor attended. This entertaining detail depends on Ovid's failure to follow the version of the story reported by Apollodorus (see on 10.560-707) according to which she 'ran in arms'. These words, and the lines that follow, may well provide an exemplification of the difference between the way an animal reacts to human beauty and the way a human does, a difference brought out at 10.548-9.

579 **like mine:** Venus' arrogance is neatly alluded to here.

583 **more swiftly:** i.e. than Atalanta.

584 ***and he feared envy*:** a much disputed problem to which no plausible solution has been found. Golding, perhaps from desperation, omits the phrase altogether.

586 **God...dare:** for a discussion of what was even then something of a cliché, see Harrison on Virg. *Aen.* 10.284. It seems to have started in a military context but was borrowed for amatory use in the spirit of *Am.* 1.9: 'Every lover is a soldier...' (*militat omnis amans...*)

588 **Aonian:** Aonia was another name for Boeotia, see on 9.122. For Hippomenes' Boeotian origins, see on 10.605-6.

589 **a Scythian arrow:** cf. e.g. Hor. *Odes* 3.8.23-4.

590 **and her very running gave her beauty:** much the same was said of Daphne at 1.530.

595-6 **just as when...*atrium*:** this simile conjures up a very modern Roman scene in this very Greek and very ancient contest; for this particular type of anachronism, much favoured by the Romans and by none more than Ovid, see on 9.307. Here, we are to imagine a Roman *atrium* (the technical term has been left untranslated partly to underline the anachronism and partly because the design of a Roman house is so idiosyncratic that words such as 'house' might well convey an inappropriate impression). The *atrium* is built round an uncovered square area; when the sun was particularly oppressive, purple awnings would be stretched over the square and would filter through, from the sun, a reddish light on the white walls below. Lucretius (4.75-83) has an interesting account of the science behind this phenomenon.

597   **the stranger:** *hospes*; i.e. Hippomenes.

      turning-point: *meta*; another Roman term, see on 10.595-6.

603   **he said:** *ait*; the delay suffered by this is almost as striking in the Latin as in the translation.

605-6 **Onchestian Megareus...king of the waters:** (stress '-est-' and 'Meg-'); Apollodorus (3.15.8) refers to a 'Megareus, son of Hippomenes, who had come from Onchestus.' To this should be added Pausanias 1.39.5 which identifies a, presumably earlier, Megareus as a son of Poseidon (Neptune). Given the Greek practice of naming boys after grandfathers, it would be natural to assume that this Megareus was the father of our Hippomenes. Onchestos was a Boeotian town known as such as early as Homer (*Il.* 2.505-10).

609   **Schoeneus' daughter:** *Schoeneïa*; i.e. Atalanta, see on 10.560-707.

617   **third in line:** *quartus*; literally 'fourth', but, as Neptune's great grandson, he is third in line by our reckoning, fourth in line by Latin's inclusive reckoning.

633-5 The reader is irresistibly reminded of Dido, in a much more sublime passage, musing on the temptations of a forbidden union with Aeneas (Virg. *Aen.* 4.15-23, West's translation):
> *If my mind had not been set and immovably fixed against joining any man*
> *in the bonds of marriage..., if I were not so utterly opposed to the marriage*
> *torch and bed, this is the one temptation to which I could possibly have suc-*
> *cumbed...this is the only man who has stirred my feelings and moved my*
> *mind to waver.*

636-7 For this kind of naivety, see on 9.457. Modern editors tend to follow the majority of the manuscripts and read *quid facit*, 'not knowing what she was doing' (which, however, would require a subjunctive, and the alleged parallels all crumble when examined closely) for *quod facit*, 'not knowing the thing she was doing'. For another woman in a similar frame of mind, consider Medea's words at 7.12-13:
> *'it is some god opposing you,' she said, 'and it's a wonder if this,*
> *or at least something like this, is not what is called to love.'*

639   **the Neptunian offspring, Hippomenes:** see on 10.605-6.

640   **Cytherea:** (stress the penultimate syllable) i.e. Venus, see on 10.529.

644   For the ekphrasis, see on 9.334.

      Tamasos: (stress the first syllable); there were two towns with similar names, one in Cyprus (this one) and one in Italy; cf. Strabo 6.1.5.

648   **rustling:** *crepitantibus*; an irresistible echo from Virgil's famous and sublime description of the Golden Bough (*Aen.* 6.209, West's translation):
> *so rustled (*crepitabat*) the golden foil in the gentle ' reeze.*

651   **visible to no one except to him:** exactly the same thing was said in the case of the first divine intervention in the *Iliad*, Athene's appearance to Achilles, (1.197-8, Lattimore's translation):
> *The goddess, standing behind Peleus' son, caught him by the fair hair,*
> *appearing to him only, for no man of the others saw her.*

652-68 **bugle call...starting-gate...turning-point...stands...applause:** *signa tubae ... carcere ... meta ... spectacula...plausu*; Ovid, even more than other Roman poets, loves to introduce the technical terms of Roman life into this sort of deliberately unsuitable context; see on 9.307; 10.595-6, 597.

659   **Megareïan hero:** i.e. Hippomenes, see on 10.605-6.

660   **the Schoeneïan maiden:** i.e. Atalanta, see on 10.560-707.

665   **fruits of the tree:** *fetibus arboreis*; Ovid uses the phrase also at 4.125 of the mulberries stained by the blood of Pyramus; he doubtless borrowed it from Virg. *G.* 1.55.

677   **pick it up ...picked up:** *tollere... sublato*; in spite of appearances, these two Latin words are parts of the same verb, *tollo*.

679-80 Ovid, here speaking through Venus, can be a very self-conscious narrator; for a particularly striking example, see 3.235 and the note on 3.206-33.

680   **led off:** *duxit*; this is both the ordinary Latin word for any sort of 'leading (off)' and also, when given an appropriate object, the standard word used of a man marrying (as at 9.498); both senses may be thought to be present here.

682   **Adonis:** the address reminds us that this whole story is being told to Adonis, and it prepares us for the return to him in another twenty-six lines; see on 12.363.

687   **Echion:** in other extant versions of the story (see on 10.560-707), it is Jupiter's temple that was violated. Since Ovid's Hippomenes came from Boeotian Onchestos (see on 10.605-6), it is reasonable to assume that he was taking Atalanta back to Boeotia and that this Echion is the same one as the Echion who, being one of the five surviving armed men who sprang from the dragon's teeth planted by Cadmus, went on to help Cadmus found Thebes (see 3.99-130); he also fathered Pentheus (3.513-4).

687-8 **Mother of the gods:** i.e. Cybele, see on 10.104. No such temple in or near Boeotia is otherwise known.

692   **covered by native pumice stone:** similar, no doubt, to Diana's grotto (3.157-60) where it is much clearer that the pumice stone forms the roof.

694   **wooden images:** a mark of great antiquity, cf. e.g. Cic. *Ver.* 4.3.7 (Greenwood's translation):

> But Verres...carried off all the statues I have mentioned from the chapel of Heius...he left not one of them behind...except one ancient figure of wood, which I believe represented Good Fortune.

696   **turret-crowned:** *turrita*; Austin (on Virg. *Aen.* 6.785, where Cybele is also called *turrita*) refers to her 'battlemented crown' and gives a full account of the term and its relation to Cybele. Ovid himself (*F.* 4.219-21) suggests that the crown was given to Cybele because she had given towers (*turres*) to the Phrygians. Commentators also allude to Lucr. 2.598-608 (Bailey's translation):

> Wherefore earth alone has been called the Great Mother of the Gods...Of her in days of old the learned poets of the Greeks sang that on a throne in her car she drove a yoke of lions...To the car they yoked wild beasts, because, however wild the brood, it ought to be conquered and softened by the loving care of parents. The top of her head they wreathed with a battlemented crown, because embattled on glorious heights she sustains towns; and dowered with this emblem even now the image of the divine Mother is carried in awesome state through great countries.

700   **shoulders forequarters:** *umeris armi*; Ovid consistently uses *humerus* for human shoulders, *armus* for the shoulders of animals; see on 12.303.

704   **lions:** see Lucr. 2.598-605 quoted above. Cf. also Virg. *Aen.* 3.111-3 (West's translation):

> This is the origin of the Great Mother...and the yoked lions that draw the chariot of the mighty goddess.

705-7 With these three lines, we return to Venus' advice to Adonis to avoid dangerous animals in the hunt, advice from which she broke off at 10.560 to tell the tale of Hippomenes and Atalanta.

708-39 Orpheus' song: Venus and Adonis (continued)

708   **and with her swans yoked:** *iunctisque...cygnis*; cf. Hor. *Odes* 3.28.15 where the same meaning, also of Venus' chariot, is achieved with the phrase *iunctis...oloribus*; see also 4.1.10. Bömer has a very long discussion about this motif.

709   **but courage is opposed to warnings:** *sed stat monitis contraria uirtus*; translators have tended to take this not as a generalization but as a comment specific to Adonis and Venus: 'but his courage was opposed to her warnings'. The Latin is ambiguous on the point.

711   **pig:** *suem*; see on 10.549.

711-5   **it...it...its...its...its:** although the Latin makes it plain that the pig is male, the translation uses 'it' and 'its' for the pig to make a clear distinction from Adonis; Latin is able to avoid any ambiguity without sacrificing the sex of the pig.

712   **the Cinyreïan young man:** i.e. Adonis, Cinyras' grandson, see on 10.298.

716   Editors rightly compare Virg. *Aen.* 5.374 (West's translation): 'and stretched him out to die (*moribundum*) on the yellow (*fulua*) sand (*harena*)'. Here again, Ovid invokes a sublime heroic moment (the end of the boxing contest at the funeral games for Anchises) in a very unheroic context. See on 9.6.

717   **through the intervening air:** *medias...per auras*; see *OLD* s.v. 'medius' 3, cf. 8.182; this seems to provide more point than 'middle air', the interpretation usually adopted (e.g. at *TLL* VIII 586.77), especially in view of 'from the high ether' (10.720) where it makes nonsense to suppose that when Venus turns round she flies higher than before. There is no doubt, however, that 'through the upper air', or the like, is more usual in this sort of passage; cf. e.g. 3.101; 5.641; 9.219; 10.178; 14.127.

720-1   Cf. Bion *Lament for Adonis* 40-2 (Reed's translation):

> *When she saw, when she spied Adonis' unstaunchable wound,*
> *when she saw the gory blood upon his languishing thigh,*
> *spreading wide her arms she keened, "Wait Adonis...*

Further discussion on Ovid's debt to Bion is to be found in Reed *passim*.

720   **ether:** see on 10.2.

721   **his body writhing:** *iactantem...corpus*; literally 'tossing his body' but the intransitive 'writhe' is the *mot juste* in English in this context; cf. 5.59-60.

723   **beat her breast with her...palms:** *percussit pectora palmis*; in the translation it was not possible to do justice to the alliterative onomatopoeia of the Latin.

725-6   Ovid is thinking of the annual festival of Adonis; a version of its hymn is given by Theocritus (15.100-44) and it was by Ovid's time apparently celebrated in Rome, see *Ars am..* 1.75; 3.85.

730   **mint:** for the story, see Strabo 8.3.14 (Jones's translation):

> *Near Pylus, towards the east, is a mountain named after Minthê, who, according to myth, became the concubine of Hades, was trampled underfoot by Corê, and was transformed into garden-mint, the plant which some call Hedyosmos* [sweet-smelling].

Strabo was a great Greek geographer of the Augustan period; his is the only other extant reference to this story.

734   **mud:** *caeno*; this is Merkel's controversial suggestion for *caelo*, 'sky', of the manuscripts. Anderson defends *caelo* vigorously but unconvincingly.

735-9   According to the scholiast to Theocritus 5.90, Adonis' transformation into an anemone was to be found in Nicander. It seems to be not otherwise extant before Ovid.

739   **winds:** there is, apparently, no earlier extant suggestion that the name 'anemone' is from *anemos*, the Greek word for 'wind'.

BOOK XI

There is a useful edition of book 11 by G.M.H. Murphy.

1-66 *The death of Orpheus*

With the end of Orpheus' mythological *tour de force* (10.148-739), we return to his own story which had broken off at 10.147. Here again, the obvious model is Virgil (*G.* 4.520-7) and, once again (see on 10.1-85), Ovid narrates what Virgil has passed over, and passes over what Virgil has narrated. Here, indeed, Ovid devotes 60 lines to a story told by Virgil in eight. Apollodorus (1.3.2, Frazer's translation) is even briefer:

> Orpheus also invented the mysteries of Dionysus, and having been torn in
> pieces by the Maenads, was buried in Pieria.

For more details, see Hill 134-5.

1   **Thracian:** see on 10.11.
     bard: *uates*; see on 10.11.

1-2   **leading...woods...beasts...rocks:** see on 10.1-85 and cf. 10.86-105.

3   **Ciconian:** the immediate source is Virgil who refers to these women as *Ciconum...matres* (*G.* 4.520); the Cicones (stress the first syllable) lived on the southern coast of Thrace and were known as early as Hom. *Il.* 2.846. Their fighting prowess is recorded in a memorable incident to be found at Hom. *Od.* 9.39-61.
     frenzied: *lymphata*; for a discussion of this unusual word, see Fordyce on Virg. *Aen.* 7.377, also N.-H. on Hor. *Odes* 1.37.14.

9   **sewn over by foliage:** *foliis praesuta*; this is an odd expression in both languages; what must be meant is that foliage miraculously grew around the spear and impeded its effectiveness.

14   **and mad Erinys:** *insanaque...Erinys*, (stress the middle syllable); a general term for a Fury to be found as early as Homer (e.g. *Il.* 9.571); this one seems very like the one seen by Austin (on Virg. *Aen.* 2.337) as especially associated with war; see also on 10.313-4.

16   **Berecyntian:** i.e. 'Phrygian'; for a full discussion of the association of this word with Bacchic worship, see N.-H. on Hor. *Odes* 1.18.13.
     pipe: *tibia*; N.-H. (on Hor. *Odes* 1.18.14) gives a full account of the instruments associated with Cybele and her wild worship.
     bent: *infracto*; a somewhat striking sense for *infractus*, but it is difficult to imagine what it could refer to except the curvature of Phrygian horns elsewhere referred to as *aduncus* at e.g. 3.533; 4.392 or *curuus* at e.g. Catul. 63.22, Virg. *Aen.* 11.737.

16-18 Cf. 3.531-7; 4.391-3.

17   **Bacchic howlings:** *Bacchei ululatus*; the word is especially associated with rituals, and with women's rituals in particular. The quadrisyllabic ending and the hiatus between the last two words of the line produce a strikingly wild effect. There is a good discussion of the similar *femineo ululatu* by Austin (on Virg. *Aen.* 4.667).

22   **Maenads:** a Greek word meaning 'mad', 'raving' which became a standard word for the female devotees of Bacchus whose nocturnal rites excited such disapproval from detractors; they are most familiar from Eur. *Bacchae*.

23   **himself:** English idiom demands the addition of this word.

24-5 **bird of night:** i.e. the owl; see on 10.453.

26   **the morning's sand:** *matutina...harena*; a standard term for the first session of the day's entertainment in the amphitheatre (see *OLD* s.v. '(h)arena' 3b). This usage develops from the sand (*harena*) on the floor of the amphitheatre; it is then easy to see how the English word 'arena' arose. For the characteristic introduction of this very Roman touch into a very alien context, see on 9.307.

28   **thyrsi:** see on 9.641.

34   **the column:** *agmine*; sc. 'of the wild women'.

37-8 **torn the oxen from their threatening horns:** i.e. so that they can pick up the horns and use them as weapons; editors, with or without emendation, assume that the reference is to tearing the oxen apart, but this seems to fit neither the context nor the language. See Hill (247, n. 23) for a fuller discussion.

38 **bard:** *uates*; see on 10.11.

39 **stretching out his hands:** the normal gesture of supplication; see on 9.210.

39-40 Orpheus' sudden inability to use his voice to effect miracles is still the result of the excessive noise of 11.15-18.

44-7 **for you...For you...for you...for you:** *te...te...te...te*; for the hymnic effect, see on 10.122-4; 6.177-9. Virgil's description of Orpheus' lament for Eurydice includes a very similar passage (*G.* 4.464-6) which must be in Ovid's mind here:

> He himself, consoling his sick love on his hollow tortoiseshell [i.e. lyre],
> sang of you, sweet wife, of you on the lonely shore with him,
> of you as the day came, of you as it departed.

47 **hair:** *comas*; the Latin word can mean either 'hair' (*OLD* s.v. 1, cf. 9.307) or 'foliage' (*OLD* s.v 3a, cf. 10.103); 'tearing the hair' is a normal part of mourning (e.g. 4.139) so that here we have a striking pun which is impossible in English, a language which has no word that can mean either 'hair' or 'foliage'.

49 **draped:** *obstrusaque*; this rare word normally means 'thrust at' or 'pushed down'; however, if it is correct here, it must something like 'draped'.

50-3 There is a fascination in the literature with the behaviour of dismembered parts of bodies; very similar are: Homer on Dolon (*Il.* 10.454-7), Virgil on Orpheus (*G.* 4.523-6) and Ovid on Emathion (5.105-6), Lampetides (another musician 5.117-8) and Philomela (6.555-61); not dissimilar are: Lucretius 3.640-7 and Virgil *Aen.* 10.395-6.

50 **Hebrus:** a river in Thrace.

51 For the parenthesis, see on 9.17.

52-3 **gave some doleful complaint...dolefully...dolefully:** *flebile nescioquid queritur...flebile...flebile*; in the Virgilian version (*G.* 4.525-6), we learn that he said:

> Eurydice...ah, unhappy Eurydice...Eurydice.

That the double repetition of *flebile* and the apparently perfunctory *flebile nescioquid* (literally: 'something or other doleful') are parody is obvious. For a fuller analysis of the relationship between this passage and the Virgilian equivalent, see Hill 134-5.

54 **they:** i.e. the head, the tongue and the lyre.

55 **Methymna:** the Hebrus empties into the Aegean sea about eighty miles due north of Methymna, which is on the northern shore of Lesbos.

58-60 This is the earliest extant account of this snake and its petrifaction; however, it may be the snake briefly alluded to at 7.358. See Forbes Irving, 299.

58 **At last:** *tandem*; Murphy wryly comments: 'Apollo's intervention on behalf of his protégé is certainly overdue.'

59 The line seems redundant and was excised by Riese.

61-6 Neither in the *Georgics* nor in the *Aeneid* (see on 11.62), is there any hint of this happy reunion in the Underworld.

61-2 **the places he had seen before:** for an account of his previous visit to the underworld, see 10.11-63.

62 **the fields of the pious:** *arua piorum*; the Elysian Fields, a place for the virtuous to live eternally; the earliest extant version is in Homer (*Od.* 4.561-9) but the topic recurs frequently thereafter; perhaps the most memorable account is Virgil's (*Aen.* 6.637-78; see also Austin's very full note). One of the inhabitants of Elysium in that account was Orpheus (645-7). At *Aen.* 5.734-5, Virgil describes Elysium as 'the pleasant councils of the pious' (*amoena piorum concilia*; for *piorum*, see also on 9.382).

63 **embraced her with eager arms:** in Virgil's account (*G.* 4.500-1), there is a last futile embrace between the lovers; while Ovid allows himself no verbal echo, it is impossible not to associate his Orpheus' happy embrace with Virgil's futile attempt.

66   **safely now:** in contrast to what happened at 10.53-63 and to Virgil's sad account at *G.* 4.490-8.

67-84 *The punishment of the Maenads*

This story is not otherwise known.

67   **Lyaeus:** a Greek cult-title of Bacchus meaning 'Loosener'; cf. 11.105, see on 3.520.

68   **priest:** *uates*; elsewhere in reference to Orpheus in books 10-11, translated 'bard'; for its range of meanings, see on 10.11.

70   **mothers who had seen:** *matres…quae uidere*; presumably the same 'young women' *nurus* we met at 11.3; Mynors (on Virg. *G.* 4.520) points out that *matres*, especially in Bacchic contexts, does not necessarily imply motherhood; furthermore, *quae uidere*, 'who had seen', is not to distinguish a less guilty group of mere onlookers from those who had actually committed the attack, but is to suggest that mere seeing would be enough to warrant the penalty.

70   **Edonian:** the Edoni were a tribe who dwelt on the borders of Thrace and Macedonia and were famous as devotees of Bacchus. See also N.-H. on Hor. *Odes* 2.7.27.

83   **stretched out arms:** *porrectaque bracchia*; the reading is owed to mediaeval correctors; if genuine, it is an even clearer example of Ovid's use of the act of supplication to produce humour; see on 9.210; the traditional reading, *longos quoque bracchia*, would give the meaning: 'and you would think that her arms really were long branches'; such a reading is not only far less interesting, it also offends against a principle of Latin verse (normally followed scrupulously by Ovid) that, if a clause contains two nouns and two adjectives, one adjective will go with one noun and the other with the other; see on 9.10.

85-145 *Midas and the golden touch*

While this is the earliest extant version of this story, there are indications (see especially on 11.90) that it is much older than Ovid.

86   **better:** i.e. better than the one that had killed Orpheus.

his: for T(i)molus as a mountain sacred to Bacchus, see Dodds on Eur. *Bacchae* 55.

Timolus: (stress the middle syllable), usually 'Tmolus' (cf. 2.217, 6.15) etc., but the extra vowel is sometimes found in Greek too), a Lydian mountain range. It was noted for its vineyards (see Virg. *G.* 2.97-8). Bacchus has left Lesbos and travelled south-east to the mainland.

87   **Pactolos:** (stress the middle syllable), a small Lydian river that flows north from mount Tmolus into the Hermus, which then flows west to empty into the Aegean just south of Phocaea. The river was reputed to carry gold dust; see Virg. *Aen.* 10.142 and Harrison, also Herod. 1.93 (de Sélincourt's translation):

> *Lydia…has few natural features of much consequence for a historian to describe, except the gold dust which is washed down from Tmolus.*

89   **Satyrs and Bacchae:** the same groups were following Bacchus at 4.25; Satyrs were goat-footed demi-gods of wild places (see further on 1.193); Bacchae were the female followers of the god.

90   **Silenus:** see Herod. 8.138 (de Sélincourt's translation):

> *…the Gardens of Midas…According to local legend it was in these gardens that Silenus was caught.*

Is this an early allusion to Ovid's story? Otherwise, Silenus is best known from Virgil (*Ecl.* 6).

91   **neat wine:** *mero*; the ancients normally mixed their wine with water; to drink it neat was regarded as uncouth.

93   **Cecropian Eumolpus:** *Cecropio Eumolpo*; the earliest extant reference is *Hom. Hymn* 2.470-476 (Evelyn-White's translation):

> *And rich-crowned Demeter…went…and to the kings who deal justice,*
> *Triptolemus and Diocles, the horse-driver, and to doughty Eumolpus and*

> *Celeus, leader of the people, she showed the conduct of her rights and*
> *taught them all her mysteries* ['orgia']...

These were the Eleusinian Mysteries, celebrated at Eleusis, near to Athens, hence 'Cecropian' (see on 6.70-1). The rhythm of the words is similar to that discussed at 11.17, except that here there is the further irregularity of a spondaic fifth foot. The effect must be to recall the sound of Bacchic worship.

orgies: *orgia*; although the word 'orgy' is, of course, derived from the Greek *orgia*, a word adopted into Latin by Catullus (64.260) as well as by Virgil (*G.* 4.251, *Aen.* 4.303; 7.403, where Fordyce is instructive), its normal usage in both classical languages is as a technical term for the rites of Bacchic worship. See further on 4.2.

97   **Lucifer**: i.e. 'Light-bringer', the Morning Star. For more details, see on 2.114; that passage and 8.1 are both very similar to this one.

99   **his youthful foster-son**: i.e. Bacchus. The relationship was alluded to as early as the second century B.C. Nicander of Colophon (*Alexiph.* 31).

105   **Liber**: the word means 'Free' and was the name of an early Italian god of vegetation later identified with Bacchus who was also known in Greek as *Lyaeus*, 'Loosener'; cf. 11.67, see also on 3.520.

106   **the Berecyntian hero**: i.e. Midas; see on 11.16.

108   The line was condemned by Merkel; a cautious desire not to climb too high into the tree seems wholly without point here; it also fits ill with the staccato effect of the succeeding lines.

109-117   **the twig: a twig...a stone: the stone...touched a clod...touch, the clod...door posts...door posts...water, the water**: *uirgam: uirga...saxum: saxum...contigit et glaebam: contactu glaebam...postibus...postes...undis, unda*; polyptoton (see on 9.44) is used with particular effect here to emphasise the transformations.

112   **a lump of gold**: *massa*; the word normally means a 'lump'; here context compels us to take it as 'lump of gold'; Bömer compares Lucan 7.753.
      Ceres: i.e. wheat, see 5.341-3; for the metonymy, see on 9.141.

114   **the Hesperides**: for the story of the Golden Apples of the Hesperides, 'the daughters of the West', see on 9.190.

117   **Danaë**: she was seduced by Jupiter disguised as a 'shower of gold' and subsequently gave birth to Perseus. See 4.610-1 and the note.

120   **baked meal**: *tostae frugis*; i.e. bread.

121-2   **rewards of Ceres...gifts of Ceres**: *Cerealia...munera...Cerealia dona*; see on 11.112. The change from *munera*, 'rewards', to *dona*, 'gifts', may be only for metrical convenience.

123   **eager teeth**: the point presumably is that when he finds that his hands turn the food to gold he tries to expose it only to his teeth.

123-4   **food...teeth...food...teeth**: the translation attempts to catch something of Ovid's jingling lines: *dapes...dente parabat...dapes...dente premebat*.

125   **the source of his gift**: *auctorem muneris*; i.e. Bacchus and so, by metonymy (see on 9.141), wine.
      mixed...with pure water: see on 11.91.

131   For the gesture of supplication, see on 9.210.
      shining: Midas' arms are now 'gold-plated'.

132   **Lenaean**: (stress the middle syllable) *Lenaee*, Greek for 'of the wine press', a frequent epithet of Bacchus; see on 4.14.

137   **the river**: the Pactolos, see on 11.87.

145   **pale...grow hard**: *rigent...pallentia*; the pallor and the growing hard are the pallor and growing hard of gold; cf. *palluit* at 11.110 and *rigebant* at 12.122.

146-93 Midas and his ass's ears

There is no extant account of this story before Ovid; however, references to Midas' ass's ears at Aristophanes *Plutus* 287 and *Greek Anthology* 5.56 show that it is traditional. For a discussion of the Ovidian version, see Hill 136-7.

146-7 dwell in...worshipping: *colebat*; the Latin word has both meanings (*OLD* s.v. 'colo' 1 and 6) and is, accordingly, used in syllepsis (sse on 9.135) here: 'he did the act of *colere* to the woods, the country and Pan'; there is, however, no English word that can mean either 'dwell in' or 'worship' so that the translation has had to use two different verbs for the one Latin one, thus losing the syllepsis.

147 Pan: a rustic divinity noted for his skill at playing the pipes that bear his name, or that of his beloved Syrinx; see 1.689-712 and the notes on 1.677. In this instrument, different pitches are obtained by moving the mouth across the ends of a set of reeds of different lengths glued together by wax. *Hom. Hymn* 19 is devoted to him.

148 the foolish mind in his heart: *stultae praecordia mentis*; literally, 'the area around the heart (*praecordia*) that belongs to his foolish mind'. As can be seen from e.g. Lucr. 3.615-7 or Cic. *Tusc.* 1.17.41, there was considerable doubt in antiquity as to whether the mind was in the head or near the heart or somewhere else. Lucretius knew it was in the breast; Cicero knew that the issue had not yet been decided.

150 looking widely over the sea: actually, Tmolus is some fifty miles from the nearest sea.

151 stretched out: the mountain is a long ridge running from north-west to south-east.

152 small Hypaepa: Sardis and Hypaepa were towns to the north and south respectively of Tmolus. Hypaepa was much smaller than Sardis; it is called 'small' (*paruis...Hypaepis*) also on the only other occasion Ovid refers to it (6.13).

153-4 songs...song: *carmina...carmen*; see on 10.443-4.

154 waxed reeds: see on 11.147.

155 The folly of rivalling the great gods in artistry has already been well established by the Pierides (5.294-678), Arachne (6.1-145) and Marsyas (6.382-400); this contest, however, has a gentler outcome.

156 under: *sub*; with this word, meaning either literally 'under' of the mountain or metaphorically 'under the authority of' of the judge, Ovid begins an account where the ambiguity between Tmolus as mountain and Tmolus as anthropomorphic divinity is fully exploited. There is a similar exercise with Sleep (see on 11.621) and with Atlas (see on 4.657-66) itself modelled on Virgil's treatment of Atlas at *Aen.* 4.246-51.

unequal contest: partly because it was between Apollo and a minor deity, partly because it was felt that barbarous music associated with the rustic pipes could not compete with the lyre of the Olympian gods.

158 hair: *coma*; here Ovid again (see on 11.47) exploits the fact that *coma* can mean either 'hair' or 'foliage'; the effect has not been reproduced in the translation.

160 the god of the flock: Pan was a shepherd (*Hom. Hymn* 19.5).

160-1 from the judge...there will be no delay: *in iudice...nulla mora est*; reminiscent of Damoetas' words just before his contest (modelled on Theocritus 6) with Menalcas: *in me mora non erit ulla* 'in me there will not be any delay' (Virg. *Ecl.* 3.52). There, however, eight lines elapse before the contest actually begins.

161-2 rustic...barbarous: see on 11.156.

162 For the parenthesis, see on 9.17.

164 to face...face: *ora...ad os*; the translation has changed the grammar to catch the repetition; see on 10.443-4.

165 He: *ille*; Apollo. There is no ambiguity in the Latin; see on 9.279.

laurel: for Apollo's association with laurel, see 1.452-567.

from Parnassus: Delphi, at the foot of Mt Parnassus was sacred to Apollo; the association between all three is at least as early as *Hom. Hymn* 3.268-9 and becomes a commonplace.

166 Tyrian murex: a shell-fish, traditionally associated with Tyre, from which purple dye was derived; see Austin on Virg. *Aen.* 4.262.

170 **learned:** *docto*; the Latin word is indelibly associated with poetry, especially poetry in the Callimachean tradition. According to Nisbet-Hubbard, in a note (on *Odes* 1.1.29) well worth consulting, it is:

> a hard word to translate; 'learned' is too heavy, and 'cultured' too pretentious.

171 **by their sweetness:** i.e. 'by the sweetness of their sounds'; the compression of thought is no less striking in the Latin than in the English.

to lower...to: *submittere*; see *OLD* s.v. 7c or 10. Bömer is probably right to think that this has nothing to do with the idiom *fasces submittere* since that involves a willing act of obeisance, not an acknowledgement of defeat. The usage is, however, clearly formal and prosaic, an example of Ovid's delight in the deliberately inappropriate expression.

174 **The Delian:** *Delius*; Apollo, who was born on Delos.

178 **only:** see on 10.373.

179 For this use of *-que*, here represented only by the colon, cf. 7.454 and see *OLD* s.v. 6.

181 **turban:** *tiaris*; this was a Persian head-dress, rather like a turban with a pointed top and ear- or cheek-flaps. Here, it serves both to conceal Midas' ass's ears and to emphasise his barbarian nature. See also Fordyce on Virg. *Aen.* 7.247. Suetonius (*Nero* 13.2) tells of Tiridates, king of Armenia, accepting a diadem from Nero in place of his *tiara* to symbolise his acceptance of the fact that it was to Rome he must look for legitimacy, not Armenia.

192 **the farmer:** *agricolam*; not a rôle that Midas' servant had ever sought.

south wind: *austro*; see on 11.663.

194-795 Troy before the Trojan War and other stories more or less related to that period or its major personalities.

194-220 Laomedon

The whole story is recorded by Apollodorus, but various allusions to parts of it by Homer make it plain that it is very ancient. I record below in parentheses the relevant Homeric references. If you choose to follow them up, you will notice various slight inconsistencies between Homer, Apollodorus and Ovid. Homer, indeed, is not entirely consistent with himself since, at *Il.* 7.452-3, there is a reference to the building of a wall for Laomedon by Poseidon and Apollo; whereas at 21.441-54, the building is done only by Poseidon, while Apollo tends Laomedon's cattle. At *Il.* 5.638-42 and 649-51, Homer records that Heracles came for the sake of promised horses and that he was cheated and sacked the city, but he makes no mention of Hesione or a sea monster. Apollodorus' version is as follows (2.5.9 and 2.6.4, Frazer's translation):

> But it chanced that the city [Troy] was then in distress consequently on the wrath of Apollo and Poseidon. For desiring to put the wantonness of Laomedon to the proof, Apollo and Poseidon assumed the likeness of men and undertook to fortify Pergamum [Troy] for wages [Il. 7.452-3]. But when they had fortified it, he would not pay them their wages [Il. 21.441-54]. Therefore Apollo sent a pestilence, and Poseidon a sea monster, which, carried up by a flood, snatched away the people of the plain. But as oracles foretold deliverance from these calamities if Laomedon would expose his daughter Hesione to be devoured by the sea monster, he exposed her by fastening her to the rocks near the sea. Seeing her exposed, Hercules promised to save her on condition of receiving from Laomedon the mares which Zeus had given in compensation for the rape of Ganymede. On Laomedon's saying that he would give them, Hercules killed the monster and saved Hesione. But when Laomedon would not give the stipulated reward, Hercules put to sea after threatening to make war on Troy [Il. 5.649-51].
>
> And having come to port at Ilium, he [Hercules] left the guard of the ships to Oicles and himself with the rest of the champions set out to attack

the city. Howbeit Laomedon marched against the ships with the multitude
and slew Oicles in battle, but being repulsed by the troops of Hercules, he
was besieged. The siege once laid, Telamon was the first to breach the
walls and enter the city, and after him Hercules...and when he had taken
the city [Il. 5.638-42]...he assigned Laomedon's daughter Hesione as a
prize to Telamon...

194   Leto's son: *Latoius*; i.e. Apollo, see Hom. *Il.* 1.9.

195   to this side: *citra*, i.e. 'to this side of the Hellespont from the point of view of a traveller going north from Tmolus'. Troy lies between Tmolus and the Hellespont, but is much nearer to the Hellespont.

Helle, Nephele's daughter: the story is conveniently told by Apollodorus (1.9.1, Frazer's translation):

Athamas...begat a son Phrixus and a daughter Helle by Nephele. And he
married a second wife, Ino, by whom he had Learchus and Melicertes. But
Ino plotted against the children of Nephele and persuaded the women to
parch the wheat...But the earth, being sown with parched wheat, did not
yield its annual crops; so Athamas sent to Delphi to enquire how he might
be delivered from the dearth. Now Ino persuaded the messengers to say it
was foretold that the infertility would cease if Phrixus were sacrificed to
Zeus. When Athamas heard that, he was forced by the inhabitants of the
land to bring Phrixus to the altar. But Nephele brought him and her
daughter up and gave them a ram with a golden fleece...and borne through
the sky by the ram they crossed land and sea. But when they were over the
sea which lies between Sigeum and the Chersonese, Helle slipped into the
deep and was drowned, and the sea was called Hellespont ['Helle's sea']
after her.

For an interesting account of Ovid's treatment of this story, see on 4.416-562.

197   Sigean...Rhoetean: Sigeum and Rhoeteum (stress the middlr syllable in both cases) are two promontories situated respectively to the north-west and to the north of Troy. Assuming that the altar is in Troy, it will stand to the right of Sigeum and the left of Rhoeteum from the point of view of an observer in Troy who is looking out to sea.

198   Panomphaean: a Greek epithet for Zeus (Jupiter) at least as early as Hom. *Il.* 8.250 and traditionally interpreted to mean 'from whom all voices (i.e. omens) come.'

Thunderer: *Tonanti*; i.e. Jupiter, cf. e.g. 1.170.

202   trident-wielding *tridentigero*; probably an Ovidian coinage (see on 9.262), like *tridentifer* 'trident-bearer' at 8.596. For Neptune's trident, see e.g. Hom. *Il.* 12.27, Virg. *Aen.* 1.145.

203-4   walls...walls: *muros...moenibus*; the repetition in the English does not reflect a repetition in the Latin. *muri* and *moenia* are standard Latin words for 'walls'; but English does not have two basic words for 'walls'; see on 9.32-4.

215   her twice perjured walls: *periura...moenia Troiae*; the phrase echoes Virgil's *periurae moenia Troiae* 'the walls of perjured Troy' (*Aen.* 5.811) where the reference is only to Laomedon's first 'perjury', to Apollo and Neptune.

217   For: *nam*; the logic appears to be that Peleus did not need to be given a bride because he was already married. That he participated in this expedition with his brother Telamon is plausible from Apollodorus' account. For their history, see on 7.476-7.

218   divine wife: see on 11.221-65.

219   grandfather: i.e. Jupiter who was the father of Aeacus, himself the father of Peleus; cf. Achilles' words at Hom. *Il.* 21.187-9 (Lattimore's translation):

'but I claim that I am of the generation of great Zeus.
The man is my father who is lord over many Myrmidons,
Peleus, Aiakos' son, but Zeus was the father of Aiakos.'

father-in-law: i.e. Nereus, Thetis was the daughter of Nereus and thus one of the Nereïds; cf. e.g. Hom. *Il.* 18.34-8, 50-1. No other man was formally married to a goddess.

not just to one: readers of the *Metamorphoses* will be able to supply examples quite readily.

219-20 just...just: see on 10.373.

221-65 *Peleus and Thetis*

Peleus' marriage to Thetis and the subsequent birth of their son, Achilles, is a story celebrated throughout ancient literature from e.g. Hom. *Il.* 18.79-87 to Catul. 64. Frazer's note on Apollodorus 3.13.5 is unusually full even for him and is also supplemented by a very wide-ranging appendix (vol. 2, pp. 383-8).

221 old Proteus: *senex... Proteus*; an exact translation of Homer's phrase for him (*Od.* 4.395) often rendered in English as 'The Old Man of the Sea'; he was indeed a sea-god famously described by Homer (*Od.* 4.384-424) where too he is accorded prophetic powers.

Goddess of the waves: Thetis, see on 11.219.

221-3 This particular prophecy is attributed elsewhere (Pind. *Isthm.* 8.31-36 and Apollod. 3.13.5) to Themis.

222-3 deeds...deeds: *actis acta*; for the polyptoton, see on 9.44. Some editors prefer *armis* 'arms' or *annis* 'years' but neither (especially the former) gives so pleasing an effect.

225 fires: *ignes*; i.e. fires of love for Thetis.

227 Aeacides: (stress the second syllable); 'son of Aeacus', i.e. Peleus; see on 11.219.

229-37 for the ekphrasis, see on 9.334.

229 Haemonia: N.-H. on Hor. *Odes* 1.37.20: 'properly an area of Thessaly, but used by the Alexandrian and Roman poets as a name for Thessaly in general.'

234 berries of both colours: see on 10.98.

235-6 (whether made by nature or by art): Diana's cave (3.155-9) was 'constructed by no art but by nature, in her genius, imitating art.' Fashions change in the perennial debate on the relative merits of nature and artifice. The Romans, unlike the Romantics, preferred artifice. Murphy rightly comments on the 'comic incongruity' of this theoretical discussion. For the parenthesis, see on 9.17.

236-44 for the apostrophe, see on 9.101.

241 customary skills: the mutability of sea divinities (no doubt a reflection on the mutability of the sea itself) is well established. Homer's story of Proteus (*Od.* 4.383-570) is largely a celebration of his powers of metamorphosis (cf. 2.9 and the note, 8.731 and the note, Virg. *G.* 4.405-52). Psamathe is another sea divinity equipped with these powers (Apollod. 3.12.6). Thetis' use of metamorphosis in a vain attempt to escape Peleus is recorded in typically oblique way by Pindar (*Nem.* 4.62-5, Sandys's translation):

> *So Peleus, having escaped the violence of fire, and the keen claws of bold lions, and the edge of their terrible teeth, wedded one of the enthroned Nereids.*

See also Periclymenus (12.536-76).

243-4 bird (and yet a bird...tree...tree: *uolucris (uolucrem... arbor... arbore*; for the polyptoton and near polyptoton, see on 9.44.

249 the Carpathian seer: *Carpathius... uates*; i.e. Proteus. Virgil (*G.* 4.387-8) had set him in the Carpathian sea; for *uates*, see on 10.11.

253-4 It is ironic that Proteus is giving exactly the same advice as Eidothea gave to Menelaus when he wanted to overcome Proteus' metamorphoses (Hom. *Od.* 4.414-24); exactly the same formulas are also found in Cyrene's instructions to her son, Aristaeus, when he wished to overcome the ever-changing Proteus (Virg. *G.* 4.387-414).

254 reshapes: *reformet*; see on 9.399.

258 Nereïd: i.e. 'Thetis', see on 11.219.

263 and said, 'It is not...: *'neque' ait...* see on 10.569.

266-409 *Peleus with Ceyx*

For the story of Peleus' exile, see Apollod. 3.12.6-13.1 (Frazer's translation):

*As Phocus excelled in athletic sports, his brothers Peleus and Telamon
plotted against him, and the lot falling on Telamon, he killed his brother in
a match by throwing a quoit at his head, and with the help of Peleus carried
the body and hid it in a wood. But the murder being detected, the two were
driven fugitives from Aegina by Aeacus... Peleus fled to Phthia to the court
of Eurytion...*

Frazer's notes discover many other versions of this exile most of which attribute the murder to
Peleus, not Telamon, but the idea that Peleus took refuge with Ceyx seems to be found only in
Ovid. Ceyx had, however, given refuge both to Hercules (Apollod. 2.7.7) and to his sons
(Apollod. 2.7.8).

268 had turned out well: *contigerant*; not a usual sense of the word, which is normally neutral
(see *OLD* s.v. 'contingo' 8), but a sense fairly easily inferred from *felix...felix*.

269 Trachis: a small town in Oetaea, about twenty miles north of Delphi. According to Homer
(*Il.* 2.682) it was part of Achilles' territory, but it was chiefly celebrated as the site of Hercules' death, the subject of Sophocles' *Trachiniae*.

271 the son of father Lucifer, Ceyx: see Apollod. 1.7.4 (Frazer's translation):
Alcyone was married by Ceyx, son of Lucifer.
For Lucifer, the Morning Star, see on 11.97.

271-2 father...father's: *genitore...patrium*; the repetition in the English does not reflect a repetition in the Latin; *pater*, from which the adjective *patrius* derives, is the standard word for
'father'; *genitor* is a somewhat more elevated word for which there is no English equivalent; in context, however, not least because of its redundancy, it does give a certain mock
grandeur to the passage; see also on 9.32-4.

273 his brother: Daedalion, whose story is about to be revealed. See on 11.291-345.

276 both...and: *-que...et*; Tarrant restores *et*; otherwise, the sentence rambles from 274 to 281
in an unacceptably disordered way.

279 olive-branch: *uelamenta*; suppliants carried olive branches wrapped in wool as a symbol of
peace; see the note on 6.101, Fordyce on Virg. *Aen.* 7.154, *OLD* s.v. 2b.

282 the Trachinian: i.e. Ceyx.

291-345 Ceyx tells the story of Chione and Daedalion

The story that Chione was visited in one night by both Apollo and Mercury who fathered respectively the twins Philammon and Autolycus is as old as Hesiod (frg. 64 M.-W.). That her father
was Daedalion and that he was transformed into a hawk is found elsewhere only in Hyginus
(200), and it is normally assumed that Hyginus is relying on Ovid here. The connexion between
Ceyx and Daedalion is found only here and is probably Ovid's invention. Further details and a
bibliography can be found at Forbes Irving, 241-2.

293 (so great is the consistency of character): see on 9.320-1.

295-6 that father...is the last to go from the sky: for Lucifer as Ceyx' father, see on 11.271;
for Lucifer as the Morning Star, see on 11.97. It is, in fact, the planet Venus which is visible
in the Northern hemisphere either just before dawn, or at dusk, when it is known as *Vesper*,
the Evening Star. *Pace* Murphy, however, 'is the last to go from the sky' is a reference to
dawn, not dusk; indeed, Ovid refers here only to the dawn. See further on 2.114.

297 My care...peace, my care...peace: *cura mihi pax...pacis mihi cura*; the word play is more
obvious in the Latin than in the translation. Some manuscripts and some editors read *culta*
which would give: 'I nurtured peace, my care...'. For the polyptoton *pax...pacis*, see on
9.44.

298 for my marriage: this apparently trivial detail foreshadows the tragic tale of Ceyx and Alcyone (stress the -y-) which will dominate the second half of this book (410-748).
No attempt has been made in the translation to catch the harsh alliteration *fuit; fratri fera*; as
Austin (on Virg. *Aen.* 6.100) points out, Quintilian (12.10.29) regarded the 'f' sound as being scarcely human.

300 **Thisbaean doves:** a learned reference to Hom. *Il.* 2.502: 'Thisbe of the many doves.' According to Leaf's note: 'Chandler was led to the discovery of the ruins of Thisbe (near the coast of the Corinthian Gulf) by the number of wild doves which haunted them.'

303 **Maia's son:** Mercury, see on 2.697-704.

304 **Delphi...Cyllenaean peak:** for Apollo's association with Delphi, see on 9.332; for Mercury's association with mount Cyllene, see *Hom. Hymn* 4.2 etc., Virg. *Aen.* 4.252.
Cyllenaeo: normally, Ovid is even stricter than other Roman poets of his time in ending a hexameter with a dactyl followed by a spondee (see *Introduction* pp. 4-5); here, the spondaic fifth foot and the quadrisyllabic end give the line a very Greek feel.

306 **hopes of love:** *spem Veneris;* see on 9.141.

307 **his staff that brings sleep:** Mercury's staff that can induce or dispel sleep is familiar from all literature; cf. e.g. Hom. *Od.* 5.47-8 (Lattimore's translation):
> *He caught up the staff, with which he mazes the eyes of those mortals*
> *whose eyes he would maze, or wakes again the sleepers.*

308 **touched...touch:** *tangit: tactu;* for the polyptoton see on 9.44.

310 **made himself like an old woman:** this is a favourite technique by which gods and goddesses induce young women to trust them. Apollo used the same device to seduce Leocothoë (4.220); for more examples, see on 3.275-8.

312 **the wing-footed god:** Mercury; cf. 1.671-5 and the note; see also Hom. *Od.* 5.44-6 (Lattimore's translation):
> *Immediately he bound upon his feet the fair sandals,*
> *golden and immortal, that carried him over the water*
> *as over the dry boundless earth abreast of the wind's blast.*

313 **Autolycus:** notorious as early as Homer; see e.g. *Od.* 19.394-7 (Lattimore's translation):
> *This [Autolycus] was his [Odysseus'] mother's noble father, who surpassed all men*
> *in thievery and the art of the oath, and the god Hermes*
> *himself had endowed him...*

Later, e.g. at Apollod. 1.9.16, he became, as in Ovid, a son of Hermes (Mercury).

314-5 **white...black...dark...bright:** *candida... nigris... candentibus atra;* Ovid enjoys polyptoton (see on 9.44); here, however, where one might expect two polyptota, Ovid chooses to vary the vocabulary instead, perhaps to indicate the trickery of Autolycus. However, *candida* and *candentibus* are cognate while 'white' and 'bright' are not.

315 **a not unworthy heir to his father's skills:** Hermes himself was noted for theft (see e.g. *Hom. Hymn* 4 *passim*), and the family tradition was maintained by Autolycus' grandson, Odysseus.

316 For the parenthesis, see on 9.17.

317 **singing voice...lyre:,** each half-brother took after his particular father.

319-20 **a brave father:...a radiant grandfather:** Daedalion and Lucifer cf. 11.271-2 and the note, 295-6. The intense word play between 11.271-2 and this passage supports the minority reading *nitenti,* as against the majority reading *Tonanti,* 'Thunderer', i.e. Jupiter (see on 11.198), which would, in any case, give a false genealogy.

321-7 This part of Chione's story is an abbreviated version of Niobe's tale (6.146-312), except that, with Niobe, the issue was fecundity, not beauty.

322 **but in her:** *at illi;* this is Diana; see on 9.279.

323 **with my deeds:** i.e., with great irony, 'if not with my beauty, then with my deeds.'

325-6 **tongue. The tongue:** *linguam. lingua;* for the polyptoton see on 9.44.

328-30 **father's...brother...father:** the text is corrupt in most manuscripts; the version adopted here is that followed by modern editors: Ceyx feels a sorrow as if he were the father, speaks words of consolation to Daedalion, his brother, who, as the true father, is inconsolable.

329 **pious:** see on 9.382.

331 Cf. 11.273 near the beginning of this tale.

343 **his courage as before:** this transition is as harsh in the Latin as it is in the English. It is tempting to suppose that a line has dropped out. Ovid is very fond of the metamorphosis that reveals an underlying truth; the reader has been prepared for this one at 11.293; cf. 10.242; see also on 1.234; 6.97; 9.320-1.

346-409 The wolf that attacked Peleus' cattle
The story of the savage wolf that slaughters Peleus' cattle until eventually turned to marble, briefly alluded to by Lycophron (91-2), is to be found in Antoninus Liberalis (38), and he attributes it to the first book of Nikander's *Heteroeumena*. Antoninus gives a very different and much more complex narrative than Ovid's; in it, the purification of Peleus for the death of Phocus was performed by Iros' son, Eurytion, whom Peleus later accidentally killed during a boar hunt (presumably the Calydonian Boar hunt; see on 11.409); banished, Peleus fled to Acastus whose wife falsely accused him of seducing her; after even more misadventures, he brought a herd of cattle and a flock of sheep to pay Iros for the loss of his son. Iros, however, refused the offering upon which the wolf attacked the sheep; then, by non-specific divine intervention, the wolf was turned to stone. Forbes Irving (299) wrongly places the story at Ovid *Met.* 11.266ff. There is every reason to suppose that it was Ovid's idea to associate this story with that of Ceyx and Alcyone.

348 **Onetor:** presumably Ovid's invention.
Phocian: Phocis was a territory to the north-west of Boeotia.
350 **disaster:** *cladis*; for this striking enjambment; see on 9.78.
351 This line is normally understood as in the translation offered; if so, its attribution to Ceyx ('the Trachinian') of a permanently trembling face is both inappropriate in context and untrue to e.g. 11.382ff. Tarrant is, accordingly, tempted to follow Heinsius and excise it. Could the line, however, be saved by translating it: 'The Trachinian too was in suspense with fear at his [i.e. Onetor's] trembling face.'? For a similar line, see 8.465.
353 **when the Sun...course:** *medio...orbe*; for the same words in a very different context, see 1.592.
358-9 **the sea...the sea:** *aequora...mari*; the repetition in the English does not reflect a repetition in the Latin. *aequora* and *mari* are standard Latin words for 'sea'; but English does not have two basic words for 'sea'; see on 9.32-4. Exactly the same issue arises at 1.291-2, 330-1; 11.702-3; at 11.427, a much harder case, I adopt a different solution.
359-64 for the ekphrasis, see on 9.334. This ekphrasis offers a suitably sinister setting for the savage violence which is to follow.
361 **the Nereïds and Nereus;** see on 11.219.
361-2 For the parenthesis, see on 9.17.
362 **of the sea:** *ponti* (another word for 'sea', see on 358-9); editors have sometimes been tempted to accept the banal manuscript variant *templi* ('of the temple'), apparently insensitive to the humour of the sailor carefully explaining the obvious to Onetor.
367 **flashing:** *fulmineos*; see on 10.550.
375 **moo-filled:** *demugitae*; another Ovidian coinage; see on 9.262; this one is particularly absurd and undercuts the horror of the narrative.
378 **arms, arms:** *arma, arma*; for the repetition of *arma*, cf. 12.241, and see Austin on Virg. *Aen.* 2.668.
379-81 **losses...losses:** *damna...damna*; such repetition is more tolerable to Roman ears than to ours; see on 10.443-4.
380-1 For the incident, see on 11.266-409.
380 **the bereaved Nereïd:** Psamathe, the mother of Phocus; cf. Hes. *Theog.* 1003-5 (Evelyn-White's translation):
> But of the daughters of Nereus, the Old man of the Sea, Psamathe, the fair
> goddess, was loved by Aeacus through golden Aphrodite and bare Phocus.
382 **The Oetaean king:** Ceyx; mt. Oeta was near Trachis, see on 11.269, 282.

385 her hair not yet fully dressed: suddenly, Ovid incongruously incorporates into Ceyx' speech mention of the Roman ladies and their obsession with hair styles that he had treated in his elegiacs; for a discussion, see Booth on *Amores* 2.8.1.

389 Aeacides: i.e. 'son of Aeacus', Peleus; see on 11.219.

390 pious: see on 9.382.

for what you both have promised: *uestri* shows that 'your' refers to more than one person (in this case, Ceyx and Alcyone); had he meant only Alcyone he would have used *tui*; here, however, English 'your' is ambiguous on this point, hence the addition of 'both'. For the promise, cf. 11.287.

392-3 A very brief ekphrasis; see on 9.334.

398 aquamarine: *caeruleam*; the colour is a dark bluish green, but the word is indelibly (but not exclusively) associated with sea divinities; wherever it is so associated, I have translated it 'aquamarine'; see on 1.275,

400 her husband: Peleus, see on 11.219.

404 she: i.e. Psamathe.

408 the Magnesians: the inhabitants of Magnesia, a coastal territory in the East of Thessaly; as 'Haemonian' makes plain (see on 11.229). This Magnesia is not to be confused with either of the cities of that name, one of which was in Lydia and the other in Caria.

409 purification for murder...Acastus: what is implicit here, that the killing was the killing of his brother Phocus, is explicit at *Fasti* 2.39-40; Apollodorus (3.13.2), however, who attributes Phocus' killing to his other brother, Telamon (see on 11.266-409), tells us that the killing in question was Peleus' involuntary killing of Eurytion during the Calydonian Boar hunt. For Acastus' rôle, and for a radically different sequence of events, see Anton. Lib. 38 (outlined in the note on 11.346-409) and the notes by Papathomopoulos.

410-748 Ceyx and Alcyone

There were two versions, one conveniently found in Apollodorus (1.7.4, Frazer's translation) but apparently traceable back to Hesiod (see Forbes Irving 239):

> *Alcyone was married by Ceyx, son of Lucifer. These perished by reason of their pride; for he said that his wife was Hera, and she said that her husband was Zeus. But Zeus turned them into birds...*

the other, clearly the one followed by Ovid, attributed to Nikander and telling of Ceyx' shipwreck followed by Alcyone's pathetic weeping until she is transformed into a halcyon (kingfisher). Whether Homer's Alcyone (*Il.* 9.555-64) is relevant here has been a matter of debate. If so, she seems surprisingly more like the innocent and pathetic Hellenistic Alcyone than the sacrilegious Hesiodic(?) one. For further details of an extremely complex issue, see Otis (1966) 392-4, (1970) 311-3, Forbes Irving 239-40.

411 the portentous stories of his brother: the stories about Daedalion told at 11.291-345.

those that came after his brother's: the subsequent stories of the wolf and its petrifaction told at 11.346-409.

412 the delight of men: *hominum oblectamina*; the text has been questioned, but the point seems to be that, although recent events might justify a visit to an oracle, Ceyx' motives are, in fact, rather frivolous. This sharpens the sense of unnecessary tragedy.

413 the Clarian god: Apollo; cf. 1.516 and see Williams on Virg. *Aen.* 3.360. Claros was the name of an oracle sacred to Apollo; it was at Colophon, which was in Ionia, on the other side of the Aegean, just north of Ephesus. Ceyx was, accordingly, obliged to make a long and dangerous sea journey. For details about the oracle, see *OCD* s.v. 'Claros'.

Phorbas: the story is not extant in earlier literature but may have been alluded to in the *Epic Cycle* if we can trust the rather oblique account to be found in the scholiast to Hom. *Il.* 23.660 most conveniently found in Davies (p. 74); much later than Ovid, a fuller account appears in *Imagines* (p. 842 (424)) attributed to one of the Philostrati.

414 Phlegyans: (stress the first syllable) noted as eternally aggressive by Homer (*Il.* 13.301-2) and as careless of Zeus at *Hom. Hymn* 3.278-80.

415 **most faithful Alcyone, he told you:** for the apostrophe, see on 9.101. At first sight, 'most faithful', *fidissima*, seems like a conventional epithet for a wife; only later do we realize how significant it is.

416 **her:** by 419, Ovid has abandoned the apostrophe and returned to normal third person narrative. However, the passage from 416 'at once...', '*cui protinus...* ', to the end of 418 is, in the Latin, ambiguous as between second and third person, thus enabling Ovid to make the transition almost imperceptibly. English, however, does not permit such an ambiguity, hence the rather harsh jump to 'her' here.

420 **pious:** *pias*; see on 9.382.

422-3 **care...without a care:** *cura...securus*, Ovid cannot resist the pun.

425 **But...I assume:** *at puto*; the phrase regularly introduces heavy irony (see *OLD* s.v. 'at' 12); Alcyone, it seems, knows of Phorbas and his Phlegyans (11.413-4) and of Ceyx' plan to go by sea to Colophon rather than, as would otherwise be more natural, by land to Delphi.

427 **sea...waters:** *aequora...ponti*; see on 11.358-9.

429 **burial-mounds without a body:** death at sea was particularly abhorred, because it prevented a proper funeral, cf. e.g. Hom. *Od.* 5.311-2 (Lattimore's translation):
> *and I would have had my rites and the Achaians given me glory.*
> *Now it is by a dismal death that I must be taken.*

See also the instructions given to Aeneas in the Underworld and the story of Palinurus at Virg. *Aen.* 6.318-83.

431 **Hippotades:** i.e. 'son of Hippotas'; this was Aeolus, king of the winds (Hom. *Od.* 10.1-79, Virg. *Aen.* 1.50-80). According to Homer (*Od.* 10.5), he had six sons and six daughters, all unnamed, but Apollodorus (1.7.3) gives him seven sons and five daughters, all named; one of the daughters is, indeed, Alcyone.

432 **prison:** *carcere*; the image is borrowed from Virgil's description of Aeolus' cave (*Aen.* 1.54).

434-5 **land...sea...sky:** the winds affect all parts of the traditional tripartite division of the world; cf. 1.5.

434 **unprotected:** *incommendata*; apparently another Ovidian coinage; see on 9.262.

435 **all of it, and all:** *omnis et omne*; for the polyptoton, see on 9.44.

435-6 **the clouds in the sky...strike...from...collisions:** *caeli... nubila... excutiunt...concursibus*; Ovid is clearly thinking of Lucretius' account of lightning (6.160-218), especially 214 and 160-1 (Bailey's translation):
> *the clouds of heaven [*nubila caeli*]*
> *It lightens likewise, when the clouds at their clashing [*concursu*] have*
> *struck out [*excussere*] many seeds of fire...*

437-8 For the parenthesis, see on 9.17.

440- **your course...of course:** *certus...certe*; an attempt to catch Ovid's repetition. It is for the reader to decide whether it is accidental or deliberate.

441 **we shall be...storm-tossed:** *iactabimur*; the word is not restricted to a maritime context but is closely associated with storms at sea, most memorably, perhaps at Virg. *Aen.* 1.3, where Austin's note is instructive. Cf. also 4.535, *OLD* s.v. 8.

442-3 **and together we shall bear...together...we shall be borne:** *pariterque feremus...pariter...feremur*; Ovid brings out the pun (see on 11.422-3, 440-1) by placing the key words at the ends of successive lines.

444 **Aeolis:** i.e. 'daughter of Aeolus', Alcyone, see on 11.431.

445 **star-like:** *sidereus*; at 11.271-2 Ceyx was said to 'bear his father's radiance in his face'; his father was, of course, Lucifer, the Morning Star, see on 11.271.
no less fire: the recent puns at 11.422-3, 440-1 and 442-3 have, perhaps, prepared us for this striking phrase which must simultaneously suggest that he has as much literal fire as his father, and as much metaphorical fire (i.e. 'love', see *OLD* s.v. 9) as his wife.

450 **her loving heart:** *amantem*, 'heart' corresponds to nothing in the Latin but its omission, normal in Latin, would be intolerable in English.

452 **by my father's fires:** see on 11.271.

466 **first:** *prima*; normally this would mean: 'she was the first to...' but here it is tempting to wonder whether it does not mean that this was the first thing she did in a series, though I know of no parallel for such a meaning. Miller takes it to refer to Ceyx' signals, but this seems most unlikely.

466-7 **when the land had sunk too far:** just for a moment, the perspective changes to that of Ceyx before returning to Alcyone's. As the land sinks down, he can no longer see her and, presumably, stops waving; but she can still see the ship for some time.

467-8 **eyes...eye:** *oculi...lumine*; there are not two different words for 'eye' in English; see on 9.32-4.

476-7 **mast...mast:** *arbore...malo*; there are not two different words for 'mast' in English; see on 9.32-4.

481 **Eurus:** the east wind; Ceyx has been sailing Eastwards towards Colophon (11.413); suddenly he is confronted by a violent head-wind; for a similar, but not identical, situation, see 7.659-64 and 8.1-2.

487 **to protect the side:** *munire latus*; the precise nature of such a precautionary practice is unclear; one idea suggested for this passage by *OLD* s.v. 'munio' 3 'to provide with a protective wall, covering etc.' is, perhaps, to be related to the Greek φράττεσθαι ναῦν identified by Taillardat (*Rev.Phil.* 39 (1965) 80-90) as a technical term for protecting a ship from damage in a storm by erecting a wicker barrier between the bridge and the deck below; cf. e.g. Aesch. *Sept.* 62-4. Murphy (on 11.475) imagines that they were stopping up the holes through which the oars had been plied.

496 **ether:** see on 10.2.

504 **Acheron:** one of the rivers of the Underworld (Hom. *Od.* 10.513 etc.).

510-3 These lines were deleted by Merkel. The lion simile certainly seems to disrupt the line of thought; after the 'battering ram or catapult' the reader expects any new simile to be also for the waves and, at first, the lion seems to be just that; the sudden realization that the lion represents the ship is disconcerting, to say the least.

513 **heights:** *alta*; this is Shackleton Bailey's suggestion for the traditional *arma* which gave a very different sense: 'it (the wave) went into the bulwarks of the ship and was much higher than they were'.

514 **wedges:** context seems to make it clear that these wedges, in conjunction with the wax, made a water-tight seal along the lengths of the planks.

519-20 **waters of the sea...waves of the sky:** the confused imagery underlines the confusion of nature.

520 **ether:** see on 10.2.

  fires: i.e. 'the stars'.

523 **thunderbolts...from the thunderbolts' fires, fires:** *fulmina; fulmineis...ignibus ignes*; for the polyptota, see on 9.44.

530 **the tenth wave:** for the belief that the tenth wave is greater than the others, see Sen. *Ag.* 502 (where Tarrant suggests that Ovid was the first to introduce the idea into Latin descriptions of storms.). There seems to be no more truth in that than in the corresponding view repeated on Britain's summer beaches that it is the seventh wave that is the greatest.

532 **walls of a captured ship:** *pace OLD* s.v. 'moenia' 3, the 'walls' here are not an otherwise unknown technical term for some part of a ship, they are part of an abbreviated simile of a city succumbing to a hostile force; in full, the simile would be: 'the tenth wave falls on the ship, as an enemy descends on captured city-walls'.

534 **they all:** i.e. 'the ship's crew'.

539 **tears:** the ancients associated weeping with a much wider range of emotions, including fear, than we do. For a full discussion, see N.-H. on Hor. *Odes* 1.3.18.

539-40 **blessed for whom funerals awaited:** see on 11.429.

554-5 **Athos...Pindus:** Athos is close to the southern tip of Acte, the most easterly of the three peninsulas of Chalcidice at the northern end of the Aegean. Since it is surrounded on three sides by the sea, it is well suited to be thrown into the sea, unlike Pindus, which is on the Thessaly-Epirus border and about as far away from the sea as it is possible to be in Greece.

556 **it:** i.e. 'the wave'.

559-61 **were holding on to...was holding on to:** *tenent; tenet*; it was impossible, in English, to catch the polyptoton (see on 9.44).

564-5 **he wanted...he wanted:** *optat*; English idiom demands the repetition which is absent in the Latin.

570 **Lucifer was dark that day:** *Lucifer obscurus... illa luce fuit*: there is complex word play here; *Lucifer* (see on 11.97) literally means 'Light-bringer' so that its juxtaposition with *obscurus*, 'dark', immediately produces an oxymoron. The effect is reinforced by Ovid's choice of *luce* (literally 'light' as in *Lucifer*) to mean 'day', a use of the word which is unremarkable in itself (see *OLD* s.v. 4) but which is arresting in this context.

573-6 The pathetic motif of the loving wife vainly preparing for her husband's return when he is already dead goes back to Homer; cf. *Iliad* 22.437-46 (Lattimore's translation):

> So she spoke in tears but the wife of Hektor had not yet
> heard: for no sure messenger had come to her and told her
> how her husband had held his ground there outside the gates;
> but she was weaving a web in the inner room of the high house,
> and folding a robe, and inworking elaborate figures.
> She called out through the house to her lovely-haired handmaidens
> to set a great cauldron over the fire, so that there would be
> hot water for Hektor's bath as he came back out of the fighting;
> poor innocent, nor knew how, far from waters for bathing,
> Pallas Athene had cut him down at the hands of Achilleus.

577 **piously:** *pia*; see on 9.382.

578 **above all...at Juno's temple:** Juno was the goddess of marriage (see on 9.762).

585 **Iris:** she was the rainbow and the messenger of the gods, especially of Juno; see Virg. *Aen.* 4.693-702 (and Austin), 5.606 (and Williams), 9.2 (and Hardie). Cf. also Shakespeare *The Tempest* 4.1.76-82.

586 **the sleep-bringing halls of Sleep:** for the transferred epithet (it is Sleep himself, not his halls, that brings sleep) see on 9.10.

Sleep: Murphy has a full note on personification in general and on this one in particular. As he observes, the ultimate sources for this particular image are to be found in Homer (*Il.* 14.231-76) and Hesiod (*Theog.* 211-2); see also Austin on Virg. *Aen.* 6.273ff. For other personifications in the *Metamorphoses*, see on 2.760-82; 8.788-808.

590 **her bow-shaped arc:** *arcuato... curuamine*; the origin of the second element of the English 'rainbow' becomes clear from this line. *arcuato* can also be spelt *arquato* which would bring out the fact that it is trisyllabic but at the cost of making the word's connexion with *arcus*, 'a bow', much less clear. Cf. Shakespeare *The Tempest* 4.1.71-2:

> the queen o' the sky
> Whose watery arch and messenger am I.

592-615 **There is...a cave...:** *est... spelunca*; for the ekphrasis, see on 9.334. This particular example is unusually long and forms an important part of a peaceful interlude between the violent storm and the highly emotional end of the story.

592 **Cimmerians:** a semi-mythical race; this passage clearly owes much to Homer's account of them (*Od.* 11.14-9, Lattimore's translation):

> There lie the community and city of Kimmerian people,
> hidden in fog and cloud, nor does Helios, the radiant
> sun, ever break through the dark, to illuminate them with his shining,
> neither when he climbs up into the starry heaven,
> nor when he wheels to return again from heaven to earth,
> but always a glum night is spread over wretched mortals.

It would be difficult to imagine more suitable neighbours for Sleep.

594 **Phoebus:** i.e. 'the Sun'; cf. e.g. 1.752.

597 **watchful bird with crested head:** the cockerel, then, as now, the announcer of sunrise.

599 **dogs...than dogs:** *canes canibusue*; for the polyptoton, see on 9.44.

 a goose, shrewder than dogs: this refers to the story of the Gauls frustrated in their attack upon the Capitol only by the timely cackling of the Sacred Geese (the story is most familiar from Livy 5.47); Ovid has referred to it once before (2.538-9), and it appears also at *Fasti* 1.453. For Ovid's characteristic anachronistic reference to Roman history, see on 9.307.

601-2 Tarrant would exclude these lines, partly because of their banality, partly because they seem to be a pastiche of other Ovidian passages.

603 **Lethe's:** Lethe was a place in the Underworld (Aristoph. *Frogs* 186) which much later was thought of as a river; Austin (on Virg. *Aen.* 6.705) observes that Virgil never uses *Lethe* (he uses various periphrases with the adjective *Lethaeus*); this passage too, with its slight periphrasis, *riuus aquae Lethes*, 'the stream of Lethe's water', does not necessarily imply that Lethe was a river (as suggested in the note on 7.152), only that there was a river associated with it.

608 **when it is turned in its socket:** *uerso...cardine*; contrast 14.781 where the threat of creaking door sockets is interestingly exploited.

616 **the virgin:** Iris; cf. Theoc. 17.134, Virg. *Aen.* 5.610.

621 **himself from himself:** *sibi se*; for the polyptoton, see on 9.44. For the artful confusion between Sleep and sleep, see on 11.156.

622 For the parenthesis, see on 9.17.

625 At 4.216, Ovid uses almost the same line to describe the restorative powers of ambrosia.

627 **Herculean Trachis:** see on 11.269.

633 **the father:** Sleep.

635 **Morpheus:** in spite of its Greek form (*Morphea* is a Greek accusative) this name appears to be an Ovidian invention; from μορφή, the Greek for 'shape' as in 'metamorphosis', Ovid has invented the name Μορφεύς (Latin *Morpheus*) and punned it with *figura*, the Latin for μορφή; he uses the name only in this episode and it seems not to recur until the middle ages when it became a commonplace for 'sleep', giving rise later, of course, to 'morphine' etc.

640-2 **gods name him Icelos, mortal folk Phobetor...Phantasos:** like Morpheus (see on 11.635), these names are Ovidian inventions; Icelos (stress the first syllable) is based on a Greek word meaning 'like', Phobetor (stress the second syllable) on a Greek word meaning 'bringer of terror', and Phantasos (stress the first syllable) on a Greek word meaning 'phantom-like'; the notion that gods might use a different name from that used by mortals is familiar from Homer (*Il.* 1.403-4, Lattimore's translation [corrected]):

> *that creature the gods name Briareus, but all men*
> *Aigaion.*

Cf. also *Il.* 2.813-4; 14.290-1. It is reasonable that gods should choose a name to reflect his skill, while mortals chose a name to reflect their terror.

645 **plebs:** for Ovid's characteristic anachronistic reference to Roman institutions, see on 9.307; for Ovid's deliberate imposition of Roman class divisions in remarkably inappropriate contexts, cf. 1.170-6, a passage quoted in the note on 6.73.

647 **Thaumantis':** Iris'; she was the daughter of Thaumas, cf. 4.480, Hes. *Theog.* 780, Virg. *Aen.* 9.5.

649 **deep coverlets:** as Bömer points out, it is hard to decide between 'deep' (i.e. 'comfortable') or 'high' (i.e. 'his bed on high', cf. 11.610). The adjective *altus* can have either meaning.

650 **He:** i.e. Morpheus; see on 10.429.

650-2 **alis...pennis:** *wings...wings*; see on 9.32-4.

660 **husband...husband's:** *coniuge coniugis*; for the polyptoton, see on 9.44.

663 **Auster:** the south wind, see on 5.285. The winds are sometimes personified, as probably here and at 12.510, sometimes not, as at 11.192, where I normally translate just 'south wind'. Sometimes the Auster is fierce, cf. 12.511, sometimes gentle, cf. 11.192.

670 **unwept for:** *indeploratum*; probably an Ovidian coinage, see on 9.262.

679-80 For the parenthesis, see on 9.17.

682 **without pausing to let it down:** it was normal to let the hair down as a first sign of grief, cf. e.g. 6.289.

690 **his former radiance in the face:** *quo prius ore nitebat*; cf. 11.271-2, when we first met Ceyx: 'Ceyx, who bore his father's radiance in his face' *patriumque nitorem ore ferens Ceyx*.

701 **without me...me:** *sine me* (ablative) *me* (accusative); for the polyptoton, see on 9.44.

701-2 **sea...sea:** *pontus...pelago*; see on 11.358-9.

705-6 **the tomb...the urn:** Ceyx' body is, she believes, lost and so not available for cremation; she anticipates her own death, after which her own cremated ashes will be placed in an urn which he will not share, but the urn will be placed in a suitably inscribed tomb dedicated to the memory of both of them.

707 **bones to bones...name to name:** *ossibus ossa...nomen nomine*; for the polyptota, see on 9.44.

714-25 These lines, among the most memorable in the *Metamorphoses*, are an exact reversal of the more conventional description at 11.461-73.

720-1 **Alas...and alas:** the repetition is not in the Latin but seems to be demanded by English idiom.

729 **man-made:** *facta manu*, literally 'made by hand', but that has an inappropriate connotation in English, suggesting a contrast with 'made by machine'.

730 **pre-exhausted:** *praedelassat*, a novel coinage to represent an Ovidian invention, see on 9.262.

731 For the parenthesis, see on 9.17.

745 **for seven days:** see Arist. *H.A.* 542b (Peck's translation):

> *Birds as a group, as has been said already, pair and breed for the most part in spring and early summer, except the halcyon. The bird breeds at the time of the winter solstice. Hence when calm weather appears at this period, the name "halcyon days" is given to the seven days preceding and the seven days following the solstice, as Simonides says in his poem:*
> As when in the windy month
> Zeus admonishes the fourteen days
> and men on earth name it the windless, the holy season,
> the season when the many-hued halcyon nurtures her young.
> *...It is said that the halcyon takes seven days to build her nest, and the other seven to lay the eggs and hatch the brood.*

For a full discussion, see D'Arcy Thompson *Birds* 46-51 and Peck's Loeb translation of Arist. *H.A.* II 368-72.

747-8 **calm sea...calm sea:** *aequore...aequor*, the basic meaning of this word is anything level and flat (*OLD* s.v. 1), so that it is used both of plains (*OLD* s.v. 1b, 3) and of the sea generally (*OLD* s.v. 2) even if, as at 11.729, it is not calm. Here, however, the smoothness is clearly stressed, as it sometimes is (*OLD* s.v. 3), and the translation must reflect that fact.

747 **Aeolus:** Alcyone's father and the king of the waves. In Homer's *Odyssey* and Virgil's *Aeneid*, he participated famously in creating storms at sea (see on 11.431). Commentators rightly note that, in spite of his authority in this area, he had no rôle at all in the storm that destroyed Ceyx. Indeed, at 11.430-2, Alcyone had warned Ceyx not to expect any favours from Aeolus just because he was his father-in-law. His intervention now is, accordingly, quite startling.

749-95 *Aesacos*

Another version of this story is to be found in Apollodorus (3.12.5, Frazer's translation):

> *But after...Ilium [Troy] was captured by Hercules...Podarces, who was called Priam, came to the throne, and he married first Arisbe, daughter of*

> *Merops, by whom he had a son Aesacus, who married Asterope, daughter of Cebren, and when she died he mourned for her and was turned into a bird. But Priam handed over Arisbe to Hyrtacus and married a second wife Hecuba, daughter of Dymas [cf. also Hom. Il. 16.717-8]...The first son born to her was Hector...*

Editors speculate on Ovid's source for the version told here. A plausible candidate is Aemilius Macer who wrote an *Ornithogonia* (a work on birds of which fragments survive) and which, Ovid tells us (*Tristia* 4.10.43-4), he heard him recite. See also D'Arcy Thompson *Birds* 27-9.

751   **The man next to him, or perhaps the same man:** note the artful care on such details, all designed to parody the standard devices to increase the suspension of disbelief. As W.S. Gilbert puts it in *Mikado*: 'Merely corroborative detail, intended to give artistic verisimilitude to an otherwise bald and unconvincing narrative.'

756-7   **Ilus...Assaracus...Ganymede...Laomedon...Priam:** see Hom. *Il.* 20.230-7 quoted in the note on 10.155-61.

758   **The one over there:** *iste*; the bird, Aesacos, from 11.751.
       Hector's brother: see on 11.749-95.

761   **Dymas' daughter:** i.e. Hecuba.
       him: i.e. Hector.

763   **Alexirhoë:** Servius (on Virg. *Aen.* 4.254) also makes her mother of Aesacos; for another view, see on 11. 749-95.
       Granicus: (stress the middle syllable); a river in the Troad (cf. Hom. *Il.* 12.21) whose chief claim to fame was that it was the site of the defeat of the Persians by Alexander the Great in 334 B.C. He is identified as Alexirhoë's father only here.
       two-horned: *bicorni*; river gods are regularly represented as horned, cf. e.g. Achelous (9.1-88) and Rhenus (Virg. *Aen.* 8.727).

766   **unambitious:** *inambitiosa*; a word found only here and, probably, another Ovidian coinage, see on 9.262. The point is, presumably, that the boy had no political ambition. For *ambitio*, see on 9.432.

768   **Hesperie:** not otherwise known.
       Cebren: another Trojan river, but unknown to Homer.

775-6   The similarity between Hesperie's story and that of Eurydice (both are fatally bitten by a snake while running from a lover) is very striking. Ovid's version of the Eurydice story (10.10) is, unlike that of Virgil, (*G.* 4.453-66), very explicit about the snake-bite (see further Hill (1992) 125); he is even more explicit here.

777-8   **Out of his mind...lifeless:** *amens exanimem*; even at this pathetic moment, Ovid cannot resist the word play implicit in this juxtaposition. The effect is impossible to reproduce in the translation; if only it could suggest mental turmoil rather than inattention, it would have been tempting to use 'mindless' with 'lifeless'.

784   **Tethys:** sometimes just a sea goddess (cf. 2.156; 9.499 and the notes), sometimes used as metonymy for 'the sea' (cf. 2.68 and the note); here both senses are brought into play.

795   **takes his name from diving into it:** *nomenque tenet, quia mergitur illo*; the word play works in both languages; the Latin for the bird is *mergus* and for diving, *mergere*; English calls the bird a 'diver'. One of the divers is indeed, called a 'merganser' from *mergere*, of course, and from *anser*, the Latin for 'goose'.

BOOK XII

1-7 Transition from Aesacos to the Trojan War

4-6   **Paris...snatched wife:** Helen; Paris' abduction of Menelaus' wife Helen was, of course, the cause of the Trojan War; see further on 11.749-95. For the use of an absentee to provide a link, cf. 1.583.

5-6   **a long war together with a snatched wife:** *rapta longum cum coniuge bellum*; for the syllepsis, see on 9.135.

6   **a thousand ships:** Homer (*Il.* 2.494-759) lists 1,186 ships; but the figure was reduced to a poetic round thousas early as Aeschylus (*Ag.* 45); for a full account, see Austin on Virg. *Aen.* 2.198.

7   **Pelasgian:** an ancient term for 'Greek', originally restricted to Greeks from the north; see Eden on Virg. *Aen.* 8.600.

8-38 The Greeks at Aulis

That the Greeks assembled at Aulis in Boeotia before crossing to Troy is familiar from as early as the *Iliad* (2.303). That Agamemnon was asked to sacrifice his daughter, Iphigenia, to Artemis (Diana) so as to achieve a good wind is possibly hinted at by Homer (*Il.* 1.108) and is a constantly recurring theme in Aeschylus' *Agamemnon*; however, as early as Hesiod (*Cat.* frg. 71), a story circulated that there was no sacrifice because either an image or an animal was substituted at the last moment. For further details, see Apollod. *Epit.* 3.21-2, Eur. *I.T.*, *OCD* s.v. 'Iphigenia'; readers of *Genesis* (22.1-18) will be reminded of a similar story from a very different tradition.

10   **fish-teeming:** there is no other extant suggestion that Aulis is particularly notable for its fish; the epithet does, however, give an epic ring to the description.

11-23   In the story of the snake and the birds, Ovid marks his entry into a Homeric section by following, unusually closely, his Homeric model (*Il.* 2.303-20, 322, 326-9, Lattimore's translation):

> ...at Aulis, when the ships of the Achaians
> were gathered bringing disaster to the Trojans and Priam,
> and we beside a spring and upon the sacred altars
> were accomplishing complete hecatombs to the immortals
> under a fair plane tree whence ran the shining water.
> There appeared a great sign; a snake, his back blood-mottled,
> a thing of horror, cast into the light by the very Olympian,
> wound its way from under the altar and made toward the plane tree.
> Thereupon were innocent children, the young of the sparrow,
> cowering underneath the leaves at the uttermost branch tip,
> eight of them, and the mother was the ninth, who bore these children.
> The snake ate them all after their pitiful screaming,
> and the mother, crying aloud for her young ones, fluttered about him,
> and as she shrilled he caught her by the wing and coiled around her.
> After he had eaten the sparrow herself with her children,
> the god who had shown the snake forth made him a monument,
> striking him stone, the son of devious-devising Kronos,
> and we standing about marvelled at the thing that had been done.
> ...
> Kalchas straightway spoke before us interpreting the gods' will:
> "...
> As this snake has eaten the sparrow herself with her children,
> eight of them, and the mother was the ninth, who bore them,
> so for years as many as this shall we fight in this place
> and in the tenth year we shall take the city of the wide ways."

13   **Danaäns:** (stress the first syllable); one of Homer's terms for the Greeks at Troy (*Il.* 1.42).

19   **Thestorides:** 'Thestor's son', i.e. Calchas, cf. Hom. *Il.* 1.69.

21   **interpreted:** *digerit*; Virgil (*Aen.* 2.182 and see Austin) uses the same word, also of Calchas.

22   **the snake:** *ille*; in such cases, where Latin's greater supply of pronouns enables it to use a pronoun without the ambiguity that would be inevitable in English, I vacillate between maintaining the original and, as here, supplying the noun; see on 9.279.

24   **Nereus:** the Old Man of the Sea (see on 11.380) and here, by metonymy (see on 9.141; 11.784), 'the sea'; see also on 2.268.

26   **because he had made the walls for the city:** for the story, see 11.199-204 and the note on 11.194-220.

30   **piety:** *pietas*; see on 9.382; here, it is the familial aspect that is stressed, the duty of Agamemnon to his daughter, Iphigenia; generally, *pietas* covers both public and private duty so that Ovid is here introducing a potentially provocative contrast.
    and kingship fatherhood: *rexque patrem*; literally, 'and the king the father' i.e. 'and the king had conquered the father'; however, in English, the switch from the abstract ('public interest…piety') produces an intolerable obscurity.

34   **Mycene's daughter:** *Mycenida*; 'Iphigenia', daughter of Agamemnon, king of Mycenae.

35   **a killing that was seemly:** i.e. an animal sacrifice as opposed to a human one; in a famous passage, Lucretius (1.80-101) uses a harrowing account of Iphigenia's sacrifice on which to base a ringing condemnation of all religion.

36   **Phoebe's:** Diana's, see on 1.11.

39-63 Rumour

Ovid here combines the ekphrasis (see on 9.334) with an elaborate personification; cf. 2.760-82 (and the note) where there is a similar passage devoted to Envy; at 9.137-9 (and see the notes), Ovid had already alluded specifically to Virgil's personification of Rumour (*Aen.* 4.173-97 and see Austin's note); here, that process is continued.

40   **the three-fold cosmos:** *triplicis…mundi*; for the idea, cf. 1.5-31 and the notes; elsewhere, I have translated *mundus* as 'world'; here, however, the proximity of *orbis* in that sense has persuaded me to use 'cosmos' which is, in fact, the Greek word for which *mundus* is the Latin equivalent. In English, 'world' can mean no more than the sphere we call 'Earth' (the sense to be found in the preceding line and elsewhere) and often, as there, represented in Latin by *orbis* (*OLD* s.v. 12), or it can mean the whole universe (variously defined) for which the Latin *mundus* (*OLD* s.v. 1b) is commonly found. *mundus* is, however, also found in the more restricted sense (*OLD* s.v. 2) and it is in that sense that it survives in modern Romance languages.

43   This line is closely based on 1.27, the description of the original ordering of the cosmos; there, however, *arce* clearly refers to the top of the vault of heaven, here, however (see 12.39-40) to a citadel, its normal sense.

44   **countless ways in and a thousand apertures:** *innumerosque aditus ac mille foramina*; here Ovid is clearly outdoing Virgil (*Aen.* 6.43): *aditus centum, ostia centum*: 'a hundred broad shafts, a hundred mouths' (West's translation).

46   **night and day it is open:** *nocte dieque patet*; Ovid takes a sublime passage from Virgil: *noctes atque dies patet atri ianua Ditis* (*Aen.* 6.127), 'night and day, the door of black Dis lies open', and re-uses it in a very different context; for other examples of this particular playfulness, see on 9.6.

52   **made…clash:** *increpuit*; for the slightly unusual sense, see *OLD* s.v. 2.

53   **the *atrium*:** see on 10.595-6; here, the anachronism is developed to include an apparent reference to the morning *salutatio* accorded to rich patrons by their venal clients thronging the great man's *atrium*; cf. e.g. Hor. *Epist.* 1.5.31.

54   **false ones mixed with true:** cf. 9.138-9 and the note.

61   **sudden:** *repens*; this is Heinsius' correction of the far less apposite *recens*, 'fresh', of the manuscripts. He compares Virg. *Aen.* 12.313 where the similar phrase, *repens discordia*, occurs.

64-71 *Protesilaüs*

The story of Protesilaüs: (stress the penultimate syllable) is familiar from Homer. (*Il.* 2.698-9, 701-2, Lattimore's translation):

> *of these in turn fighting Protesilaos was leader*
> *while he lived; but now the black earth had closed him under*
> ...
> *...a Dardanian man had killed him*
> *as he leapt from his ship, far the first of all the Achaians.*

Homer does not identify *Protesilaüs'* killer but Ovid was not the first to suggest that it was Hector. The details are collected by Frazer in his note on Apollod. *Epit.* 3.30.

70   **Achaian:** often used, as here and in Homer (e.g. *Il.* 2.702 quoted above), to mean Greek in general (cf. 4.606); for other uses, see on 5.306.

71-145 *Cycnus*

That the Cycnus who was Poseidon's (Neptune's) son was killed by Achilles seems to have been known to the author of the *Cypria*, one of the poems of the Epic Cycle (see Evelyn-White, p. 495, Davies, *Procli Cypriorum Enarratio* 69); no one else reports a metamorphosis, and Forbes Irving (258) speculates that it may be an Ovidian invention. The sequel to this story occurs at 12.580-619.

71-2   **And already the Sigean shores were growing red:** *et iam Sigea rubebant litora*; this clearly caps Virgil's description (*Aen.* 2.312): *Sigea igni freta lata relucent*, 'and the broad waters of the strait of Sigeum reflected the flames'; Virgil's *relucent* referred to the reflection of flames, Ovid's *rubebant* (borrowed in this sense form Virg. *Aen.* 8.695) to the reddening of the place from the flow of blood.

71   **Sigean:** see on 11.197.

74-5   **his Pelian speartip:** cf. Hom. *Il.* 16.140-4 (Lattimore's translation):

> *only he [Patroclus] did not take the spear of blameless Aeacides [Achilles],*
> *huge, heavy, thick, which no one else of all the Achaians*
> *could handle, but Achilleus alone knew how to wield it;*
> *the Pelian ash spear which Cheiron had brought to his father*
> *from high on Pelion to be death for fighters.*

76-7   **(for Hector had been postponed to the tenth year):** for the humorous aside, see on 9.17.

80-1   For another example of what might seem rather cold comfort, see on 5.191-2 where other examples are collected.

82   **Aeacides:** descendant of Aeacus, i.e. 'Achilles'; see on 11.219.

86   **goddess:** Thetis, Achilles' mother, see on 11.221-65.

88   **(For he was surprised):** for the humorous aside, see on 9.17.

93-4   I.e. it is better not to be the son of a minor sea-goddess, the Nereïd Thetis, as Achilles was (see on 11.219), if one can be the son of Neptune, the supreme sea god who rules Nereus, as Cycnus was (cf. 12.72).

96-7   **nine round oxhides...the tenth:** a similar tale is told of Aeneas trying to pierce through Achilles' new shield made for him by the limping Hephaestus (Vulcan) at Hom. *Il.* 20.269-72 (Lattimore's translation):

> *he did drive the spear through two folds, but there were three left*
> *still, since the god of the dragging feet had made five folds on it,*
> *two of bronze on the outside and on the inside two of tin*
> *and between them the single gold...*

We are not told anything about Achilles' original shield which must be the one at issue here; however, ten oxhides does seem very many, especially when we remember that even the mighty Ajax made do with seven (*Il.* 7.245).

102   **he:** Achilles, see on 9.279; 12.22.

102-4   For a description of bullfighting at Rome, see Pliny *N.H.* 8.182. For the anachronism, see on 9.307.

109   **Lyrnesos:** (stress the middle syllable); see Hom. *Il.* 2.688-91 (Lattimore's translation):
> *since he, swift-footed Achilleus, lay where the ships were,*
> *angered over the girl of the lovely hair, Briseis,*
> *whom after much hard work he had taken away from Lyrnessos*
> *after he had sacked Lyrnessos...*

      Tenedos: (stress the first syllable); see Hom. *Il.* 11.623-4 (Lattimore's translation):
> *And lovely-haired Hekamede made them a potion, she whom*
> *the old man [Nestor] won from Tenedos, when Achilleus stormed it.*

110   **Eëtionian Thebes:** see Hom. *Il.* 11.414-6 (Lattimore's translation), Andromache is speaking:
> *It was brilliant Achilleus who slew my father, Eëtion,*
> *when he stormed the strong-founded citadel of the Kilikians,*
> *Thebe of the towering gates.*

111   **Caïcus:** (stress the middle syllable); a river of Mysia; cf. Hes. *Theog.* 343, Strabo (13.1.69) offers a full discussion of its precise situation.

112   **Telephus:** (stress the first syllable); the story is most conveniently found at Apollod. *Epit.* 3.17-20 (Frazer's translation):
> *But not knowing the course to steer for Troy, they [the Greeks] put in to Mysia and ravaged it, supposing it to be Troy. Now Telephus...was king of the Mysians, and seeing the country pillaged, he armed the Mysians, chased the Greeks in a crowd to the ships, and killed many...But when Achilles rushed at him, Telephus did not abide the onset and was pursued, and in the pursuit he was entangled in a vine-branch and wounded with a spear in the thigh. Departing from Mysia, the Greeks put to sea...and landed in their own countries...and after their retirement from Mysia to Greece eight years elapsed before they again returned to Argos and came to Aulis.*
>
> *Having again assembled at Aulis...they were in great perplexity about the voyage because they had no leader who could show them the way to Troy. But Telephus, because his wound was unhealed, and Apollo had told him that he would be cured when the one who wounded him should turn physician, came from Mysia to Argos, clad in rags, and begged the help of Achilles, promising to show the course to steer for Troy. So Achilles healed him by scraping off the rust of his Pelian spear.*

As Frazer explains, this is an example of a folk-lore remedy where something from the particular object that caused the problem is thought also to be able to effect a cure. Cicero (*Flac.* 29.72) alludes to a slightly different version of this story.

116   **Menoetes:** he and his story are otherwise unknown, though the name may well be borrowed from Virg. *Aen.* 12.517-20..
      plebs: see on 9.307.

117-8   **chest...chest:** *pectora...pectore*; for the repetition, see on 10.443-4.

118-9   **he...he:** Menoetes...Achilles, see on 9.279.

122   **ash spear:** a characteristic weapon of Homeric heroes on both sides of the conflict (e.g. *Il.* 6.449, 19.388ff.), and especially associated with Achilles, see on 12.74-5.

130-1   **blade...sword...blade:** *ense...gladio...ferrum*; English has two common words for 'sword', but not three; see on 9.32-4.

133   **three or four times:** *ter quater*; see on 9.217.

141   **he...his:** Achilles...Cycnus', see on 9.279.

145 **whose name:** *Cycnus*, the Latin (and, in the form 'Cycnos, the Greek) for 'swan'.

146-579 Achilles' victory celebration includes the telling of heroic stories.
146-67 Introduction
148-9 For the playful repetition, cf. 6.327-8.
149 **Argive:** *Argolicas*, i.e. 'Greek', the word is the Latin equivalent for one of the common words in Homer (e.g. *Il.* 1.79) for the Greeks.
ditches: *fossas*, the standard Roman military term for defensive earthworks and thus, perhaps, another anachronism, see on 9.307; on the other hand, in the *Iliad* (18.228), there was a ditch to protect the Greek ships to which this may be an allusion.
151 **Pallas:** Minerva, the Roman equivalent of Pallas Athene, cf. e.g. Hom. *Il.* 1.200.
153 **ether:** see on 10.2.
155 **reclined on their couches:** *discubuere toris*; more Roman anachronism, see on 9.307. This particular phrase is repeated from 8.566.
156 **relieved their cares and thirst:** for the syllepsis, see on 9.135.
162-3 **else...else:** *potius*; English idiom demands the repetition, Latin does not.

168-209, 459-531 First story: Caeneus
The name, in Greek, means 'new'. The story is told by Apollodorus (*Epit.* 1.22, Frazer's translation):

> *Caeneus was formerly a woman, but after that Poseidon had intercourse with her, she asked to become an invulnerable man; wherefore in the battle with the centaurs he thought scorn of wounds and killed many of the centaurs; but the rest of them surrounded him and by striking him with fir-trees buried him in the earth.*

A simpler version, omitting the sex change and the other miraculous elements, is to be found at Ap. Rhod. 1.57-64. Austin (on Virg. *Aen.* 6.448) gives a full history of the story from its first appearance in Hesiod; he believes that the metamorphosis into a bird, at 12.524-31, is an Ovidian invention; it certainly links this story even more closely to that of Cycnus. See also on 12.210-535.

169 **Nestor:** at his first appearance in the *Metamorphoses* (8.313), he was 'still in his first years', a striking contrast to the well known garrulous old man familiar from Homer both in the *Iliad* (e.g. 1.245-84; 24.624-30) and the *Odyssey* (e.g. 3 *passim*). It is that Nestor, the one who can always outdo any young man's story, that we meet here. At *Il.* 1.264, Caineus appears in a long list of those, like the then youthful Nestor, who had fought with the Lapiths against the Centaurs; see further on 12.210-535.
170 **pierceable:** *forabilis*; probably another Ovidian coinage, see on 9.262.
171 **Perrhaebian:** Perrhaebia was an area in Thessaly used here to mean 'Thessalian'; as will emerge, Caeneus was one of the Lapiths, who lived in Thessaly. However, it may be more relevant here to note that the Perrhaebians occur in the Homeric Catalogue of Ships (*Il.* 2.749) in the contingent next to that led by Polypoetes and Leonteus, grandson of Caeneus (*Il.* 2.746).
174 **Othrys:** a mountain in the far south of Thessaly.
188 **two hundred years...third age:** *annos bis centum...tertia aetas*; cf. Hom. *Il.* 1.250-2 (Lattimore's translation, corrected):

> *In his [Nestor's] time two generations of mortal men had perished,*
> *those who had earler grown up with him and had been born*
> *in sacred Pylos, and he was king in the third age.*

This becomes a commonplace; when, for instance, Propertius (2.13.46) says that Nestor lived for three *saecla*, it would be natural to interpret the word to mean 'generations' (*OLD* s.v. 5) and not 'centuries' (*OLD* s.v. 6). Ovid may well be mischievously misinterpreting such passages to produce an even older Nestor than the traditional one. For further details see N.-H. on Hor. *Odes* 2.9.13.

189 Caenis, the Elateïan (stress the -e-) **offspring:** she was 'Caenis' when a woman and 'Caeneus' when a man; Hyginus (14.4) records that Caeneus was the son of Elatus.

194 your: *tuae*; in the Latin, the postponement of this word to the very end of the sentence and its extremely wide separation from *matris*, 'mother' gives it great emphasis. The effect is not achieved in the translation. For the story of Peleus and Thetis (Achilles' parents), see on 11.221-65.

197 The slightly absurd parenthesis is made supremely comic by the expanded echo three lines later, see on 9.17.

198 love: *Veneris*; for the metonymy, see on 9.141.

206 him: an attempt to represent Ovid's amusing sudden switch to the masculine with the word *saucius*, 'afflicted'.

208 Atrax' son: Caeneus, either from Atrax, an early king of Thessaly and so a remote ancestor, or from the river or town of that name, cf. *Thessalides*, 'daughters of Thessaly' (11.190).

209 Peneïan: (stress the second '-e-'); the Peneus was an important river in Thessaly, see on 1.452-567, 569; 7.223.

210-535 Second story: The Battle of the Lapiths and Centaurs

The story of the battle between the Lapiths and the Centaurs is at least as old as Homer. At *Iliad* 1.261-71, a brief account is given, as here, by Nestor who also, of course, claims to have been involved; see on 12.169; at *Odyssey* 21.295-8, Antinoös tells the story as a precautionary tale against drunkenness (Lattimore's translation):

> *It was wine also that drove the Centaur, famous Eurytion,*
> *distracted in the palace of great-hearted Peirithoös*
> *when he visited the Lapiths. His brain went wild with drinking,*
> *and in his fury he did much harm in the house of Peirithoös.*

Ps.-Hesiod *Shield* (178-90) gives a brief account of the battle, including Theseus (182), Pirithoüs (179) and Caeneus (179), but not his fate; other names from that account of the fight that survive into Ovid's are noted as they occur. There is another brief allusion in Pindar (fr. 166, Snell = Ath. 11.476b); once again, however, the narrative is not explicitly related to the wedding of Pirithoüs and Hippodamia. Diodorus Siculus tells us of two distinct battles between the Lapiths and Centaurs, one (4.12.3-7) involved Heracles (see on 9.98-133, 191; 12.536-79), but had nothing to do with the wedding, the other (4.70.3-4) is the first extant version which associates the battle with the wedding of Pirithoüs and Hippodamia. Both the temple of Zeus at Olympia and the Parthenon at Athens bore sculptures depicting the battle. Ovid produces many verbal echoes here of his earlier account of the brawl at the wedding of Perseus and Andromeda (5.1-235). There are also many names that are borrowed from that battle for this one (see on 5.38; 12.250, 254, 262, 271, 290, 302, 306, 321, 333, 379, 380, 450, 457) and three (see on 12.302, 303, 334) borrowed from the list of Acoetes' sailors at 3.670ff. One special case is discussed at 12.353. All the other names occur elsewhere in literature (for the details, see Bömer), but not as Lapiths or Centaurs.

210 bold Ixion's son: (stress the middle syllable), i.e. 'the son of bold Ixion'; for the boldness, see on 9.123; the son, Pirithoüs (stress the second syllable), was king of the Lapiths, see on 12.210-535, and a notorious blasphemer, see on 8.612.
Hippodame: (stress the second syllable); 'Horsebreaker'; Greek names of this sort sometimes end in *-dame* and sometimes in *-dam(e)ia*, see West on Hes. *Theog.* 244, 250; the name occurs once again in the *Metamorphoses* (12.224), and in both cases the form *-dame* is preferred. At *Her.* 16.248, Ovid uses the *-damia* form for Pirithoüs' wife as he does consistently (*Her.* 8.70, 15.266, *Am.* 3.2.16, *Ars am.* 2.8) for the Hippodamia who married Pelops.

211 and...the cloudborn beasts: *nubigenasque feros*; the Centaurs, who had the body of a horse and the head and shoulders of a man; for their birth from a cloud, see on 9.123; *nubigena*, 'cloudborn', is not an Ovidian coinage but was used of the Centaurs by Virgil (*Aen.* 7.674; 8.293).

213 were present, present...was I: *aderant, aderamus*; for the polyptoton, see on 9.44.

215 **Hymenaeos:** here, the wedding song, see on 9.762.

the *atrium*: for the word, see on 10.595-6; for the deliberate Roman anachronism, see on 9.307.

218 **and we almost nullified the omen:** as emerges in the next lines, the customary praise heaped on the bride in the previous line and a half so inflamed Eurytus' jealous rage that he almost undid all the benefits of the praise she had received.

219 **most savage of the savage:** *saeuorum saeuissime*; for the polyptoton, see on 9.44.

220 **Eurytus:** (stress the first syllable); 'Full-flowing'; elsewhere, a distinction is made between Eurytus, the king of Oechalia (as at 9.356), and Eurytion, the centaur (as at *A.A.* 1.593, Prop. 2.23.31); for the particular savagery of this Centaur, see Hom. *Od.* 21.295-8 quoted in the note on 12.210-553.

228 **while I live:** like Orestes and Pylades, Pirithoüs and Theseus were a famous type of friendship, cf. 8.405, 12.338-44. They appear together at Hom. *Od.* 11.631; for a discussion, see on 8.303, Frazer on Apollod. 2.5.12.

230-1 These lines, omitted by two of the most important manuscripts, seem to fit ill into the narrative and to bring the conflict to a premature conclusion. Merkel, in 1861, was the first to excise them; most editors have followed suit.

235-458 These lines give us an astonishing range of hideous wounds; it is difficult to resist the impression that Ovid is going out of his way to outdo his predecessors, notably Homer and Virgil, in their accounts of such brutality in battle. The impression is reinforced by the multiplicity of verbal echoes to, especially, the *Iliad* and the *Aeneid* as noted below.

235-6 **an ancient mixing bowl encrusted with high-relief figures:** *signis exstantibus asper antiquus crater*; Greeks and Romans heated their wine and mixed it with water before serving it. This required a large mixing-bowl (*crater* in Greek and Latin; the shape caused the word to be used metaphorically of the depression at the summit of a volcano even in antiquity; for further details, see on 5.424). Similar vessels, described with similar vocabulary, are to be found in Pindar (*Isthm.* 6.40), Virgil (*Aen.* 5.267; 9.263) and Propertius (2.6.17-8), as well as earlier in the *Metamorphoses* (5.80-2).

236 **vast, vaster:** *uastum uastior*; for the polyptoton, see on 9.44.

237 **Aegides:** (stress the middle syllable); the son of Aegeus, i.e. Theseus, see on 7.402-24.

240 **and kicked:** *calcitrat*; for the enjambment, see on 9.78. In the translation, the insertion of 'lay' in the previous line and the consequential addition of 'and' (neither is in the Latin, but English idiom seems to demand both) slightly weakens the effect.

bi-limbed: *bimembres*; also used of the Centaurs by Virgil (*Aen.* 8.293); Centaurs had two sets of front limbs, equine front legs and human arms, see e.g. the Parthenon frieze..

241 **To arms, to arms:** *arma, arma*; see on 11.378.

245 Neither of these Centaurs, **Ophion** (stress the middle syllable) and **Amycus** (stress the first syllable), is otherwise known.

246 **inner rooms:** *penetralia*; Golding's 'brydehouse' makes explicit what Ovid leaves as implicit.

250 **Celadon:** (stress the first syllable); 'Roaring'; not otherwise known as the name of one of the Lapiths. This is, however, (cf. 5.144) the first of Ovid's borrowings of names from his description of the battle at the wedding of Perseus and Andromeda at 5.1-235; the others are listed in the note on 12.210-535; see also on 5.38.

254 **Pellaean:** Pelle was the capital of Macedonia; normally, the adjective means essentially Macedonian, whereas the Lapiths came from Thessaly, see on 12.171.

Pelates: (stress the first syllable); 'Neighbour' or 'Invader'; the name, not otherwise known as the name of a Lapith, is borrowed from 5.123; see on 12.210-535; 5.38.

255 **him:** i.e. Amycus.

260 **Gryneus:** a Centaur, not otherwise known.

262 **Broteas:** (stress the first syllable); the name is borrowed from 5.107, but is not otherwise known as a Lapith's; see on 12.210-535; 5.38.

Orion: (stress the middle syllable); the name occurs at Ps.Hes. *Shield* 186 in the list of Centaurs involved in the battle with the Lapiths; see on 12.210-535.

Orion; Orion's: *Orion; Orio*; for the polyptoton, see on 9.44.

263 **Mycale:** (stress the first syllable); she recurs at Sen. *Her. O.* 523-7 not as Orion's mother but, indeed, as a Thessalian witch who can bring the moon down; for more on that trick, see on 7.207.

266 **Exadius:** (stress the second syllable); the name occurs at Hom. *Il.* 1.264 in Nestor's list of Lapiths involved in the battle with the Centaurs; see on 12.169.

271 **Rhoetus:** the situation with this name is more complicated than appears in my note on 5.38. Two similar names are recorded: Rhoecus and Rhoetus. According to Callimachus (*Hymn* 3.222-4) and Apollodorus (3.9.2), two Centaurs, Rhoikos and Hylaeos, tried to ravish Atalanta but were shot dead by her arrows. Virgil (*G.* 2.455-7) attributes the death of the Centaurs, Rhoecus (or Rhoetus), Pholus and Hylaeus to the abuse of alcohol. However, while that could be associated with the notorious drunkenness that led to the battle of the Lapiths and Centaurs, it could hardly, as Mynors observes, be associated with the Atalanta story. And if it were, it would mean that the Centaur had died twice. Horace (*Odes* 2.19.23; 3.4.55) knows of a Giant called Rhoetus, Lucan (6.390) of a Centaur called Rhoecus (or Rhoetus). Editors solve the problem variously: Mynors (following what is more implicit than explicit in Housman) restricts Rhoecus to Centaurs (he simply tolerates the double deaths) and applies Rhoetus to all other characters, including the Rutulian Rhoetus at 9.344-5 (where, as Hardie observes, there are close parallels with *G.* 2.455-7, a fact that tells against two different spellings), and the Marsian Rhoetus at 10.388. N.-H., on the other hand, are more sceptical about distinguishing between Centaurs and others in this way. Despite my remarks above, I would not be keen to distinguish a Centaur called Rhoecus who was killed by Atalanta from another Centaur called Rhoetus who fought against the Lapiths. I would, however, want to spell the Rhoetus at 5.38 in the same way as the Rhoetus here, given the extensive way in which Ovid has mined that passage for proper names here, see on 12.210-535. As Housman implies in his note on Luc. 6.390, there is more likely to be confusion between -*c*- and -*t*- in Latin than between κ and τ in Greek, so that Latin manuscript evidence is of little moment, though, as it happens, the manuscript evidence here is for *Rhoetus*. Given that no one is recommending *Rhoeci* at 5.38, I prefer *Rhoetus* here.

272 **Charaxus:** (stress the middle syllable); a Lapith, not otherwise known.

273-81 **hair...hair...locks:** *capillo...crines...crinibus*; English does not have another common word for 'hair' except 'locks', and 'locks', in that sense, must be accompanied by an adjective; see on 9.32-4.

276-9 Once more, Ovid returns to one of Homer's most familiar similes quoted in the note on 9.170-1.

284 **Cometes:** (stress the middle syllable); 'Long-haired'; a Lapith, not otherwise known.

287 **and...halfburnt:** *semicremoque*; apparently, another Ovidian coinage; see on 9.262.

288 **three times or four:** *terque quaterque*; see on 9.217.

289 **blow:** for the enjambment, see on 9.78. In this case, the translation puts the word for *ictu* into enjambment, rather than 'broke', the word for *rupit*, but the effect is much the same.

290 **Euagrus:** (stress the middle syllable), 'Lucky-hunter'; a Lapith, not otherwise known.

Corythus: (stress the first syllable), 'Helmeted'; another otherwise unknown Lapith; the name is borrowed from 5.125; see on 12.210-535; 5.38.

Dryas: 'Woods-dweller'; the name occurs at Hom. *Il.* 1.263 in Nestor's list of Lapiths involved in the battle with the Centaurs; see on 12.169.

291-2 **the first down:** traditionally, at the coming of the first down, a young man is at his most attractive (cf. 12.395-6, see on 9.398); it is, accordingly, especially poignant that such a boy should be killed in war, an idea fully developed by Virgil at *Aen.* 9.181ff. (and see Hardie) and 10.324-30 (and see Harrison).

296-9 **you too...:** for the apostrophe, see on 9.101.

298 **outcome:** *exitus*; for the enjambment; see on 9.78.
299 **fire-hardened:** *obusta*; Virgil (*Aen.* 7.506; 11.894) uses the word similarly.
302 **Orneüs:** (stress the '-e-'); a Centaur, not otherwise known.
    Lycabas: (stress the first syllable), 'Light-path'; another otherwise unknown Centaur; his name is borrowed from 3.673 in the list of Acoetes' sailors and from 5.60; see on 12.210-535; 5.38.
    Medon: 'Lord'; another otherwise unknown Centaur; the name is borrowed from 3.671 in the list of Acoetes' sailors; see on 12.210-535.
303 **forequarter:** Ovid consistently uses *umerus* for human shoulders, *armus* for the shoulders of animals; in the case of Centaurs (who have two sets of shoulders, see on 12.240), *armus* refers to the horse shoulder, or forequarter, and *umerus* to the human shoulder, as is elegantly revealed at 12.396.
    Thaumas 'Wonder'**...Pisenor:** two more otherwise unknown Centaurs; Pisenor is stressed on the middle syllable.
305 **Mermeros:** (stress the first syllable), 'Mischievous'; unknown otherwise either as a Centaur or as a fast runner.
306 **Pholus:** a Centaur known to Virgil (*G.* 2.456, *Aen.* 8.294); see also on 12.271.
    Melaneus: (stress the first syllable), 'Black'; another otherwise unknown Centaur; the name is borrowed from 5.128; see on 12.210-535; 5.38.
    Abas: another otherwise unknown Centaur; the name is borrowed from 5.126; see on 12.210-535; 5.38.
308 **Asbolus:** (stress the first syllable), 'Soot'; the name occurs at Ps.Hes. *Shield* 185 in the list of Centaurs involved in the battle with the Lapiths; see on 12.210-535. The name occurs in one Ovidian manuscript; the others read *Astylos* or some variant of that name, a name not otherwise associated with Centaurs (or Lapiths). Ovid's practice makes it impossible to be dogmatic in choosing between these names.
    Nessus: a truly famous Centaur whose story, including his fatal encounter with Hercules' bow, is recounted at 9.98-133. Generally speaking, the stories in the *Metamorphoses* are told in chronological order. Here, however, we are at the Trojan War listening to the elderly Nestor recounting the tales of his youth including this one that antedates the period described as far back as the beginning of book 9.
310 **Eurynomus** (quadrysyllabic, stress the second syllable), 'Wide-pastured'**...Lycidas** (stress the first syllable)**...Areos** (stress the middle syllable), 'Belonging-to-Ares',**...Imbreus** (disyllabic), 'Rainy': Bömer believes all these names, as names of Centaurs, to be Ovidian inventions.
312 **full in the face. Full in the face:** *aduersos. aduersum*; for the polyptoton, see on 9.44; it underlines the humour of the passage.
    you too: for the apostrophe, see on 9.101.
    Crenaeus: (stress the middle syllable), 'Of-a-fountain'; a Centaur, not otherwise known.
317 **in all his veins:** *cunctis...uenis*; in Lucretius' account of sleep, there is a passage which is surely relevant here (4.955-6, Bailey's translation):
    Again, sleep follows after food, because food brings about just what air
    *does, while it is being spread in all the veins [*in uenas...omnis*].*
    unawakened: *inexperrectus*; another Ovidian coinage; see on 9.262.
    Aphidas: (stress the middle syllable), 'Unsparing'; a Centaur, not otherwise known.
319 **Ossaean:** 'from Ossa', a Thessalian mountain; see on 1.154-5.
321 **Phorbas:** 'Pasturing'; an otherwise unknown Lapith; the name is borrowed from 5.74; see on 12.210-535; 5.38.
327 **Petraeus:** (stress the middle syllable), 'Rocky'; the name occurs at Ps.Hes. *Shield* 185 in the list of Centaurs involved in the battle with the Lapiths; see on 12.210-535.
332-3 **By Pirithoüs' prowess...by Pirithoüs' prowess:** for this sort of playful repetition, see on 12.148-9.
332 **Lycus:** 'Wolf'; a Centaur, not otherwise known.

333 **Chromis:** an otherwise unknown Centaur; the name is borrowed from 5.103; see on 12.210-535; 5.38.

334 **Dictys:** an otherwise unknown Centaur; the name occurs at 3.615 in the list of sailors with Acoetes; see on 12.210-535.

Helops: an otherwise unknown Centaur.

336 **right...left:** *dextra laeuam*; the translation has been unable to reproduce the juxtaposition which, by drawing attention to this inconsequential detail in such an unmistakable way, adds to the undercutting humour that pervades this whole account.

337 **from a high mountain ridge:** *ab ancipiti...acumine montis*; the *acumen* is normally a peak; *anceps*, as *OLD* (s.v. 1c) tentatively suggests, probably means 'precipitous on both sides'; this seems to suggest a high ridge; those familiar with the English Lake District may be reminded of Striding Edge and its numerous monuments to those who have fallen off, one, at least, 'while following the foxhounds'.

338-44 This incident, in which Theseus comes to the rescue of Pirithoüs, is another example of their well known friendship, see on 12.228.

338 **Ixion's son:** Pirithoüs, see on 12. 210.

341 **Aphareus:** (stress the first syllable); an otherwise unknown Centaur.

342 **Aegides:** Theseus, see on 12.237.

345 **Bienor's:** (stress the middle syllable); the manuscripts are divided between *Bienoris* and *Bianoris*; the choice is not easy; *Bienor* is found at Hom. *Il.* 9.92, *Bianor* at Virg. *Ecl.* 9.60, neither as a Centaur's name. Bömer gives fuller details.

346 **back:** for the enjambment, see on 9.78. In this case, the translation puts the word for *tergo* into enjambment, rather than 'jumped on', the word for *insilit*, but the effect is much the same.

except himself: Ovid cannot resist this ingenious joke.

349-50 **with a...club. With the club:** *robore...robore*; Ovid draws attention to the word by placing it at the beginning of two consecutive lines; the translation substitutes the effect of juxtaposition over the end of one line and the beginning of the next.

350 **Nedymnus:** (stress the middle syllable); an otherwise unknown Centaur.

351 **Lycotas:** *Lycotan*; (stress the middle syllable); an otherwise unknown Centaur. Some manuscripts read *Lycopen* which would give 'Lycopes', but that too is not otherwise known as a Centaur's name.

Hippasos: (stress the first syllable), 'Horsey'; an otherwise unknown Centaur.

352 **Rhipeus:** otherwise unknown as the name of a Centaur, but the name is perhaps borrowed from an especially poignant story at Virg. *Aen.* 2.426-8.

353 **Thereus:** an otherwise unknown Centaur name except that it appears as that of one of the fallen Centaurs in the account by Diodorus Siculus (4.12.7) of the first (see on 12.210-535) battle of the Lapiths and Centaurs. His name is derived from the Greek for 'wild beast', as befits Ovid's account of his habits.

355 **Demoleon:** (stress the second syllable), 'Lion-people'; an otherwise unknown Centaur.

356 ***thorn-bush*:** *dumo*; what does it mean? According to *OLD* it occurs in the singular here only; that, combined with the fact that it seems to make little sense must arouse suspicions. I am surprised that no one seems to have suggested *sed humo diuellere duro*, 'but he was trying to wrench away a pine tree full of years from the solid earth.'

360 **(so he himself wanted it to be believed):** Nestor, like a modern sceptic, withholds his own authority from this suggestion of divine intervention.

361 **Crantor's:** 'Ruler'; otherwise unknown either as a Lapith or as Peleus' armour-bearer.

363 **your father's...Achilles:** a reminder that this is all part of a narrative delivered during the Trojan War by Nestor to Achilles and the other Achaean heroes, cf. 12.440, 520-1. Homer (*Od.* 11.333-5) and Virgil (*Aen.* 2.506) also interrupt long narratives by, respectively, Odysseus and Aeneas in the same way and for the same reason; cf. 10.682.

364 **Dolopes:** in the *Iliad'*s only reference to the Dolopes, Homer reveals that they were indeed controlled by Peleus, (*Il.* 9.483-4, Lattimore's translation):

> He [Peleus] made me [Phoenix] a rich man, and granted me many people,
> and I lived lord over the Dolopes, in remotest Phthia...

The Dolopes are also to be found at Virg. Aen. 2.7 etc.

Amyntor: 'Avenger'; according to Homer (Il. 9.448), he was Phoenix' father and Phoenix had fled from him because they had quarrelled over a woman. It is possible to reconcile Homer's account with Ovid's by assuming either that after Peleus defeated Amyntor he reinstated him as a sort of vassal king of the Dolopians and Phoenix eventually succeeded his father, or that Peleus took Phoenix' side against Amyntor and, after defeating him, replaced him on the Dolopian throne with Phoenix. For other more gruesome accounts of the relationship between Amyntor and Phoenix, see Apollod. 3.13.8 with Frazer's notes.

365   **Aeacides:** (stress the second syllable); 'son of Aeacus', i.e. Peleus; see on 11.219.

370   **the rib cage:** *laterum cratem*; literally, 'the flanks' basket', cf. Virg. Aen. 12.508; the Latin metaphor, 'basket' corresponds to the English metaphor, 'cage'.

371   **trembling:** for the enjambment, see on 9.78.

373   **gave strength to his courage:** *uires animo dabat*; cf. 12.383.

375   **He:** i.e. Peleus.

376-7   **weapons...through the forequarters:** *arma per armos*; there is no way to render the Latin pun in the translation; for **forequarters**, see on 12.303.

377   **one...two:** *uno duo*; for the failure of the translation to reproduce the juxtaposition, see on 12. 336.

      two breasts: i.e. his human breast and his equine breast.

378   **Phlegraeos:** (stress the second syllable), 'Phlegraean'; an otherwise unknown Centaur.

      Hyles: 'From the wood', an otherwise unknown Centaur.

379   **from long range:** *eminus*; for the enjambment, see on 9.78.

      Iphinoüs: (stress the second syllable), 'Strong-minded'; an otherwise unknown Centaur.

      Clanis: an otherwise unknown Centaur; the name is borrowed from 5.141; see on 12.210-535; 5.38.

      close combat: *collato Marte*; literally 'with Mars joined', an otherwise unparalleled expression. For the metonymy, see on 9.141.

380   **Dorylas:** (stress the first syllable), 'Spearpeople'; an otherwise unknown Centaur, the name is borrowed from 5.130; see on 12.210-535; 5.38.

383   **courage gave me strength:** *uires animus dabat*; cf. 12.373.

387   **there was a cry:** *fit clamor*; is this Dorylas' cry of pain (cf. 6.661; 9.294) or the Lapiths' cry of triumph (cf. 8.420; 10.656)? The Latin is ambiguous, translators are divided.

390-1   **dragging...dragged...trampled...trampled:** *traxit tractaque...calcauit calcataque*; the double polyptoton (see on 9.44) moves the narrative along in a particularly brutal way.

393-428 *Interlude on the love between Cyllaros and Hylonome*

Neither their names, as Centaurs, nor their story can be found elsewhere; however, as Bömer observes, tragic love is a favourite theme of Ovid's in the *Metamorphoses*; Bömer compares Pyramus and Thisbe (4.55-166), Cadmus and Harmonia (4.563-603), Athis and Lycabas (5.47-73), Philemon and Baucis (8.611-724), Orpheus and Eurydice (10.1-11.84).

393   **and your beauty:** for the apostrophe, see on 9.101.

      Cyllaros: (stress the first syllable); see on 12.393-428..

394   **to that kind:** *naturae...illi*; i.e. to Centaurs.

395   **his beard was beginning:** for the significance of this, see on 12.291-2.

      golden, gold: *aureus, aurea*; for the polyptoton, see on 9.44.

396-7   **shoulders...forequarters...shoulders:** *umeris...armos...umerique*; see on 12.303.

400   **neck and head:** i.e. a horse's neck and head to replace the human ones.

401   **Castor:** the brother of Pollux, both sons of Tyndareus; Castor's interest in horses is recorded as early as Homer (Il. 3.237, Lattimore's translation):

> Kastor, breaker of horses, and the strong boxer, Polydeuces.

Both brothers were frequently represented on or with horses; cf. e.g. Livy 9.43.22 and see *LIMC* vol. III 1, pp. 569-72, III 2, pp.456-60. It is tempting to imagine that here Ovid is thinking of the statues of the brothers which are widely supposed to have stood by the *Lacus Iuturnae* (cf. *Fasti* 1.706-8), see Sande 115.

405 **Hylonome:** (quadrisyllabic; stress the second syllable) 'Forest-haunting', as Ovid goes on to emphasise; see on 12.393-428.

410 **rosemary:** *rore maris*; literally, 'dew of the sea', the Latin phrase was Anglicized and Christianized by the mid-fifteenth century.

413 **Pagasaean:** Pagasae was a town on the borders of Magnesia and Thessaly where the Argo was built (Ap. Rhod. 1.238).

414 **her shoulder on the left side:** her right shoulder was, presumably, left free for hurling weapons.

416-8 **Their love was equal...together...together...together, together:** *par amor est illis...una...simul...pariter, pariter*; in context, *una, simul* and *pariter* are synonymous, reinforcing *par*, 'equal', but the English 'together' has no suitable synonym.

419 **The perpetrator is unclear:** *auctor in incerto est*; cf. Virg. *Aen.* 12.320: *incertum qua pulsa manu* 'it is unclear by what hand it was thrown'.

421 **you, Cyllaros:** for the apostrophe, see on 9.101.

424-5 **and brought her lips to his:** *oraque ad ora admouet*; literally 'brought mouth to mouth' but that phrase has entirely inappropriate associations.

431 **Phaeocomes:** (stress the second syllable), 'Dark-haired'; an otherwise unknown Centaur. For the enjambment that seems so to suggest terror in his name, see on 9.78.

432 **which two pairs of oxen would hardly move:** at *Fasti* 1.564, the stone in front of Cacus' cave is such that five pairs of oxen would hardly have moved it.

433 **Tectaphos,** (stress the first syllable) **Olen's son:** these two Lapiths are not otherwise known.

434-8 These lines have only late manuscript support and are generally regarded as non-Ovidian.

440 **your father:** Peleus, see on 11.219. Once again (see on 12.363, 520-1), we are reminded that this is part of Nestor's reminiscences to Achilles and the other Achaeans at the beginning of the Trojan War.

441 **Chthonius** (stress the first syllable), 'Of-the-earth'...**Teleboas** (stress the second syllable), 'Far-shouter'; two otherwise unknown Centaurs.

443 **javelin. With the javelin:** *iaculum. iaculo*; for the polyptoton, see on 9.44.

445 **Pergamum:** strictly speaking, this was the name of Troy's citadel (Hom. *Il.* 4.508); it was, however, widely used just to mean Troy.

448 **just:** for Latin's idiomatic omission of this (for us) necessary detail, see on 10.373.

449 **Periphas:** (stress the first syllable); this is recorded as a Lapith name at Diod. Sic. 4.69.3.

450 **Pyraethus:** (stress the second syllable), 'Of-the-watch-fire'; an otherwise unknown Centaur.
Ampyx: 'Bridle'; an otherwise unknown Lapith, the name is borrowed from 5.184; see on 12.210-535; 5.38.

451 **Echeclus:** (stress the second syllable); an otherwise unkⁿown Centaur.

452 **Macareus:** (stress the first syllable), 'Blessing'; an otherwise unknown Lapith.
Pelethronian: Pelethron was a wooded valley under Mount Pelion, but here probably means no more than 'Thessalian'; for further detail, see Mynors on Virg. *G.* 3.115.

453 **Erigdupus:** (stress the penultimate syllable), 'Thundering'; an otherwise unknown Centaur.

454 **Nessean:** for Nessus, see on 12.308.
Cymelus: (stress the middle syllable); an otherwise unknown Lapith.
Ampyx' son, Mopsus: *Ampyciden Mopsum*; Mopsus was the name of a famous seer (or, perhaps, of more than one seer, see *OCD*); he appears at Ps.Hes. *Shield* 181 in the list of Lapiths involved in the battle with the Centaurs, see on 12.210-535; he was the Argonauts' seer (Ap. Rhod. 1.65-6 etc.); according to Ovid, he also participated in the Calydonian Boar Hunt (8.316). This Ampyx is probably not the same one that is to be found at 12.450; it is

possible too that his name is spelt *Ampycus*, the form *Ampycides* could mean 'son of Ampyx' or 'son of Ampycus'.

Mopsus; when Mopsus: *Mopsum; Mopso*; for the polyptoton, see on 9.44.

457 **Hodites:** (stress the middle syllable) 'Traveller'; an otherwise unknown Centaur, the name is borrowed from 5.97; see on 12.210-535; 5.38.

459-531 Resumption of Caeneus' story
See on 12.210-535

459-60 **Styphelus** (stress the first syllable) 'Hard', **Bromus** 'Loud-noise', **Antimachus** (stress the second syllable) 'Fighting against', **Elymus:** (stress the first syllable) 'Sheath'; four otherwise unknown Centaurs.

460 **and axebearing:** *securiferumque*; the word is not found elsewhere and may be an Ovidian coinage, see on 9.262.

Pyracmos: (stress the middle syllable) 'Fire-anvil'; not otherwise known as a Centaur's name but it may be an Ovidian second declension adaptation of Virgil's Centaur, the third decelension Pyracmon (*Aen.* 8.425).

462 **Emathian:** Emathia was a region of Macedonia; cf. Homer *Il.* 14.225-6 (Lattimore's translation, corrected):
while Hera in a flash of speed left the peak of Olympus
and came down to Pieria and Emathia the lovely...
Halesus: (stress the middle syllable); an otherwise unknown Lapith.

463 **Latreus:** 'Barker'; an otherwise unknown Centaur.

464 **enormous:** for the enjambment, see on 9.78.

470-6 For the story behind these insults, see 12.189-209.

470 **Caenis:** see on 12.189.

474 **what you were born, or what you have suffered:** *quid sis nata...uel quid sis passa*; Latreus helpfully chooses the feminine form of both verbs to underline his point; it is impossible neatly to reproduce the effect in English.

475-6 **take your distaff...wars to men:** irresistibly reminiscent of Hector's words to Andromache (Hom. *Il.* 6.490-2, Lattimore's translation):
> Go therefore back to our house, and take up your work,
> The loom and the distaff, and see to.it that your haindmaidens
> ply their work also; but the men must see to the fighting...

479 **Phyllean:** 'of the Thessalian city of Phyllus' or just 'Thessalian'; this is Caeneus again, see on 12.171.

482-3 **sword...sword:** *gladium; gladio*; for the polyptoton, see on 9.44.

487 **the groans of struck marble:** *gemitus...marmoris icti*; as becomes clear from *OLD*, this word is normally used of the sounds made by men or animals in pain or distress; however, *OLD* continues by listing a group of passages (including this one) where the word is said to be used of 'A low or hollow sound emitted by things'; this special category is, however, an illusion; here the sense clearly is that the body gave out the sort of *gemitus* you would expect from marble, i.e. no *gemitus* at all but a clanking sound; the joke relies on *gemitus* being the expected word until one remembers about Caeneus' special skin. The other quoted passages are similar: at *Aen.* 2.53, Virgil's wooden horse gives out a *gemitus* because, as the readers know, there are men inside it; at *Aen.* 12.713, Virgil is personifying the earth, when it utters a *gemitus,* as a fellow sufferer with the men of both sides in the fearful battle; at *Theb.* 3.594, Statius is comparing the shouts of warlike men with the roaring (*gemitus*) of the sea; his point will be lost if the sea's sound does not closely resemble the sounds made by men.

493 **and...wound on wound:** *uulnusque in uulnere*; for the polyptoton, see on 9.44.

497 **unpierced and unbloodied:** *imperfossus...inque cruentatus*; both words are probably Ovidian coinages; see on 9.262.

499 **Monychus:** (stress the first syllable), 'Single-hoof'; the word is a Homeric formulaic adjective for the horse, cf. e.g. *Il.* 5.236.

501 **what he was:** i.e. something less than a man.

503 **strongest animals of all:** *fortissima rerum...animalia*; for this fairly rare use of *rerum* with a superlative adjective to mean 'the most...in the world', see *OLD* s.v. 'res' 4b.

504-6 The ironic train of thought is that the Centaurs cannot really be the children of Ixion (see on 9.123) and the goddess Nephele if they are unable to defeat the ex-woman, Caeneus.

509 **and its weight will do the wounding:** the idea is that, if Caeneus cannot be wounded by a sharp weapon, he may succumb to pressure applied by a heavy weight.

511 **Auster:** the south wind; for the personification and violence, see on 11.663.

519 **to roll away:** *euoluere*; picks up 'Roll...over' *inuoluite* at 12.507.

512-3 **Othrys...Pelion:** two mountains closely associated with the Centaurs, see on 7.352 and 353; 12.74-5, 452.

520-1 **lofty Ida which, look, we can see:** once again (cf. 12.363, 440), we are reminded that this is a long account by Nestor to his Achaean companions delivered outside Troy just before the beginning of the Trojan War. For the geography, see on 10.71.

524 **a bird:** see on 12.168-209, 459-531.

526 **too:** English idiom demands the addition of this word; there is nothing to correspond to it in the Latin.

526-9 **it...it...it:** the Latin offers the feminine but that is probably only because the Latin for 'bird' *auis* is feminine and is making no suggestion of a return to the female sex; perhaps to confirm that, the account ends with the male name, Caeneus, not the female, Caenis.

531 **Caeneus:** here too, the meaning of the name, 'new', may be in the reader's mind; see on 168-209, 459-531.

535 **flight and darkness:** *fuga noxque*; literally 'flight and night' but the jingle is not acceptable.

536-79 Nestor, Tlepolemos and Periclymenus

At the end of Nestor's account, we are back with the Achaeans outside Troy (see on 12.363); one of these, Tlepolemus, Hercules' son, berates Nestor for his alleged neglect of Hercules' prowess against Centaurs. This complaint provokes Nestor into a passionate outburst against Hercules, culminating in the story of Nestor's brother, Periclymenus (stress the middle syllable). For Tlepolemus' presence at the Trojan War and his parentage, see, from the Homeric Catalogue of Ships, *Il.* 2.653-4, (Lattimore's translation):

> Herakles' son, Tlepolemos the huge and mighty
> led from Rhodes nine ships with the proud men from Rhodes aboard them...

The Catalogue follows with a rather unsavoury account of Tlepolemus' character entirely consistent with his portrayal here. For Hercules' only known encounters with Centaurs, see on 9.98-133, 191; 12.210-535. For the story of Periclymenus, see Apollod. 1.9.9 (Frazer's translation):

> ...Neleus, being banished, came to Messene, and founded Pylos, and...had...sons, to wit, Taurus...Nestor and Periclymenus, whom Poseidon granted the power of changing his shape. And when Hercules was ravaging Pylus, in the fight Periclymenus turned himself into a lion, a snake, and a bee but was slain by Hercules with the other sons of Neleus. Nestor alone was saved...

To this should be added, from one of Nestor's Homeric speeches, *Il.* 11.689-92 (Lattimore's translation):

> For Herakles had come in strength against us and beaten us
> in the years before, and all the bravest among us had been killed.
> For we who were sons of lordly Neleus had been twelve, and now
> I alone was left of these, and all the others had perished...

536 **the Pylian:** Nestor, he came from 'sandy Pylos' (Hom. *Il.* 1.247-8).

541 **cloudborn:** Centaurs, see on 12.211.

542-3 Why compel me to remember evils and to lay bare sorrows hidden by the years: as Harrison points out, this is a close imitation of Virg. *Aen.* 10.63-4:

quid me alta silentia cogis
rumpere et obductum uerbis uulgare dolorem?

According to Servius, *obductum* is a metaphor of scarring over a wound; hence, West translates:

> *The scars have formed over my wounds. Why do you make me speak and re-*
> *open them?*

Ovid's use here of *rescindere*, 'tear open', 'lay bare', would certainly confirm Servius' view (cf. also Hor. *Epist.* 1.3.32). There is, however, some doubt as to the text; *rescindere* is found only in a few late manuscripts; the rest are divided between *rest(r)ing(u)ere*, 'suppress' or 'bind', *resciscere*, 'get to know' and *retexere*, 'undo' or 'retrace'.

547-8 Deïphobus (stress the second syllable)...**Pulydamas** (stress the second syllable)...**Hector:** three of the greatest of the Trojan heroes; during the military climax of the *Iliad*, the fight between Achilles and Hector (*Il.* 22.1-366), Athene decided to trick Hector by pretending to be a helpful Trojan hero; the disguise she adopted was to make herself look like Hector's brother, Deïphobus, presumably because he would inspire real, but false, confidence, as indeed he did (*Il.* 22.225-305). Pulydamas was the wisest of the Trojan heroes; at *Il.* 18.254-313 he had advised Hector to withdraw into the city, but Hector had spurned his advice; in a rare editorial comment, Homer observes (*Il.* 18.310-3, Lattimore's translation):

> *So spoke Hektor, and the Trojans thundered to hear him;*
> *fools, since Pallas Athene had taken away the wits from them.*
> *They gave their applause to Hektor in his counsel of evil,*
> *but none to Poulydamas, who had spoken good sense before them.*

Shortly before he dies at Achilles' hands, Hector delivers a speech full of pathos which begins with these relevant lines (*Il.* 22.99-104, Lattimore's translation):

> *'Ah me! If I go now inside the wall and the gateway,*
> *Poulydamas will be the first to put a reproach upon me,*
> *since he tried to make me lead the Trojans inside the city*
> *on that accursed night when brilliant Achilleus rose up,*
> *and I would not obey him, but that would have been far better.*
> *Now, since by my own recklessness I have ruined my people...'*

All this is, of course, in the future from the point of view of Ovid's narrative here.

550-1 blameless cities, both Elis and Pylos: according to Nestor as reported by Homer (*Il.* 11.670-761), Elis and its people (the Epeians) were far from blameless and had been defeated not by Hercules but by Nestor and the Pylians after great provocation; Hercules had, however, indeed destroyed Pylos (see the note on 12.536-79) which Nestor, its most famous son (see on 12.536), naturally regarded as 'blameless'.

552 penates: see on 9.307, 446.

554 twice six: for the twelve sons of Neleus and their fate, see Hom. *Il.* 11.691-2 quoted in the note on 12.536-79.

556-8 Mutability is especially associated with marine gods, see on 11.241.

558 the founder of Neleus' blood line: Neptune was, in fact, Neleus' father; the complex tale is fully related by Homer (*Od.* 11.235-59).

561 For the eagle as Jupiter's special bird, see on 10.154-61, Austin on Virg. *Aen.* 1.394; for the eagle as the carrier of thunderbolts, see on 10.158.

564 Tyrinthian: Hercules, see on 9.66.

574 Rhodian: Tlepolemus led the fleet from Rhodes, see Hom. *Il.* 2.653-4, quoted in the note on 12.536-79.

577 the Neleïan: Nestor, son of Neleus, see on 12.536-79.

578 gift of Bacchus: *munere Bacchi*; perhaps another metonymy (see on 9.141) giving the sense 'gift of wine', perhaps 'Bacchus' gift' i.e. 'wine'.

580-619 *The death of Achilles*
For this story, consider Hector's dying words to Achilles in the *Iliad* (22.358-60, Lattimore's translation):

> *Be careful now; for I might be made into the gods' curse*
> *upon you, on that day when Paris and Phoibos Apollo*
> *destroy you in the Skaian gates, for all your valour.*

580 spear: *cuspide*; this must be Neptune's trident, see on 12.595.

581 his son: Cycnus, Neptune's son, whose story was told at 12.71-145.

582 Phaëthon's bird: the swan, because of Cycnus, son of Sthenelus, who was so upset by the death of Phaëthon that he pined away till turned into a swan (2.367-80). He was, of course, a different Cycnus (see on 2.367) both from Neptune's son and from the Cycnus of Hyrie (see on 7.371).

583 in a less than civilized way: *plus quam ciuiliter*; literally 'in a more than civilized way' but the English idiom works the other way round.

584 And now, when the war had been dragged out for about two quinquennia: like Homer, Ovid will ignore the first nine years of the Trojan War; cf. Agamemnon's words near the beginning of the *Iliad* (2.134-5, Lattimore's translation):

> *And now nine years of mighty Zeus have gone by, and the timbers*
> *of our ships have rotted away and the cables are broken.*

once again, however (see on 10.1-11.84), though Ovid will, like Homer, concentrate on the war's tenth year, he will, to a considerable extent, omit what Homer discusses and concentrate on what Homer omits.

585 unshorn: a Homeric picture of Apollo (*Il.* 20.39) and ubiquitous in literature and art thereafter; for more details, see N.-H. on Hor. Odes 1.21.2.
Smintheus: a title for Apollo used by his priest, Chryses, right at the beginning of the *Iliad* (1.39), but not thereafter.

586-96 Neptune (Poseidon), from the *Iliad* on, had always been hostile to the Trojans (see on 12.591); nevertheless, incensed by Achilles' killing of his son Cycnus (12.71-145, 581-2) he urges Apollo, who had, in any case, always supported the Trojans (see on 12.591), to kill Achilles. For conflict between Neptune and Apollo, see on 12.595-6.

586 my brother's sons: Jupiter was the brother of Neptune (i.e. Poseidon, Hom. *Il.* 15.187-8), and Apollo was one of the many sons of Jupiter (i.e. Zeus, Hom. *Il.* 1.9).

587 vainly: for the story of the building of the Trojan Walls by Apollo and Neptune, and why they thought that it was in vain, see 11.199-206.

587-90 walls...walls: *moenia...muros*; see on 11.203-4.

591 dragged around his own Pergamum: in the *Iliad*, Poseidon (Neptune) specifically refuses to contemplate any intervention against Achilles' maltreatment of Hector's body (24.25-27); Apollo, on the other hand, took steps to prevent Hector's body from being further damaged (24.18-22) and initiated a debate (24.33-54) that led finally to the gods' decision to permit Priam's ransoming of the body from Achilles. According to Homer (*Il.* 24.14-21), Achilles dragged Hector's corpse around Patroclus' tomb; the view that he was dragged round the walls of Troy is best known from Virgil (*Aen.* 1.483-4); however, the change of scene was not original to him, see Austin and Eur. *Andr.* 107-8.

595 with my trident: *triplici...cuspide*; literally, 'with my triple spear'; for Neptune's trident, see e.g. Hom. *Il.* 12.27, Virg. *Aen.* 1.145.

595-6 not allowed...my enemy: perhaps a reference to Zeus' words to Iris, his messenger, (Hom. *Il.* 15.158-61, Lattimore's translation):

> *Go on your way now, swift Iris, to the lord Poseidon*
> *and give him all this message nor be a false messenger. Tell him*
> *that he must now quit the war and the fighting, and go back*

among the generations of gods, or into the bright sea.
The message was duly delivered at 15.171ff. However, at 20.23-5, the gods were specifically told that they could intervene in the war, and Apollo and Poseidon would have come to blows but for Apollo's restraint (21.435-469).

598 **veiled in a cloud:** for gods to come so into the presence of humans is an epic cliché; see e.g. Hom. *Il.* 15.308.

602 **plebeian:** for the anachronism, see 9.307.

603 **Aeacides:** 'Aeacus' grandson' i.e. Achilles; see on 11.219.

604 **Pelides:** 'Peleus' son' i.e. Achilles; see on 11.219.

605-6 **he...his...him...his:** Apollo...Paris'...Achilles...Apollo's; even in the Latin, the context is required fully to resolve the ambiguity.

609 **timid:** Paris' reputation is found as early as Homer (cf. e.g. *Il.* 3.421-446).

610 **you:** for the apostrophe, see on 9.101.
a womanish battle: *femineo...Marte*; literally, 'womanish Mars', for the metonymy, see on 9.141; the battle is 'womanish' because it is fought against Paris whose effeminacy was so savagely attacked by Homer's Hector (*Il.* 3.39-57), a passage closely imitated by Horace (*Odes* 1.15.13-20).

611 **you would have preferred to fall:** instead of the other way round; for the story, see Apollodorus *Epit.* 5.1 (Frazer's translation):

> *Penthesilia [Queen of the Amazons]...slew many, and amongst them*
> *Machaon, and was afterwards herself killed by Achilles, who fell in love*
> *with the Amazon after her death and slew Thersites for jeering at him.*

the double axe of Thermodon: *Thermodontiaca...bipenni*; the Amazons lived by the river Thermodon (see on 9.189); for the double axe, cf. Virg. *Aen.* 11.648-51 (West's translation):

> *There in the middle of all this bloodshed, exulting in it, was the Amazon*
> *Camilla with the quiver on her shoulder, and one side bared for battle.*
> *Sometimes the pliant spears came thick from her hand; sometimes, unwea-*
> *ried, she caught up her mighty double axe* [bipennem].

612 **glory and protection:** *decus et tutela*, a phrase also used by Ovid (*Fast.* 4.415), in a remarkable contrast, of a statue of Priapus protecting a garden; the phrase is a synonymous variation of Virgil's *decus et tutamen* (*Aen.* 5.262) used of a suit of armour and much later borrowed to serve as a substitute for milling on coins, most recently, some British pound coins.

614 **the very god...the very one:** Hephaestus (Vulcan), the divine blacksmith, had made Achilles' armour for him (Hom. *Il.* 18.468-616) and was the god of fire.
had armed...had cremated: *armarat...cremarat*; the Latin verbs make an undercutting jingle that has eluded the translation.

620-13.398 The contest over the arms of Achilles.

Homer gives us our earliest extant reference to the story; Odysseus sees Ajax hanging back when the other ghosts are crowding round the pit he dug and filled with blood to summon them up (*Od.* 11.543-51, Lattimore's translation):

> *Only the soul of Telamonian Aias stood off*
> *at a distance from me, angry still over the decision*
> *I won against him, when beside the ships we disputed*
> *our case for the arms of Achilles. His queenly mother*
> *set them as prize, and the sons of the Trojans, with Pallas Athene,*
> *judged; and I wish I had never won in a contest like this,*
> *so high a head has gone under the ground for the sake of that armor,*
> *Aias, who for beauty and for achievement surpassed*
> *all the Danaans next to the stately son of Peleus.*

Frazer (on Apollod. *Epit.* 5.6) gives a survey of the extant fragments from the Epic Cycle and beyond. For Ovid, as becomes clear in book 13, the story gives a wonderful opportunity for a brilliant exercise in competitive rhetoric.

621   **arms, arms:** *armis arma*, for the polyptoton, see on 9.44.

622   **Tydides:** (stress the middle syllable), 'son of Tydeus', i.e. Diomedes, cf. e.g. Hom. *Il.* 4.365-400.

622-3 Ajax, son of Oileus: the 'lesser' Ajax, not the son of Telamon; cf. e.g. Hom. *Il.* 23.473-98.

623   **the lesser Atrides:** (stress the middle syllable), the lesser 'son of Atreus', i.e. Menelaus, cf. e.g. Hom. *Il.* 7.92-119.

623-4 the one greater in age and war: i.e. the greater 'son of Atreus', Agamemnon, cf. e.g. Hom. *Il.* 2.434-40.

624   **Telamon's** (stress the first syllable) **son:** the 'greater' Ajax, cf. e.g. Hom. *Il.* 7.233-43.

625   **Laërtes':** (stress the middle syllable): i.e. 'Laërtes' son', Ulixes; cf. e.g. Hom. *Od.* 24.205-364.

626   **Tantalides:** (stress the second syllable), 'descendant of Tantalus' i.e. Agamemnon. Tantalus' son, Pelops (see on 6.401-11) was the father of Atreus, and Atreus was the father of Agamemnon (and Menelaus).

BIBLIOGRAPHY

To save space in the notes, authors frequently cited are cited only by name and page number together with, where more than work is involved, date of publication or other suitable indication. The references are fully expanded here.

LIMC	*Lexicon Iconographicum Mythologiae Classicae,* Zurich and Munich, 1981-97.
N.-H.	See **Nisbet-Hubbard.**
OCD	*The Oxford Classical Dictionary Third Edition edited by Simon Hornblower and Antony Spawforth,* Oxford, 1996.
OLD	*Oxford Latin Dictionary edited by P.G.W. Glare,* Oxford, 1968-82.
TLL	*Thesaurus Linguae Latinae,* 1900-
Anderson	*Ovid's Metamorphoses Books 6-10 Edited, with Introduction and Commentary, by William S. Anderson,* Norman, Oklahoma, 1972.
———	*P. Ovidii Nasonis Metamorphoses edidit William S. Anderson,* Stutgardiae et Lipsiae, 1996.
Austin	*P. Vergili Maronis Aeneidos Liber Primus with a commentary by R.G. Austin,* Oxford, 1971.
———	*P. Vergili Maronis Aeneidos Liber Secundus with a commentary by R.G. Austin,* Oxford, 1964.
———	*P. Vergili Maronis Aeneidos Liber Quartus edited with a commentary by R.G. Austin,* Oxford, 1955.
———	*P. Vergili Maronis Aeneidos Liber Sextus with a commentary by R.G. Austin,* Oxford, 1977.
Bailey	*Titi Lucreti Cari de Natura Deorum libri sex Edited with Prolegomena, Critical Apparatus Translation, and Commentary by Cyril Bailey,* Oxford, 1947.
Barlow	*Euripides Heracles with Introduction, Translation and Commentary by Shirley A. Barlow,* Warminster, 1996.
Bömer	*P. Ouidius Naso Metamorphoses Kommentar von Franz Bömer,* Heidelberg, 1969-86.
Booth	*Ovid the Second Book of* Amores *Edited with translation and commentary by Joan Booth,* Warminster, 1991.
Burman	*Publii Ovidii Nasonis opera omnia....cura et studio Petri Burmanni,* Amstelodami, 1727.
Courtney	*A Commentary on the Satires of Juvenal,* London, 1980.
D'Arcy Thompson	See Thompson
Davies	*Epicorum Graecorum Fragmenta edidit* Malcolm Davies, Göttingen, 1988.

de Sélincourt	*Herodotus the Histories translated with an introduction by Aubrey de Sélincourt*, (Penguin Classics), Harmondsworth, 1954, 1972.
Dodds	*Euripides Bacchae Edited with Intoduction and Commentary by E.R. Dodds*, Oxford, (second edition), 1960.
————	*Plato Gorgias, a Revised Text with Introduction and Commentary by E.R. Dodds*, Oxford, 1959.
Easterling	*Sophocles Trachiniae edited by P.E. Easterling*, Cambridge, 1982.
Evelyn-White	*Hesiod the Homeric Hymns and Homerica with an English translation by Hugh G. Evelyn-White* (Loeb Classical Library), London and Cambridge, Mass., 1914.
Forbes Irving	*Metamorphosis in Greek Myths, P.M.C. Forbes Irving*, Oxford 1990.
Fordyce	*Catullus A Commentary by C.J. Fordyce*, Oxford, 1961.
————	*P. Vergili Maronis Aeneidos Libri VII-VIII with a commentary by C.J. Fordyce*, Oxford, 1977.
Fränkel	*Ovid, a Poet between two Worlds, Hermann Fränkel*, Berkeley and Los Angeles, 1945.
Frazer	*Apollodorus The Library with an English Translation by James George Frazer* (Loeb Classical Library), London and Cambridge, Mass., 1921.
Galinsky	G. Karl Galinsky, 'Hercules Ouidianus (Metamorphoses 9.1-272)' *Wiener Studien* 85 (1972) 93-116
Godwin	*Catullus Poems 61-68 edited with introduction, translation and commentary by John Godwin*, Warminster, 1995.
Golding	*The xv Bookes of P. Ouidius Naso, entytuled Metamorphosis, translated oute of Latin into English meeter, by Arthur Golding gentleman, a worke very pleasaunt and delectable*, London, 1567. See also *Ovid's Metamorphoses The Arthur Golding Translation 1567 edited, with an introduction and notes, by John Frederick Nims*, New York, 1965.
Greenwood	*The Verrine Orations with an English Translation by L.H.G. Greenwood* (Loeb Classical Library), London and Cambridge, Mass., 1935.
Gregory	*Ovid The Metamorphoses A complete new Version by Horace Gregory*, New York, 1958.
Hardie	*Virgil Aeneid Book IX edited by Philip Hardie* [Cambridge Greek and Latin Classics] Cambridge, 1994.
Harrison	*Vergil Aeneid 10 with Introduction, Translation and Commentary by S.J. Harrison*, Oxford, 1991.
Heinsius	*Operum P. Ovidii Nasonis edito nova N. Heinsius...recensuit ac notas addidit*, Amstelodami, 1661.

Henderson *Ovid Metamorphoses III, with Introduction, Notes and Vocabulary by A.A.R. Henderson,* Bristol, 1979.

Hessayon *The Tree and Shrub Expert Dr D.G. Hessayon*, pbi Publications, Waltham Cross, 1983.

Hill D.E. Hill, 'From Orpheus to Ass's Ears' *Author and Audience in Latin Literature edited by Tony Woodman and Jonathan Powell,* Cambridge, 1992.

Hollis *Ovid Metamorphoses Book VIII edited with an introduction and commentary by A. S. Hollis,* Oxford, 1970.

Housman *M. Annaei Lucani Belli Ciuilis libri decem editorum in usum edidit* A.E Housman, Oxford and Cambridge, Mass., second edition, 1927.

Jebb *Bacchylides The Poems and Fragments*, edited etc. by Richard C. Jebb, Cambridge, 1905.

Jones *The Geography of Strabo with an English translation by Horace Leonard Jones* (Loeb Classical Library), London and Cambridge, Mass., 1917.

Kenney E.J. Kenney, 'Ovidiana', *CQ* 43 (1997) 458-67.

Kovacs *Euripides Children of Heracles Hippolytus Andromache Hecuba edited and translated by David Kovacs* (Loeb Classical Library), London and Cambridge, Mass., 1995.

———— *Euripides Supplian Women, Electra Heracles edited and translated by David Kovacs* (Loeb Classical Library), London and Cambridge, Mass., 1998.

Lattimore *The Iliad of Homer Translated with an introduction by Richmond Lattimore,* Chicago, 1951.

———— *The Odyssey of Homer Translated with an introduction by Richmond Lattimore,* New York, Evanston and London, 1965.

Leaf *The Iliad edited with English notes and introduction by Walter Leaf*, London, 1886.

McKeown *Ovid Amores Text Prolegomena and Commentary in Four volumes*, Leeds, 1989-

Mair *Callimachus Hymns and Epigrams Lycophron with an English translation by A.W. Mair Aratus with an English translation by G.R. Mair* (Loeb Classical Library), London and Cambridge, Mass., 1921.

Mayer *Lucan Civil War VIII Edited with a Commentary by R. Mayer,* Warminster, 1981.

Merkel *P. Ovidius Naso ex recognitione R. Merkelii,* Lipsiae, 1881.

Miller *Ovid Metamorphoses with an English translation by Frank Justus Miller* (Loeb Classical Library), London and Cambridge, Mass., 1916.

Mozley *Statius with an English translation by J.H. Mozley* (Loeb Classical Library), London and Cambridge, Mass., 1928.

Muecke	*Horace Satires II, with an Introduction, Translation and Commentary*, Warminster, 1993.
Murphy	*Ovid Metamorphoses Book XI edited with an introduction and commentary by G.M.H. Murphy*, Oxford, 1972.
Mynors	*Virgil Georgics Edited with a Commentary by* R.A.B. Mynors, Oxford, 1990.
Nisbet-Hubbard	*A commentary on Horace: Odes Book 1, by R.G.M. Nisbet and Margaret Hubbard*, Oxford, 1970
———————	*A commentary on Horace: Odes Book II, by R.G.M. Nisbet and Margaret Hubbard*, Oxford, 1978.
Oldfather	*Diodorus of Sicily with an English translation by C.H. Oldfather* (Loeb Classical Library), London and Cambridge, Mass., 1933.
Otis	*Ovid as an Epic Poet by Brooks Otis*, Cambridge, 1966 (1st edition), 1970 (2nd edition).
Papathomopoulos	*Antoninus Liberalis Les Métamorphoses Texte établi traduit et commonté par Manolis Papathomopoulos,* (Collection…Budé) Paris, 1968.
Peck	*Aristotle Historia Animalium in Three Volumes with an English Translation by A.L. Peck*, (Loeb Classical Library), London and Cambridge, Mass., 1970.
Pease	*Publi Vergili Maronis Aeneidos Liber Quartus edited by Arthur Stanley Pease*, Cambridge, Mass., 1935.
Petersmann	Hubert Petersmann, *'Lucina Nixusque Pares'*, *Rh.Mus.* 30 (1990) 157-75.
Rackham	*Cicero de Natura Deorum Academica with an English Translation by H. Rackham*, (Loeb Classical Library), London and Cambridge, Mass., 1933.
Rand	*Ovid and his Influence by Edward Kennard Rand*, London, 1925, New York, 1963.
Reed	*Bion of Smyrna The Fragments and the Adonis edited with Introduction and Commentary by J.D. Reed*, Cambridge, 1997.
Reid	*The Oxford Guide to Classical Mythology in the Arts, 1300-1990s, Jane Davidson Reid,* New York and Oxford, 1993.
Sage	*Livy with an English translation by Evan T Sage* (Loeb Classical Library), London and Cambidge, Mass., 1936.
Sande	Siri Sande, 'Il tempo del Foro Romano: l'età Augustea' *Castores L'immagine dei Dioscuri a Roma a cura di Leila Nista*, Roma, 1994.
Sandys	*The Odes of Pindar with an introduction and an English translation by Sir John Sandys* (Loeb Classical Library), London and New York, 1915.
Shackleton Bailey	D. R. Shackleton Bailey, 'Notes on Ovid, *Metamorphoses'*, *Phoenix* 35 (1981) 332-7.

Skutsch	*The Annals of Q. Ennius Edited with Introduction and Commentary by Otto Skutsch*, Oxford, 1985.
Storr	*Sophocles With an English Translation by F. Storr* (Loeb Classical Library), London and Cambridge, Mass., 1913.
Tarrant	*Seneca Agamemnon Edited with Commentary by R.J. Tarrant*, Cambridge, 1976.
————	See Preface p. viii.
Thompson	*A Glossary of Greek Birds, a new edition by D'Arcy Wentworth Thompson*, London, 1936.
Vahlen	*Ennianae Poesis Reliquiae iteratis curis recensuit Ioannes Vahlen*, Lipsiae, 1928.
Warmington	*Remains of Old Latin Edited and Translated by E.H. Warmington*, (Loeb Classical Library), London and Cambridge, Mass., 1935.
Weir Smyth	*Aeschylus with an English translation by Herbert Weir Smyth* (Loeb Classical Library), London and New York, 1922.
Wilkinson	*Ovid Recalled by L. P. Wilkinson*, Cambridge, 1995.
————	'The world of the Metamorphoses' in *Ovidiana, recherches sur Ovide Publiées à l'occasion du bimillénaire de la naissance du poète par N.I. Herescu*, Paris, 1958.
West	*Hesiod Theogony edited with prolegomena and commentary by M.L. West*, Oxford, 1966.
West	*Horace Odes I. Carpe Diem. Text, Translation and Commentary David West*, Oxford, 1995.
———	*Virgil The Aeneid a new prose translation by David West*, (Penguin Classics), Harmondsworth, 1990.
Williams	*P. Vergili Maronis Aeneidos Liber Tertius edited with a comentary by R.D. Williams*, Oxford, 1962.
————	*P. Vergili Maronis Aeneidos Liber Quintus edited with a comentary by R.D. Williams*, Oxford, 1960.

INDEX

This index is to head words in the explanatory notes. The references refer to the line numbers of the translation and are rarely, if ever, more than one line from the Latin reference.